Missouri Genealogical Gleanings

1840 and Beyond
Volume 5

Sherida K. Eddlemon

HERITAGE BOOKS
2009

HERITAGE BOOKS
AN IMPRINT OF HERITAGE BOOKS, INC.

Books, CDs, and more—Worldwide

For our listing of thousands of titles see our website
at
www.HeritageBooks.com

Published 2009 by
HERITAGE BOOKS, INC.
Publishing Division
100 Railroad Ave. #104
Westminster, Maryland 21157

Copyright © 1998 Sherida K. Eddlemon

All rights reserved. No part of this book may be reproduced or transmitted in any form or by any means, electronic or mechanical, including photocopying, recording or by any information storage and retrieval system without written permission from the author, except for the inclusion of brief quotations in a review.

International Standard Book Numbers
Paperbound: 978-0-7884-0984-4
Clothbound: 978-0-7884-8220-5

DEDICATION

To the biggest surprise of my life, my daughter, Rhena Ann Victoria South, born September 14, 1995

TABLE OF CONTENTS

	Page

ATCHINSON COUNTY
(Founded 1843 from Holt County)

1850 Census Index	114
Democratic Committee Members, 1933	130

BUCHANNAN COUNTY
(Founded 1838 from the Platte Purchase)

1840 Census Index	78
Newspaper Editors, 1903	162

BUTLER COUNTY
(Founded 1849 from Wayne County)

Will of John C. Smart	47

CALDWELL COUNTY
(Founded 1836 from Ray County)

Persons Listed as Land Owners on the 1897 Atlas	131
Newspaper Editors, 1903	163

CAPE GIRARDEAU COUNTY
(Founded 1812 Original District)

Newspaper Editors, 1903	163

CARTER COUNTY
(Founded 1859 from Ripley and Shannon Counties)

Marriage Book A, 1881 - 1890	96

CHARITON COUNTY
(Founded 1820 from Howard County)

Land Owners' Atlas	178

GRUNDY COUNTY
(Founded 1841 from Livingston County)

Members of the Trenton Lodge of Free Masons, 1865	130
Charter Members, Galt Lodge, 1890	146

LACLEDE COUNTY
(Founded 1849 from Camden, Pulaski and Wright Counties)

Charter Members of Washington Christian Church	149
Charter Memberss of White Oak Pond Cumberland Church, 1868	162

MADISON COUNTY
(Founded 1818 from Cape Girardeau and Ste. Genevieve Counties)

Marriage Records, 1840 - 1850	52

MORGAN COUNTY
(Founded 1833 from Cooper County)

Miscellaneous Birth and Death Records	94

NODAWAY COUNTY
(Founded 1841 from Andrew County)

Individuals listed on 1850 Census	149

PETTIS COUNTY
(Founded 1833 from Cooper and Saline Counties)

Sedalia, 1914 Yearbook	75

POLK COUNTY
(Founded 1835 from Greene)

Historical Sketch from the *"Bolivar Herald,"* 1876	163

ST. LOUIS COUNTY
(Founded 1812, Original District)

Daybook of Dr. W. J. Harris	10
Persons Listed on the Golden Jubilee Souvenir of Loretto, Florissant, 1897	106

STONE COUNTY
(Founded 1851 from Taney County)

1870 Mortality Schedule   147

SULLIVAN COUNTY
(Founded 1843 from Linn County)

Green City High School Commencement, 1898   13
Green City High School Playbill, 1938   23

TANEY COUNTY
(Founded 1837 from Greene County)

Members of the Democratic Committee, 1932   146

TEXAS COUNTY
(Founded 1845 from Shannon and Wright Counties)

Pupils of Rocky Branch Normal Music School, 1914   129
Postmasters of Dykes   131
Postmasters of Hazelton   149
Postmasters of Cabool   162
Charter Members of the Freedom Baptist Church, 1916   197

MISCELLANEOUS MISSOURIANA

Register of Faculty, High Schools, 1889 1
Abstracts of some Military Correspondence of the
    Battle of Wilson's Creek   14
Letter of J. C. Morris, 1863   20
Missouri Arizona WPA Records   22
WPA Interview of Allen Chrisman   22
WPA Interview of Mary E. Burleson   23
Letters of Benjamin Lippincott   25
Principals and Presidents, Private Schools, 1898-1899   49
Missourians from Benton and Blount Co., TN that served
    in World War I   66
Conductors of Colored Institutes, 1899   66
Persons Indicating Missouri as their Place of Origin on
    the 1855 Territorial Census of Kansas   67
Missouri Marriages mention in Pottawatomie, Kansas in
    William G. Cutler's *"History of the State of Kansas"*   75
Missourians on the Arapahoe County, Colorado 1870

Mortality Schedule	78
Missourians on the Ellis County, Texas, 1860 Mortality Schedule	78
Missourians on the Jack County, Texas Voter's List, 1867-1869	78
Missourians Killed in Action or Missing in Action, Regular Army, Korean War	87
Missourians at the Civil War Veteran Reunion, Centerville, Appanoose Co., Iowa	107
Missouri Confederate Dead at Rock Island Civil War Prison Camp	107
Missourians Listed on th4 1870 Mortality Schedule, Pueblo, Colorado	131
Missourians buried at Lexington National Cemetery	147
Missourians on the 1860 Mortality Schedule, Livingston County, Kentucky	147
Missouri Civil War Veterans in Illinois	148
Missourians Buried at Danville, Kentucky National Cemetery	149

PREFACE

Missouri was a gateway to the west. Both the Santa Fe Trail to the southwest and the Oregon Trail to the northwest began at Independence, Missouri. Settlers and new immigrants from Germany, Switzerland, Ireland, England, Poland, Bohemia and Italy flooded into Missouri when statehood was granted in 1821. Many of these new arrivals often did not list a destination on the ship passenger list. If a destination was indicated, it may mean that their were other relatives already there or that the family had already purchased property in advance.

Kansas was part of the Missouri Territory until 1821, but it was not until 1854 that the territory of Kansas was created luring new immigrants and settlers from Illinois, Ohio, Indiana and Missouri. So many Missourians relocated to Kansas that in 1855 Kansas was voted into the Union as a slave state.

Missouri was plagued with outlaws and raiders that had their beginnings even before the Civil War. The 1857 Dred Scott Decision helped to inflame the anti-slavery feelings in Missouri. During the Civil War, raiders and outlaws such as William Clarke Quantrill, Frank and Jesse James and the Cole Younger gangs terrorized Missouri. In the eyes of some these outlaws were heroes, but the law prevailed in the end.

Each new Gold Rush lured more people to Missouri on their way to make their fortune. There was a California Gold Rush in 1848; the Colorado Gold Rush in 1858 and the Klondike Gold Rush in the Yukon in 1896-1897. Many lost sons went to look for gold as well as whole families with only a child born in Missouri to show their passing through the state.

St. Joseph, Missouri was the starting point for the Pony Express. It promised delivery of the mail to Sacramento, California in eight to ten days. Although it was only in operation for eighteen months, these riders gained a glamorous spot in Missouri history.

Although there are extant census records for Missouri starting in 1830 many travelers and pioneering settlers were missed in the census years or only lived in the state between the census years. The purpose of this collection is to help the researcher pinpoint his ancestor between the census years.

All names appear as written on the records including the abbreviations of given names. The surnames appearing in the parentheses are included in the index. No attempt has been made to make corrections in spelling. Cemetery listings and mortality schedules include only persons born in 1840 or later.

In some instances it was necessary to use abbreviations.
They are as follows:

m - Month	y - Year
d - Day/Died	RD - Recorded Date
b - Born	CLK - Clerk
D - Date	GR - Grantor
GE - Grantee	IN - Instrument
P - Page	I - Issue
R - Range	C - Court Cases
AP - Application	Dis - Dismissed
MOC - Missouri Connection	SUS - Suspended
TWP - Township	APP - Appraiser
A - Age	St - Martial Status
BP - Birth Place	RES - Residence
OC - Occupation	ADM/AD - Admission
MD - Marriage Date	MG - Minister
CMTS - Comments	SVC - Service
SVCCP - Service Branch	FAC - Faculty
YSUP - Years Superintendent	SUP - Superintendent
SEC - Secretary	Reg - Regiment
PO - Post Office	

Good luck in finding your ancestors within these pages.

DATES TO REMEMBER

1821	Missouri became the 24th state.
1835	Samuel K. Clemens or Mark Twain was born.
1837	Missouri gained six northwestern counties with the Platte Purchase.
1846	Mexican War
1848	California Gold Rush
1849	St. Louis Cholera Epidemic
1854	Kansas Territory was created.
1855	So many Missourians moved to Kansas that it was voted in as a slave state.
1857	Dred Scott Decision
1858	Colorado Gold Rush
1858	Butterfield Stage Line ran from St. Louis, MO to San Francisco, CA.
1860 - 1861	Pony Express mail run from St. Joseph, MO to Sacramento, CA.
1863	Some State registration of births and deaths began, but very scattered.
1861 - 1865	Civil War
1865	New Missouri constitution was created with a "Test Oath" clause denying southern sympathizers the right to vote.
1865	Wm. C. Quantrill, guerilla raider, was killed.
1870	Great Mississippi steamboat race between the "Robert E. Lee" and the "Natchez" from St. Louis to New Orleans.
1870 - 1872	Missouri-Kansas-Texas Railroad in operation.
1875	Sixty-eight men were elected to draft a new

Missouri constitution.

1883 - 1893 County Clerks were required to register births and deaths, but not enforced.

1889 Oklahoma Land Rush

1896 - 1897 Gold Rush to the Klondike District of the Yukon.

1911 Full compliance for the State registration of births and deaths.

Missouri High Schools, 1889, Register of Faculty, Eddlemon Collection.

Adrian: (SUP) A. L. Ives, (YSUP) 2, (SEC) J. F. Herrel, (FAC) A. L. Ives.

Albany: (SUP) J. H. Markley, (YSUP) 8, (SEC) J. F. Patton, (FAC) C. M. Walton, J. H. Markley.

Appleton City: (SUP) W. J. Wright, (YSUP) 1, (SEC) R. N. Burns, (FAC) K. H. Logan, W. J. Wright.

Ash Grove: (SUP) Alfred Page, (YSUP) 3, (SEC) J. H. Penyman, (FAC) Alfred Page, Frances Stancill.

Aurora: (SUP) D. L. Amburgh, (YSUP) 3, (SEC) S. G. Elliott, (FAC) P. B. Hood, F. L. Appleby, D. L. Amburgh.

Bethany: (SUP) J. R. Hale, (YSUP) 6, (SEC) A. S. Cumming, (FAC) J. R. Hale, Anna B. Tull, Kate McClement, Bertha Greer.

Belton: (SUP) A. W. Wirt, (YSUP) 7, (SEC) J. H. White, (FAC) A. A. Wirt, Ida Woodruff.

Billings: (SUP) A. C. Farley, (YSUP) 2, (SEC) Wm. Watkinson, (FAC) A. C. Farley, Mattie Pearce.

Bloomfield: (SUP) I. H. Hughes, (YSUP) 2, (SEC) J. H. Richardson, (FAC) S. S. Thomas, I. H. Hughes.

Boliver: (SUP) S. A. Hoover, (YSUP) 2, (SEC) S. Odor, (FAC) Mrs. W. S. White, S. A. Hoover.

Bolckow: (SUP) A. J. Rowland, (YSUP) 1, (SEC) C. M. Davis, (FAC) A. J. Rowland.

Bonne Terre: (SUP) L. N. Gray, (YSUP) 2, (SEC) J. W. Helber, (FAC) E. B. Wheeler, L. E. Smith, J. C. Edwards.

Boonville: (SUP) W. A. Annin, (YSUP) 1, (SEC) Wm. Mittelback, (FAC) H. A. Edwards, Melinda Montague, Emma Stegner, W. A. Annin.

Bowling Green: (SUP) W. J. Rowley, (YSUP) 10, (SEC) S. G. Pollard, (FAC) Mary Tulley, W. J. Rowley.

Braymer: (SUP) J. H. Eckelberry, (YSUP) 2, (SEC) J. A. Rathburn. (FAC) J. H. Eckelberry.

Breckinridge: (SUP) E. C. Orr, (YSUP) 3, (SEC) C. W. Curran, (FAC) E. C. Orr.

Brookfield: (SUP) J. U. White, (YSUP) 1, (SEC) J. A. Arbuthnot, (FAC) H. R. McCullough, May Hickman, Florence Trumbo, J. U. White.

Browning: (SUP) A. P. Vaughn, (YSUP) 1, (SEC) J. L. Kille, (FAC) A. P. Vaughn, Cora Buchanan.

Brunswick: (SUP) C. L. Buckmaster, (YSUP) 4, (SEC) M. A. Knappenberger, (FAC) W. S. Drace, C. L. Buckmaster.

Buffalo: (SUP) W. A. Wilkinson, (YSUP) 2, (SEC) A. R. Miller, (FAC) W. A. Wilkinson, Mrs. M. O'Bannon.

Burlington Junction: (SUP) H. G. Davis, (YSUP) 1, (SEC) A. S. Bollinger, (FAC) H. G. Davis, Lida Corken.

Butler: (SUP) J. M. Taylor, (YSUP)1, (SEC) W. W. Rose, (SEC) A. C.

Gwinn, Emma Depee, Teresa Patterson.

Cabool: (SUP) H. C. Moore, (YSUP) 1, (SEC) R. P. Hubbard, (SEC) Ada Fluharty, H. C. Moore.

Cameron: (SUP) Brutus Riggs, (YSUP) 7, (SEC) J. W. Parry, (FAC) Bertha Ensign, Mattie Ware, Brutus Riggs.

California: (SUP) J. W. Major, (YSUP) 1, (SEC) H. E. Blakeman, (FAC) Henry Hernleben, Leona Brown, J. W. Major.

Canton: (SUP) A. O. Moore, (YSUP) 5, (SEC) H. C. Chinn, (FAC) E. K. Fretwell, Mrs. A. Maupin, A. O. Moore.

Carrollton: (SUP) E. H. Stroeter, (YSUP) 2, (SEC) W. R. Creel, (FAC) C. A. Phillips, Anna R. Quisenberry, Hattie Averill, Geo. Dietrich.

Carthage: (SUP) W. J. Stevens, (YSUP) 5, (SEC) M. J. McClurg, (FAC) Edwain Gray, S. W. Howland, J. J. Hunt, Mabel P. Dow, A. F. Hendrix, Esther Pratt, Carrie Hammmons, Loula Van Neman, Blanche K. Chase, Florence Fabyam, J. W. Whybark, Winifred Bryan.

Caruthersville: (SUP) Lee W. Rood, (YSUP) 5, (SEC) H. C. Schult, (FAC) Dixie Dix, Lee W. Rood.

Centralia: (SUP) W. A. Muir, (YSUP) 6, (SEC) W. A. McCallister, (FAC) E. S. Patterson, Frank Sanford, W. A. Muir.

Charleston: (SUP) A. R. Boone, (YSUP) 6, (SEC) E. Shelby, (FAC) A. R. Boone.

Chamois: (SUP) J. L. Bankson, (YSUP) 1, (SEC) W. P. Joachim, (FAC) J. L. Bankson, A. A. Speer, J. W. Hoffman.

Chillicothe: (SUP) Oliver Stigall, (YSUP) 3, (SEC) J. M. Dunn, (FAC) J. W. Barton, Belle H. Reed, Josephine Norville, Daisy Gordon, Ethel Salle, Oliver Stigall.

Clarence: (SUP) Beulah Bruner, (YSUP) 5, (SEC) M. Whitby, (FAC) Beulah Bruner, Nona Maupin.

Clarksville: (SUP) Dollie Oglesby, (YSUP) 1, (SEC) A. T. Jamison, (FAC) Dollie Oglesby.

Clinton: (SUP) F. B. Owen, (YSUP) 1, (SEC) T. W. Collins, (FAC) H. L. Green, Arthur Lee, J. R. Newton, Eugenia Kennedy.

Cole Camp: (SUP) R. M. Scotten, (YSUP) 3, (SEC) Geo. Kieffer, (FAC) R. M. Scotten.

Columbia: (SUP) R. H. Emberson, (YSUP) 5, (SEC) J. L. Henry, (FAC) E. B. Cauthorn, Myrtle Barnett, Inez Riggs, Peter Potter, Mary Barnett, R. H. Emberson, H. A. Clark.

Craig: (SUP) W. Lee Jordan, (YSUP) 1, (SEC) C. W. Anibal, (FAC) W. Lee Jordan.

Deep Water: (SUP) D. Walker Smith, (YSUP) 2, (SEC) J. M. Woodward, Lou Gaines, May Goodwin, D. Walker Smith.

DeSoto: (SUP) A. B. Carroll, (YSUP) 1, (SEC) M. R. Baruthouse, (FAC) C. K. Bliss, Anna McClure, A. B. Carroll.

DeWitt: (SUP) A. S. Green, (YSUP) 1, (SEC) Minnis Griffith, (FAC) A. S. Green.

Dexter: (SUP) C. M. Hall, (YSUP) 3, (SEC) A. J. Thrower, (FAC) C. M. Hall.

Edina: (SUP) A. R. Coburn, (YSUP) 1, (SEC) C. R. Fowler, (FAC) Mrs. A. X. Brown, A. R. Coburn.

El Dorado Springs: (SUP) A. W. Duff, (YSUP) 1, (SEC) G. Hainine, (FAC) Minnie Amsden, A. W. Duff.

Eldon: (SUP) W. S. Platt, (YSUP) 2, (SEC) P. S. Whitacre, (FAC) W. S. Platt.

Elsberry: (SUP) B. P. Taylor, (YSUP) 2, (SEC) W. W. Watts, (FAC) B. P. Taylor.

Everton: (SUP) George Melcher, (YSUP) 2, (SEC) Howard Ragsdale, (FAC) C. T. Bell, George Melcher.

Excelsior Springs: (SUP) J. F. Kennedy, (YSUP) 7, (SEC) Wm. Crocket, (FAC) Leslie Bates, J. F. Kennedy.

Fairfax: (SUP) A. E. Kennedy, (YSUP) 1, (SEC) N. F. Dragoo, (FAC) A. E. Kennedy.

Fayette: (SUP) J. L. Lynch, (YSUP) 2, (SEC) H. A. Norris, (FAC) M. Deatherage, J. L. Lynch.

Fillmore: (SUP) Rupert Peters, (YSUP) 1, (SEC) E. W. Davis, (FAC) Rupert Peters

Fredericktown: (SUP) T. E. Joyce, (YSUP) 3, (SEC) F. J. Parkin, (FAC) T. E. Joyce, Emmet Williams.

Fulton: (SUP) J. C. Humphrey, (YSUP) 2, (SEC) J. W. McIntire, (FAC) J. S. Morrison, Dollie Carter, J. C. Humphrey.

Gallatin: (SUP) A. R. Alexander, (YSUP) 4, (SEC) J. W. Alexander, (FAC) R. W. Ginnings, Osta Feurt, A. R. Alexander.

Glasgow: (SUP) A. F. Willis, (YSUP) 5, (SEC) H. C. Cockerill, (FAC) A. F. Willis, Nettie Sears.

Golden City: (SUP) W. R. Crowther, (YSUP) 5, (SEC) G. T. Thompson, (FAC) Ambrose Johnson, W. R. Crowther.

Grant City: (SUP) H. N. Stamper, (YSUP) 3, (SEC) L. M. Phipps, (FAC) C. J. Witmer, Sylvester Taylor, H. N. Stamper.

Greenfield: (SUP) I. N. Evrard, (YSUP) 1, (SEC) J. A. Davis, (FAC) Frankie Eastin, C. E. Bell, I. N. Evrard.

Hamilton: (SUP) W. C. Holman, (YSUP) 1, (SEC) T. A. Filson, (FAC) B. C. Brous, Daisy When, W. C. Holman.

Hannibal: (SUP) R. B. D. Simonson, (YSUP) 8, (SEC) J. W. Whaley, (FAC) Gertrude Ashmore, Barbara Mullen, Mary V. Ellis, Adalaide Brown, Mrs. Dean Dulany, F. F. Winchester, Roy Galsgow, Cora Reid, R. B. D. Simonson, J. H. Pelham, Julia Lewis.

Harrisonville: (SUP) A. T. Fisher, (YSUP) 6, (SEC) D. C. Barnett, (FAC)

J. Q. Cope, M. J. Patterson, Nettie Lamm, A. T. Fisher.
Hermann: (SUP) C. C. Thudium, (YSUP) 6, (SEC) A. B. Walker, (FAC) Lottie Riley, H. C. Von Struve, Eugene Twendle.
Higbee: (SUP) Claude B. Adams, (YSUP) 1, (SEC) Jno. Saunders, (FAC) W. D. Welch, Claude B. Adams.
Higginsville: (SUP) W. C. Sebring, (YSUP) 3, (SEC) S. J. Kleinschmidt, (FAC) J. K. Fletcher, Ada McDaniel, W. C. Sebring.
Holden: (SUP) P. A. Boulton, (YSUP) 1, (SEC) Wm. Mayhew, (FAC) P. A. Boulton, Lizzie Hammond.
Houston: (SUP) R. E. Barnard, (YSUP) 2, (SEC) E. J. Tweed, (FAC) R. E. Barnard, Marietta Tweed.
Hume: (SUP) G. W. Pendergraft, (YSUP) 2, (SEC) A. M. Wallace, (FAC) G. W. Pendergraft, Arthur Barron.
Humansville: (SUP) J. A. Bloomer, (YSUP) 2, (SEC) A. H. Ham, (FAC) F. L. Stufflebam, J. A. Bloomer.
Independence: (SUP) G. M. Holliday, (YSUP) 1, (SEC) R. D. Wirt, (FAC) W. L. C. Palmer, Matilda D. Brown, Ardelia Palmer, Myra W. Ewin, Bertha Entrekin, Gussie Hunt.
Ironton: (SUP) R. E. Wilkinson, (YSUP) 3, (SEC) W. H. Delano, (FAC) R. E. Wilkinson.
Jackson: (SUP) B. F. Lusk, (YSUP) 8, (SEC) Fred Geyert, (FAC) B. F. Lusk.
Jamesport: (SUP) H. H. Edmiston, (YSUP) 3, (SEC) M. F. Stipes, (FAC) Dorothy Buren, H. H. Edmiston.
Jefferson City: (SUP) J. W. Richardson, (YSUP) 1, (SEC) A. M. Hough, (FAC) S. A. Baker, S. I, Arhur, T. A. Binford.
Joplin: (SUP) J. D. Eliff, (YSUP) 3, (SEC) J. C. Faulkender, (FAC) J. M. Gwinn, J. Otilla Kahn, L. L. Lichliter, Elise Geier, Rena Keith, A. D. Whealdon, Blanche Carpenter.
Kahoka: (SUP) H. A. Higgins, (YSUP) 4, (SEC) C. A. Stevenson, (FAC) Jessie Roy, H. A. Higgins.
Kansas City (Westport): (SUP) J. M. Greenwood, (YSUP) 25, (SEC) W. E. Benson, (FAC) S. A. Underwood, Anne C. Wilder, W. H. Whitten, Sophia Watson, Mary E. Bowles, J. S. Ankeney, Florence G. Neale, Margaret DeWitt, Elizabeth E. Dobbin, P. K. Dillenbeck, Jr., Stella F. Hodsheir.
Kansas City (Central): (SUP) J. M. Greenwood, (YSUP) 25, (SEC) W. E. Benson, (FAC)E. C. White, L. I. Cammack, R. A. Mibnxkwitz, F. H. Ayres, A. F. Smith, L. L. L. Hanks, Mary E. Wilder, C. H. Nowlin, F. N. Peters, E. M. Bainter, H. H. Holmes, Ellen E. Fox, J. W. White, Eva Z. Steinberg, Kate Harriman, A. F. Jacquemot, Margaret H. Jones, Esther Crowe, A. E. Douglass, Jessie L. Thatcher, S. E. Kelsey, B. A. Sutermeister, E. E. Rush, Louise Morey, Feda Von Unwerth, W. H.

Ficklin, Gerturde Semans, Nettie Semans, Laura I. Whipple, Bertha Bain, Porter Graves, Sarah E. Steele, Zina D. Snyder, Eleanor M. Denny, Gertrude Johnson, R. Jennie Adams, Wm. Weber, Carrie E. Voorhees, Effie Buck, Sophia Rosenberger, Anna Spence, Wm. Luby, P. K. Dillenback, Ruby Archer, Burton Reid, Eda Darnall, Leonora Yeager, Vivian Armstrong, Mrs. C. H. Wheeler, Mignon Crowder.

Kansas City (Manual Trg.): (SUP) J. M. Greenwood, (SEC) W. E. Benson; (FAC) G. B. Morrison, E. D. Phillips, Jas. A. Merrill, Jas. C. Richardson, A. A. Dodd, Stanley H. Moore, B. T, Chase, Herbert M. Page, Geo. Arrowsmith, P. B. S. Peters, R. F. Knight, Mary Fisher, Anna C. Gilday, M. Alice Murphy, Clifton Sloan, Armand Miller, Josephine G. Casey, Bertha H. Bacheller, C. M. Thompson, Hansford McCurdy, Della Drake, Sallie C. Elston, Sallie VanMetre, Olive B, Wilson, Stella Jenkins, Wallace B. Shields, Floy Campbell, Jessie L. Griffith, Katherine M. Dunn, Ethel Osgood, Mrs. Ella Sargent, Mrs. A. C. Lavine, Barry Fulton, O. E. Herring, J. M. Kent.

Kansas City (Lincoln): (SUP) J. M. Greenwood, (SEC) W. E. Benson, (FAC) G. N. Grisham, Anna H. Jones, David Croswait, Wm. H. Dawley, Jr., W. E. Griffin, Daisy L. Jackson.

Kearney: (SUP) B. F. Brown, (YSUP) 3, (SEC) C. L. Eberts, (FAC) Cora L. Walker, B. F. Brown.

Kingston: (SUP) J. E. Herriott, (YSUP) 4, (SEC) C. S. McLaughlin, (FAC) J. E. Herriott.

Kirksville: (SUP) C. S. Brother, (YSUP) 2, (SEC) F. L. Link, (FAC) O. H. Lind, Lena Trowbridge, Ida Brashear, Harry Laughlin, Horace Ivie.

Kirkwood: (SUP) R. G. Kinkead, (YSUP) 1, (SEC) H. W. Hough, (FAC) R. G. Kinkead, Susanna Williams, Frances M. Wilde, Ethnal (sic) Flournoy, Mary E. Griffith.

La Monte: (SUP) J. N. McElvain, (YSUP) 1, (SEC) J. S. White, (FAC) J. N. McElvain.

Lancaster: (SUP) Alfred H. Smith, (YSUP) 1, (SEC) E. Higbee, (FAC) Alfred H. Smith, Rosa Crump, Wm. K. Seitz, E. G. Alexander. 0

La Plata: (SUP) L. B. Osborne, (YSUP) 1, (SEC) J Walter Heninger, Hattie Baity, L. B. Osborne.

Lathrop: (SUP) J. W. Barley, (YSUP) 1, (SEC) G. Grant, (FAC) J. W. Barley, F. D. Hamilton, Belle Peckover.

Lebanon: (SUP) F. W. Ploger, (YSUP) 4, (SEC) J. McKnight, (FAC) F. W. Ploger, Fannie Gleason, Jennie Mustard.

Lexington: (SUP) H. D. Demand, (YSUP) 14, (SEC) T. J. Baudon, (FAC) Nannie Shaw, Florence Arnold, H. D. Demand.

Liberal: (SUP) N. A. Mackey, (YSUP) 4, (SEC) W. J. Lavery, (FAC) N. A. Mackey.

Liberty: (SUP) V. E. Halcomb, (YSUP) 4, (SEC) F. H. Trimble, (FAC)

C. O. Nelson, Virginia Newlee, Bessie Lane, V. E. Halcomb.
Linneus: (SUP) H. B. Bence, (YSUP) 7, (SEC) L. C. Phillips, (FAC) H. B. Bence.
Lockwood: (SUP) D. W. Bird, (YSUP) 4, (SEC) W. H. Pierce, (FAC) D. W. Bird, Estella Sittler.
Louisiana: (SUP) A. W. Riggs, (YSUP) 4, (SEC) Taylor Frier, (FAC) R. R. Rowley, Margaret Knight, A. W. Riggs.
Macon: (SUP) W. F. Jamison, (YSUP) 3, (SEC) W. S. Herman, (FAC) Henry King, Anna Pile, V. C. Coulter, W. F. Jamison.
Maitland: (SUP) J. E. Crosen, (YSUP) 7, (SEC) J. U. Crosen, Maud McKnight.
Malden: (SUP) C. W. Fisher, (YSUP) 1, (SEC) W. S. Gardner, (FAC) C. W. Fisher.
Malta Bend: (SUP) W. C. Fisher (sic), (YSUP) 1, (SEC) H. F. Knapp, (FAC) W. C. Fisher.
Marionville: (SUP) B. F. Woodford, (YSUP) 1, (SEC) A. Doggett, (FAC) B. F. Woodford, Carrie Turrentine.
Marshfield: (SUP) H. E. Blaine, (YSUP) 1, (SEC) J. J. Bollinger, (FAC) H. E. Blaine, F. P. Miller.
Marshall: (SUP) T. E. Spencer, (YSUP) 15, (SEC) J. A. Fisher, (FAC) L. M. Nelson, Elizabeth Whitaker, May Duggins, A. R. James, J. M. Roberts, G. M. Furguson, Elizabeth Rucker, Nora Robertson.
Maryville: (SUP) B. F. Ducan, (YSUP) 4, (SEC) W. C. Frank, (FAC) C. A. Hawkins, Dr. F. R. Anthony, Miss M. B. Potter, Miss Ida Dutton, B. F. Duncan.
Meadville: (SUP) D. A. Randall, (YSUP) 2, (SEC) W. L. Botts, (FAC) D. A. Randall, Alma Loomis.
Memphis: (SUP) A. P. Settle, (YSUP) 3, (SEC) W. T. Reddish, (FAC) J. O. Boyd, E. E. Huffman, A. P. Settle.
Mexico: (SUP) D. A. McMillan, (YSUP) 10, (SEC) J. H. Sallee, (FAC) Martha Shea, J. W. Scott, Mary Houston, Anna Hinde, Carrie Baldwin, Clare Grantham, D. A. McMillan.
Miami: (SUP) E. C. Fisher, (YSUP) 1, (SEC) A. R. Edwards, (SEC) G. W. Carpenter, W. E. Tuner, E. C. Fisher.
Moberly: (SUP) J. A. Whiteford, (YSUP) 5, (SEC) J. R. Lowell, (SEC) J. C. Lilly, Orienne Harriss, A. B. Chamler, Edwin Elliott, A. C. Bush, Laura Balthis, Fannie Nise.
Monroe City: (SUP) R. S. Nichols, (YSUP) 6, (SEC) T. J. Sharp, (FAC) Della Harwood, Mattie L. Weaver, R. S. Nichols.
Montgomery City: (SUP) W. C. Williams, (YSUP) 4, (SEC) J. D. Barnett, (SEC) Dora Hams, J. O. Henderson, Jennie Baker, W. C. Williams.
Mound City: (SUP) J. P. Coleman, (YSUP) 5, (SEC) B. P. Smith, (FAC) B. C. Maxwell, Ethel Bardeaux, J. P. Coleman.

Mountain Grove: (SUP) W. H. Lunch, (YSUP) 11, (SEC) W. S. Candler, (FAC) W. H. Lynch, W. T. Dodson, C. A. Stephens.
Nevada: (SUP) J. C. Pike, (YSUP) 1, (SEC) W. R. L. Ellis, (FAC) W. E. Veerkamp, Virgina Sutherland, Ethel Swearingen, Howard P. Finks, R. F. Bryan.
New Haven: (SUP) M. T. Connally, (YSUP) 10, (SEC) W. C. Gerding, (FAC) M. T. Connally.
New London: (SUP) R. E. Downing, (YSUP) 1, (SEC) William Christian, (AC) Jack Briscoe, R. E. Downing.
New Madrid: (SUP) W. L. Barnard, (YSUP) 1, (SEC) M. J. Conran, (FAC) W. L. Barnard.
Norborne: (SUP) Arthur Bruton, (YSUP) 3, (SEC) W. H. Hess, (FAC) S. E. Seaton, Arthur Bruton.
Oak Grove: (SUP) W. T. Hoover, (YSUP) 1, (SEC) W. A. Warren, (FAC) W. T. Hoover, Annie Franklin.
Osceola: (SUP) M. F. Butler, (YSUP) ?, (SEC) Lee Shrynberry, (FAC) M. F. Butler.
Ozark: (SUP) R. E. Morris, (YSUP) 2, (SEC) J. F. Adams. (FAC) R. E. Morris.
Palmyra: (SUP) J. M. McMurry, (YSUP) 26, (SEC) David Willock, (FAC) Miss A. Meagher.
Paris: (SUP) W. D. Christian, (YSUP) 16, (SEC) T. T. Rodes, (FAC) J. M. Green, Nell Stone, W. D. Christian.
Pattonsburg: (SUP) J. L. Gallatin, (YSUP) 1, (SEC) F. E. Venable, (FAC) Mollie Wynn, J. L. Gallatin.
Perry: (SUP) W. L. Oliver, (YSUP) 1, (SEC) B. J. Coil, (FAC) W. L. Oliver.
Pierce City: (SUP) D. L. Newkirk, (YSUP) W. A. Rhea, (FAC) Bertha Barber, Marg. Williamson, Lillian Paxton, D. L. Newkirk.
Pilot Knob: (SUP) J. M. Hawkins, (YSUP) 3, (SEC) P. A. Jaquith, (FAC) J. M. Hawkins.
Plattsburg: (SUP) P. H. Crafton, (YSUP) 9, (SEC) Ed. McWilliams, (FAC) J. D. Marr, P. H. Crafton.
Pleasant Hill: (SUP) R. L. Walker, (YSUP) 3, (SEC) E. A. Gowdy, (FAC) Dora Pyles, Kizzie Lowe, R. L. Walker.
Poplar Bluff: (SUP) Jno. T. Withers, (YSUP) 6, (SEC) Lemuel Mills, (FAC) H. G. Builteman, J. R. H. Napper.
Princeton: (SUP) G. W. Brown, (YSUP) 2, (SEC) J. M. Hayes, (FAC) Millicent Griffith, Miss Florence Oliver, G. W. Brown.
Queen City: (SUP) P. O. Sansberry, (YSUP) 1, (SEC) J. O. Coffey, (FAC) P. O. Sansberry.
Richmond: (SUP) B. G. Shackelford, (YSUP) 1, (SEC) W. M. Allison, (FAC) J. E. Dunn, G. H. Evans, B. G. Shackelford.

Ridgeway: (SUP) Mark Burrows, (YSUP) 5, (SEC) E. T. Hopkins, (FAC) Mark Burrows, Frank L. Wiley.
Rock Port: (SUP) W. W. Gallaher, (YSUP) 3, (SEC) W. T. Buckham, (FAC) Jno. Groves, Leola E. Coggins, W. W. Gallaher.
Rolla: (SUP) L. B. Baughman, (YSUP) 5, (SEC) Albert Newman, (FAC) Mollie Renny, L. B. Baughman.
St. Charles: (SUP) Joseph Herring, (YSUP) 2, (SEC) L. M. Breker, (FAC) W. C. Barron, Joseph Herring.
Salisbury: (SUP) N. P. Noel, (YSUP) 2, (SEC) S. F. Trammel, (FAC) W. P. Noel, Emma Smith.
Salem: (SUP) S. T. Sherry, (YSUP) 1, (SEC) J. L. Smith, (FAC) F. H. Groom, S. T. Sherry.
Sarcoxie: (SUP) W. R. McElree, (YSUP) 2, (SEC) W. T. Sabert, (FAC) W. E. McElree, Gertrude Johnston, Miss E. J. Newell.
Savannah: (SUP) L. M. Garrett, (YSUP) 5, (SEC) C. C. Somerville, (FAC) L. M. Garrett, E. E. Zimmerman, Nora Holt.
Schell City: (SUP) M. A. Cleveland, (YSUP) 1, (SEC) W. F. Maring, (FAC) M. A. Cleveland.
Seneca: (SUP) J. C. Hennon, (YSUP) 1, (SEC) W. O. Buck, (FAC) C. A. Neet, J. C. Hennon.
Sedalia: (SUP) G. V. Buchanan, (YSUP) 7, (SEC) A. W. McKensie, (FAC) J. D. Wilson, Mattie M. Letts, La Pette Dugan, L. P. Coleman, F. M. Bailey, S. W. Longan, Irvin Rautenstrauch, Gertrude McKinley, Leda S. Kelly, Laura McGowan.
Shelbina: (SUP) S. E. Stout, (YSUP) 1, (SEC) J. R. Lyell, (FAC) H. A. Hill, Roy Beeman, S. E. Stout.
Shelbyville: (SUP) Ira Richardson, (YSUP) 3, (SEC) J. T. Perry, (FAC) Betty McNeill, S. C. Myers, Ira Richardson.
Sheridan: (SUP) W. C. Ogier, (YSUP) 1, (SEC) T. C. Tiblels, (FAC) W. C. Ogier.
Smithville: (SUP) W. E. A. Aul, (YSUP) 2, (SEC) J. W. Wilkerson, (FRAC) W. E. A. Aul.
Southwest City: (SUP) J. A. Woodford, (YSUP) 1, (SEC) W. T. Watters, (FAC) Mrs. J. M. Paul, J. A. Woodford.
Springfield: (SUP) J. Fairbanks, (YSUP) 25, (SEC) M. Bowerman, (FAC) E. E. Dodd, S. M. Barrett, Edna A. Abbott, Cora B. Ott, W. D. Higdon, Nena Baxter, E. K. John, Daisy Ford, J. H. Norton, Charles E. Marston, Georgie W. Hardy.
Stewartville: (SUP) E. H. Homberger, (YSUP) 3, (SEC) J. A. Deppen, (FAC) E. H. Homberger.
Stanberry: (SUP) Robt. L. Knie, (YSUP) 2, (SEC) J. F. Baker, (FAC) Geo. L Gray, R. L. Knie.
Stockton: (SUP) J. A. Burke, (YSUP) 1, (SEC) W. E. Craig, (FAC)

Corda Bradley, J. A. Burke.
Sweet Springs: (SUP) M. A. O'Rear, (YSUP) 2, (SEC) P. D. Vandyke, (FAC) M. A. O'Rear, E. N. Shackleford.
St. James: (SUP) James Hess, (YSUP) 2, (SEC) Chas. Roster, (FAC) James Hess.
Sturgeon: (SUP) F. M. Patterson, (YSUP) 3, (SEC) J. W. Hulett, (FAC) F. M. Patterson, Nannie Summers.
Saint Joseph: (SUP) E. B. Neeley, (YSUP) 36, (SEC) H. H. Smith, (FAC) C. E. Miller, Geo. O. Crothers, Etta L. Knowles, Mary E. B. Neeley, Mary M. Porter, Florence B. Lyon, Edith M. Rhoades, R. H. Chambers, Graces Travers, Olga Mueller, R. H. Jordan, Jean A. Shafer, Jno. S. Stokes, L. M. Sherman, Mary E. Rains,
St. Louis: (SUP) F. Louis Soldan, (YSUP) 5, (SEC) C. L. Hammerstein, (FAC) Wm. J. S. Bryan, Wm. Schuyler, Wm. Butler, Paul Peltier, Wm. M. Bryant, R. C. Dunhoupt, J. W. Spargo, L. N. Judson, F. W. Potjoff, Susan V. Beeson, Amelia C. Fruchte, Alice D. Choate, Evelyn G. Gilfillan, K. E. Shoughnessy, Emma P. Simmons, W. H. Vaughn, Helen E. Peabody, Laura M. Oviatt, Isabella Andrews, Mary V. Osburn, J. B. Quinn, Lillian Heltzell, Marg. Lawitsky, F. W. Fink, F. O. Sylvester, G. P. Know, Marg. F. Baker, Carrie E. Griffith, Ella Fenley, Pauline Mueller, Gertrude Garrigues, Jennie M. Jones, L. D. Hildenbrandt, Paul Miller, Anna L. Matthews, W. A. Godbey, Anna Hickey, W. S. V. Sibert, Julia D. Dunn, Laura Hichman, Margaret Glenn, Hetty Parsell, R. B. White, Melinda Calvert, C. B. Curtis, S. A. Douglass, Marg. Shoughnessy, S. A. Douglass, C. F. Baker, C. D. Frank, H. W. Thayer, Miss A. E. Carr, Mary Ettner, Julia Dang, Rosalie Kaufman, Isabel Mulford, Isabel Wilcox, Jennie Chase, Anna R. Waney, Bertha J. Schneider, Esther Mills, Ellen Kendall, Lillie Ernst, Mary B. Brown, Antoinette Taylor, Marie Garasche, Lillian Brown.
St. Louis (Sumner): (SUP) L. Louis Soldan, (YSUP) 5, (SEC) C. L. Hammerstein, (FAC) O. M. Waring, A. J. Gossing, P. H. Clark, F. J. Roberson, E. E. Campbell, A. W. Scott, Minnie C. Mitchell, J. L. Usher, Corienne Gibson, Alice Easton.
Tarkio: (SUP) J. F. Starr, (YSUP) 1, (SEC) John Gerlas, (FAC) J. F. Starr, Miss Caro Lynn, Belle McKalup.
Thayer: (SUP) F. N. Dyer, (YSUP) 3, (SEC) Geo. M. Duest, (FAC) Flor. O'Doneghea, F. N. Dyer.
Tipton: (SUP) B. S. Couch, (YSUP) 6, (SEC) Dr. W. R. Patterson, (FAC) B. S. Couch, Georgia L. Fowler.
Trenton: (SUP) L. Tomlin, (YSUP) 2, (SEC) C. A. Foster, (FAC) B. F. N. G. Rogers, L. F. Smith. Lizzie Brainerd.
Triplett: (SUP) Oscar Ingold, (YSUP) 1, (SEC) G. H. Dobyns, Oscar

Ingold.
Unionville: (SUP) H. D. Kistler, (YSUP) 1, (SEC) C. A. Middleton, (FAC) D. C. Guffey.
Urich: (SUP) E. M. Hall, (YSUP) 8, (SEC) M. V. Trails, (FAC) E. M. Halls.
Vandalia: (SUP) T. B. Ford, (YSUP) 3, (SEC) Jno. McIntire, (FAC) S. S. Carroll, T. B. Ford, Louisa Wardin.
Verona: (SUP) I. P. Orahood, (YSUP) 3, (SEC) S. A. Briggs, (FAC) J. P. Orahood.
Washington: (SUP) J. N. Tankersly, (YSUP) 2, (SEC) E. W. Gallenkamp, (FAC) J. W. Tankersly, Ella Busch.
Walker: (SUP) I. L. Marquis, (YSUP) 1, (SEC) G. H. Mahbey, (FAC) I. L. Marquis.
Warrenton: (SUP) J. B. Garber, (YSUP) 2, (SEC) C. F. Poisse, (FAC) S. G. Roberson, J. B. Garber.
Webster Groves: (SUP) Sarah J. Milligan, (YSUP) 13, (SEC) W. H. Simmons, (FAC) Sarah J. Milligan, Mary Bryan, Mary W. Mills, Celia Hodges, Amy Clyde.
Webb City: (SUP) A. G. Young, (YSUP) 5, (SEC) J. C. Williams, (FAC) J. W. Storms, Lydia Wampler, Mary Davis, Estella Wangelin.
Wentzville: (SUP) W. J. Dysart, (YSUP) 2, (SEC) J. H. Daniel, (FAC) W. J. Dysart.
West Plains: (SUP) B. B. Cassell, (YSUP) 2, (SEC) J. R. Galloway, (FAC) B, B. Cassell, Mrs. M. Winningham.
Winston: (SUP) F. W. Williams, (YSUP) 6, (SEC) W. S. Mallory, (FAC) F. W. Williams.
Willow Springs: (SUP) E. L. Hume, (YSUP) 3, (SEC) G. W. Campbell, (FAC) E. L. Hume.
Wellsville: (SUP) J. W. Dunlap, (YSUP) 3, (SEC) C. P. Wise, (FAC) J. W. Dunlap, Ethel Maxwell, Mildred Hawkins.

St. Louis County, Missouri, St. Louis City, Daybook Of Dr. W. John Harris
    Aldrich, Isabel: (D) Jul. 28, 1895, (A) 36Y.
    Babbitt, Elizabeth Halt: (D) Oct. 18, 1897, (A) 3M.
    Beach, Henry O.: (D) Nov. 11, 1903, (A) 76Y.
    Beggs, Wm.: (D) Apr. 18, 1890, (A) 88Y.
    Beggs, Emma R.: (D) Jun. 29, 1898, (A) 84Y.
    Bell, Mary Ruth: (D) May 19, 1896, (A) 4M.
    Bell, Margaret: (D) Aug. 12, 1899, (A) 60Y, (BP) Scotland.
    Biddleman, Helen E.: (D) Oct. 1, 1891, (A) 18Y.
    Bingham, David Ralston: (D) Jan, 29, 1899, (A) 1Y.
    Bishop, Abba J.: (D) Jun. 24, 1895, (SEX) Female.

Blydes, Margaret: (D) Jul. 2, 1897, (A) 27Y.
Bradford, Carrie T.: (D) Feb. 25, 1899, (A) 50Y.
Brandt, Myrtle Irene: (D) Jun. 28, 1891, (A) 6M.
Brandt, George: (D) Jul. 20, 1893, (A) 4M.
Brenning, Catherine L.: (D) Jan, 6, 1902, (A) 68Y.
Brown, Mrs. Frank: (D) Dec. 28, 1894, (A) 52Y.
Cambell, Richard B.: (D) Sep. 18, 1893, (A) 50Y.
Carn, Robert E. (B) Aug. 9, 1827, (D) Sep. 8, 1900, (A) 73Y, (BP) KY.
Cernick, Mrs. Augusta: (D) Apr. 11, 1898, (A) 50Y.
Infant Child Of C. H. and L. Wickard: (D) Dec. 20, 1897
Infant Child Of H. W. Larberge: (D) Dec. 8, 1890, (A) One Day.
Infant Child Of C. H. Howard: (B and D) Stillborn, Feb. 20, 1896.
Infant Child Of Mr and Mrs. Brainard: (D) Oct. 10, 1899.
Infant Child Of C. Ingerson: (B and D) Stillborn, Nov. 3, 1896.
Infant Child Of Charles and Elizabeth Gunn: (D) May 18, 1900.
Cross, Sarah I.: (D) Nov. 8, 1895 (A) 72Y.
Cumming, Robert: (D) Apr. 20, 1891 (A) 3Y.
Curtis, Jr., John Henry: (D) Sep. 16, 1895 (A) 2y.
Davis, Mary E.: (D) Jul. 17, 1896 (A) 67Y.
De Bernates, E. J. (A) 75Y.
Debolt, Helen G.: (D) Dec. Jul. 1895 (A) 3Y.
Deisten, Theresa: (D) Apr. 14, 1897 (A) 54Y.
Dickengd, Jorge E.: (D) Feb. 2, 1890 (A) 40Y.
Dowling, Eunice A.: (D) Sep 1, 1902 (A) 64Y.
Downes, Thomas: (D) Sep. 17, 1890 (A) 3M.
Duley, Essie: (D) Jun. 5, 1894 (A) 28Y, (Cmts) Music Teacher
Eames, Florence: (B) May 1, 1858: (D) Jul. 16, 1900 (A) 42Y.
Ellison, Agnes: (D) Nov. 22, 1893 (A) 32Y.
Ethington, Gordon: (D) Jan, 28, 1899 (A) 9M.
Fargy, Martha: (B) Mar 7, 1811, (D) Jun. 10, 1901 (A) 90Y, (BP) Ireland
Field, Frank: (D) Oct. 9, 1890 (A) 2Y.
Field, Edna V.: (D) Dec. 6, 1890 (A) 1M.
Flint, Ollie: (D) Feb. 28, 1900 (A) 23Y.
Ford, John Odell: (D) Jan, 13, 1898, (A) 75Y.
Ford, Charles: (D) Oct. . 4, 1899, (A) 45Y.
French, E.E.: (D) Apr. 1, 1898, (A) 55Y.
Fulton, R.E.: (D) Jun. 3, 1898, (A) 26Y.
Greenwood, Edward S.: (D) Aug. 8, 1902, (A) 69Y.
Greve, Catherine Elizabeth: (D) Apr. 3, 1899, (A) 70Y.
Greve, Martin H.: (D) Oct. 21, 1901, (A) 32Y.
Gunn, Emma Glenn: (D) Nov. 30, 1903, (A) 67Y.

Goddard, Annie C. W.: (D) Sep. 4, 1891, (A) 5Y.
Harkness, Grace: (D) Feb. 18, 1895, (A) 1Y.
Harvey, Annie E.: (D) Jan, 19, 1898, (A) 70Y.
Hearnes, Sylvester: (D) May 13, 1896, (A) 1D.
Herthel, George: (D) Jun. 21, 1899, (A) 48Y.
Hinchman, Laura: (D) Jan. 18, 1903, (A) 46Y.
Hiob, Henry: (D) Oct. . 20, 1891, (A) 20Y.
Hobie, Wm.: (D) May 19, 1896, (A) 83Y.
Hughes, Mrs. Belle: (D) Feb. 9, 1902, (A) 37Y.
Hunter, Daniel F.: (D) Dec. 2, 1903, (A) 71Y.
Isbell, Claud: (D) Feb. 1, 1902, (A) 19Y.
Jackson, Mrs. A.: (D) Aug. 21, 1898
Johnson, Barton W.: (D) May 24, 1894, (A) 60Y.
Jones, Mrs. C. J.: (D) Feb. 6, 1892, (A) 70Y.
Jones, Wm. (B) 1839, (D) May 21, 1901, (A) 62Y, (BP) England.
Jones, Howard: (D) Dec. 29, 1903, (A) 65Y.
Kerns, Katherine: (D) Dec. 21, 1895, (A) 30Y.
Kerns, Ellen Margaret: (D) Dec. 27, 1895, (A) 11D.
Kerns, Johanna: (D) Sep. 24, 1889, (A) 65Y, (BP) Germany.
Koern, Matthew: (D) Mar. 2, 1891, (A) 75Y, (BP) Germany.
Kindermann, Elizabeth: (D) Oct. 6, 1894, (A) 44Y.
Kinsey, Phillie Durand: (D) Nov. 3, 1896, (A) 24Y.
Klyce, Cora V.: (D) Oct. 4, 1903, (A) 45Y.
Langschmidt, William: (D) Nov. 3, 1894
Ledlie, John F.: (D) Feb. 20, 1890, (A) 56Y.
Lice, Ella Van: (B) Aug. 9, 1863: (D) Sep. 22, 1900, (A) 39Y.
Lindsly, Joseph B.: (D) Mar. 5, 1890, (A) 69Y.
Lindsly, Fred B.: (D) Dec. 21, 1889, (A) 5Y, (BP) St. Louis,
Lyon, Mary E.: (D) May 16, 1891, (A) 66Y.
Lyon, James: (D) Jul. Oct. 1897, (A) 72Y.
Martin, George Wray: (D) Feb. 23, 1903, (A) 1Y.
Macdonald, David: (D) Jul. 15, 1893, (A) 80Y.
Mare, Edwin Francis: (D) Mar.18, 1900, (A) 1Y.
Matlock, Margaret: (D) Jan, 18, 1892, (A) 56Y.
Mccargo, John: (D) May 14, 1898, (A) 33Y.
Mclean, Linda Mae: (D) Oct. . 8, 1894
Mcmahan, Lottie: (D) Dec. 28, 1897
Mccullah, Katherine H.: (D) Jun. 6, 1900, (A) 57Y.
Miller, James: (D) Jun. 26, 1893, (A) 76Y.
Missinger, Maud Gertrude: (D) Feb. 5, 1900, (A) 31Y.
Morrison, John J.: (D) Oct. . 25, 1895, (A) 8Y.
Muller, Odelia J.: (D) Oct. . 20, 1899, (A) 53Y.
Munroe, Isabel: (D) Aug. 9, 1891: (D) 4Y.

Noyes, Mary R. B. Dec. 6, 1825: (D) Jan, 28, 1900, (A) 74Y.
Palfrey, Mary B.: (D) Feb. 20, 1902, (A) 52Y.
Palmer, Nancy R.: (D) Mar. 30, 1903, (A) 93Y.
Parker, Sarah Turner: (D) 3, 28, 1902, (A) 74Y.
Pearson, Isaac M.: (D) Jan, 18, 1899, (A) 56Y.
Powell, Abraham William: (D) Aug. 6, 1895, (A) 31Y.
Prewitt, Sherman: (D) Aug. 21, 1898, (A) 1Y.
Pritchard, Elizabeth B. C.: (D) Aug. 30, 1899, (A) 48Y.
Rosslen, Joseph: (D) Nov. 16, 1890, (A) 29Y.
Roth, Oscar William: (D) Apr. 9, 1895, (A) 7M.
Rozier, Harriet G.: (D) Jan, 11, 1896, (A) 76Y.
Scott, W. D.: (D) Jan, 16, 1890
Scott, Matson: (D) Feb. 14, 1894, (A) 28Y.
Shirley, Emily: (D) Apr. 13, 1900, (A) 79Y.
Slough, John W.: (D) Apr. 14, 1902, (A) 54Y.
Smith, Charles Martin: (D) Sep. 24, 1890.
Smith, Thaddeus S.: (D) Feb. 14, 1897, (A) 56Y.
Smith, Sarah M.: (D) Mar. 23, 1900, (A) 80Y.
Spotswood, Elizabeth: (D) Apr. 24, 1897
Strain, Sarah M.: (D) Jul. 24, 1899, (A) 55Y.
Taylor, Fred W.: (D) Apr. 22, 1893, (A) 3Y.
Taylor, Martha: (D) Dec. 26, 1895, (A) 42Y.
Waterman, Henry D.: (D) Apr. 15, 1891, (A) 63Y.
Watson, John Thomas: (D) Mar. 15, 1896, (A) 68Y.
Weston, Clarrisa: (D) Dec. 30, 1895, (A) 80Y.
Weston, Annie E.: (D) Jul. 29, 1903, (A) 63Y.
Wilde, Henry T.: (D) Jul. 12, 1900, (A) 74Y.
Wilson, Louis Carpenter: (D) Jun. 17, 1890, (A) 3m.
Wind, Fred E.: (D) Oct. 9, 1890, (A) 3m.
Wray, Lulu S.: (D) Aug. 3, 1902, (A) 40Y.
Wright, Roy Horace: (D) Feb. 9, 1900, (A) 16Y.

Green City High School Commencement, May 13, 1898, Sullivan County, Missouri.
Order of Excerises: Ruby Mayfield, Rev. L. E. Wheeler, J. F. Morrissey, J. O. Williamson, Supt. M. W. McKanna, Chas. Walker, Harold Martin, Rev. J. W. Cabbage, Eva Kauzlarich, sponsor.
Graduates: Kenneth Fasron, President; Margaret Bookout, Vice-President; Panst Porter, Sec. Treas.; Wayne Ammerman, Wayne Bankus, Loraaine Bingham Dunlap, Millard Chapman, Williard Chapman, Lelah Chappell, Fontell Conner, Dwight Courtney, Noel DeWitt, Clayton Eckles, Martin Frank, Eveyln Frazier, Alden Gifford, Leonard Hampton, Maurince Hayes, Benny Law, LeNelle Mardis,

Harold Martin, Alpha Miller, Ada Beryl Moore, Lee Maupin, Shelton Muir, Juanita Page, Donald Pigg, Leman Powell, Basil Seymour, Alma Tharp, Arthur Wiles, Bennie Woy, Blaine White, Gertrude Zeigler.

Abstracts of the military correspondence of the Battle of Wilson's Creek, Missouri, Hdqrs. U.S. Troops, Mcculla's Farm, 24 Miles From Springfield, Fayetteville Road, August 4, 1861. Correspondence Of N. Lyon, Brig.-Gen., Commanding. Capt. John C. Kelton, Asst. Adjt. Gen., Hdqrs. Dept. Of The West, Saint Louis, Mo.

Mentioned: Hayden's farm. The rebel forces under Rains were some 3,000 strong. Captain Totten.

I should still hope to retain Springfield and hold out against the enemy in this region but for the expiration of the term of the three-months' volunteers, of whom Colonel Bates' First Iowa Regiment claiming discharge on the 14th instant. Colonel Salomon's Fifth Missouri Regiment at different periods by companies from the 9th to the 18th instant. and a considerable portion of Colonel Sigel's regiment in a similar manner. My force will be reduced to about 3,500 men., badly clothed and without a prospect of supplies

Camp On Wilson's Creek, Greene County, Mo., August 11, 1861. Military Correspondence Of De Rosey Carroll, Colonel -First Cavalry Regiment, Arkansas Volunteers. Brig. Gen. N. B. Pearce.

Mentioned: Captain Lewis' Company: 2 killed, 5 wounded. Two of Captain Lewis' Company wounded thought to be mortally so.
Captain Park's Company: 1 killed, 3 wounded, 1 missing.
Captain Walker's Company: 4: wounded, 3 missing. Captain Walker
  wounded, but will recover.
Captain Withers' Company: 2 killed.
Captain Perkins' Company: 4 wounded, 4 missing.
Captain McKissick's Company: 4 wounded, 2 missing.
Captain Kelly's Company: 1 missing.
Captain Armstrong's Company: 1 wounded, 8 missing.

Headquarters Second Division Mo. S. G., Camp At Springfield, August 12, 1861. Correspondence of James S. Rains, Brigadier-General, Comdg. Second Division, Mo. S. G. Col. Thomas L. Snead, Acting Assistant Adjutant-General.

Mentioned: For an hour this brigade resisted the fire of the enemy's artillery and infantry before being sustained, and under their gallant leader, Colonel Cawthorn.

Colonel Graves' regiment was detached to sustain Captain Woodruff's battery. The remainder under Colonel Weightman, was engaged in the thickest of the fight on the hill. Here, while examining the position of the enemy, he fell mortally wounded, pierced by four balls. Here also, nearly at the same time, fell the leader of the Republican invaders, Major-General Lyon, under a fire from the Fifth Infantry.

Captain Bledsoe's artillery, under command of Lieutenant-Colonel Rosser, was ordered across the creek. Lieutenant-Colonel Maclean, my aide-de-camp, examined the position of Colonel Sigel's battery. He gave a report to Lieutenant-Colonel Rosser who was charged and captured by the Louisiana regiment and other infantry, among whom was Major Murray's battalion, of the First Brigade.

Colonel Dyer, acting quartermaster-general, served with distinction.

Hdqrs. First Brigade, Second Division, Mo. S. G., August, 1861.
Cor- respondence of John R. Graves, Colonel, Comdg. First Brigade, Second Division, Mo. S. G.

Mentioned: Colonel Weightman fell at the head of his brigade. Colonel Weightman ordered us into the line of battle. Colonel Hurst, of the Third Regiment, and Colonel Clarkson, of the Fifth Regiment, were led directly across Wilson's Creek. Colonel Weightman fell mortally wounded at the head of his column. Colonel Rosser, commanding the First Regiment and Fourth Battalion with Captain Bledsoe's artillery was attacked by Siegel. Captain Bledsoe succeeded in disabling a portion of the enemy's guns. Colonel Rosser, together with the Louisiana regiment, led by General McCulloch in person, drove the enemy from their guns.

Colonels Hurst's and Clarkson's commands were ordered across the creek. Colonel Graves' regiment under Major Brasher, was ordered to support Captain Woodruff's battery.

I must notice especially the cool deliberation and courageous deportment of Colonels Hurst and Clarkson; also Lieutenant-Colonels Rosser, Crawford, and Tracy; also the great courage of Adjutant Gordon, of this brigade, who was severely wounded in discharging his duties. Major Martin also rendered great service in delivering orders wherever duty called him; also Major Morris, who gave valuable information of the position of the enemy, though quite sick at the time; also Adjutant Trigman and volunteer aides Donaldson and Whitfield, who did great service in delivering orders; also F. L. Graves, who rendered valuable service.

I mention with satisfaction the discretion and soldierly bearing of Captains McKenny and Muse, of the First Regiment of Infantry; Captains Hall, Vaughan, and McElrath, of the Fourth Battalion, and Captains Cockrell, Mings, Cunningham, King, Galliher, and Newton, of the Third Regiment of Infantry; also the discretion and bravery at the most trying time of the conflict of Lieutenants Foster, Fewell, Gibbs, Wynn, McClean, Barr, McMahan, Harper, and Martin, of the Fourth

Battalion; also the promptness of Adjutant Hornwood and Sergeant-Major Murray, in delivering orders, of the First Regiment of Infantry, and Adjutant Beltzhoover, of the Fourth Battalion. And I must mention the daring bravery of Sergeant-Major Murray. He was taken prisoner by Sigel while executing an order, and as soon as the enemy commenced retreating before the galling fire of the Bledsoe Artillery he mounted one of their cannon and cheered the Louisiana regiment, exclaiming that the enemy was in full retreat.

I must also mention the gallantry of Lieutenant Waddell, Sergeants Anderson and Bunker, and three privates of the Third Regiment of Infantry, who were taken prisoners the morning before the fight, and we were exposed to a strong fire in front on the enemy's ranks. When the enemy commenced retreating, the prisoners mounted one of Sigel's guns and dragged it into our lines.

Hdqrs. Army Of The West, Camp Cary Gratz, Near Rolla, Mo., August 20, 1861. Correspondence Of S. D. Sturgis, Major, First Cavalry, Commanding To The Assistant Adjutant-General, Headquarters Western Department.

Mentioned: The command was to move in two columns, composed as follows: The first, under General Lyon, consisted of one battalion regular infantry, under Captain Plummer--Companies B, C, and D, First Infantry, Captains Gilbert, Plummer, and Huston--with one company of rifle recruits, under Lieutenant Wood; Major Osterhaus' battalion, Second Missouri Volunteers, two companies; Captain Totten's light battery, six pieces, and Captain Wood's mounted company of the Second Kansas Volunteers, with Lieutenant Canfield's company, First Cavalry, regulars. This constituted the First Brigade, under Major Sturgis.

The Second Brigade, under Lieutenant-Colonel Andrews, First Missouri Volunteers, was composed of Captain Steele's battalion of regulars, Companies B and E, Second Infantry; one company of recruits, under Lieutenant Lothrop, Fourth Artillery; one company of recruits, under Sergeant Morine; Lieutenant Du Bois' light battery, consisting of four pieces, one of which was a 12-pounder gun, and the First Missouri Volunteers.

The Third Brigade was made up of the First and Second Kansas Volunteers, under Deitzler, Colonel Mitchell commanding the latter regiment. The First Regiment Iowa Volunteers, with some 200 mounted Home Guards completed the column under General Lyon. The second column, under Colonel Sigel, consisted of the Third and Fifth Regiments Missouri Volunteers; one company of cavalry, under Captain Cart; one company Second Dragoons, under Lieutenant Farrand, First Infantry.

Wherever the battle most fiercely raged there was General Lyon to be found, and there, too, was Major Schofield, his principal staff officer. The coolness and equanimity with which he moved from point to point carrying orders was a theme of universal admiration. I cannot speak too highly of the invaluable services of Major Schofield and the confidence his example inspired.

Captain Granger, acting assistant adjutant-general on my staff, rendered such excellent aid in various ways, that a full mention of those services would render this report too voluminous for an official statement. Captain Granger was hard at work at some important service.His energy and industry seemed inexhaustible. To the important services rendered by him I beg to call the attention of the commanding general.

The services of Captain Totten, re so emphatically interwoven with the various operations of the day as to appear in many, if not all the subreports, and his name deserves to become a "household word. Lieutenant Sokalski also deserves great credit for the energy with which he managed the pieces of his section. I cannot speak in too high praise of the coolness and accuracy with which Lieutenant Du Bois handled his guns, and of the valuable services he rendered throughout the entire conflict.

The following-named officers came under my personal observation during the day, and deserve especial mention for the zeal and courage they displayed, although it would prolong this report to too great a length if I should particularize in each individual case: Lieutenant Conrad, Second Infantry, A. C. S. to General Lyon, wounded; Major Wherry, volunteer aide-de-camp to General Lyon; Major Shepard, volunteer aide-de-camp to General Lyon; Mr. E. Cozzens, volunteer aide-de-camp to myself.

General Sweeny, inspector-general. This gallant officer was especially distinguished by his zeal in rallying broken fragments of various regiments even after receiving a severe wound in the leg, and leading them into the hottest of the fight.

Assistant Surgeon Sprague, medical department, attended the wounded with as much self-possession as though no battle was raging around him.

Surgeon Cornyn, First Missouri Volunteers, not only took charge of the wounded as they were brought to him, but found time to use a musket with good effect from time to time against the enemy.

Colonel Deitzler, First Kansas.' He led his regiment into a galling fire as coolly and as handsomely as if on drill. He was wounded twice.

Major Halderman, First Kansas. Early in the action he led four companies of his regiment which had been held in reserve gallantly, cheering them on with the cry of "Forward, men, for Kansas and the old flag!"

Colonel Mitchell, of the Second Kansas. He fell severely wounded in the thickest of the fight. As he was carried from the field, he met a member of my staff, and called out, "For God's sake, support my regiment."

Lieutenant-Colonel Blair, Second Kansas. This excellent soldier took command of the regiment when Colonel Mitchell was wounded. Under a most deadly fire from the enemy rode along the front of his line, encouraging his men, to the great admiration of all who saw him. Major Cloud, Second Kansas; Lieutenant-Colonel Andrews, First Missouri; Lieutenant-Colonel Merritt, First Iowa; Major Porter, First Iowa; Captain Herron, First Iowa.

The gallantry of the following officers was conspicuous from the beginning to the close of the battle: Captain Plummer, First Infantry; Captain Gilbert, First Infantry; Captain Huston, First Infantry; Lieutenant Wood, First Infantry; Captain Steele, Second Infantry; Lieutenant Lothrop, Fourth Artillery; Lieutenant Canfield, First Cavalry

Camp Near Rolla, Mo., August 17, 1861. Correspondence Of Fred'k Steele, Captain, Second Infantry, Commanding Battalion To Capt. G. Granger, R. M. R., A. A. G., Hdqrs. Army Of The West, Near Rolla, Mo.

Mentioned: The battalion was composed of Companies B and E, Second Infantry, commanded by First Sergeants Griffin and G. H. McLaughlin; a company of General Service Recruits, commanded by First Lieut. W. L. Lothrop, Fourth Artillery, and a company of Mounted Rifles, recruits, commanded by Lance Sergeant Morine. Capt. C. C. Gilbert, First Infantry, joined my battalion with a part of his company. We made arrangements to repel a threatened assault on the battery in front, which was repelled without our becoming engaged with the enemy. Major Sturgis then ordered me to form line of battle and advance upon the enemy's front. Lieutenant Lothrop was in command of a company of skirmishers on the brow of the hill to our left and front.

I wish to call the attention of the major commanding to the gallant conduct of Capt. C. C. Gilbert, First Infantry; of First Lieut. Lothrop, Fourth Artillery, and of George H. McLaughlin, first sergeant, commanding Company E, Second Infantry. Sergeant McLaughlin received the highest commendations of all the officers present. I also mention the first sergeant of Captain Gilbert's Company. Mandazy who was killed in the last assault of the enemy; also First Sergeant Griffin, commanding Company B, Second Infantry, and Lance Sergeant

Morine, commanding the company of Mounted Rifle recruits, each of whom behaved with distinguished gallantry. Sergeant Morine was mortally wounded, and died on the field.

William H. Merritt, Lieutenant-Colonel, Commanding, August 10, 1861 To J. M. Schofield, Acting Adjutant-General.

Mentioned: On the 9th instant the First Regiment of Iowa Volunteers, was under command of Lieut. Col. William H. Merritt, Col. J. F. Bates being sick. We were supported on the right by Companies A, F, D, and E, of the Iowa troops, under command of Major Porter, and on the left by one company of regular infantry, under command of Captain Lothrop.

It is with great pleasure that I acknowledge valuable aid and assistance from Maj. A. B. Porter, Adjt. George W. Waldron, who was wounded in the leg, and Sergt. Maj. Charles Compton, and to express my unbounded admiration of the heroic conduct displayed by both officers and men. Before concluding this report I must bear testimony to the gallant and meritorious conduct of Capt. A. L. Mason, of Company C, who fell in a charge at the head of his company.

Abstract of military correspondence of an engagement near Carthage, MO.

Camp Lee, Cowskin Prairie, Mo., July 16, 1861. James Mccown, Col., Comdg. First Bat'n Second Cav., Eighth Div. Mo. S. G. To Brigadier-General Rains.

Mentioned: My battalion of cavalry consisted of Company A, commanded by Captain Crenshaw; Company B, commanded by Captain Johnson; Company C, commanded by Captain King, and Company D, commanded by Captain McCowan. I was ordered up by Brigadier-General Rains in the direction of the enemy's battery for the purpose of making a charge. Upon being joined by General Rains, I understood from him we were to charge upon the enemy's battery on a given signal from the commanding officer of cavalry on the east wing. Private George W. O'Haver, of Captain Crenshaw's company had his left arm shot off aand of which wound he died at the end of two days; his horse was also wounded, Private Elijah Wood, of Captain McCowan's company had his left leg shot off, but in a fair way to recover. Six horses killed in Captain McCowan's company; several slightly wounded.

While halted for the purpose of ascertaining the position of the enemy near the timber on Spring River, we received shots from the enemy's battery, one of which wounded Private John Byler, of Captain McCowan's company, in the left thigh and leg, and also wounded his horse. All of our movements during the engagement were according to the orders of Brigadier-General Rains.

Salem, Mo., September 13, 1863, 8 P.M. Correspondence Of L. E. Whybark, Captain, Comdg. Detachment Fifth Missouri State Militia Cavalry To Lieut. Col. Joseph P. Eppstein, Commanding -Fifth Missouri State Militia Cavalry.
    Mentioned: Colonel Freeman and his band of thieves. Lieut. Charles Koch just returned and made the following report: In compliance with orders received from headquarters detachment Fifth Missouri State Militia Cavalry, I started, together with Lieutenant .] Eddleman and 80 men of Companies C and M, Fifth Missouri State Militia Cavalry, at about 6 a.m., in pursuit of the rebel force which attempted to attack our camp last night. We followed their trail with the utmost possible speed, and ascertained of the inhabitants of houses which we passed that their force was from 200 to 300 strong. They did not keep any road, but went right through the woods and over the mountains, so that we were several times obliged to dismount to get our horses down the cliffs. After three hours' hard ride, making about '20 miles in that time, we had the satisfaction to see the force right before us, on a hill, ready for a fight. While myself, with the men of Company C, attacked in the front, Lieutenant Eddleman, with the men of Company M, made a flank movement on the right flank, charging on the enemy at the same time, as well as my command from the front. The rebels could not stand this combined charge, and, after about twenty minutes' resistance, fled in every direction. Rebel loss, 14 killed, and wounded a good many more, as we found in the pursuit many signs of blood. Among the killed was Captain Post, whose recruiting commission I herewith enclose. No others were recognized. The rebels were commanded by Colonel Freeman, and had in their company William Orchard and a certain Duckworth, from this place. Our loss was 3 men wounded of Company M, one of them severely in the knee; also one citizen, Mr. Copeland, who voluntarily joined Company C, and was shot in the thigh. We also have to report the supposed capture of a private of Company M, who got wounded, and, being unable to follow any farther, started homeward with other wounded, and supposed is captured, as they were followed by a part of the rebels, and his horse gave out, and nothing has been heard from him since, while the others have arrived in camp.I must say that Lieuts. Charles Koch and Eddleman and men deserve the greatest of praise for their coolness and promptness in pursuing the rebels.

Special Collections Department, University Libraries, Virginia Tech
Camp near Lanjer, Ark. J. C. Morris., May 10, 1863.
My Dear Amanda,
    It has been a long time since I had an opportunity of writing to you,

and I gladly avail myself of the present opportunity. I am not certain that I will have a chance of sending this but I will write a few lines any how and try and get it off to let you know that I am among the living.

We have been on a raid into Ms. but I have not time to give you the particulars of our trip. I will write in a few days if I can get a chance to send it and write you a long one. I just came off of picket and found the boys all writing to send by a man that has been discharged who is going to start home this morning. I was quite sick three or four days while in Mo. but have entirely recovered. We captured a good many prisoners while in Mo. and killed a good many. We went up as high as Jackson 8 or 10 miles above Cape Girardeau. We fought them nearly all day at the Cape on Sunday two weeks ago today. The yanks boasted that we would never get back to Ark but they were badly mistaken, for we are back again and have sustained but very light loss, we never lost a man out of our company and only one or two out of the regt. I wish I had time to give you a full description of our trip. It would be very interesting to you I know; but you will have to put up with this little scrawl for the present. I am in hopes that I will get a whole package of letters from you in a few days. I never wanted to see you half as bad in all my life as I do now. I would give anything in the world to see you and the children. I have no idea when I will have that pleasure. We can't get any news here - do not know what is going on in the outside world. The boys will all write as soon as they get a chance to send them off.

We will remain in this vicinity, I expect for some time to recruit our horses. Our horses are sadly worsted. We found plenty to eat and to feed our horses on in Mo but hardly even had time to feed or eat as we traveled almost insesantly night and day. We could get any amount of bacon of the very best kind at 10 cts and every thing else in proportion.

I must close for fear I do not get to send my letter off. Write often I will get them some time. I will write every chance, do not be uneasy when you do not get letters, for when we are scouting around as we have been it is impossible to write or to send them off if we did write. Give my love to the old Lady and all the friends. My love and a thousand kisses to my own sweet Amanda and our little boys. How my heart yearns for thou that are so near and dear to me. Goodbye my own sweet wife, for the present. Direct to Little Rock as ---.

As ever your devoted and loving Husband, J.C. Morris. Mrs. A.N. Morris.

<u>Missourians in the Arizona WPA Records.</u>

Bush, Nellie Trent: (B) Nov 28, 1888, (BP) Cedar Co, (HUS) Joseph E. Bush , (MD) Dec 25, 1912
Cameron, Ralph Henry: (B) Oct 21, 1863, (BP) Southport, MO, (WF) Ida May Spaulding, San Juan, WA, (MD) Nov 25, 1895.
Childers, James W.: (B)1859, (BP) MO.
Faulkner, Jesse William: (B) May 21, 1877, (BP) St. James, Phelps Co., MO.
Hayden,Chas T.: (B) 1849, (BP) MO, (D) 1907, (DP) Tempe, AZ.
Heydon,C. Arlin: (B) May 24, 1889, (BP) Bolivar, MO, (WF) Ruth Elizabeth Crenshaw, Fulton,MO, (MD) May 21, 1913.
Horn, Tom: (B) Nov 21, 1860, (BP) Memphis, MO.
O'Neill, William O. "Bucky": (B) Feb 2, 1860, (BP) St. Louis, MO.
Oglesby, Edwin B.: (B) Aug 4, 1875, (BP) Bowling Green, MO, (WF) Frances Lewis Thomas.
Oldaker, Elizbeth Seargeant: (BP) Marshall, MO, (HUS) Emery E. Oldaker, (ND) Oct 16, 1913.

WPA Interview of Allen Chrisman by R Albert Burks, December 20, 1938.

Date and time of interview: Dec. 20, 1938. 10:00p.m. - 12:45 p.m. Personal information: (RACE) Negro; (BP) Andrew, Missouri, (B) 1870, No. in Family: Three; Lived in Filmore, Missouri 1870-90; St. Joseph 1890 - 1918; Farmer and teamster all of his years; mending harness; Methodist; Tall, angular browned skin individual. Hair and mustache; recovering from a paralysis stroke which has left him partially lame in right arm and leg.

Interview: "I am sixty-seven years old and before I had this stroke I don't believe I've had a sick day, that is, exceptin ' a cold or something like that. I guess that's the reason I'm frettin' so.

I was born in Andrew County, Missouri sixty-seven years ago and when I was big enough to do anything. I was set to weedin' out the garden down on dads farm or helpin' with the chores around the place.

My father and some more folks decided to move to Filmore County, Missouri, when I was about twelve, so dad loaded our stuff in two wagons, and hitched up the teams. My brother drove one and he the otherand we started for our new home. We lived there for a good many years in fact I came to Lincoln from their twenty-eight years ago.

I had learned when I was a kid how to take care of horses and until I had this stroke I've always tended my own teams. If one of them got sick I always knew what to do.

Whenever some of the farmer's mares was getting ready to fold they would always call me. If a mare couldn't fold natural, I knew what to do, and I would do the cleaning after the colt was born. I had my preparations that I used to keep out infections. I've never lost one of my horses exceptin' when they was so old they couldn't live no longer. I don't know how my teams going to get along now that I can't tend to them. Even if folks mean to be a help they can't take care of a fellah's team like he would hisself. The doctor says if I quit worrin' and rest up it won't be long before I can get back to work. I've always made a gair living teamen', and I only hope I can get out and do some plowin' next spring.

Sullivan County, Missouri, Greene City High School Play, "The Cat Came Back," Green City, Tuesday, February 5, 1938.

Student Name	Part in Play
Dorence Wray	Gerald Gardner, the Groom
James Busick	Tim Gallager, Groom'd Friend
Donald Woy	Tanaka, Japanese Butler
Esta Rouse	Mrs. Bridget Maloney
Helen Terry	Keona Gardner, the Bride
Beatrice Bankus	Mrs. Letetia Peters
Thomas Porter	Peter Peters
Carola Singley	Lily, the Maid
Maryland Shoop	Doria Kelly
LaVerne Cable	Alonzo Jackson
Melvin Downing	Billy Scanlon, Grocer Boy
Maxine Long	Mrs. Oberkamp
Chas. Nowels	Stage Manager
Nelson Thompson	Assistant Stage Manager
Helen Pitkin	Director
Martha Lou Fisher	Cat Dance

WPA Interview of Mrs. Mary E Burleson, Aged 78 years, Carrizozo, New Mexico by Edith L. Crawford.

The Government train we came to New Mexico in had about one hundred prairie schooners in it. Of this number four belonged to my family. My grandfather and grandmother Searcy, with six girls and one boy and my father, O. K. Chittenden, with my mother brother Tom and myself. I was five years old and my brother was about one year old. My grandfather and my father sold their farms in West Fort, Missouri . We brought all our supplies along with us. We had our flour in barrels, our own meat, lard and sugar. We were not allowed to stop and hunt buffalo on the way out here on account of the Indians. The women made the bread out of sourdough and used Soda. There was no such thing as baking powder in those days. The men baked the bread in dutch ovens over the camp fires. When we stopped at night the schooners with families were put into a circle and the Government schooners would form a circle around the family wagons. In between the two circles they put the oxen and horses, to keep the Indians from getting them. Every night the men took turns standing guard. All the soldiers rode horses. Every few days the train would stop and everybody would get rested. The feet of the oxen would get so sore that they could not go without resting them every few days. When the train stopped it was nearly always at water and the women would do their washing. The train used cow and buffalo chips and anything they could find to burn. The men did all this as the women and children were never allowed far from schooners on account of Indians. We did not milk our cow as she had to be worked along with the oxen. Our schooners had cow hides fastened underneath and our cooking utensils were packed in them. Our drinking ater was carried in barrels tied to the sides of the schooners.

We had no trouble of any kind on our trip but we were always in fear of the Indians as other trains had been attacked by them. Mr. Tom Boggs, the foreman of the Government train, told us that there was a band of Indians just ahead of our train. The Indians had attacked a train not long before we came along and had killed the people, stolen the horses and cattle and burned the wagons. We saw what was left of the wagons as we passed by.

We left the wagon train on Raton Pass. Enoch Tipton who was a relative of my grandmother, and who had persuaded my grandfather and father to come out to this country, met us on Raton Pass. We stopped at his place at Tiptonville, New Mexico. Enoch Tipton had come out here sometime before from West Port, Missouri . I do not remember just when he came or how he happened to settle here. Tiptonville is the same place as Mora, New Mexico is now. My father and grandfather farmed a year at Tiptonville. When we found our new home hard dirt floors and a dirt roof my mother was so very homesick to go back to Missouri where we had a nice farm home. My mother had brought her spinning wheel with her. She spun all the yarn for our clothes and knitted all our socks and stockings. My father and grandfather made a loom for her and she made us two carpets for our floors to keep the baby from getting so awful dirty on the floor. We had brought some seed cane with us and my father and grandfather made a homemade syrup mill and made syrup, the first ever made in that country. The mill was a crude affair made of logs and drawn by a horse. The juice was pressed out with the logs and put in a vat and cooked into syrup. People came from miles around to see this mill.

We always saved all our beef and mutton tallow to make our candles. We brought our moulds from Missouri with us. We made our wicks out of cotton strings. We tied a large knot in the end of the wick, slipped the mould over the wick and poured the hot tallow into the mould. When the tallow got cold we cut the knot off and slipped the candle out of the mould. Our candle moulds were the first ones brought into that part of the country, and all the neighbors borrowed them to mould their candles.

My father moved to Ute Creek, New Mexico, in 1867, when they struck placer gold there, and he put in a country store to supply the needs of the miners and the people who were rushing to the gold strike. A man by the name of Stevens, I can't remember any other name as everyone called him "Steve", wheeled a wheelbarrow all the way from the State of Maine to Colorado. In this wheelbarrow he had his bed, his clothes and his provisions. He did not stay long in Colorado. He came on to Tiptonville and put in a toll road to Ute Creek and my father took care of the toll gate for him. They charged $1.00 for a wagon, .50 for a horse and rider 25 for a person on foot. Mr. Stevens made a lot of money as there were lots of miners rushing to Ute Creek looking for gold.

When my brother and I were old enough to go to school we had to walk three miles. My mother was always so afraid of wild animals and Indians. We had a big bull dog who used to go with us to school. When he got tired waiting for us he would go home and when it was time for us to get home he would come to meet us. We lived down in a valley and had to go over a big hill and he would wait for us on top of this hill. We went to school at Ute Creek. The Indians were not so hostile as when we first came to New Mexico. It was the Apache and Ute Indians who gave so much trouble and sometimes the Kiowas and Cheyennes would slip in and make raids on the settlers.

My father was from Connecticutt originally and came to West Port, Mo., and married my mother there. She was Elizabeth Searcy. I am the last one left of the Searcy and Chittenden families. My brother Jap who was born after we came to New Mexico died in Gallup, New Mexico, in 1926.

<u>Letters of Benjamin Lippincott, Journeyed from Independence, Missouri to Sutter's Fort, California, in 1846.</u>
Ciudad de los Angelos, Feby 6, 1847, John L. Stephens, Esqr.
Dr. Sir,
I take advantage of Gov. Fremont's dispatch to address you for the second time only owing to want of certain communications. My tour from New York has been one wild adventure with all the changes of an ardous trip, intermingled with some pleasures and instruction.

May 10, 1846, we left the rendezvous on Indian Creek, 25 miles west of Independence. Colonel Russell was voted the command of the party in opposition to Ex-Gov. Boggs. Captain Kuykendall of Santa Fe, New Mexico expedition was appointed 1st Lieut. Mr. Curry, assistant editor of the St. Louis Reveille, aid, and myself quartermaster. Sixty nine wagons comprised our company. With the exception of Col. Russell's mess and our own, they were all families. Edwin Bryant Esqr., cousin of W.C. Bryant, R.T. Jacobs, son of wealthy John J. Jacobs, Louisville, and Col R. formed one mess of the bachelors. Francis Powers Esqr. of Boston, Jefferson with whom I left New York, and myself the other; after three days journey we kicked Jefferson out of the company which I never regretted afterward, although at the time inclined to stay with him.

We had fitted out with a first rate wagon and six mules, with harness complete, others were all ox teams. On arriving at the Kansas river, we became discontented at the slow progress of the caravan with one other wagon left the main body, our own pilot, to overtake an Oregon Co. we heard was one week ahead. Our friends parted reluctantly with us. Not expecting to meet until in California, but it was ordered otherwise. We succeeded in joining the head company after traveling some 300 miles, occasionally meeting Kaw Indians to whom we gave tobacco and other trifles. Some Shoshonees we met returning from the Buffalo country loaded with meat for which we traded and gave in return beads, knives, etc. Mr. Powers and myself had the credit of being better fitted out than any wagons on the road and had the satisfaction of being associated with an amiable, pleasant companion, industrious and perserving who resembled E.H. Williams more than any individual I ever met.

At Phalen's Bluffs, on the south fork of the Platte, 17 head of horses and mules were stolen by the Pawnees, as grand a set of double refined horse thieves as the Prairies can produce. Here we were, our team broken up and 500 miles from nowhere, however, by dint of trade, we obtained oneyoke of oxen which we put at the wheel--of our two mules left we put in advance.

A consultation was held, five individuals were selected to hunt for the lost animals, myself among the number. Imagine a gentleman, four in hand, ploughing the western prairie, although we met such a loss, the ludicrous appearance of Powers with a pair of reins in one hand and an ox goad in the other, could not but excite some merriment. Off started the wagons, leaving us to scout the adjacent prairies and hills with some four days of provisions. We separated in the heart of the Pawnee hunting grounds, three riding to the south and Mr. Burgess from S. Carolina and myself to steer due east, the course from which we had just come. We found the trail of our horses and followed it some 80 miles, until lost among Buffalo tracks. We would frequently ride within 10 feet of some old bull sunning himself under the lea of a sand hill, but a near approach to them was so frequent we ceased to notice them.

What an undertaking, roaming in a strange land in quest of a thieving band of Indians. The number we did not even think of amid barren and arid waste. The growth of which was the prickly pear and bitter worm wood, interspersed with a little grass sufficient to keep life in our animals and water! Several nights we camped near stagnant pools, the odor of which was loathsome. I can compare these pools to nothing but a barn yard puddle, trod and mixed up by buffalo. We may have landed in Arkansaw but for luckily striking the trail which I knew. Quite an argument between Mr. Burgess and myself over which end of the trail to take--I finally convinced him and we turned our faces west again, unsuccessful in our hunt--exhausted with fatigue and provisions gone. We dismounted and drove our animals ahead of us. They became so tired. I succeeded in killing a fat Buffalo cow, from which we took sufficient to last us until we reached the waggons--Our companions, who had taken the other course, we had no knowledge of and finally the eighth day after leaving our company, we again found snugly camped on the north fork of the Platte and the others had returned to camp the like unsuccessful after 3 days search--we supposed the distance we had travelled about 300 miles.

One adventure is worth relating--while making for the grassy bottom of the Platte fast at night--we discoverd two Indians on the bank of the stream. We agreed to approach them and take them prisoners--supposing them to be armed with only bows and arrows--but the knaves saw us when about 300 yards from them--discharged a gun at Mr. Burgess and fled--I dismounted and took a crack at the devils, but did not hit--for fear of interception from a larger body in the night--we travelled fifteen miles farther and camped.

At Fort Laramie Powers and myself separated, he concluding to go to Oregon--I retained the wagon and cattle--he the mules and his share of provisions--in the states my trade would have been $75 the best bargain, but in the wilderness it was different. The mules were good pack animals for which he desired them. I loaned my waggon and cattle to an emigrant whose team was nearly exhausted and waggon broken down. With him I joined with now, no care, no trouble, hauling my trunks, ammunition, guns, harness, etc.

From this time on, no incident worthy of notice transpired, excepting the breaking up and forming of new companies. In the meantime, the rear companies had overtaken us--Russell resigned his control and with some 7 or 8 others packed through from Laramie--I stayed with the waggons, commenced trading in horses with mountain men and Souix Indians and found myself in possession of 7 head when we left Laramie--my note book is some 600 miles from here, consequently dates I cannot remember.

On arriving at Bridger's trading post on the Black fork of the Rio Colorado of the west--we found Lansford W. Hastings author of a work on California and Oregon, who had discovered a nearer route by some 300 miles, by way of the Salt Lake and great desert leaving the old route and Fort Hall to the North. He succeeded in inducing 1/2 of the emigration to follow him, but his statements to me was so unsatisfactory, concerning the route that our company followed the old trail, knowing that was passable--the result showed after travelling at least 300 miles farther--we came in ahead, our teams in better order, our provisions now plenty.

Oh! the fishing, speckled trout and the salmon trout were my daily prey--with a yankee rod and reel I astonished the Hoosiers--a singular fact, not a trout to be taken in the streams east of the South pass, but in every brook in the west I caught trout--even Mary's or Ogdens river which sinks in the desert--running a meandering course of 300 miles sometime flowing and again the bed entirely dry even in such a stream I took trout weighing upwards of 3 pounds.

On the same stream, the Shoshonee Indians, a tribe of the Snakes, committed many depredations on the emigrants. Frquently shooting at the men and at night killing cattle. They drove off several head of our cattle, killing some and wounding others. At a meeting of our company, it was resolved to attack the devils, recover our cattle if we could and chasten them severely and accordingly our little army praraded, numbering 17 men all told, only two others and myself on horseback, 14 on foot. The Indians had possession of a large track of rushes very high and thick. Their number at the lowest estimate was put down at 150, but I am confident it was a tribe of 300 souls, who had placed themselves in that position to prey on the emigrants.

We sallied forth and came within long rifle shot. I was selected to fire the first shot. I chose my ground, fired, every man disappeared, supposed to have been hit. Upon which the well known Indian yell was raised and onward we rushed driving them before us. Our first charge resulted in our killing two Indians, on our side two men were wounded with arrows and one horse, our leader slightly wounded in the wrist. Upon consultation we resolved to charge, your humble servant then leading, which resulted in dislodging them from their stronghold, and forcing them to the hills and rocks. No loss on our side, 3 Indians wounded. Up to this time we had been fighting them some four hours.

Our men elated with success, demanded again to be led on with a view to take some prisoners as hostages for their future good conduct--After driving about 50 of their warriors in the rocks we imprudently charged to within ten feet, and not less than 20 arrows were aimed at me alone--I escaped unhurt, but discharged "Yucatan" well loaded with buckshot in their faces.

We drew back about 30 yards from the redskins and opened a sure fire on them killing four more, but during the action, a Mr. Wm. P. Sallee of St. Louis, a brave, cool and determined Gentleman, received a mortal wound, of which he died 3 days after, and so keen were the devils to kill him that no less than four arrows pierced him at the same timeand his horse was also killed under him. Nor did I escape a slight token of their regard.

I had dismounted and exchanged "Yucatan" for a rifle with which I was operating. I had successfully dodged all their arrows, when a gun to my right bursted which drew my eye for a moment from the foe who took advantage of the opportunity and shot me through the right leg below the knee cap. It struck the bone, pierced thru beneath the sinew and there was I, most beautifully feathered--I immediately grasped the barbed point that protruded and drew the arrow its length through to which I attribute my quick recovery, the feathers wiping out all poisonous matter from the wound. 14 days from then I hobbled out on a pair of crutches made of willow and an old ox bow and 6 days from that threw them aside and have felt no inconvenience from the wound since, save when exposed and drenched with rain. Some 8 or 10 days previous to my arrival at Sutter's Fort, I was taken ill with the camp fever, of which after two weeks sickness I recovered.

From Sutter's Fort on the Sacramento, I started down that beautiful river, across the bay of Francisco to Yerba Buena on the south side. Where I hired a boat, invested my funds in groceries, and returned to Sutter's Fort, sailing the boat myself to trade with the emigrants. Being engaged ten days in which time with my small capital I cleared $107. The next 3 weeks I was traveling from one part of the Bay to another always with goods, trading for hides and produce, at the expiration of that time, Fremont and his little army started for lower California to quell an insurrection broken out there, Messrs Jacobs and Bryant whom I before mentioned had raised a company of Tule Indians, wrote me desiring that I would join them. Col. Russell obtained for me a commission under Fremont, Jacob, Captain, Bryant and myself Lts. of the Indians. We left the head of the Bay--joined Col. Fremont 120 miles at the mission of St. Johns There we commenced a memorable campaign. One which could only have been conducted by our indefatigable leader.

On our arrival at Sutter's Fort, the American Flag was flying and on my arrival at Yerba Buena it was there waving. The U.S. Sloop of War Portsmouth, Capt. Montgomery, the Warren, Capt. Hull, and the Savannah, Capt. Mervin were lying in port with some seven or 8 merchantmen and whalers.

The Bay exceeds any port or harbor I ever saw and the present site is well adapted for a commercial location. Com. Stockton in the Congress had sailed the day before for Lower California, where Fremont, who was then raising volunteers from the Emigrants, was to cooperate with him. Fremont had already been made Governor by Stockton and a civil Government was being formed whtn this revolution commenced which brought out the present array.

On the Salinas Plains near Monterey, a company of 54 Americans under Burrows were attacked by 165 Californians. The Americans with their awful weapons, the rifle, defeated the enemy with the loss of three men killed. Among the rest the brave Burrows. The loss of the Californians as I was informed by Thomas O. Larkin, our former consul, who was a prisoner at the time and necessarily a spectator, stated their loss at 16 killed and wounded, our company did not join the main body till after this fight. Our reception at Camp by Col. Fremont was gratifying; from the first days march we were made the advance guard and retained that position until we entered this City of the Angels, whimsically so called by Com. Stockton, a batch of adobe houses covering an area of a mile square with some 900 inhabitants.

I was freqently detached by the Col.--with a foraging troop and was successful in capturing horses and frequently prisoners. Our passage across the St. Barbara Mountain with four pieces of heavy artillery was a bold and glorious achievement and entitled our noble leader to the praise of his countrymen. At the Rencon where the mountains run into the sea and only low tide could we pass was also another daring exploit. The schooner, Julia Ann with two guns was sent horses and frequently prisoners. Our passage across the St. Barbara Mountain with four pieces of heavy artillery was a bold and glorious achievement and entitled our noble leader to the praise of his countrymen. At the Rencon where the mountains run into the sea and only low tide could we pass was also another daring exploit. The schooner, Julia Ann with two guns was sent at the The California Gen. Flores had challenged Fremont. Here we were only 400 strong, advancing towards an enemy 1600 strong and the best horsemen in the world. But Flores, having a more contemptable opinion of the marines and sailors than he had of riflemen, judiciously attacked the Commodore on the 8th of January, but withdrew after sustaining considerable loss. On the 9th they again attacked the Co. who how had formed a juncture with Gen. Kearny with his 500 dragoons, but was defeated with the loss of 60 killed and wounded. The Comd. loss was but 3 killed and wounded. This victory enabled Stockton to take this place. He entered the Town four days before our arrival; the Spainards, however, would not surrender to him, they captiulated with our leader and surrendered their armies. Col. Fremont is again Gov. Com. Stockton has marched to Santiago on the coast and Gen. Kearny to San Pedro.

It appears Kearny arrived here with instructions to conquer the country and institute a civil government, his orders from Government were dated the 6th of lst June, Stockton was invested with the same power, only of prior date. Stockton contended he had conquered the country and appointed a Govr. and neither Fremont nor Stockton did recongnise Kearny's authority, no doubt you will see accounts in the papers at length, as I know communications have been forwarded from here to the press. Col. Russell is Sec of State and a council of 3 Americans and 2 natives been appointed to put our laws in execution. They are appointed by the Gov. for this and next year, after that the election goes to the people. Capt. Jacob returned to the states via Panama. E. Bryant than whom a more sterling man never lived, returns by the mountains. He has been taking notes, intends publishing his work as soon as he can, of his arrival at the states and from the war. I say a better account of the country will not be necessary.

I am now Asst. Qtrmaster, holding my comn. still of Lt. Both officers have gone, a part of the Battalion disbanded, but the Indians still here and under my control.

Not an idle day has passed since I arrived in Cala. and to you again I do return sincere thanks for the opportunity in launching out on the rough seas of life. Should it meet your approbation and you wish to start one of your nephews to this country, a certain and sure competency await any individual who would now invest money in anything. Whether you contemplate such an adventure now, I know not-- Vehicles selling at home from 80 to 100 is worth 400 to $500— machines thrashing, cornshellers, mining or cradling machines 200 percent above cost and charges can be realized. Dry goods of all kinds, hardware, in fact, the country is destitute of all merchandise.I have in my possession an article from Thomas O. Larkin, former consuland the best merchant in the country, guaranteeing to raise and put in my possession $4,000 which amount I am to invest in goods at the Sandwich Islands.

The appointment of Asst. Qmaster has been offered me. But I wish only to remain in employ temporarily. Mr. Larkin is above; he expects to be here soon in the Hawaiian Barque, Don Quixote, Commander Paty, with whom I sail for the Island.My letter of introduction has been of the utmost importance to me. At once being made acquainted with all the prominent business men of the country. The amount due me from Government and funds and property on hand amounts to not one cent less than 900 Dol. Mr. Larkin is now building a large store and warehouse at Yerba Buena which will be open for a produce and Genl. Assortment Store. I have secured two lots in the town, the seat of Government at present or for the time is located here, but will be removed north after this session.California is all that I expected, both as regards soil and grazing purposes but for an agricultual country it is not well adapted. Some rich mines of Lead and Silver have been discovered and mining operations will commence soon as the Govnt. is throughly settled. The resources of this country are immense, but under the control of the natives never would have been brought out. Now the Anglo-Saxon race predominating, everything looks up and even the lazy indolent Spaniard who before thought work a disgrace will be sure striving to earn, if fact they must work now or the Yankee will root them out and soon have their property.The express by which I forward this starts in the morning, with the noted Kit Carson, Gov. Fremont's guide as bearer of dispatches. I would write E.H.W. Mother, or some of the boys but must defer it until I arrive at the Sandwich Islands.

I am very desireous to hear from home, to receive any papers or news would be very acceptable. When you hear from me again, I shall be some 600 miles north doing business with all to gain and not much to lose. Commodore Sloat left the coast before my arrival, consequently your friend's kind letter is still in my possession. With respects and remembrance to all I conclude, hoping you may enjoy the same blessing "health" I now have. Remember me affectionately to all your family and to my good mother. Send her word that Ben is trying to do well. Affectionately,Benj. S. Lippincott

Letter Number 2.Ciudad de Los Angeles, Feb. 7, 1847, E. H. Williams, Esq.,

This will serve to introduce you to adjutant, L.T. Talbot, Bearer of Dispatches from Gov. Fremont to U.S. Govnt. Any Attention paid Mr. Talbot will be duly appreciated by your affectionate Bub.Benj. S. Lippincott

Letter Number 3,Ciudad de Los Angeles,March 22nd1847

Dear Bub,This will serve to introduce to your acquaintance, Col. Wm. H. Russell, Sec. of State of California, under Gov. Fremont. You will find him a pleasant, affable, and instructing acquaintance. If so an opportunity should offer that you could introduce the Colonel to Mother and Amelia, it will be a source of gratification to me. He will be enabled to inform all concerning this "El Dorado" of the west. No doubt through Jno. L. Stephens Esq., you heard from be dated February--since that time, I have remained here occupied as Assistant Quartermaster in the California Battalion and consequently one of Gov. Fremont's staff. My salary is good and amply sufficient for all present wants. My prospects too are flattering.

The Gov. detailed me to accompany him to the States on secret duty to the Capital. but considering the expenses of traveling and elapse of time before I again returned to California, although my salary still continues and expenses paid, I would arrive here about as I would start. I accordingly respectfully declined the appointment, although I might gain "notoriety."Quite a complicated political machinery is now in operation here as well as in the States. Commodore Stockton arrived on this coast sometime early last May, with instructions in case of war with Mexico to conquer the country and establish a civil government. At the same time Major Fremont received his commission of Lieut. Col. Fremont and was to cooperate with the Commodore. Recruiting officers were sent to meet the immigrants who to a man enlisted. Myself, Gov. Boggs, Capt. Reed, and one or two others did not at the time on account of sickness.

I could then as early as Nov. last have obtained a Captaincy, but my health was an obstacle and again I desired to enter the broils of contending parties as little as I could--Stockton sailed for the southern coast and Fremont with 450 as hawk-eyed riflemen as ever pulled triggers marched down through the country. Oh! that campaign and the spirits that formed that little army, fatigue, endurance, toil, hunger, and often time drenched with the heavy rains was all overcome and on we came.Com. Stockton landed his marines and sailors numbering 400 men at San Diego, 165 miles south of this and marched his men on foot to meet Fremont, on the memorable plains of Kowango.

But we had been detained for want of horses traveling over 600 miles in the most inclement season that Stockton, who was about five days travel nearer the focus: viz City of Angels, was met by the enemy on the 8th and 9th Jany and a severe skirmish ensued, which resulted in the defeat of the Mexicans and consequently he marched triumphantly in the city. Notwithstanding their defeat, the Mexicans on superior horses were not captured. They immediately presented themselves to Fremont who was now within 2 days of the city and surrendered which mortified the naval officers--The idea of their capitulating with the "barefoot Battalion."

What brought me amongst them is simply this, while selling a small consigment of goods at the head of Francisco Bay, a messanger came with a request from Col. Fremont to proceed to Yerba Buena and there procure a cannon, ammunition, etc. and deliver it to an officer who in the meantime would arrive at the head of the Bay. On my return with the gun, my feelings were enlisted for the cause and I proceeded with the escort to Camp Johns, 120 miles south. Here Fremont tendered me with a Lieutcy in Co. H which I accepted and from that time on was in more perilous service than any other co. constantly as advance guard, except when on a horse raising exped-ition. With a detachment of 10 as rascally redskins as ever drew breth, I succeeded in taking three prisoners and they were the first brought in camp in the campaign.

So here am I now about 600 miles south of San Francisco hale, hearty, and busy. But the politics. It appears that General Kearny with same instructions from Gov. as "Fighting Bob" arrived just after the conquest of the country and demanded to be recognized Governor. That was a pill neither Stockton and Fremont would swallow, accordingly for the time he withdrew, but still intent on the Governship. While this counciling was going on at Angeles, the Gov. sends another Governor in the person of Col. Mason from Virginia, who arrived at Monterey some 500 miles north of this. Com. Shubrick also arrived and succeeded Stockton, Biddle also arrived. Now the jealousy of the naval commanders to Stockton is well known and Kearney thinking to enlist them, proceeded immediately to Monterey. There after a long consultation Kearny was pronounced Governor, issued his proclamation and as a superior officer, ordered Fremont to report to him instantly. Fremont wisely relinquished his authority without transgressing any law, either civil or military and this morning started north. What the results will be time will develop. but all the officers concur in the opinion that Fremont is entitled to the Governorship and we are now daily looking for the return dispatch that was forwarded to Washington after the capitulation. The Union naval officer "in mass" are in favor of Fremont. A son of Louis McClane was a major in our Battalion, but Shubrick very cavallierly ordered him afloat and other similar instances. The popularity of Fremont among the natives is unbounded.

Threats are even made if Fremont is not Governor, they will raise another insurrection. Colonel Russell is now on secret business on this same subject. Col. Benton is father-in-law to Fremont. Calhoun is his warm friend, and through Russell formerly marshall of Missouri he expects to conciliate the Whig Party. So long as good pay, so long am I here, etc. I might have been more strongly induced to return but oh, that horrid trip over the mountains. If I do return, it will either be by sea or by Panama, but as I think at present some two or three years must elapse. In a commercial point of view, this country must attract considerable attention Francisco Bay particularly, but on beauty and safety exeed your far famed harbour. The principal trade is from the Sandwich Islands and goods of all descriptions are enormously high. The first ten days I was in the country I proceeded from Sutter's Fort on the Sacramento, to Francisco Bay and there invested my funds after which I cleared in hard cash 107 doll. Again the next ten weeks while selling goods, some on consignment, some my own at head of bay, I cleared 120 dols. These are not occasional instances but daily occurances and will until an influx of Genuine Yankees and their wares flood the country.

The resources of the country are not yet developed. Mines for instance abound in all quarters, lead in the north and at no future day a great trade will be opened with China. In this section gold and silver abound. This country like all that has been the scene of war the last 12 years, constant revolution has occurred which not only draw forth all the money, but decrease the stock which is hide and tallow the staple product tend to ruin the country. A description of the town's manners and customs of the inhabitants might employ me for some time and the accound would be exactly the description of Kendall's Santa Fe expedition or Hasting's work on California.

My letters were of material benefit at once introducing be to many business men, and consequent advantages. I have seen California from the head waters of Sacramento to San Diego, but it does not suit me. Want of timber, want of water, want of communication except on horse back or by sea, and greatest of all objections a want of agricultural country. As a grazing district it exceeds any I have ever seen, and a man that does not own from 3 to 20 leagues, has no rancho or farm at all. The Catholics with all their pomp and ceremony flourish here, but the Mormons who are fast congregating here create some jealousy.

Now if Shep want health and to improve his affairs, let him start to Independence and from there here, astonishing as it may seem, invalids from the states pronounced passed medical aid have started on this trip regained their health and now are enjoying the best of health. No exaggeration when I say they kill a bullock, hang it up at their door, the air so pure and there it] remains in their warmest weather until eaten by he family. I could write many a page. Wheter great inducement to return is my desire to see mother, to see all, but I know I would be sacrificing my expenses and eat up my earning. I have never been from home, that my desire was so strong to return. Col. Fremont's offer made me unsettled and vacillating for a week, but my conclusion is settled and here I stay.

My warmest thanks for all your kindness and my love to "all," don't let the least chances pass without writing and I shall answer every opportunity. Remember me kindly to Fletcher and introduce the Col. to him, also to Jno. L. Stephens Esq. and say to him, his kindness to me is remembered and I shall write him the first opportunity.I introduced Major Talbot to you who left here on my express in February. You will find him much of a Gentl. Wm. H. Hanford was desirous to hear from me, tell him to come and see this country and no danger of his being dissatisfied. Now if Wm. would induce Bloom Hannond to invest every cent he could raise for staple articles of any kind for this market, he would make a good adventure.

Many are the advantages open for any adventurer who invests his funds in your market. Mr. Frank Ward, a New Yorker, sailed in the Brooklyn, before I started, with $1500 in goods and now commands amuch of a Gentl. Wm. H. Hanford was desirous to hear from me, tell remember Uncle Ben to all the little ones and tell them he often thinks of them. To Mother, Amelia, Clarence, the boys all, all my love, Your affectionate Brother, Benj. S. Lippincott

Letter Number 4, Colton Hall, September 25th, 1849, Monterey, Jno. L. Stephens Esq.

Dear Jn.Your letter by Mr. Beale came today to hand and I feel gratified by your notice I am now occupying a seat in the Convention of California from the San Joaquin District--having been elected during my absence to this place, and the honor being conferred I could do no less than attend this body--although sacrificing much valuable time.I have been as active to accomplish my desires as my means would adm it had not "Dame fortune" deserted me when I disposed of my property to come home prior to the bursting of our "gold bubble," I might now have been in the states with more than a competency. As it is, I lose nothing by preserving and am in hopes to gather a small share of the harvest here.

A discovery has lately been made by Col. Fremont in my opinion equal to the first discovery of gold here, viz, the discovery of a vein at the head of the River Mariposa on which is situated his ranch purchased from the former Mexican Gov. Alvarado, proving to the world our mines can never be exhausted--new discoveries are being made daily, and our population is increasing rapidly. We have now been sitting since the 3rd Sept. having present 44 members from the ten districts and will probably close our labour by the 1st Oct. but I am fearful not in time to send our Constitution to Washington by the Oct steamer.

The slave question is forever settled here, no involuntary servitude and we have even gone so far as to exclude the free Negro race from emigrating here. The incorporation of Banks and monopolies have received their ?????. Our seat of Gov. will be located most probably at

San Jose de Guadaloupe and our elections for state officers as well as Senators and Representatives will be held at the same time the Constitution will be put before the people for their acceptance or refection. The election will come off the first week in November. The most prominent candidate for the Senate is Col. Fremont who will certainly receive a larger vote than any man in this country. He will fill the office of commissioner to settle our Southern boundary until another is appointed, considering his services were demanded before the appointment arrived.

You must not consider me vain when I write there is no man in our district who can cut a wider swath than I can and I am determined to use my influence for his elevation. California may through him receive her dues--but I am decidedly opposed to assist in hoisting any man to that office who has never seen it rain in this country. We have some shrewd old political hacks who even concocted a ticket of Panama for the future representation of Cal. We do not fear them and they will probably receive as sure a defeat as the occasion calls for.

Now my own prospects. I have since my return secured lots in San Jose, Stockton, and New York of the Pacific besides now locating a town on the San Joaquin, the prospects of which are flattering--having also purchased with others part of Castro's grant at the head of navigation in the San Joaquin, intending to lay out another town by the time steamers are put on that river. That co. is composed of Blair, Hammond, Fremont, ?????, and myself. I drew this co. together and the material with little expense is among us to compete with any co. in California for the advance of this district. Last April I established on the Tuolumne river a trading post as a gap to the Merced and Mariposa mines, controlling all the Indians between the Tuolumne and Merced river by which a lucrative business has been done. But two days ago a reprot was brought me [that] our Indians had gathered in one day 38 pounds of gold, but I have no certain a/c from my partners of their success since I have been here.

Last April we were the first to settle so far south, but one short month and thousands had crowded in below us, necessarily drawing business and trade to our door. I am anxious the elections were over, desirous of wintering in the mountains, having closed out all interest in San Francisco and owning no property except at San Jose south of the San Joaquin of any value. When I returned from Mazatlan last Feby. I fortunately found myself part owner of a water and Beach lot in San Francisco and the other owners I immediately bought out, the lot then costing me $400. In the last week of August, I sold the same lot for $9000, every foot under water--San Francisco will eventually be much injured by locations further up the Bay. But its present advanced state and the amount of capital invested there, will hold business until steam navigation is introduced and all our rivers navigated and steam tow boats to take shipping afore San Francisco Bay and up to Pablo Bay through Carquenez Straits to Benecia or Marteniz and possibly through Suisune Bay to New York of the Pacific.

The emigration is now arriving and many ore settling in our district and quite a friendly contention exists whether Sacramento or San Joaquin has the greatest population. Those two as by apportionment of delegation and apportionment of representation in our Legislature those districts will be equal to the other eleven. Being on the Special Committee for reporting a constitution, I can promise the strengths of this new state will be in the hands of those two districts. Thomas Lloyd Vermule whose family you may know is also a delegate here from my district. He will probably be in the first Legislature.

I have not attempted to distinguish myself by speechifying here but have reserved a silence in my seat and out of doors will turn my hand to none in using desirable influence--A still lounge shows some wisdom--If I could but sit by you one hour it would be more satisfactory to both and many interesting points that do not now strike me would form a continuity of thought and conversation be developed and my great excuse for not writing or keeping up a correspondence is an inability to do so to my satisfaction. The time is nothing, the labor a pleasure, but habit is confirmed and a greater task I could not undertake. But to you a duty prompts.

The policy of purchasing or ordering goods in New York is impractable besides the great proportion of our trade consumes nothing but Mexican goods, the Indians having aped the fashions of the Californiansl. Our trade is extensive as I first started. We are the pioneers in that quarter and it was not until Fremont came up the valley from the Soluth did people feel it safe to work in small detached parties. His name was "Legion" and on rushed the "Diggers." Aside from the influence I controlled people came confidently forward which has resulted in such immense discoveries to the south. That I can go to the first Senate of this new state I do not doubt and to you I say I can, but I am not desirous of that fame.

My feeling have been much gratified at taking my seat here, proving to my friends at home that I have grown with this country, but my pocket must be better lined and time is too precious although the pay would be considered an object in any other state, "honor thrown in. "I have now 31 lots at the place where the seat of Gov. will be located, San Jose, bought last May and not quite a ?????. I have in Stockton, one of our most thriving inland commercial towns 13 lots variously valued from $400 to $1500 dolls and upon the introduction of steamers will advance 50 pr. ct. Other valuable property I have besides my regular business and not one cent in debt so you see a foundation is now laid that by attention the coming winter I shall again be "about." The remnant of the $500 dolls. you so kindly advanced me rolled itself into a Ball of such magnitude that now the property drawn together by me ln that small remnant I had in my pocket when I landed at San Francisco would now amt. to at S. Francisco valuation over $200,000.

What prompted me to sell was a desire to come home, induced by constant solicitations from my family, but it is passed, and here am I at it again, led by "hope" and a sanguine disposition of future success--at any rate a satisfaction I am not idle. The Monmouth ????? Mining Co., composed of Red Bankers principally, have not as a Co. been successful, finding, as many have who arrived here with the expectation of picking up gold any where without trouble find it a more serious matter than anticipated. I do not think candidly our mineral resources have as yet been half developed, new arriving that gold is being found now on the coast range--hertofore alone found on the Sierra Nevada. Again at the head of Trinity Bay gold has been discovered and the mines generally rich, besides our vast silver and quicksilver mines.

Should you be desirous of a splendid operation forward immediately a steamer of the same style as the ?????. $40,000 would be paid this day for her in full blast here and steamers of that description will for a long time be in demand. 100 steamers for the Bay and rivers will only increase instead of diminishing business. Europe has not awakened and what will we do for transportation for our population. Again should the steamboat business be over done in the Bay, such a boat as the one built to cross New York Bay would be the very boat for our coast trade from San Francisco, Monterey, San Luis Obispo, Santa Barbara, San Pedro and San Diego.

The moment our Gov. is established, the mail contract for the coast the passengers and freight would form a most lucrative business. It certainly will pay should such a scheme not be put in operation until the elapse of eight months--All the boats now afloat are inadequate and too little power. Think of this and should you by inquiry and information be induced to enter into it I should be happy to hear by return steamer and then will state the interest I should desire in the speculation.Sept. 26th--Col. Fremont leaves for San Francisco this morning and I find him a steady business young man.

Much respected and thought of by his friends--Ned Beale is here, he will probably come flying with our Constitution to Washington. We have told him here he can take a seat in our first Legislature, but a young wife at home is the "magnet." Please remember me affectionately to Uncle and your family, and should you see any of my family, say my health is unimpaired and hopes alluring. I shall write them by Beale.Very respectfully, yr obdt servt,Benj. S. Lippincott

Letter Number 5, Convention Hall, Sept. no Oct. 1st, 1849

Sister Amelia: To you I again drop a few lines, my antipathy for corresponding certainly originates more from thoughtlessness, than from a desire to communicate with you all, but one letter can say to all that I enjoy the same good health and prospering slowly. On the other side you have a design for the seal of the new State of California--with my usual desire of copying, I imitated the design recommended by the committee, and thought that none would appreciate it more, than yourself. Here I go in my wild way of introducing to you almost an enigman without in the first place stating your brother is a member of the Great California Convention. Elected by the people and met to frame the constitution for this new start--the particulars of which will probably be printed in journals at home.

I was elected from San Joaquin district one of the two richest portions of California and receiving one more vote than any delegate from the same district. T. Lloyd Vermule sits along side of me and I can assure you no disgrace to our representation. So you will see I am again in politics, but only for the consummation of one object; vis-a-vis, to prove tomy friends at home that I have warm friends here, and those who support me.

Again I am desirous to see Col. Fremont, a Senator from this state, who will certainly come on as soon as we are admitted. We have much talent here and many aspiring and prominent men, but they have "never seen it rain here yet." Mr. Beale now rooms with me and will come on the "wings of Mercury" with our Constitution when completed. He will call and see you if in New York .Col. Fremont and family are here.

I had the pleasure to hear from Mrs. F. the other day that a chair at her table was always vacant for me. Oh, what a splendid lady--you would be pleased with her. She is certainly instructive and amusing and Oh! how bitter when she chooses. My prospects are the same and when I last wrote home my business in the mines has proved lucrative and my investments in land good. We have removed the seat of Gov. to San Jose de Guadalupe, where fortunately I owned 31 lots, which only advanced 20 percent. I sold my last lot in San Francisco on the first of September, which cost me $400, for $2,000 dols. This I have reinvested. You will soon hear of a new town called "Eureka," which I have the honor of locating and having surveyed. It is situated in my district nearer the southern mines than any other town. Mr. Blair, a partner, steams the San Joaquin, has arrived to run exclusively to our town, and and Col. Fremont, also a partner, has discovered a mine, not a placer, which pours out riches inexhaustible, but a short distance from the site.Ned Beal is very anxious to have me accompany him home, but I would sacrifice so much and the previous lesson has tahught me to be patient.

I was desirous to see you all, which induced me to sell out before which property now is worth over $200,000 dols.--should I be successful, this winter, will come to see you all in the spring as communication is now so easy by the Isthmus.A Mr. Savage, Foster, and myself formed a Co. which went in operation last April--and just the other day news came to me they had with the Indians under our control, got out 38 pounds of gold in one day, but I have no positive assurance of this fact, but have no doubt they are very successful. I recd. from Jno L. Stephens a long letter, he has condescended, last steamer, offering any assistance, but prosperity does not need it--however--I advised him to make a spec. offering to take an equal share. What his answer will be I cannot say, but he may possibly accept. The house is adjourned and I am waiting at my room.

Ned lies dozing on the bed, waiting with anxiety the results of our labours. (*Note: Letter is unfinished.*)

Letter Number 6,San Francisco,Jan. 8th, 1850,.Jno. L. Stephens

It affords me pleasure to introduce to your acquaintance Genl. Thos. I. Green. The Genl. had the honor representing one of our most populous districts in the first Senate of California. You will glean from him desirable intelligence in relation to this "term." A scheme is now an foot to locate the capital of Cal. Capital and influence is not wanting--the Genl. will explain fully. I shall write you particulars by this steamer in the care of the Genl., who will see you at Panama. David Broderick Esq. of this city joins me in our remembrance to you.

With due respect,Yr. obdt. sertBenj. S. Lippincott

Letter Number 7, Senate Chamber, January 26, 1851, Sunday Morning

Dear Sister, Your affectionate letter of the 10th November is before me and how to employ the morning better than writing home I know not. How is it I never heard of Hattie's marriage, your letter bearing the first information. With all my heart I wish her happiness, and do not doubt from the character her husband bears that she will enjoy her share.Ere' this, Shep is amongst you and a gratification it must be to Mother. I have not written as punctually since his return. I heard from Charles a short time since. He was still in the mines, and I feel thankful he is located in the most thickly populated district on account of the recent Indian disturbances.

My former partner has been driven from his camp on the Fresno and three young men murdered by the Indians and all his property was burnt. Since a battle has been fought in which some 50 Indians were killed, and subsequently they in large numbers attacked another settlement in the night and massacred 76 Americans. The Gov. has ordered out troops to aid the miners, and we have been the last two days legislating to create a "war fund" to defray expenses. I rear the war will be protracted as the Indians, counting all the tribes from Sacramento to Tulare lake number about 9000 who subsist principally on roots and acorns and can take refuge in the impregnable fastnesses of the Sierra Nevada.

Charles was well and should I hear he is not successful will send for him. Will you allow Mr. Vanity to day a little about himself? Gov. P.H. Burnett resigned some two weeks since and the Lieut. Gov. Jno. McDougal installed as Gov. consequently a Lieut. Gov. as president of the Senate was wanted. There were many aspirants in our body. I declined a nomination but recd a majority of the votes. I then requested each member not to support me. But Genl. Douglass, a warm friend and another senator would vote for me, so that if you see the vote you must not think I would allow myself to be run and defeated. Mr. Broderick, who is a New Yorker, I warmly supported. Much feeling exists here between Northerners and Southerners. This ultra-radicalism I despise, particularly a fanatical Southerner.

Quite a compliment was paid me a few days since. The title of Col. is prefixed to my name. The first intimation I had was in the State Journal, that the Hon. B.S.L. and Col. J. Neely Johnson were appointed aid de camps to his excellency, Gov. McDougal. How heart rending is the news about those two little boys. Do send for them and put them to school. I will forward $1000 to Shep for than purpose. That puppy Leonard ought to be cowhided within an inch of hs life. My feelings have not been as much ruffled in a long time as when your letter cautiously speaks of his cruelty. Something should be done--a day of retribution will come when he must answer for this inhuman conduct. I wrote to your cubs and directed them to superscribe to me as the capital.

Overtures of great interest have been made me by aspirants--for instance a position worth $6000 per annum and perquisites, but I hold off. The legislation is within one or two of a tie as regards politics. I have acted independent and with two friends whom I control, can wield the balance of power. Fremont is very friendly and polite. T. Butler King calls in my room most every day. The small potatoes are still more friendly and ever obsequious--so much for management.

I have been thinking seriously of making a flying trip home this spring--circumstances will govern. I am desirous of seeing you all. What would you say: to see an hombre weighing about 186 pounds, hearty and hale, stalk in among you some day ?Although I begin to count the years, and they number too many?, I feel the dame bouyancey of spirits as when at 18. My health is excellent. This climate suits me. Think of the 26th Jany, sitting here with my window up and the birds singing gayly and such succession of days. Everyone who remains 2 or 3 winters in this state will never be satisfied with the cold northeasters and snoe and sleet of your latitudes.

Monday Morning, 27th Jany-- Another fine day and here am I at me desk penning again. The Gov. appointment I yesterday mentioned has jus been reported--We have a mass of business before us which will occasion a log session--how position opens new eyes to the intriues of the world. So many advances mad so differently and all emanating from some interested motive. On the 4th of Feby, a grand flare up comes off.

I send Annie a ticket. Tell her if she only had wings how soon she would fly over. Tell Ned he's a dutchman and won't write to Uncle Ben. I suppose your little ones are all at school. By the by, I made arrangements this morning to send E.H. W. instead of Shep $1000 which is all the same. Please expend it for the little boys of Clem, Willy, and Eugene. Let Hart use his judgment. I will strive and write Mother a few lines by this steamer. I can judge of her anxiety to hear from us and will try and reciprocate all favors from home. As ever, your affectionate Brother, Benj. S. Lippincott, My love to all!!

Letter Number 8, San Jose Jany 28th, 1851, Senate Chambers, Jno L. Stephens, Esq.

Dr. Jn.Your last favor was recd just previous to the convening of the Legislature. In relation to the Vallejo Scheme, I have secured from Genl. Vallejo and Capt. Frisbee (his agent) two shares--one for yourself and myself, and the other between Col Geo McDougal and myself. The bill for the removal of the capital from this place has passed our body by a vote of eleven to two. Fears are entertained for its safety in this house, but I can assure you, young politicians as we are, deeper intrigue we never resorted to. This is a school calculated to make one better acquainted with human nature than any I have ever been connected with.

You will notice our friend D.W. Broderick Esq. is our president, the Lieut. Gov. filling the place of P.H. Burnett who resigned. I was waited upon by a committee to take the appointment and also by David, but declined. Much feeling exists between Northern and Southern members. This ultraism of the South and fanaticism of the North I despise and have kept aloof from either party.

My course has been independent. The Legislature is very nearly a tie and with two friends who go with me, I shall be ble to paralize the action of wither unless the movements are formidable. Questions have been made me by prominent men aiming at the Senatorship, but always through third persons.

Apon all occasions I listen. The candidates now before us are J.C. Fremont, Jno. W. Geary, Jno B. Nelles, T. Butler King, and Soloman Heydenfelt. All have their strong friends, and should each party conform to a caucus nomination, I predict a Democrat will be returned. I was shown a letter written by King this morning intended to this steamer, recommending to Millard Filmore my appointment as one of the U.S. Commissioners to settle the old Cal. claims. It was not at my request, but would accept--it may have been a "feeler."

Constant intimacy with these Gents. show the influence at work and Gov. patronage is freely distributed. I was not sufficiently explicit in relation to the seat of Gov. The city is divided into thirty shares, and for each share secured to the shareholders, it is necessary they should give bonds for the payment of $7500 dolls per share to be paid in two years from the time the Gov. signs the Bill or so soon as property can be sold, the proceeds to be paid to the Board of Directors. All this I can easily arrange already many are desirous to take hold and advance for an interest. I have no doubt a most profitable investment will be made again. The induences used by Genl Green as agent for influential individuals at home are carrying their due weight. You will observe by the papers the disturbance with the Indians. I fear a protracted war. They number 8 or 9000--subsisting on roots and acorns and takiing refuge in their mountain fastnesses.

The Governor has ordered out a force in connection with a force dispatched by Genl P.F. Smith. I have just recd from Senator Woodsworth a recommendation to President Fillmore in favor of myself as a commissioner to settle claims of our citizens against the U.S. Govt. It was signed by every senator. I understand there is also one in circulation in the House. It will do no harm to forward them. 29th Jany.

T. B. King has opened privately a serious question in relation to the Quicksilver mines of this place. The Almaden Mine yields now at the rate of $1,200,000 per annum and other equally rich veins are in the vicinity. I have certain knowledge of some facts that should prove profitable--More anon.Before the receipt of your letter, I had your circular published in the "Herald" and forwarded some copies to your, desiring to draw attention here to the completion of your giant work in which our people are vitally interested.

Any service I can be, I will willingly lend my attention. Some of my plans must obtain, for instance, being chairman of the committee on public buildings and state prisons. I have a scheme to report a bill in which the Gov. will have the appointing power of superintendents and be authorized to let to parties the care of the prisoners for their clothing and subsistence, in the lieu of the labor to be performed--at the rate of laboor here a most profitable arrangement will be made--of course through third persons.

Your old friend Dennis is dong well. I never meet him that he does not speak of you--Please give my best respects he will say if you write. I also met Jno. Mc????. He has done well.

Casserly who brought a letter form you has his paper in full blast in San Francisco. Please remember me to Uncle Benj. By last mail I had recd from home all well. With due respect, Your obdt servt.Benjamin S. Lippincott

Letter Number 9, San Francisco, July 14th, 1852, Jno L. Stephens Esq.

Dear Jn.Your letter of June 23rd was received through the hands of ????? Stephens this morning. Now in relation to any property or share of property coming to me from my father's estate in which you may be interested, I freely and willingly accord to you the authority on my part to do as in your judgment you may think best and will willingly ratify when I return to the states anything that may have been doe by you predicated upon my assent thereto. I shall strive and be at home the following year.

My shoulder is now at the wheel again. I am not involved nor can I command a heavy amount neither can I ever relinquish the desire to come out of California better than when I entered it. You no doubt will be interested in my present--I am now engaged in superintending the state prison labor. Having an interest myself, aside from the salary of $400 a month. We are employing them at a steam brick works owned by the co. and I have made with the labor 43,000 bricks per day and can compete with any concern in Cal. for contracts. We have offered our proposition to the Pacific Steamship Co. at Benecia to supply material for their works and other contracts supplying builders in this city. The site of the State prison has been changed from Vallejo to within 500 yds of our grounds. The land purchased by the state commissioners the deed made and delivered the state and paid for offers will be accepted this week to furnish material.

Now some of the com. are interested with us. "We may by chance get the contract. At any rate my time is employed and I receive good pay for it. I have been dabbling in several things and plan a foothold yet Some of the money cannot burn.

Politcally too independent to ask for anything and to be a party hack? Too senile and hypocritical for me. Although there are many prominent men here who owe their advancement partly to me whose influence I might command, but nothing is made at it, unless one stoops to downright stealing. Such as I have witnessed here. I await the time when with pleasure, I can sit down and rehearse to you the course of many of our prominent men here and the general listing of many you know.

The last fire in June one year ago hurt me indirectly, but I will not complain--good health stout heart, and a desire to do what is right will yet bring me along. This life is a long rough road and will not do to travel too fast. One's "mule" might get "tender footed." I gave Lieut. Gov. Purdy and Mr. A.H. Sibley a letter each to you. Do engage them in conversation you will find they can post you in relation to matters here. Will you please remember me kindly to your father--A grand Dem. ratification meeting took place in the plaza. More unanimity could not have been expected. California will give Pierce four thousand majority.

Mr. Purdy will call to see you; he can give you more information than I could write on a piece of paper. He is one of our most pipular men and deservedly so. Sibley is a Whig and if he returns here in time will get the Whig nomination for Mayor of this city. If you meet any of my people will you please remember me to them. I am a poor correspondent and seldom write. One longing wish I have, to see by good old mother once more. With due respect, As ever, Benj. S. Lippincott

Letter Number 10,Santa Barbara, May 18th, 1853, Mr. B. D. Wilson.

Dear Sir, Your favor came to hand after some delay and I did not answer it expecting every week to start for Los Angeles, but not being able to get farther south this time, I hasten to write you in relation to the subject we were speaking of.

You wrote that the spring had partially dried up; it must certainly fine vent somewhere in the same neighborhood and should you succeed in procuring possession, I will pay half the expenses by a draft on my through Palmer, Cook, and Co. Machinery and apparatus has been forwared to this state by Gov. Purdy's brother who will be prepared to operate as soon as he arrives. I feel assured in stating to you nothing can be lost by a moderate outlay to secure the right to the spring and a small quantity of land adjacent. Should you judge it of sufficient importance to claim your time and attention for a short time, please acquaint me respectfully, Yr. obdt. servt.Benj. S. Lippincott

Letter Number 11, Sacramento, 28th March, 1854, Mr. J.W. Mandeville.

Sir Enclosed I send a letter from Mrs. D.A Enyart. Please peruse it and at your earliest convenience I would respectfully request an interview. Mr. Enyart is desirous to have an answer and I am as equally desirous that an amicable understanding should be had between you.Can you call at the Orleans, say this afternoon at 4 or 5 o'clock. respectfullyYr. etc. Benj. S. Lippincott

Letter Number 12, San Francisco, Nov. 5th, 1855

Friend Houghton, In relation to the matter of the young man we spoke of, Mr. Broderick has told me if you will forward to him or to Gov. Bigler the recommendation to mercy in his favor, it shall be promptly attended to. Do not fail to pay attention to this. Of course I feel much interest in it, but would not have Vermule know it. It is a sad thing and enough to break his poor mother's heart. Your early attention is respecfully requested--Yr. Obt. Servt.Benj. S. Lippincott

Letter Number 13, New York, August 10th, 1855

Dear Uncle, I have called upon Mr. Burger, 51 Courtland St., one of Mr. Dayton's administrators and he paid the [?] after talking a short time, he wishes particularly to see you about releasing Mr. Dayton's estate and taking two other parties with of whim he says are as good as the estate. His object is to get released from serving as administrator until the end of the lease. If as he says, he will give two persons of either of whom are as good and better than the Est. I can see no objection to canceling the lease and letting them settle the Est. Tomorrow I will deposit the money as per your request at the Merchants Bank. Yours, B. S. Lippincott

Will of John C. Smart, Recorded July 15, 1861, Butler County, Missouri, Book C, pp. 125-126

To the children of Sarah Smart, children being John Morrow and Ester Catherine Morrow an amount in cash equal to the value of their portion of their fathers estate at the time John C. Smart married their mother. Also within this will is the giving the power of attorney to James W. Morrow while John C. Smart is at war. Also assigns James W. Morrow Executor and Administrator of will should John get killed in the civil war.

To all to whom these presents may concern be it known that owing to the confused condition of State and Government affairs and the fact of civil war in our midst I have deemed it my duty which I owe to myself and my family to volunteer in defence of what I deem to be my rights intending to defend those rights to the best of my abilities: in view of all these matters and the uncertainty of life and the certainty of death at home or abroad and all these things being considered I have determined to make an agent to attend to all my public business and in all cases to act as my attorney in fact to sue and for me and in my name to accept service of process and defend or compromise all in any suits according to his best discretion and in case of my death to be my Executor and Administrator until the appointment hereby made shall be worked either by my dismisal from Military Service or by document of revocation under my hand and Seal upon request of such agent or otherwise and to ? the Ends and interests and for the purposes aforesaid I do hereby nominate constitute and appoint James W. Morrow of Butler County Missouri and his executors and administrators my true and lawful agent and agents attorney and attorneys in their or his own name or names or in any name as circumstances may require to ask demand sue for recover and receive all money debts dues and demands now owing due or becoming due to me and stand thereof upon the following trusts.

First To pay all my just and lawful debts so far as he may be in of the means.

Secondly, In the event of death or any casuality to see that my wife's two children John Morrow and Easter Catherine Morrow get from My Estate as much in value of property in cash as they had from their Father's Estate when I married their Mother!

Thirdly I desire my said agent to do the best he can towards giving all my children such advantages of education as may be in his power.

My Thomas Cannon to have the same advantages of Education as my own Children and an Equal share of my Estate with my own children after providing for said John and E Catherine Morrow as above mentioned in at least on hundred and fifty dollars.

Fourthly I desire My wife Sarah Smart to have my home farm during her natural life and that at her death the same be Equally divided among My children the above Cannon to have no more than above forwiled.

Fifthly- I desire and empower My said agent to use and Excercise his discretion in all things relating to the matters and hereby intrusted to him and all things that may in future arise Lastly- I declare that my said agent his heirs Executors and Administrators Shall Not be answerable or responsible for any lose which may happen to the ????. Nor for any more Money than he or they shall actually receive Nor for any loss or injury happening escept (sic) by his or their willful or default I mean in all above that my present wife and children by her Shall have the farm on which I now live. Attest, John C. Smart,

I the undersigned I Samuel H. Thomson a Justice of the Peace acting in and for the County aforesaid do certify that the 13th day of July A.D. 1861 before me came John Co. Smart who is personally known to me to be person described in and who Esceeuted (sic) the forgoing instrument and whose name is subscribed to the same as the Maker thereof and he acknowledged that he Esecuted the same for the purposes therein set forth Samuel H Thomson Justice of the Peace, Filed for Record in My Office on the 15th day of July A.D.

1861. Transcribed from Book C. and Pages 125 and 126 September 22nd A.D. 1870 Isaac B. Tubb, Clerk

Principals or Presidents of Private Schools in Missouri, 1898-1899, Eddlemon Collection.

Central College: Fayette, Male, M. E. South, E. B. Craighead.
Westminster College: Fulton, Male, Presbyterian, J. H. MaCraken.
William Jewell College: Liberty, Male, Baptist, J. P. Green.
Missouri Valley College: Marshall, Mixed, Cumberland Presbyterian, Wm. H. Black.
Washington University: St. Louis, Mixed, W. S. Chaplin.
Springfield: Drury College, Mixed, Congregational, Homer T. Fuller.
Canton: Christian University, Mixed, Disciples, Clinton Lockhart.
Parkville: Park College, Mixed, Presbyterian, L. M. McAfee.
St. Louis: Christian Brothers College, Male, Roman Catholic, Brother Emery.
Tarkio: Tarkio College, Mixed, United Presbyterian, J. A. Thompson.
Warrenton: Central Wesleyan College, Mixed, Methodist Episcopal, Geo. H. Addicks.
Glasgow: Pritchett College, Mixed, C. C. Hemenway.
St. Louis: St. Louis University, Male, Roman Catholic, J. F. X. Hoeffer.
Albany: Central Christian College, Mixed, Disciples, Zuinglius Moore.
Albany: Northwest Missouri College, Mixed, M. E. Church, W. H. Pritchett.
Appleton City: Appleton City Academy, Mixed, G. A. Theilman.
Bolivar: Southwest Baptist College, Mixed, Baptist, James Rice.
Boonville: Megguler Seminary, Female, Miss Julia Megguler.
Boonville: Kemper Military School, Male, T. A. Johnston.
Brookfield: Brookfield College, Male, Presbyterian, Harry C. Myers.
Caledonia: Bellevue Collegiate Institute, Mixed, Methodist, H. A. Smith.
Camden Point: Female Orphan School, Female, Disciples, A. O. Riall.
Camden Point: Camden Point Military Institute, Male, W. N. Stagner.
Cameron: Missouri Wesleyan College, Mixed, Methodist, C. F. Spray.
Carthage: The Fitting School, Mixed, Presbyterian, L. E. Robinson.
Chillicothe: Normal, Business and Shorthand College, Mixed, Allen Moore.

Clarksburg: Hooper Institute, Male, S. H. Pollard.
Columbia: University Academy, Male, J. B. Welch.
Concordia: St. Paul's College, Male, Evang. Lutheran, J. H. C. Kaeppel.
Farmington: Carleton College, Mixed, Meth. Eposcopal, J. J. Martin.
Fayette: Howard Payne College, Female, M. E. South, H. D. Groves.
Fredericktown: Marvin Collegiate Institute, Mixed, M. E. South, N. B. Henry.
Fulton: Synodical Female College, Female, Presbyterian, T. P. Walton.
Fulton: Orphan School, Female, Disciples, James B. Jones
Gallatin: Grand River College, Mixed, Baptist, J. H. Hatton.
Glencoe: La Salle Institute, Male, Catholic, Brother Gerardus.
Holden: Saint Cecilia Seminary, Mixed, Sr. M. Purification.
Iberia: Iberia Academy, Mixed, Congregational, G. B. Smith.
Independence: Woodland College, Mixed, Disciples, Geo. S. Bryant.
Jefferson City: St. Peter's Parochial School, Mixed, Catholic, O. J. S. Hoog.
Jennings: St. Louis Seminary, Female, B. T. Blewett.
Joplin: Joplin Business College, Mixed, W. B. Joiner.
Kansas City: Kansas City Dental College, Male, A. H. Thompson.
Kidder: Kidder Insitute, Mixed, Congregational, G. W. Shaw.
Kirksville: Columbian School of Osteopathy, Mixed, M. L. Ward.
Kirksville: American School of Osteopathy, A. T. Still.
Kirkwood: Kirkwood Military Academy, Male, E. C. Haight.
Laddonia: Collins Academy, Mixed, E. A. Collins.
Lexington.: Central Female College, Female, M.E. South, Z. M. Williams.
Lexington: Wenteorth Military Academy, Male, Sandford Sellers.
Marionville: Marionville Collegiate Institute, Mixed, Meth. Episcopal, L. G. Reser.
Marshall: Missouri Valley College Academy, Mixed, Cumberland Presbyterian, Wm. H. Black.
Mexico: Hardin College, Female, Baptist, J. W. Million.
Moberly: St. Mary's Academy, Mixed, Roman Catholic, Sister Caroline.
Morrisville: Morrisville Academy, Mixed, M. E. South, J. J. Pritchett.
Moundville: Cooper College, Mixed, C. H. Miles.
Mount Vernon: Mount Vernon Academy, Mixed, Presbyterian, Elizabeth Park.
Neosho: Scarrett Collegiate Insitute, Mixed, M. E. South, W. C. Hill.
Nevada: Cottey College, Female, M. E. South, Mrs. V. A. Stockard.

Odessa: Odessa College, Mixed, None, J. R. McChesney.
O'Fallon: Woodlawn Institute, Mixed, Presbyterian, W. T. Howison.
Palmyra: Centenary College, Mixed, M. E. South, Jas. A. Lanius.
Platte City: Gaylord Institute, Female, Mrs. T. W. Park.
Plattsburg: Plattsburg College, Mixed, German Baptist, S. Z. Sharp.
Richmond: Woodson Institute, Mixed, M. E. South, B. G. Shackleford.
St. Joseph: St. Joseph Commerical College, Male, Roman Catholic, Bro. E. Lewis.
St. Joseph: Sacred Heart Academy, Female, Roman Catholic, Madame M. Vernice.
St. Louis: Walther College, Mixed, Lutheran, Aug. C. Burgdorf.
St. Louis: Hosmer Hall, Female, Miss. M. H. Mathews.
St. Louis: Academy of the Visitation, Female, Catholic, Sister Aquin Martin.
St. Louis: Mary Insitute, Female, E. H. Sears.
St. Louis: Bishop Roberson Hall, Female, Episcopal, Sister Catherine.
St. Louis: Smith Academy, Male, Chas. P. Curd.
St. Louis: Ste. De Chantol Academy of the Visitation, Female, Roman Catholic, Sr. Jane F. Fletcher.
St. Louis: Jones Commerical College, Mixed, J. G. Bohmer.
St. Louis: Missouri Dental College, Male, A. H. Fuller.
St. Louis: Bryant and Stratton College, Mixed, W. M. Carpenter.
St Louis, Concordia College, Male, Lutheran, Francis Pieper.
St. Louis: St. Louis Medical College, Mixed, Dr. H. B. Mudd.
St. Louis: Barnes' Business College, Mixed, Arthur J. barnes.
St. Louis: Manuel Training School, Male, C. M. Woodward.
St. Louis: Rugby Academy, Male, Denham Arnold.
Salisbury: North Missouri Academy, Mixed, G. C. Briggs.
Sedalia: Central Business College, Mixed, C. M. Robbins.
Sedalia: Geo. R. Smith College, Mixed, A. Meth. Episcopal, E. A. Robinson.
Springfield: Loretta Academy, Female, Catholic, Sister of Loretto.
Springfield: Drury College Academy, Mixed, Congregational, Clark P. Howland.
Weaubleau: Christian College, Mixed, Disciples, J. Whitaker.
Wringarten: Our Lady of Help, Mixed, Catholic, J. H. Muehlsiepen
West Plains: West Plains College, Mixed, J. T. Outen.

Madison County, Missouri, Marriages, 1840-1850, Books B and C.

Abernatha, William and Penn, Matilda, (MD) Jan.26,1845, (BK) B.
Addison, James and Harriss, Mandy, (MD) Aug. 30,1847, (BK) B.

Allen, N. B. and Bollinger, Sarah, (MD) Dec. 30, 1841, (BK) B.
Allred, John and Vincent, Hannah, (MD) Oct. 9, 1846, (BK) B
Anderson, James and Harris, Martha, (MD) Apr.8, 1841, (BK) B.
Anthony, Joseph F. and Dill, Emily, (MD) May 30, 1843, (BK) B.
Anthony, Josiah M. and Bennett, Sarahan, (MD) Oct. 22,1843, (BK) B.
Arnett, Duncan and Caruthers, Eliza, (MD) Dec. 17, 1840, (BK) B
Arnold, William and Okes, Mary Martha M., (MD) Jul. 15,1841, (BK) B.
Ashlock, Lewis Lacey and Sutten, Salina, (MD) Apr.15, 1847, (MD) B
Bagnell, Isaac and Hill, Mary, (MD) May 21,1843, (BK) B.
Baldwin, Vardy and Shoults, Emily, (MD) Dec. 24,1846, (BK) B.
Banker, John C. and McDermith, Mary Ann, (MD) Apr.14,1846, (BK) B.
Beaver, Logan and Jackson, Emma, (MD) Jun. 12,1845, (BK) B.
Belmar, John and O'Bannon, Mrs. Margaret, (MD) Apr.22,1841, (BK) B.
Berd, Hartehorn and Eten, Arminty, (MD) Aug. 11,1846, (BK) B.
Bernier, Louis and Ranfro, Roothy, (MD) Jul. 1,1845, (BK) B.
Berry, John and Belmire, Elizabeth, (MD) Dec. 17,1840, (BK) B.
Berryman, James and Haris, Matilda, (MD) May18,1845 (BK) B.
Berryman, James G. and McFaddin, Margarett L., (MD) Jan. 8,184?, (BK) B.
Beve, Antony and Tesserou, Clarissa, (MD) Feb. 8,1842, (BK) B.
Blanton, Benj F., (BK) B.erryman, Alcey Jane, (MD) Jul. 30,1840, (BK) B.
Boan, Willson and Lashant, Judy, (MD) Dec. 27,1846, (BK) B.
Boardwine, Lewis E. and Smith, Anna, (MD) Feb. 13,1842, (BK) B.
Booth, J. J. Dr. and Starn, Harriet, (MD) Jan. 19,1845, (BK) B.
Boswell, John and Matthews, Talitha, (MD) Feb. 19,1846, (BK) B.
Bott, Luke and Moore, Jo Anna, (MD) Jul. 8,1845, (BK) B.
Boyd, John and Lincoln, Sarah, (MD) Feb. 9,1845, (BK) B.
Brady, Uriah and Frizell, Mary Ann, (MD) Sep. 14,1845, (BK) B.
Brewin, Jonathan, and Bivens, Sarah, (MD) May 9,1847, (BK) B.
Brewin, Jonathan and Reaves, Rachal, (MD) Jan. 28,1844, (BK) B.
Bright, Benjamin A.W. and Whitner, Rachel, (MD) Aug. 26,1845, (BK) B.
Brittain, Samuel and Anthony, Sarah, (MD) Jan. 11,1844, (BK) B.
Brown, James and Stark, Elizabeth, (MD) Jan. 1,1846, (BK) B.
Brown, James and Willet, Sina, (MD) Feb. 13,1842, (BK) B.
Buckner, John and Huff, Polly, (MD) May 16,1841, (BK) B.

Bullard, Aaron and Steely, Ann, (MD) Sep. 1,1840, (BK) B.
Burns, John, (MD) Mayburn, Eveline, (MD) Oct. 27,1845, (BK) B.
Burns, Milten and Oldham, Julian, (MD) Sep. 4,1845, (BK) B.
Butenholer, Peter and Asmon, Mary, (MD) Feb. 24,1846, (BK) B.
Caillote, Alexis, (BK) B.eeves, Elizabeth, (MD) Mar. 3,1840, (BK) B.
Calaman, John and Saunders, Mary, (MD) Dec. 20,1842, (BK) B.
Callaway, John and Murray, Salina, (MD) Sep. 9,1844, (BK) B.
Callaway, Powel, (BK) B.erryman, Mary E., (MD) Sep. 12,1844, (BK) B.
Carmack, Jonathan, (BK) C.astile, Nancy, (MD) Dec. 4,1846, (BK) B.
Carrol, William and Pecktol, Dortha, (MD) Jan. 15,1843, (BK) B.
Casteal, John and Parker, Matilda, (MD) Aug. 6,1846, (BK) B.
Chilton, James and Thompson, Mary Ann, (MD) Mar. 21,1841, (BK) B.
Chinaworth, John and Lorans, Sarah, (MD) Feb. 16,1843, (BK) B.
Clay, Eliazor G. and Shelton, Susan, (MD) Nov. 9,1841, (BK) B.
Clevelen, Charles and Miller, Eliza W., (MD) Feb. 26,1846, (BK) B.
Collier, Miles Harper and Short, Mary Swan, (MD) Sep. 23,1843, (BK) B.
Colliner, John and Sherner, Mary, (MD) Jul. 24,1846, (BK) B.
Compton, Andrew and Deguire, Theodisa, (MD) Jan. 4,1840, (BK) B.
Compton, Stephen and Deguire, Matilda, (MD) Apr. 14,1846, (BK) B.
Compton, William V. and Lewis, Gemima, (MD) Mar. 30,1845, (BK) B.
Cox, Aris and Vincent, Dorcas, (MD) Jan. 5,1846, (BK) B.
Craddock, Thomas and Lanius, Malinda, (MD) Aug. 19,1841, (BK) B.
Culegher, Isaac and Williams, Dematsia, (MD) Nov. 29,184?, (BK) B.
Darnell, William W. and Underwood, Mary, (MD) Feb. 11,1844, (BK) B.
Deguire, Francis and St. Gemme, Eleanor, (MD) Apr. 16,1844, (BK) B.
Denbo, John, and Brooke, Sarah and Jan. 18,1845, (BK) B.
Donally, James, and Cook, Susan, (MD) Jan. 3,1844, (BK) B.
Dreier, Conrad Dietrick and Latgen, Caroline W. and 7,18,1847, (BK) B.

Duncan, Rice, and Burcham, Hannah, (MD) Feb. 28,1845, (BK) B.
Dunn, Elial and Laine, Winey, (MD) Jul. 21,1843, (BK) B.
Eaton, Washington and Miller, Elizabeth C. W., (MD) May 11,184?, (BK) B.
Edmonds, Charles and Harris, Permela A., (MD) Mar. 22,1846, (BK) B.
Edwards, William and Davis, Adeline, (MD) Aug. 20,1843, (BK) B.
Edwards, William and Ragin, Nancy, (MD) May 14,1846, (BK) B.
Evans, Moses B. Rev. and Cooper, Ellen, (MD) Feb. 20,1840, (BK) B.
Falkner, Joseph F. and Perringer, Ann, (MD) Sep. 27,1846, (BK) B.
Farr, John and England, Mary, (MD) Jul. 22,1841, (BK) B.
Farr, Madison C. and Cravens, Ellen, (MD) Dec. 23,1841, (BK) B.
Finch, William and Menees, Louisa, (MD) Aug. 12,1841, (BK) B.
Fitzpatrick, James, and Callaway, Elizabeth, (MD) Sep. 26,1844, (BK) B.
Fletcher, Alexander and Folmire ?, Nancy, (MD) Nov. 1,1842, (BK) B.
Foster, Edwin K. and Bennett, Nancy A., (MD) Oct. 7,1847, (BK) B.
Fox, David M. and Kelly, Eliza, (MD) Jan. 25,1841, (BK) B.
Frazier, William and Allen, Harriet, (MD) Dec. 9,1841, (BK) B.
Frier, Erastus A. and Wilkins, Harriett, (MD) Oct. 22,1840, (BK) B.
Frizell, Thomas and Allen, Rebecca, (MD) Oct. 3,1841, (BK) B.
Graham, Elijah, and Bess, Catharine, (MD) Mar. 11,1841, (BK) B.
Graham, James and Whitener, Polly, (MD) Mar. 29,1838, (BK) B.
Graham, William W. and Poller, Martha Ann, (MD) Aug. 14,1844, (BK) B.
Grayham, Pleasant and Burns, Elizabeth, (MD) Jul. 6,1841, (BK) B.
Green, John and James, Mary Ann, (MD) Aug. 6,1843, (BK) B.
Griffen, Andrew and Maize, Luvina, (MD) Jul. 11,1844, (BK) B.
Griffin, David N. and Ronalds, Margaret, (MD) Jul. 21,1842, (BK) B.
Grigsby, Thomas B., (BK) C.ollier, Emeline, (MD) Aug. 15,1844, (BK) B.
Grovner, William and Yonger, Fredericake, (MD) Nov. 12,1846, (BK) B.

Hamblin, George and Roggers, Catharine, (MD) Jun. 10,1847, (BK) B.
Hamelton, William and Brown, Manda (MD) Dec.18,1845, (BK) B.
Harriss, Christopher C. and Potter, Sary, (MD) Feb. 5,1843, (BK) B.
Hawkins, Thomas and Harper, Elizabeth Mrs, (MD) Jun. 24,1845, (BK) B.
Hay, Gabriel and Langsher, Elizabeth, (MD) Jun. 6,1847, (BK) B.
Hayden, John P. and Pease, Frances F., (MD) Mar. 24,1842, (BK) B.
Hayes, Daniel J. and Whitner, Mary M., (MD) Mar. 7,1847, (BK) B.
Hayes, John and Lisle, Meddy Maria, (MD) Dec. 8,1846, (BK) B.
Hertzinger, John and Fath, Louisa, (MD) Apr. 15,1847, (BK) B.
Holder, Isaac and Brown, Nancy, (MD) Sep. 12,1841, (BK) B.
Holt, James H. and Cobb, Polly, (MD) Apr. 20,1841, (BK) B.
Holter, Jacob and Werner, Margarita, (MD) May 16,1843, (BK) B.
Hovies, Caleb and Spain, Nancy, (MD) Jan. 1,1847, (BK) B.
Huff, Isaac, and Buckner, Jane, (MD) Jul. 17,1843, (BK) B.
Huff, James and Napeyear, Ruthey, (MD) Apr. 1,1841, (BK) B.
Huff, John and Jones, Marget, (MD) Oct. 20,1844, (BK) B.
Hulson, James, and Barron, Elizabeth, (MD) Jun. 4,1840, (BK) B.
Huver, Jacob and Davalt, Mary, (MD) Dec. 5,1841, (BK) B.
Ishmel, Micagher and Bounds, Sarah Ann, (MD) Mar. 31,1844, (BK) B.
Israil, Langley and Johnson, Sarah, (MD) Apr. 12,1843, (BK) B.
Johnson, Joseph and Moss, Mariah, (MD) May 19,1844, (BK) B.
Johnson, Joshua and Cain, Susan, (MD) Jun. 30,1846, (BK) B.
Jones, John K. and Devault, Marjarett, (MD) Oct. 22,1840, (BK) B.
Jones, Stephens and Berryman, Elizabeth, (MD) Mar. 7,1840, (BK) B.
Jonson, John J. and Graham, Elizabeth, (MD) Apr. 21,1842, (BK) B.
Keele, Abraham M. and Johnson, Shulotty, (MD) May 25,1843,] (BK) B.
Kelly, George and Whitner, Lucinda, (MD) Jan. 12,1843, (BK) B.
Kempers, Yelvester and O'Bannon, Mary Ann and 6,18,1844, (BK) B.
Kennett, Jacob and Herzinger, Caroline, (MD) Jun. 30,1845, (BK) B.

Kidwell, Lewis G. and Glen, Nancy D., (MD) May 31,1847, (BK) B.
Lacey, John M. and Buckner, Sophia, (MD) Jul. 17,1847, (BK) B.
Lachance, Michael and Renfro, Rachael, (MD) Sep. 7,1841, (BK) B.
Lance, Anthony and Henderson, Elizabeth and 2,18,1845, (BK) B.
Laniers, Jacob and Long, Nancy, (MD) Jul. 23,1839, (BK) B.
Lanius, Daniel P. and Cain, Elizabeth M., (MD) Apr. 25,1847, (BK) B.
Leclare, Syprian and Cooper, Sara, (MD) Sep. 1,1846, (BK) B.
Lee, Andrew J. and Hardin, Elizabeth, (MD) Jun. 8,1846, (BK) B.
Lewis, Funney and Perringer, Nancy, (MD) Jan. 21,1838, (BK) B.
Lincoln, Elijah Marshall and North, Almira, (MD) Mar. 4,1847, (BK) B.
Lindsay, James and Frier, Carline C., (MD) Oct. 4,1838, (BK) B.
Linkhorn, William and Revell, Sarah, (MD) Sep. 27,1846, (BK) B.
Long, Horace M. and Tong, Harriet, (MD) Jun. 21,1838, (BK) B.
Lorance, David and O'Bannon, Lucinda, (MD) Apr. 8,1841, (BK) B.
Lot, James and Perringer, Eveline, (MD) Jan. 7,1847, (BK) B.
Louis, John and Deen, Emline, (MD) May 9,1842, (BK) B.
Marshall, James and Whitworth, Charity, (MD) Apr. 9,1846, (BK) B.
Mathews, Ansel and Carmack, Sary, (MD) Sep. 27,1846, (BK) B.
Mathews, John Jones and St. Gemme, Pelagie, (MD) Nov. 22,1842, (BK) B.
Matkin, Leroy and Polk, Rebecah, (MD) Nov. 3,1842, (BK) B.
Matthews, Russel R. and Mury, Rebecky, (MD) Apr. 5,1846, (BK) B.
Matthews, Russell and Pruit, Matilda, (MD) Oct. 29,1840, (BK) B.
McDade, Matthew and Miller, Amey M., (MD) Jul. 11,1841, (BK) B.
McDade, Matthew and Watson, Nancy, (MD) Oct. 7,1846, (BK) B.
McDowel, James and Polk, Matilda, (MD) Mar. 28,1844, (BK) B.
Miller, Jacob and Harris, Martha, (MD) Mar. 24,1840, (BK) B.
Miller, Jacob and King, Mary Ann, (MD) Jul. 7,1845, (BK) B.
Montgomery, Thomas and Provence, Jane, (MD) Jan. 31,1843, (BK) B.
Moon, Leonard and Reeder, Ann, (MD) Oct. 4,1842, (BK) B.

Mooney, Amos, and Compton, Martha Jane, (MD) Nov. 28,1844, (BK) B.
Moor, Elbert and Ragin, Elizabeth, (MD) Nov. 24,1840, (BK) B.
Moor, Westly and Potter, Fereba, (MD) Aug. 8,1843, (BK) B.
Moore, William and Walker, Araminta, (MD) Feb. 16,1845, (BK) B.
Mullen, Morgan and Berry, Matilda, (MD) Feb. 25,1843, (BK) B.
Mungle, Isaac and Lantz, Lovina, (MD) Oct. 10,1847, (BK) B.
Murry, Calvin and Lance, Luvicy, (MD) Sep. 3,1845, (BK) B.
Myers, William H. and Sutton, Elizabeth, (MD) Jun. 2,1844, (BK) B.
Needhardt, Erastus and Dinger, Eve, (MD) Nov. 15,1843, (BK) B.
Newcom, Benne H. and Harriss, Nancy and 1,18,1844, (BK) B.
Nifong, Washing, andCarathers, Elizabeth, (MD) Jan. 25,1842, (BK) B.
Nightfong, Jefferson, and Caruthers, Amanda, (MD) Sep. 19, 1844, (BK) B.
Noell, Edward G. and Perkins, Elizabeth, (MD) Feb. 26,1846, (BK) B.
Oldham, Thomas H. and Burns, Sarah Ann, (MD) Dec. 4,1845, (BK) B.
Page, Robert P. and Finch, Sarah, (MD) Sep. 16,1842, (BK) B.
Parker, William and McDaniel, Matilda, (MD) Mar. 19,1847, (BK) B.
Parkey, William and Twitty, Margaret, (MD) Jul. 16,1843, (BK) B.
Parkin, Thomas and Parkin, Emily, (MD) Jul. 11,1844, (BK) B.
Parks, Richard and Langley, Celia, (MD) Sep. 13,1842, (BK) B.
Patten, Peter and More, Patsy, (MD) Aug. 10,1843, (BK) B.
Perringer, Lenard and Murry, Agnes Peiliza, (MD) Oct. 19,1845, (BK) B.
Polk, William and Ashlock, Mary An, (MD) Aug. 13,1846, (BK) B.
Pratte, Onessin and Valle, Edilia, (MD) Nov. 23,1841, (BK) B.
Pruett, Willam and Sharp, Polly P., (MD) Dec. 5,1843, (BK) B.
Reed, David, and Cooper, Eleander, (MD) Nov. 4,1841, (BK) B.
Reed, James, and Berry, Nancy, (MD) Jan. 22,1841, (BK) B.
Reed, Joseph and Swearengin, Jane, (MD) Jan. 14,184?, (BK) B.
Reed, Robert and Crawford, Minerva, (MD) Aug. 6,1840, (BK) B.
Revel, Isaac and Razor, Elizabeth, (MD) Mar. 25,1847, (BK) B.
Revel, Jackson and Lincoln, Cordelia, (MD) Feb. 23,1843, (BK) B.

Reves, Caswell and Parke, Eliza, (MD) Sep. 22,1844, (BK) B.
Reynolds, Benjamin F. and Beaird, Elizabeth, (MD) Sep. 16,1847, (BK) B.
Rhodes, Isaac and Watts, Lucinda, (MD) Aug. 20,1840, (BK) B.
Rickman, James E. and Whitner, Elizabeth, (MD) Feb. 1,1844, (BK) B.
Row, William and Newkirk, Emily Jnae, (MD) Aug. 27,1840, (BK) B.
Rule, John, and Craddick, Elizabeth, (MD) Oct. 27,1844, (BK) B.
Sanders, Edward J. and Sitze, Artamissa, (MD) Aug. 20,1846, (BK) B.
Sauntman, William and Skaggs, Martha, (MD) Jun. 13,1847, (BK) B.
Seals, John and Oen, Anna, (MD) Jul. 15,1841, (BK) B.
Sebastin, William and Miller, Amanda C., (MD) Mar. 12,1840, (BK) B.
Sebastion, William and Miller, Juley Ann, (MD) Mar. 26,1840, (BK) B.
Settle, Anderson M. and Barrett, Elizabeth, (MD) Jul. 25,1844, (BK) B.
Settle, Peter and Street, Rachael, (MD) Apr. 1,1847, (BK) B.
Sharp, Anthony H. and Sinclair, Rebecca, (MD) Mar. 9,1843, (BK) B.
Shelton, Jaret and Kemper, Judith, (MD) Jul. 4,1844, (BK) B.
Sherner, Benedict and Berhoff, Louisa, (MD) Jul. 24,1846, (BK) B.
Shetley, William H. and Brotherton, Sarah, (MD) Dec. 19,1844, (BK) B.
Sinkler, Daniel B. and Graham, Melvina, (MD) Feb. 27,184?, (BK) B.
Sitze, Eli and Underwood, Polly, (MD) Dec. 6,1840, (BK) B.
Skaggs, James and Bett, Elizabeth, (MD) Oct. 7,1846, (BK) B.
Smith, James and Henderson, Lavina, (MD) Nov. 16,1843, (BK) B.
Smith, James and Johnson, Kathrye, (MD) Apr. 2,1845, (BK) B.
Smith, William and Watts, Malinda, (MD) Jul. 19,1847, (BK) B.
Spain, Marshall D. and Collier, Rebecca, (MD) Dec. 27,1840, (BK) B.
Spane, John and Odom, Carline, (MD) Nov. 17,1842, (BK) B.
Spiva, Elisha and Matthews, Rossann, (MD) Oct. 8,1845, (BK) B.
Stealey, John and Frohn, Sophia Mrs, (MD) Feb. 12,1842, (BK) B.
Stephens, Isaac B. and Hancock, Martha J., (MD) Feb. 15,184?,

(BK) B.
Stevenson, Robert and Hix, Nancy, (MD) Jan. 14,1847, (BK) B.
Stone, Micajah and Cartlon ?, Susan, (MD) Sep. 12,1847, (BK) B.
Story, John and Grounds, Elizabeth, (MD) Oct. 27,1845, (BK) B.
Stuard, George and Griffith, Elizabeth J., (MD) Feb. 16,1840, (BK) B.
Sullivan, Frederick L. and Valle, Josephine, (MD) Aug. 29,1843, (BK) B.
Sutton, David and Huff, Nancy, (MD) Oct. 7,1841, (BK) B.
Taylor, Thomas and Brady, Polly, (MD) Dec. 14,1845, (BK) B.
Tittle, James and Johnson, Sary, (MD) Sep. 14,1847, (BK) B.
Tong, Hiram and Allen, Eugenia, (MD) Mar. 8,1843, (BK) B.
Tong, Hiram N. and Baird, Mary Ann, (MD) Oct. 16,1845, (BK) B.
Tong, William and Hill, Margaret, (MD) Aug. 10,1843, (BK) B.
Underwood, Abner and Sitze, Joanna, (MD) Jan. 31,1841, (BK) B.
Underwood, John and Easton, Lucinda, (MD) Aug. 12,1845, (BK) B.
Upman, William and Lomseck, Rachel, (MD) Jan. 23,1847, (BK) B.
Valle, Francis and Tessereau, Louisa, (MD) Nov. 26,1845, (BK) B.
Valle, John and Overfield, (MD) Feb. 8,1842, (BK) B.
Waggoner, Joseph and Grovner, Margaret, (MD) Oct. 27,1846, (BK) B.
Walker, Henry and Cooper, Sarah Ann, (MD) Sep. 23,1841, (BK) B.
Wallace, Andrew and Martin, Rachael Matilda , (MD) Aug. 28,184?, (BK) B.
Warreman ?, John and Watts, Louisa, (MD) Nov. 29,1846, (BK) B.
Watson, William and Trip, Margaret, (MD) Mar. 23,1847, (BK) B.
Watts, James and Berry, Elizabeth, (MD) Sep. 23,1841, (BK) B.
Watts, Reuben and Sitzes, Nancy, (MD) Mar. 28,1844, (BK) B.
Weber, John and Warnecke, Mina, (MD) Nov. 24,1843, (BK) B.
White, William and Arnet, Elizabeth, (MD) Dec. 20,1846, (BK) B.
Whitener, Benjamin and Kelly, Priscilla, (MD) Mar. 10,1842, (BK) B.
Whitner, Absalem K., (BK) B.ess, Mahala, (MD) Sep. 17,1846, (BK) B.
Wilkinson, Larkin and Peterman, Sarah B., (MD) Dec. 2,1841, (BK) B.
Williams, George W. and Williams, Sarah, (MD) Dec. 24,1846,

(BK) B.
Willis, Wiley and Lashant, Rachael, (MD) Feb. 9,1847, (BK) B.
Wilson, Bazel and Vance, Lucinda, (MD) Mar. 23,1843, (BK) B.
Winbarger, Skiler ? and George, Mary, (MD) Oct. 14,1847, (BK) B.
Wood, George W. and Callaway, Frances, (MD) Mar. 5,1840, (BK) B.
Young, Preston F. and Mathis, Eleander, (MD) Jan. 22,1843, (BK) B.
Young, Randolph G. and Vincen, Mary Ann, (MD) Feb. 3,1844, (BK) B.
Ziegler, Conrad C. and Bossier, Helvina, (MD) Oct. 29,1840, (BK) B.
Akers, Washington and Cox, Elizabeth, (MD) Sep. 1,1850, (BK) C.
Allcorn, William and Hampton, Kezzy, (MD) Nov. 14,1849, (BK) C.
Allen, Damascus and McGuire, Elizabeth, (MD) May 2,1848, (BK) C.
Arnett, William and Pinkley, Elizabeth, (MD) Oct. 8,1849, (BK) C.
Austin, Jonas and Murray, Sarah, (MD) Jul. 5,1849, (BK) C.
Barns, Felix G. and Oldham, Emeline, (MD) Oct. 5,1848, (BK) C.
Barrett, John and Ivy, Mary Jane, (MD) Apr. 30,1848, (BK) C.
Barton, Jacob B. and Lunsford, July Ann, (MD) Jun. 22,1848, (BK) C.
Beckett, Samuel, and Bond, Catherine, (MD) Jul. 23,1848, (BK) C.
Beckett, Thomas and White, Eliza, (MD) Jul. 23,1848, (BK) C.
Beeve, Felix and Lachance, Aspacia, (MD) Sep. 19,1848, (BK) C.
Beeve, Joseph and Lachance, Odil, (MD) Nov. 28,1848, (BK) C.
Bennett, John S. and Graham, Elizabeth, (MD) Aug. 1,1850, (BK) C.
Bennett, Newkum and Harris, Sary, (MD) Jan. 9,1849, (BK) C.
Bess, Thomas D. and Sitzes, Polly, (MD) Sep. 3,1850, (BK) C.
Bewer, John and Sander, Agguste, (MD) Sep. 18,1849, (BK) C.
Bird, Antony and Lachance, Catherine, (MD) Feb. 28,1848, (BK) C.
Bloom, James and Skaggs, Mary Elizabeth, (MD) Jul. 29,1849, (BK) C.
Bollinger, William and Williams, Nancy, (MD) Jul. 6,1848, (BK) C.
Booth, David V. and Grounds, Centha, (MD) Jan. 27,1850, (BK) C.

Botts, Isaac and Thompson, Martha, (MD) Nov. 4,1847, (BK) C.
Brewer, Howel and Sutton, Nancy, (MD) Dec. 27,1848, (BK) C.
Brewer, Nimrod, Jr. and Stricklin, Susan, (MD) Nov. 14,184?, (BK) C.
Brown, Sterlin and Morgan, Elizabeth Mrs., (MD) Oct. 4,1849, (BK) C.
Buckner, Lewis and Key, Nancy, (MD) Jan. 23,1850, (BK) C.
Campbell, Henry and Moon, Mary Ann, (MD) Oct. 14,1849, (BK) C.
Carmack ?, Francis M. and Castiel, Elizabeth, (MD) Aug. 19,1849, (BK) C.
Casteal, Andrew and McDowal, Nancy, (MD) Jan. 23,1848, (BK) C.
Castile, George M.C., (BK) C.armack, Miriam, (MD) Mar. 5,1848, (BK) C.
Causby, Wm. Henderson and Goodman, Sarah Ann, (MD) Dec. 4,1849, (BK) C.
Cincleare, Thomas and Harris, Julian, (MD) Dec. 19,1850, (BK) C.
Clackston, Thomas and Vincent, Rachel, (MD) May 8,1848, (BK) C.
Coates, Thomas and Ayres, Ann Eliza, (MD) May 12,1849, (BK) C.
Cobb, William T. and Clubb, Lavina, (MD) Dec. 10,1850, (BK) C.
Collier, Drewry and Hofman, Elizabeth, (MD) Jan. ??, 1849, (BK) C.
Collier, Samuel and Vellars, Caroline, (MD) Nov. 22,1849, (BK) C.
Comes, Fealdin, and Clifton, Sarah Jane, (MD) Sep. 23,1849, (BK) C.
Cooper, Robert and Chilton, Mary Ann, (MD) Nov. 30,1848, (BK) C.
Cotner, John, Jr. and Steward, Rebecky, (MD) Nov. 9,1848, (BK) C.
Cox, John B. and Smith, Jane, (MD) Dec. 27,1847, (BK) C.
Davis, Charles, and Cooper, Amanda, (MD) Feb. 11,1849, (BK) C.
Deguire, Paul W. and Dill, Emily, (MD) Oct. 20,1848, (BK) C.
Dillen, Joseph P., and Cain, Catharine W., (MD) Mar. 23,1848, (BK) C.
Dimond, Josef and Easton, Mrs. Olibeveline, (MD) May 5,1849, (BK) C.
Dollen, William and Woods, Sary Ann, (MD) Oct. 28,1850, (BK)

C.
Douglas, John and Oldham, Christianna, (MD) Feb. 14,1849, (BK) C.
Dudley, William L. and Graham, Mary, (MD) Mar. 24,1850, (BK) C.
Eaton, Ovel M. and Cacy, Sarah Jane, (MD) Dec. 23,1850, (BK) C.
Federly, Henry and Moyers, Esther, (MD) Jan. 11,1849, (BK) C.
Forgarson, Hooke and Thomason, Mary, (MD) Jun. 8,1849, (BK) C.
Forndon ?, John and Harris, Mary, (MD) Oct. 5,1848, (BK) C.
France, Geddin, and Caulreed, Mattes, (MD) Nov. 20,1847, (BK) C.
Francis, Leonard, and Bonds, Mary Jane, (MD) Mar. 9,1848, (BK) C.
Freday, Frederic and Renier, Odelier, (MD) Mar. 15,1849, (BK) C.
Frizel, Salathael and Smith, Judy, (MD) Aug. 23,1849, (BK) C.
Garner, Isaac F. and Bess, Patience C., (MD) Dec. 3,1850, (BK) C.
George, James and Powel, Nancy Mrs, (MD) Feb. 24,1850, (BK) C.
Gepperich, William and Bunning, Henrietta, (MD) Dec. 7,1849, (BK) C.
Gholson, John N. and Molloy, Louisa Mrs, (MD) Feb. 19,1849, (BK) C.
Goodman, John H. and Horton, Nancy J., (MD) Aug. 23,1850, (BK) C.
Graham, William and Waggoner, Nancy Jane, (MD) Jul. 20,1849, (BK) C.
Gregoire, Charles and Janis, Mary, (MD) Nov. 6,1849, (BK) C.
Grotoff, Antony and Munderhoff, Christina, (MD) Oct. 19,1848, (BK) C.
Hackman, Henry and Drier, Sophia, (MD) May 1,1848, (BK) C.
Haris, Eli, and Barett, Taletha, (MD) Jan. 7,1849, (BK) C.
Harris, John and Denton, Elizabeth, (MD) Apr. 29,1849, (BK) C.
Harris, Zachariah J., (BK) B.erryman, Frances A., (MD) Oct. 12,1848, (BK) C.
Harris, Zadok G. and Peas, Malissa, (MD) Jan. 6,1848, (BK) C.
Haun, Alfred and Whitner, Elizabeth C., (MD) Mar. 16,1848, (BK) C.
Hehn, John and Knoche, Catharine, (MD) Jun. 5,1848, (BK) C.
Helton, John and Drake, Eliza, (MD) Sep. 19,1848, (BK) C.
Hembe, James and Oldham, Melinda J. Mrs, (MD) Oct. 21,1849,

(BK) C.
Hensly ?, John C. and Miller, Jane N., (MD) Aug. 20,1850, (BK) C.
Heux, Joseph and Shultz, Elizabeth, (MD) Oct. 2,1850, (BK) C.
Hook, Joseph Henry and Tessereau, Marcellite, (MD) Oct. 22,1850, (BK) C.
Howard, Clemuel and Arnet, Selina, (MD) Dec. 21,1848, (BK) C.
Huddleston, William, and Brewer, Eliza, (MD) Sep. 20,1848, (BK) C.
Huff, William and Hampton, Caroline, (MD) Oct. 14,1849, (BK) C.
Jackson, Carroll and Peace, Elizabeth, (MD) Dec. 8,1850, (BK) C.
Jackson, William, (BK) B.edes, Elisabeth, (MD) Sep. 14,1848, (BK) C.
Jonson, Nehemiah and Mathews, Martha, (MD) Feb. 12,1850, (BK) C.
Jordan, Levy and Denbow, Ann Jane, (MD) Oct. 7,1849, (BK) C.
Kelly, Henderson and Collins, Ledonia, (MD) Apr. 16,1848, (BK) C.
Kemper, John and O'Bannon, Elizabeth, (MD) Nov. 23,1848, (BK) C.
Keny, James and Eoff, Luceann, (MD) Aug. 30,1849, (BK) C.
Kinnion, Albert and Allen, Ann Elizabeth, (MD) Oct. 26,1847, (BK) C.
Lachance, Fluare and Swairangain, Margrate, (MD) Aug. 23,1848, (BK) C.
Lincoln, Andrew J. and Masters, Margaret, (MD) Dec. 19,1847, (BK) C.
Lohrie, Jacob and Shouth, Catharine, (MD) Jun. 11,1848, (BK) C.
Lunsford, Noah, and Barton, Martha J., (MD) Jul. 6,1848, (BK) C.
Marler, Duke and Walker, Lucinda, (MD) Dec. 3,1848, (BK) C.
Marlow, Allen and Trip ?, Nancy, (MD) Feb. 13,1848, (BK) C.
Marlow, Duke and Sharp, Isabella, (MD) Oct. 13,1850, (BK) C.
Marlow, Joseph and Hasler, Sally, (MD) Mar. 1,1849, (BK) C.
Master, John and Welburn, Gemima Ann, (MD) Dec. 26,1850, (BK) C.
McBride, John, (BK) B.erryman, Margaret, (MD) Nov. 24,1850, (BK) C.
McSween ?, Daniel and Tong, Julian Ann, (MD) Oct. 19,1848, (BK) C.
McVey, James A. and Sitzes, Sarah, (MD) Nov. 5,1850, (BK) C.
Meyer, Conrad and Weise, Catherine, (MD) Dec. 28,1848, (BK)

C.
Miller, George W. and Hemby, Louisa J., (MD) Dec. 28,1848, (BK) C.
Miller, John and Story, Lucinda, (MD) Mar. 23,1848, (BK) C.
Miller, William Eldridge and Hammack, Amanda Eliz, (MD) Sep. 16,1849, (BK) C.
Morgan, Riley and Moore, Melinda, (MD) Dec. 22,1850, (BK) C.
Mouser, Franklin and Moore, Margaret, (MD) Feb. 3,1848, (BK) C.
Moyers, Michael and Cheack ?, Sarah, (MD) Aug. 20,1850, (BK) C.
Murry, Lewis and Weber, Caroline, (MD) Nov. 23,184?, (BK) C.
Murry, William, Jr. and Hosler, Elizabeth, (MD) Aug. 26,1849, (BK) C.
Nalle, Greenberry B. and Hill, Mary, (MD) Mar. 14,1850, (BK) C.
Parks, James and Taylor, Sarah, (MD) Jun. 20,1850, (BK) C.
Parks, William C., (BK) B.oze, Mary Frances, (MD) Jan. 17,1850, (BK) C.
Peace, Fayette and Nall, Susan, (MD) Aug. 31,1848, (BK) C.
Pendey, Abraham C., (BK) B.urrows, Mary Ann, (MD) Dec. 16,1849, (BK) C.
Reder, Andrew and Deguire, Mary, (MD) Dec. 31,1849, (BK) C.
Reed, Leonard and Beal, Mary Ann, (MD) Aug. 9,1849, (BK) C.
Reede, William T. and Williams, Lurana, (MD) Oct. 25,1849, (BK) C.
Revel, Elbert and Razor, Sally, (MD) May 2,1849, (BK) C.
Rogers ?, Frederick and Steritt, Weary ?, (MD) Dec. 8,1848, (BK) C.
Samuels, Henry and Shelton, Cordelia, (MD) May 9,1848, (BK) C.
Samuels, James and Gareheart, Ellen, (MD) Jun. 20,1850, (BK) C.
Seal, Robert and Dunn, Jane, (MD) Feb. 28,1850, (BK) C.
Sell, George and Burcham, Susan C., (MD) Mar. 11,1849, (BK) C.
Sharp, Finas and Young, Nancy Jane, (MD) Dec. 30,1847, (BK) C.
Sharp, John and Sutten, Elizabeth Ann, (MD) Mar. 30,1848, (BK) C.
Sharp, William M., (BK) C.hambers, Mary Ann, (MD) Mar. 23,1848, (BK) C.
Shaw, Philip A., and Cox, Emelia, (MD) Sep. 23,1848, (BK) C.
Simmans, Andrew and Francis, Lusceny, (MD) Apr. 5,1848, (BK) C.
Sinclair, William A. and Johnson, Wiley Elen, (MD) Mar. 10,1848, (BK) C.
Sitze, John F. and Whitener, Eleanor, (MD) May 31,1849, (BK) C.

Skaggs, Erastus and Peterman, Nancy Ann, (MD) Oct. 15,1850, (BK) C.
Slater, Roberson M. and Mathews, Susan Ann, (MD) Mar. 13, 1850, (BK) C.
Smith, George and Willis, Sintha, (MD) Apr. 16,1850, (BK) C.
Smith, John, Jr. and Renalds, Eady, (MD) Jul. 26,1848, (BK) C.
Spain, Bazley D. and Haynes, Mary, (MD) Sep. 24,1848, (BK) C.
Spiva, Elisha and Reaves, Brotha, (MD) Feb. 14,1849, (BK) C.
Spiva, John B. and Whitworth, Hannah B., (MD) Jun. 8,1848, (BK) C.
St, Gemme Raphael and Harber, Lemirah, (MD) Oct. 10,1849, (BK) C.
Stevens, Thomas B. and Smith, Lovely, (MD) Jul. 24,1849, (BK) C.
Stricklen, Thos. P. and Hameblen, Nancy, (MD) Mar. 22,1849, (BK) C.
Sutten, James and Gatewood, Polly, (MD) Jul. 20,1848, (BK) C.
Sutton, Jesse and Fields, Rebecca Olley, (MD) May 15,1850, (BK) C.
Teel, Andrew and Hyde, Eliza, (MD) Apr. 15,1849, (BK) C.
Tessereau ?, Felix and McCallum, Nancy, (MD) Nov. 17,1849, (BK) C.
Tessereau, Bernard and Lachance, Elizabeth, (MD) Jul. 15,1850, (BK) C.
Tripp, Willey and Hart, Jane, (MD) Apr. 3,1849, (BK) C.
Volentine, Soloman and Moore, Detitha C., (MD) Feb. 3,1848, (BK) C.
Wagener, Godfry and Weber, Catherin, (MD) Jun. 13,1850, (BK) C.
Werner, Andrew and Weber, Mary, (MD) Oct. 26,1849, (BK) C.
Wever, John Adam and Schoute, Elizabeth, (MD) Mar. 2,1848, (BK) C.
Wilcox, Jessee and Ellis, Sarah, (MD) Jan. 27,1848, (BK) C.
Wiley, Barnet and Cravens, Angeline, (MD) Jan. 24,1850, (BK) C.
Wiley, John Washington and Shoemate, Nancy C., (MD) May 20,1849, (BK) C.
Williams, Ezekiel and Parks, Sela Mrs, (MD) Oct. 31,1850, (BK) C.
Wilson, Joseph and Cravens, Docas ?, (MD) Mar. 9,1848, (BK) C.
Winebarger, Samuel and Deguire, Marcelete, (MD) Nov. 29,1848, (BK) C.
Woolford, Frederick and Ruble, Martha, (MD) May 6,1849, (BK)

C.

Missourians in Tennessee, World War I Veteran List.
Benton Co., TN
Akin, Bivvin M.: (A) 22Y, (BP) Steel, MO, (P) 1.
Jenkins, William B.: (A) 28Y, (BP) Clarkton, MO, (CMTS) Dead, (P) 50
Wiseman, Grover C.: (A) 24Y, (BP) East Prairie, MO, (P) 42.
Blount Co., TN
Jones, Charlie H.: (A) 23Y, (BP) Ozark Co., MO, (P) 35.

Colored Institutes, Missouri, 1899, Eddlemon Collection.

Place Held	Conductor
Boonville	C. G. Williams
Cape Girardeau	Jno. S. Cobb
Carrolton	J. Silas Harris
Charleston	H. G. Elam
Chillicothe	L. M. Scholl
Columbia	Arthur Craddock
Farmington	J. C. Staten
Fayette	A. R. Chinn
Fulton	W. C. Payne
Hannibal	J. H. Pelham
Hartville	G. H. I. Nelson
Jefferson City	B. F. Allen
Keytsville	W. H. Harrison
Lexington	Geo. H. Green
Louisiana	Jacob M. Cockfield
Marshall	A. W. Craddock
Place Held	Conductor
Monroe City	Greene Thompson
Montgomery City	G. S. Abbington
Neosho	J. M. Clendennin
St. Charles	W. B. Highgate
Sedalia	Shelton French
Springfield	W. H. McAdams

Kansas, 1855 Territorial Census, Persons Indicating Missouri as Their Place of Origin
First District
James B. Abbot, Michael R. Albin, Anson E. Alverson, C. W. Babcock, Edwin Bond, Harrison Budily, David C. Buffum, Thomas Burton, Hugh Cammeron, A. E. Colman, Hiram Crane, Peter

Crockett, A. Cronee, James H. Crooks, Robert A. Cummins, Delano Curlew, James Curlew, Lucas Curlew, William Curry, John C. Davidson, Sylvester H. Davis, Carloss M. Day, William Evans, Henry W. Feck, John H. Fernan, George Gilbert, Simartin V. Harnsby, Samuel C. Harrington, Samuel N. Hartwell, Leonard G. Higgins, Forester Hill, Benjamin F. Hopper, Benjamin Johnson, Erastus D. Ladd, Charles Link, Cuthburt McBee, Benjamin F. McDonnel, John McFarland, ??? McGlenn, David Mencham, Zeno B. Page, Samuel C. Pomeroy, David Purmton, William Randolph, Henry Reed, George W. Reid, Turner Sampson, Calvin H. Sarvin, Henry C. Sebastion, Arnab Seducke, Jackson Sellers, John E. Stewart, Abraham Still, James M. Still, Thomas J. Stone, James Sullivan, Clarkson M. Wallace, William Whitlock, Jerry Whitson, John P. Wood.

Second District

J. S. Bacon, Lafayette Barret, Fields Bledsoe, George W. Brians, Jacob Brown, O. H. Browne, A. J. Buck, Thomas Burnett, B. Callaghan, Henry A. Callue, Robert Callue, John Carroll, John W. Chamberlin, A. B. Collett, Frederick Cook, Jonathan Crummer, James R. Davis, Wm. M. Davis, David Dickey, Nehemiah Dorrell, Wm. Douglas, Paris Ellison, James Evans, Drury Fletcher, Westley Garrett, G. W. Garss, Beverly Gentry, J. W. Goodwin, William M. Harper, James H. Harrison, Fleming Hatton, D. H. Heindricks, James W. Heix, Abraham Hendricks, James Hendricks, John Hockler, John Howard, Orange Howard, D. S. Howe, A. J. Howland, Samuel Hufaker, Thomas Husley, Samuel Jones, William Justice, Madison Kincade, James Kutes, Henry Lacey, F. E. Lahay, Townsend Lahay, Kinsey Lanum, Joseph Lewis, George W. Lynn, John Mason, Moses McCall, John G. McClanahan, Joel Montgomery, K. J. Murchison, Levi Orvins, Martin Palmer, Thomas Phillips, James Powell, Jonathan Prather, W. W. Randolph, Enoch Reed, James Reed, Littleton Reed, George Rhodes, Tipton Robinson, Thomas M. Rogers, Madison Rule, John F. Russell, William H. Russell, William Shirley, Thomas Simmons, Wm. R. Simmons, Augustine Smith, John M. Smith, M. Somers, Grant Spurlock, Absolom St. Davis, Green Swezer, John O. Talbot, Amanus Todhunter, Devoe Todhunter, Evan Todhunter, John Todhunter, Thomas Todhunter, Valentine Todhunter, James Turner, Joseph Vance, S. J. Wafal, George W. Ward, Willis S. Warder, Peter Wendell, Absolem White, Andrew White, James S. White, James Williams, Thomas B. Wisdom, Albert Yates.

Third District

William R. Boggs, Solomon Coker, Linsus T. Cook, Christopher Coplin, Richard Cox, Duke W. Hunter, James McConnell, Elamore Shetter, John Taylin, Joseph West.

Fourth District

F. Barnes, J. M. Bernard, M. Carter, C. Clark, F. M. Coleman, A. Dale, W. M. Haris, C. Harmony, D. Hendricks, J. C. Hughes, J. F. Javens, J. Keren, D. J. Keser, G. Y. Keser, J. H. Lochridge, D. Pultz, J. D. Skidmore, A. Williams.

Fifth District

Benjamin C. Adkins, James Adkins, Francis J. Agnew, Fonts Alexander, B. H. Ames, Philip Anderson, John H. Arbuckee, Wm. A. Austin, Philip Ball, Elder Barnolly, Hiram Beckett, John A. Beckett, James Beets, Joseph Black, Isaac Bledsoe, John Bledsoe, George Bradbury, James Bradbury, John Bradbury, Robert Brady, John C. Brooks, John E. Brown, Saml. Brown, Benjamin Bunch, David Bunch, Henry Bunner, Clabron Burnett, John Buts, Jas. W. Carmon, Aaron Case, David Casteel, James L. Childers, Isaac Churk, John H. Cleaton, Lott Coffman, Sam'l Covey, James W. Cox, Josiah H. Damson, James Daniel, Jonah Daniel, Josiah Daniels, Robert M. Daniels, Henry Davidosn, Brisco Davis, David Dehoney, John H. Dervint, Saml. Dillon, Jasper Dingen, G. B. Donell, Thos. Donell, Wm. Doolin, John R. Driskell, William Driskell, James Dudley, Thos. J. Duncan, John Dunigan, Moses Dunigan, Henry Eidson, John W. Elliott, Lewis Elliott, Clayton Ellis, Cliften Ellis, John Esteps, Joseph Everhart, Jeremiah Farmer, Leander Fawts, William Field, C. S. Fleming, David P. Fleming, James Fleming, John D. Fleming, Samuel Fleming, Benj. Ford, Benj. F. Ford, Calvin Ford, James P. Fox, Jas. Fox, Henry France, John W. Freaks, Perry Freaks, Robert Freaks, Wm. Gadling, Valentine Ganarva, Joseph Gasaway, Marcus Gill, Henry Gillespie, Fineas T. Glover, Richard Golden, Joseph Good, Amos H. Goodwin, Joseph B. Goodwin, William Goodwin, G. H. Gordon, Richard Graves, James W. Greer, Wm. S. Gregory, Shade Halcum, James Halloway, F. A. Hamilton, Milton Hampton, Julius Hansbraugh, Caleb W. Hargis, Robert Hargrave, Wm. L. Harris, Isaac S. Hartman, S. M. Hayes, Thos. Heath, Middleton Hensley, Wm. J. Hensley, John Hicklan, Mr. Hill, John A. Hix, Joseph Hogans, Joseph Howard, Jonathan S. Huff, Wm. Hunt, Harris Jackson, Isaac P. Jackson, John Jackson, John Jr. Jackson, Marion P. Jackson, Silas R. Jackson, Wm. Jackson, Isaac Jacob, Alexander James, John W. Jameson, Peter Johnson, Wm. Jones, Wm. R. Jones, James S. Kags, John M. Keeton, Ephraim Kincaide, William C. Kirk, Wm. Landen, M. G. Lankford, Alfred Law, Francis P. Levine, Henry Littlejohn, Jackson Long, Robert

Long, L. M. Love, James Lucenson, Ingram Luck, David Lykins, Henry L. Lyon, George Mallox, Francis Marion, Thomas McAboys, Ennis McDaniel, Jessee R. McDaniel, John G. McDaniel, John R. McDaniel, Henry McKinney, Abram Medlin, John Medlin, Lemuel Medlin, Wilson Medlin, Wm. Medlin, William Moore, John G. Morse, Wm. Murray, Francis Myers, Embrey Nelson, Sam'l Nichols, Nicholas Nisinger, Reuben E. Noel, Andrew Owens, John Par, D. F. Park, Wm. Park, James O. Parker, J. W. Parks, Henry D. Parson, James Parson, Charles Polk, Thos. Polk, P. C. Poole, Peter J. Potts, D. S. Ragan, Calvin Randall, H. S. Randall, Gwin Ray, Jas. G. Ray, Champion Reesley, John Rese, Ambers Reslly, Barry Richardson, Samuel L. Ring, Wm. Ring, Jas. B. Roach, Jas. Roberts, John Robinson, Zacharia Roe, Joseph Sanders, Jesse Sears, Thos. Sears, John Shannon, Wm. Shugars, Wm. Skidwell, Alfred Smith, Harrison Smith, Hickman Smith, William Sparkman, Robert E. Spotwood, Wm. H. Stanford, Saml. Stanton, John Steel, Geo. T. Stein, Wiram Stephens, Wm. Stephens, John Stergeon, Allen Stewart, Thomas Stolen, Wm. Surman, John H. Tate, Lewis Thomas, Wm. Thomas, Joseph E. Tindall, Edmund L. Trygle, Elisha Tucker, Wm. Turner, Andrew Tyler, John Vanhorn, James Wade, Samuel Wade, Chas. Wagoner, Jas. Walker, Joseph E. Watkins, John H. Whistler, Bloomer White, Stephen White, John Wikle, Thomas Wilburn, Thomas Williams, W. B. Williams, Wm. Wires, John Witzong, Albert Woodson.

Sixth District

John Adkins, Joseph Alexander, William Alexander, James Arnett, Nathan Arnett, Thomas B. Arnott, John Barnes, Samuel Bearer, Noah W. Bennett, George Blake, Adam Boyd, Reuben Boyd, John Brown, James Burgess, George Butler, John Cail, Thomas Carter, John Cates, Matthew Cellars, Andrew Conville, E. B. Cook, John Culton, Thomas Dorland, Samuel Drennon, James Dreeser, Robert Edwards, G. J. Endicott, Jonathan Evans, Stephen Fisher, Issac Fleetwood, Miles Fleetwood, Reuben Fleetwood, Elisha Fly, John Fly, Daniel Francis, Jesse Fowler, Samuel S. Gilmore, William Godfrey, Thomas Graves, James Gunthey, John Gunthey, John Hix, Henry Humphreys, Thomas P. Ingham, Daniel B. James, Thomas James, L. Janny, William Janny, Washington Jones, Peter Lebaun, Fielder Lewis, James M. Linn, William Margrove, L. McKiney, Jeremiah McNew, John N. Minor, Jacob Miller, Issac Mills, Charles Mitchell, Cowan Mitchell, Jerome Moody, Philander S. Moore, Samuel Moore, Lewis Mooyard, William Morgan, Enoch Osborne, Thomas Osburn, Alfred Ousboin, William Painter, Reuben Parker, James

Pickeral, Thomas Pickeral, B. Piles, George Price, James Ray, James B. Ray, William Ray, Jackson Russell, Samuel Russell, George Simons, John Simpson, Hans Smidt, Charles Smith, James Smith, Joseph Smith, Aaron W. Snider, Jacob Snider, Henry Snider, Abrer Sooter, William Sooter, Solomon Spears, Reuben Spratt, Charles Stephen, Thomas Sumers, Aaron Thompson, George Tinker, James Turner, Francis Twombly, William Underhill, James Upton, Lemuel Vestall, John Wakefield, George Wakefield, Arthur Ward, Davis Ward, Harrop Ward, William Weaver, Joseph Welch, Peter Welch, Benjamin Williams, James Williams, John Williams, William Williams, Hir. T. Wilson, William Young.

Seventh District

John Akins, James Akins, F. McGee, C. C. Coots, J. H. Ratcliffe, Elliott Cusiger, Matthias A. Reed, William Hanley, Ely Snyder, John W. Webb, William Webb, William B. Jones, Frank Dufrene, Jackson Lovelace, Clayborn Lyking, George W. Berry, George Watny, Charles Watny, M. W. McGee.

Eight District

Lawrence Brook, George W. Butcher, Allen Crowley, Monon Crowley, Edward Davis, George Davis, John Devort, Charles T. Gillmore, W.D. Harris, William H. Hogan, George S. Huffaker, Thomas A. Huffaker, Alfred Hyden, Thomas Johnson, Jesse King, John A. Kelley, James Monkass, Emanuel Mosen, John Ratcliff, Richard Williams.

Nineth District

John N. Dyer, William A. Lowe, Fred Sonnamaker, Robert Wilson.

Tenth District

George W. Eubanks, Henry Mechlman, Henry Sheriff, Jacob Sheareir, Lewis Sanders, Gustave Stahl, James Lowry, Tunis Roscie, Samuel D. Dyer, W. C. Dyer, Alvan Dyer, Marshall A. Garrett, Samuel P. Allen, Joseph Hayes, Samuel Hayes, James Bishop, Aborn Martin, Joseph Stewart, Enoch G. Hinton, Antony Tasseer, Henry Rummell, Michael Flois, Mathew Flois.

Eleventh District

John E. D. Avis, Julias Berger, Robert Berger, George Munthely, George F. Hubbard, William Hubbard, Jerry Sweat, John Donaldson, William P. McCuse, Daniel Bowly, Francis J. Marshall, A. G. Woodward, John G. Clarke, John Jones, Sr., Daniel Jones, David Evans, William Evans, Edward Jones, David Jones, Samuel Jones, S. N. B. Holmes, James Lucas, E. S. Bishop, Agnes McClelland, John Robbens, Oliver Jesse, C. D. Stockwel.

Twelfth District

Udlem Alley, Bowlen Baker, Walter D. Beels, Moses Bellmore, John Blouchard, E. G. Booth, Lewis Cattin, Saml. Crozeer, Antona Deslous, Daniel Doneen, Joseph Fox, Andrew Frongan, Maurice Gellond, Henrie Hollenboch, Peter Karleskind, Andrew Lecompte, James Mathews, Joseph Mathews, J. B. Meige, R. C. Miller, W. W. Moore, John Newton, Olie Oldson, Joseph Papen, Ellunne Papin, Lowe Papin, Perry Polk, William Purkitt, Peter Rudhomme, James Slesin, E. M. Sloan, John L. Toburs, Joseph Vertefeille, Benjamin Winkle, George Winkle, John Winkle, George L. Young.

Thirteenth District

William Arthur, James Atkinson, May Barton, Benjamin Bogston, Holman Bonfield, Phelix Braden, Henry Bretz, Franklin Browning, Robert Carter, Thomas Carter, Charles Casy, James Chandler, Prater Chandler, Richard Chandler, J. H. Clemmons, Aaron Cook, John Cunningham, John Davis, G. M. Dyze, Joseph Elliott, John Evans, James Gardner, Hubbard Holder, James Hopewell, Napoleon Hopewell, William Hunter, William Jibbs, F. John, James Jont, Richard Jont, James Kirkendall, William Kirkendall, John Mear, John Miller, Thomas Mooney, A. J. Morrow, William Nations, J. W. Pate, Albro Pemberton, James Piles, Shelby Piles, Adam Post, M. E. Riddle, J. B. Ross, Henry Seals, E. B. Trap, W. H. Trap, M. Walker, George White, Smith White.

Fourteenth District

William Michaels, James Michaels, Robert Ewin, Winburt F. Chudys, Calvin Louis, Bonard Brady, John Landies, Joseph W. Batie, John W. Foreman, James L. Foreman, Lewis C. W. Foreman, James W. Holland, S. K. Miller, Aaron Gibbons, John P. Cordineer, John Carson, James Morrison, Elys Hamilton, Zedock Martin, William Smith, Washington F. Martin, Silvester Madison, Richard Henderson, Thomas Sweeten, Isaac Martin, Joshua Sanders, Calvin N. Newman, Richard Tuck, Richard Rest, Samuel Collins, Paris Dunning, John Stanton, William M. Peppers, W. W. Huddle, Norman Alexander, Michael McCormac, Robert Clory, John Clory, John Donley, Dennis Mullen, Jameh (sic) O'Connell, H. N. Beauchamp, William K. Shaw, J. W. Collins, Anderson Cox, Anderson Cook, Jacob Goshon, Matthew Fitzpatrick, John Grace, William Gains, Edward Deacon, Henry Moore, Parker A. Hooper, James C. Ditymore, Melchior Brown, Joel Byron, Peter Mintcèr, Josephus Nett, G. R. Wilson, A. G. Rice, George Gay, Charles Millaman, Harvey W. Forman, William Vivis, William Sugg, Francis Bushnell, Nelson Rodgers, Anthony Gravil, Joseph Better, John Hullen, John B. Roy, Samel M. Irvin, Cornelius McClain, Henry Buch, E.P. Richardson, J. S. Pemberton, Oliver Bealer, Jackson Bealer, Charter Searles, Thomas Davis, Eli Galbard, John McKauler,

John Edward, John Greenfield, Daniel Million, Nicholas White, E. W. B. Rodgers, Silsas Stone, L. H. Pendleton, Uriah Griffith, Thomas W. Matterson, James Matterson, R. W. Witsett, George H. Breyson, Mathew Ilse, William Newman, Jesse Brown, Jesse Brown, David Howard, A. Jamison, G. H. Jamison, William Rhodes, George Rhodes, Jacob Driesselmier, D. B. Welding, Robert McSpiring, Aaron Barnes, Hamilton J. Johnson, Nelson Abby, John M. Tracy, William H. Hye, Charles Ritcher, Charles Eggars, Samuel Kirkpatrick, John Copland, Laster Copland, Q. Lewis, William Chamberlain, Patrick Wright, Jonathan Hurt, Cary B. Whitehead, G. B. Jones, Ephraim McCleland, Leander McCleland, John G. McCleland, Stephen N. Bell, Amett Gromes, Ab Gromes, James Gromes, Joseph H. Cislifee, Newton R. Carter, Nason F. Moss, Mirah Curtis, James Campbell, Mark Yogan, M. T. Sweeny, John Dryle, Franklin Kream, William P. Richardson, Benjamin Duncan, John W. Stevens, Edward Schmider, William Skelton, John Smith, Anderson Gladdin, Sayburn Gladdin, Henry Dolon, Benjamin Todd, Polete Levsee, Obadiah Nermier, Doctor Wells, P. T. Transaway, William H. Allen, James Sollers, Mathias Rapp, John M. Hartman, Robert Rody, Charles Schilmer, Richard Baber, Joseph Ashley, Bertus Pryer, Henry Lashiena, Edward Maron, Joseph Peter, Hezekiah Jackson, James B. Anderson, Frederick Trent, William Jordon, John W. Sr Smith, Joseph Crippen, William Sharper, Charles Rodgers, Benjamin H. Brock, Sheron Lawhorn, James Lawhorn, Henry Wilson, James Craft, Robert L. Morris, Q. W. Davis, E. S. Stinson, S. E. Morris, T. M. Morris, Richard Morris, James Lovell, Lias Roark, Madison Osbourn, Morgan Osborn[sic], James N. Miller, Garnett Kelley, Arnot Tribble, Thomas Howell, Jackson Feilds[sic], Henry Adams, Donland Marrow, Elijah Merril, James Gabriel, Richard Ward, Russel Hazelhanan, Pleasant Hanan, Richard Shankes, Thomas Duvanet, Jacob Inglehart, Andrew Tribble, James P. Harper, Robon Shannon, James Boston, Pat Tindle, Daniel Tindle, John Wallace, B. Gardinner, John Bolen, Jefrey (sic) M. Palmer, Joel P. Blair, William Deys, James R. Whitehead, John H. Whitehead, Daniel Montgomery, Henry S. Creal, Thomas Willbahan, Peter Hover, Henry Thompson, Luther Dillon, Benjamin Hardin, Albert Head, Tassney Ralph, E. Blackston, A. Hayes, James B. O'Toole, James O'Toole, William Arthur, Jacob Yonder, John I. Brady, Henderson Shallwood, Anderson Hill, Milton E. Bryant, John Trotman, Antwise Tere, William McGreer, William Palmer, George Palmer, William McGrew, Henry Rhodes, Robert Myres, Archibald Willis, William Brittain, John D. Noble, Jacob Sharp, Francis Flanigin, Jeffrey Landon, Benjamin Fry, Andrew B. Armstrong, John Armstrong, Green McCafferty, John B. McCafferty, Osborn Huling, James Riley,

Constance Poena, Eli Copeland, William Copeland, John C. Copeland, William Rhodes, George P. Rhodes, Hamilton Osbourne, Benjamin Haglewood, John Lovelandy, Elijah Lovelady, H. P. Ruscal, Winston Thomas.

Fifteenth District

James Brooks, Jonah Lacy, Horace Haley, Calvin Brown, D. A. N. Grover, Charles Grover, William Dyse, J. M. Martin, J. P. Basket, S. W. Tunnel, A. G. Boyd, A. J. Walker, A. C. Hayne, E. S. Wilhite, D. Suell, A. M. Price, W. S. Blanton, E. H. Evans, Isaiah Austin, J. C. Ellis, J. W. Freeland, John Freeland, B. F. Freeland, Uriah Higby, Thomas Dearnier, William Novel, J. W. Atkinson, James Knox, William Kirkman, Robert Joler, Washington Haze, C. Bishop, James Beagle, E. D. Bishop, John Norton, R. W. Thompson, John Cook, E. J. Myers, M. Elliott, G. W. Thompson, G. W. Myers, M. B. Myers, G. S. Davis, Richard Davis, J. J. Thompson, J. F. Sapp, Daniel Sapp, Allen Henson, John Jones, John Bowman, Jonathan Smith, James Douglas, B. Douglas, Robert Smith, H. C. Bradley, John Bailey, Franklin Goddard, Thomas Goddard, Allen Pullen, David Hunt, Benjamin Wallace, E. Downing, William Downing, James Smith, J. H. Kisinger, John Light, Levi Robins, Job Robins, Peter Wade, James Cronens, William Kence, Francis Stutz, Barbery Dowry, J. O. Hawley, J. B. Perry, George B. Wells, William Wade, William Pennick, James Frily, Stephen Frily, Jesse Frily, Francis Noyes, Jim Johnson, George Sharp, William Sharp, Robert Isaacs, Silas Snoddy, Silas Willa, John Snoddy, R. M. Lisby, James Cunningham, James Losten, George Hollingsworth, L. Yokem, Grafton Thomason, S. Dickens, David Pennick, N. J. Allen, M. A. Branfield, Jesse Shepard, H. H. Williams, J. D. Durony, Andrew Chenyworth, Jonathan Congreve, G. F. Challas, John Parker, John Flannery, J. S. Wiser, A. H. Allen, J. H. Stringfellow, James Donnel, W. D. Adams, R. S. Kelly, Ira Norris, William Hensler, Charles Eckles, Michael Wilkin, Martin Jones, E. J. Narvey, J. J. Brown, C. B. Graham, William Morton, Henry Snider, John Taylor, Joseph Taylor, Patrick Hancock, Eph. Farwell, John Snider, F. L. Stutz, Christ. Harn, B. L. Rich, J. H. Gilbert, John Chandler, David Fiser, Luther Dickerson, William Mcvay, Dudley Mcvay, F. M. Mcvay, Joseph Mcvay, Weal Higby, Bond Thomas, Daniel Thomas, John Large, William Crawford, Gilbert Mulford, Thomas Pickton, M. Moony, H. F. Power, John House, Samuel Bixler, S. F. Kay, Alexander Cotterel, M. Coale, H. B. Gale, J. R. Jones, William Dilla, James Henderson, Samuel Wallace, J. M. Wallace, John Thornbury, Pleasant Thornbury, William Cummings, John Waddle, James Cooly, J. M. McBride, Abner Henson, F. M. Potter, Y. B. Gates, M. T. Baily, J. W. Baily, William Baily, O. Wammack, Allen

Wammack, T. T. Kelly, J. A. Henderson, James Lewis, J. M. Freeland, F. M. Stanly, N. W. Hodges, Thomas Sumpter, J. B. Passly, Robert Parks, J. E. Beckner, J. D. Carban, ??? Jones, Martin Rickle, John Norton, M. A. Jones, J. M. Dean, J. M. Layton, S. S. Layton, C. E. McDonald, Nathaniel Stephens, M. A. Stephens, William Boon, H. C. Boon.

Sixteenth District

James Findley, Benj. H. Twombley, David Dodge, Jos. P. Dunham, John Dunham, Caleb Dunham, John Luck, L. R. Pharr, J. Howald, Wm. H. Adams, Hy. Smith, L. J. Eastin, L. N. Reed, R. R. Reed, Wm. Saunders, Ed. Saunders, Geo. H. Keller, A. T. Kyle, A. T. Pattee, Geo. Brubaker, Wm. Pierce, F. S. Abney, John Harris, Isaac Williams, Alvah Gregory, S. Scruggs, Hiram Rich, L. A. Wiggins, Thomas Blakely, G. Gladdon, Jac. McWinders, Riley Todd, Clark Trite, John Tyler, Joseph McGee, William Large, William Meloy, A. C. Fulks, Daniel Brasfield, James Davis, B. B. Mize, John C. Newton, Asa Smith, R. Moxley, Alexander Russell, John Mire, C. F. Hammond, H. B. Kelley, George Leiggan, William Sparks, William Gaberts, Joseph Waddill, C. Linville, James Hutchings, Joseph Hix, Goodwin Howell, John Moore, J. Kinfrow, Hud. Scott, S. M. Hickman, S. Pankake, W. Bohart, John Haxwell, Thomas Scott, F. G. Bradin, James Pyle, John H. Micher, Joseph Elliott, Francis Browning, S. McMurtny, Thomas Tritt, William Pierson, Thomas Wright, George S. Winn, Montgomery Giernn, Michael Levinn, Lew Steps, Eli Hanlin, Stephen Sparks, Jno. Sparks, Jacob Adamson, James Bradley, James C. Brown, William Bukam, F. A. Hart, D. A. Mitchell, A. Payne, S.D. Pitcher, Edward Rankin, Lawni Rankin, O. Register, Jeremiah Clarke, John Harris, Hudson Howland, B. M. Crust, George Dallas, David Creek, David Shearin, James Mam, William Large, C. C. Harrison, R. P. Briggs, F. A. Roberts, Charles H. Allen, J. M. Tyner, J. G. Henderson, John Kissinger, Joseph Scaggs, James Wells, Andrew Skaggs, Thomas Stearns, John Allen, James Noble, A. L. Downey, ? ??Iddings, ??? Wilkinson, Merrill Davis, John Hartsell, William Davis, Joel S. Moore, G. Redmund, George W. Thompson, D. Thompson, William Hooper, J. Shilby Pyle, Thomas C. Bishop, F. S. Arterberry, James H. Garritt, Joseph Bowls, George W. Walker, Thomas Laige, William Coomnan, F. Paget, E. F. Stafford, John H. Dennis, H. C. Norton, George B. Northup, A. P. Leary, S. Philips, Stephen Hunt, Christ. Earle, Will G. Woons, George Cokley, Solomon Thomas, Robert Rogers, A. Brady, W. H. Lawson, Alfred Lort, Jonathan Hall, Roberts Nathan, George B. White, Nathan Adams, W. W. Jefferson, W. A. McDonell, Israel Gibson.

Seventeenth District

Thomas Johnson, J. Dummer, R. C. Meeks, Robert Brown, Augustus Charles, William Donaldson, Joseph Akin, John Boles, Samuel Ganett, Perk. Randall, John Owens, Doctor Buchhauman, Isaac Panish, C. Chouteau, L. Chouteau, Charles Boles, James Mathews, Joseph Fager, Henry I. Kaufmon, Charles Snider, S. B. Dusser, O. H. P. Reppta, E. F. Buckman, Talton Blass, William Rutlidge, B. F. Robinson, Judge Bouton, James B. Bornette, John Elbert, Daniel Frazuer, George Bagan, James Gladden, Francis Berry.

Marriages Of Early Settlers Of Pottawatomie County, As Recorded In William G. Cutler's "History Of The State Of Kansas," with Missouri Connections

John Chelander married in St. Joseph, Mo., June 24, 1871, to Miss Bregitta Olson.

William Clark twice married, first to Miss Mary A. Churchman, of Livingston County, Mo., on the 6th of March, 1859, and January 14, 1877, he was again married at Louisville, to Miss Lucinda A. Gann.

Jacob H. Hard was married July 22, 1854, in Weston, Mo, to Miss Barbara Weist.

Guy Harrington married in Jackson County, Mo., July 13, 1874 to Miss Mollie Jessup.

Phillip Immenschuh was married February 18, 1858, at Weston, Mo., to Miss Gertrude Repp.

D. B. Kitts married at Hannibal, Mo., December 31, 1845, to Miss Susan George. She lived but a year and a half, and again, November 16, 1849, he married Miss Jane George, the sister of his former wife.

John P. Koentz, M. D., married in October, 1865, at Little Santa Fe, Mo., to Miss Sarah M. White.

Hugh Sutherland married at St. Louis, Mo., January, 1851, to Miss Hannah Mary Strickland.

Sedalia High School, 1914, Yearbook, Sedalia, Pettis County, Missouri.

Name	Comments
Hattie Anderson	Teacher History
Elizabeth Bowers	Teacher Latin
S. H. Brown	Teacher Chemistry; Physics
Eunice Cousley	Teacher English
F. O. Duncan	Teacher Mathematics
Ellen Goebel	Teacher German
Daniel Lewis	Teacher Commercial

Name	Comments
Letha M. Lowen	Teacher Mathematics
Mary L. McCluney	Teacher Asst. English
Mattie Montgomery	Teacher Asst. Mathematics
Juliette Moss	Teacher Assistant English
A. G. Norris	Teacher Manuel Training; Mechanical Drawing
George Reeves	Teacher Natural Science
Daniel Shutts	Teacher Physical Geography
Tillie Snell	Teacher Domestic Science
Frank Armstrong	Student
Nina Babcock	Student
Margaret Bapple	Student
Lawrence Barnett	Student
Joseph Bast	Student
Herman Bloess	Student
John Bockleman	Student
Sadie Bowser	Student
Mary Boyle	Student
Raymond Brandt	Student
Sylvania Bryan	Student
J. Clarence Burk	Student
John Carlisle	Student
Boyd Carroll	Student
Roy Chancey	Student
Edith Crosslin	Student
Robert Cunningham	Student
Jewel Davis	Student
Lee Dowd	Student
Theodore Easton	Student
Wilbur Fisher	Student
Frances Garmen	Student
Ruby Glover	Student
Lois Green	Student
Mary Green	Student
Edith Hardin	Student
Mildred Hardin	Student
Beulah Harris	Student
Bertha Harvey	Student
George Herndon	Student
Wilson Hicks	Student
Myrtle Holmesley	Student
Will Hudson	Student

Name	Comments
Ivan Irwin	Student
Minta Jacobs	Student
Nora Keuper	Student
S. M. Kolbohn	Student
Leona Kroschen	Student
Walter M'Climans	Student
Vivian M'Curdy	Student
Zana M'Neil	Student
Dorothy Mackey	Student
Nannie Manker	Student
Forest Meyers	Student
Earl Miller	Student
Glen Miller	Student
Goldie Monsees	Student
Hannah Monsees	Student
Kalo Monsees	Student
Helen Morris	Student
Bessie Neitzert	Student
Florence Pace	Student
Edith Regan	Student
Clara Rutledge	Student
Jeanette Skinner	Student
Mildred Slagle	Student
Luckett Smith	Student
Leslie Snyder	Student
William Steele	Student
Beulah Stevenson	Student
Elizabeth Sturges	Student
Lynn Taylor	Student
Ray Thomas	Student
Vallye Tongate	Student
Ruby Turner	Student
Clara Van Hoff	Student
Naomi Walch	Student
Stanley Walker	Student
Nellie White	Student
Stella Williams	Student

Missourians on the Arapahoe County, Colorado, 1870 Mortality Schedule

Richardson, Lenore : (A) 2Y, (SEX) F (D) Jan, (BP) MO, (CMTS) Bronchitis.

Missourians on the Ellis County, Texas, 1860 Mortality Schedule
M. Harpold: (A) 1Y, (SEX) F, white, (BP) Mo, (D) Nov, (CMTS) Scarlet fever.
W. H. Bridgeman: (A) 13Y, (SEX) F, white, (BP) Mo, (D) Jan. (CMTS) Typhoid fever.
August Hood: (A) 1Y, (SEX) M, white, (BP) Mo, (D) Sept., (CMTS) Teething Diarrhea.
Rachel Lee: (A) 25Y, (SEX) F, married, (BP) Mo, (D) Nov., (CMTS) Cause unknown.
E. C. Henry: (A) 10Y, (SEX) F, (BP) Mo., (D) Jul. (CMTS) Typoid fever.

Missourians on the Jack County, Texas, Voters List, 1867 - 1869

Name	In St.	In Co.	In Prect.	Native
John W. Brummett	8Y	8Y	--	Missouri
Moses Damron	20Y	10Y	10Y	Missouri
Isaac Lynn	26Y	12Y	12Y	Missouri
Ulyssus M. Johnson	6Y	6Y	6Y	Missouri
Peter Lynn	23Y	12Y	12Y	Missouri

Buchanan County, Missouri, 1840 Census Index
Barnabus Adkins, (P) 150; Landey Alford, (P) 144; John Allen, (P) 154; Lewis Allen, (P) 141; William Alley, (P) 146; John H Allison, (P) 160; Humphrey Allison, (P) 159; William Allison, (P) 160; Edward Allison, (P) 143; Henry Almond, (P) 147; William Alnut, (P) 169; Joshua Anderson, (P) 158; James Anderson, (P) 166; William Anderson, (P) 144; Everhart Antle, (P) 142; Archibald Argyete, (P) 158; William Arnett, (P) 147; Eli Arnold, (P) 169; Singleton Asher, (P) 156; Ashel Ashley, (P) 148; Isacc Auzier, (P) 172; Thomas Auzier, (P) 172; Richard Bagbey, (P) 170; Thomas Bainton, (P) 167; Morris Baker, (P) 160; Thomas Baker, (P) 159; Zebediah Baker, (P) 155; Andrew Baker, (P) 168; Elijah W Ballard, (P) 153; Joseph Baltimore, (P) 145; Gallant Banes, (P) 150; John Baney, (P) 141; John Bano, (P) 140; Jesse Barker, (P) 143; George W Barnes, (P) 164; Benjamin Barnes, (P) 160; James Barnes, (P) 160; Jessee Barnett, (P) 170; James Barnett, (P) 170; John Barnett, (P) 170; David Barrier, (P) 142; Charles Beasley, (P) 151; Walter Beavin, (P) 155; James C. Beck, (P) 148; Benjamin Beckett, (P) 164; Stephen Bedford, (P) 164; John E. Bedford, (P) 165; Hugh B Begnold, (P) 167; John Belcheo, (P) 167; Leander Belieso, (P) 139; Micajah B Belieu, (P) 158; John Belk, (P) 142; Loya Bell, (P) 173; John Bell, (P) 157; Elisha Bennett, (P) 148; Silas Bennett, (P) 143; Edward Bent, (P) 144; Nahun Bent, (P) 144;

Peter S. Benton, (P) 148; Joseph Bercy, (P) 148; John Bermont, (P) 142; Martin Berry, (P) 161; Silas W. Berry, (P) 161; Azeriah Berryhill, (P) 170; John Berryhill, (P) 170; Emanuel Best, (P) 156; John Best, (P) 156; Silas Best, (P) 153; Mahala Best, (P) 142; David Best, (P) 147; George Bibb, (P) 171; John D. Bichey, (P) 168; William H Bichey, (P) 167; John Biggin, (P) 145; Thomas Bilderback, (P) 173; Adam Bingle, (P) 164; Hutson Bivin, (P) 151; Andrew Black, (P) 163; John W Black, (P) 163; James Blackman, (P) 159; James Blakley, (P) 142; George Blankenship, (P) 145; William Blankenship, (P) 149; Kennard Blaseton, (P) 162; Austin Bledsoe, (P) 172; Voluntine Bledsoe, (P) 164; William Bledsoe, (P) 172; Daniel Blevin, (P) 163; Stephen Blevins, (P) 169; Wilburn Bobins, (P) 146; John Bobins, (P) 143; John Bohannon, (P) 163; Philip Bohart, (P) 155; Jacob Bohart, (P) 155; Opton Bohres, (P) 148; Thomas Boitston, (P) 165; Kasper Bomard, (P) 141; John Bomard, (P) 141; Asa Boss, (P) 147; Eave Bowgers, (P) 142; James A Bowling, (P) 140; William Bowman, (P) 140; Henry Bowyers, (P) 171; Peter Bowyers Sr, (P) 171; Robert J. Boyd, (P) 173; James Boyd, (P) 163; Charles Boyers, (P) 154; Peter Boyes, (P) 171; James Bradford, (P) 148; John Brady, (P) 143; Thomas Bragg, (P) 172; William Bragg, (P) 162; Josiah Brawley, (P) 165; John W. Bridgman, (P) 172; William Bries, (P) 145; Peter Brines, (P) 149; George Brittle, (P) 171; Jacob Brittle, (P) 171; Emanuel Brittle, (P) 171; George Brock, (P) 148; Benjamin H. Brock, (P) 141; Isaac Brown, (P) 166; William L. Brown, (P) 161; Thomas A. Brown, (P) 158; Gideon L. Brown, (P) 157; Edward C. Brown, (P) 166; Thomas Brown, (P) 143; David Brown, (P) 159; Henry H. Bruce, (P) 168; George Bucknell, (P) 141; Elijah Bunton, (P) 153; Samuel Burgess, (P) 156; James Burnett, (P) 159; William Burns, (P) 147; Jeremiah Burns, (P) 151; John Burris, (P) 163; Ennis Burris, (P) 163; William T. Bush, (P) 150; George Bush, (P) 153; James Cains, (P) 142; Jessie Calvert, (P) 147; James Calvin, (P) 139; Samuel B. Campbell, (P) 144; Anderson S. Camron, (P) 151; Calvin S. Camron, (P) 147; James H. Canter, (P) 161; Charles Caples, (P) 140; James Carnes, (P) 138; Benjamin Carnes, (P) 162; Whissle Carpenter, (P) 170; Elias Cary, (P) 140; Abijah Cary, (P) 140; Josiah Casebeer, (P) 143; Dyer Cash, (P) 159; Benjamin Cash, (P) 148; Franklin D. Cashady, (P) 148; Charles Cates, (P) 168; Alphord Cates, (P) 168; Benjamin F. Catlet, (P) 168; Owen Cawlfield, (P) 141; Dennis Chance, (P) 153; Richard Chaney, (P) 164; Richard Chaney, (P) 165; Daniel Chapel, (P) 142; Thomas I.Che, (P) 164; John Citihen ?, (P) 144; Isacc Clanton, (P) 172; Joel H. Clanton, (P) 172; Henry Clark, (P) 149; Barnes Clark, (P) 142; John R. Clark, (P) 171; William L. Clark, (P) 142; Daniel H. Clark, (P) 165; Jacob Clark, (P) 140; William H.

Clasby, (P) 163; GreenBerry Clay, (P) 166; Rachel Cleek, (P) 171; John Cleek, (P) 171; Conrad Cliffield, (P) 145; John Clouser, (P) 155; Jonathan M. Cobb, (P) 150; Mary Cobb, (P) 144; Jacob Coffman, (P) 151; Thomas F. Coffman, (P) 151; Leroy Coffman, (P) 151; William Cogdell, (P) 155; Jacob Cogdell, (P) 155; David Cogdell, (P) 159; Elizabeth Coil, (P) 167; Simeon Coil, (P) 167; Allen Coleleasure, (P) 164; William Combs, (P) 171; William C. Connett, (P) 158; Edward Cook, (P) 141; Henry Cook, (P) 138; Asa Cook, (P) 157; Eli Copeland, (P) 166; John Copland, (P) 173; Hugh Copland, (P) 167; Benjamin Cornelius, (P) 142; Newton Cowen, (P) 161; John F. Cox, (P) 150; Thomas Crabtree, (P) 168; John Cromwell, (P) 159; Alford G. Cropp, (P) 144; James Crowley, (P) 152; John Croy, (P) 173; Nathan Culp, (P) 151; Eli G. Cummins, (P) 165; Christophe Cunningham, (P) 169; William Curl, (P) 161; David Curl, (P) 157; James Curl, (P) 157; John Daniels, Jr., (P) 165; John Daniels, Sr., (P) 165; John W. Davidson, (P) 155; Edward M. Davidson, (P) 155; Joseph Davidson, (P) 156; Hannah Davidson, (P) 156; Resin Davis, (P) 158; Mathew L. Davis, (P) 155; Ishmael Davis, (P) 172; Sarah Davis, (P) 161; John D. Davis, (P) 163; James Davis, (P) 138; Jacob Davis, (P) 153; James Davis, (P) 166; James Davison, (P) 141; Edward Davison, (P) 141; Anderson Davison, (P) 141; David Davison, (P) 145; Lucas Dawson, (P) 173; Voluntine Day, (P) 160; Nicholas Deakins, (P) 153; William Deakins, (P) 153; Powell Dean, (P) 171; George Dial, (P) 145; Benjamin H. Dickson, (P) 168; Moses Dike, (P) 148; John S. Dill, (P) 147; Ralph Dison, (P) 141; Enoch Dixon, (P) 167; John Donell, (P) 167; James Donell, (P) 169; Robert Donnell, (P) 157; James Donovan, (P) 158; Erastus Downing, (P) 148; Morgan Dryden, (P) 165; John Dryden, (P) 165; Henry Duff, (P) 147; Thomas Duke, (P) 150; Robert Duncan, (P) 158; John Duncan, (P) 144; Charles Duncan, (P) 143; Catherine Dungan, (P) 142; Richard Dunn, (P) 148; James Dunn, (P) 148; William Dunning, (P) 159; Francis Durell, (P) 167; Benjamin K. Dyer, (P) 144; Jonathan Earls, (P) 153; John Easley, (P) 151; Edward Easton, (P) 148; James Edgar, (P) 158; Samuel W. Edwards, (P) 161; James P. Edwards, (P) 172; Samuel E. Edwards, (P) 168; William Edwards, (P) 169; John Elington, (P) 146; William Elliott, (P) 165; Robert Elliott, (P) 147; Willis Elliott, (P) 163; William Ellis, (P) 150; James Ellison, (P) 161; Robert English, (P) 162; Daniel Eplinger, (P) 140; Harrison Erickson, (P) 164; William J Erickson, (P) 162; John Erickson, (P) 164; Conrad Esininger, (P) 146; Joel Estes, (P) 147; William Estes, (P) 167; John Estes, (P) 168; Archibald Estes, (P) 147; David M. Evans, (P) 170; John Evans, (P) 150; Weston I. Everett, (P) 172; John A. Ewell, (P) 160; Margaret Farley, (P) 145; Zachariah Fennea, (P) 155; William Fenny, (P) 172;

Jefferson Ferrel, (P) 157; Samuel D. Ferrel, (P) 156; Daniel Ferril, (P) 150; Ezekiael Fidler, (P) 166; James Fidler, (P) 166; William Field, (P) 172; Clark Fields, (P) 148; Stephen Fields, (P) 163; Humphrey Finch, (P) 163; Jessee Finch, (P) 159; Colby Finley, (P) 145; Lee Fitzgerald, (P) 155; John B Flannery, (P) 160; William Flannery, (P) 173; William E. Flannery, (P) 159; Charles Fletcher, (P) 166; Jessee Fletcher, (P) 164; John Fletcher, (P) 166; Thomas Fletcher, (P) 166; Henry Fosher, (P) 154; Henry Foster, (P) 149; Dugen Fouts, (P) 172; John Fowler, (P) 172; William Fowler, (P) 170; John Fowler, (P) 170; William Fowles, (P) 155; Nathan Frakes, (P) 154; Joshua Frazee, (P) 149; Solomon Frazure, (P) 173; John W Freeman, (P) 151; Nathan Freeman, (P) 153; Sanford Freland, (P) 156; Isiah Frigett, (P) 157; Gilbert H. Frost, (P) 153; Jonathan C. Fugett, (P) 165; John Fulks, (P) 147; James Fulton, (P) 147; Richard Fulton, (P) 168; James Fulton, (P) 168; William Furgison, (P) 148; Mikael Gabbert, (P) 154; Willis Gaines, (P) 151; Isaac Gann, (P) 156; John Gann, (P) 156; Isam S. Gardner, (P) 162; John Garret, (P) 171; William Garret, (P) 171; Euriah Gaston, (P) 162; Zachariah Gaston, (P) 162; Nathan Gates, (P) 157; Edmund W. Gee, (P) 147; Matison Geere, (P) 161; John W Gentry, (P) 150; Price Gesst, (P) 164; James Gibson, (P) 154; George Gibson, (P) 172; George Gibson, (P) 172; James Gibson, (P) 170; William Giddens, (P) 170; Mitchell Gilam, (P) 139; Henry Gill, (P) 161; Nicholas Gillam, (P) 151; Thomas Gillet, (P) 168; Joseph Gilmore, (P) 158; James I. Gilmore, (P) 172; James Gilmore, (P) 171; Robert Gilmore, (P) 168; Samuel M. Gilmore, (P) 173; Milphord Gilmore, (P) 168; Isaac Givens, (P) 166; William Glaze, (P) 157; Hugh Glen, (P) 171; John Goodnight, (P) 150; Mikael Graham, (P) 139; Alexander Graham, (P) 139; David Grant, (P) 152; Thomas Gray, (P) 148; Timothy Green, (P) 146; Leonard Green, (P) 144; Andrew Gregory, (P) 142; Lewis Gresham, (P) 163; Joel Griffey, (P) 150; John Griffith, (P) 148; Samuel Grit, (P) 151; Solomon Gromes, (P) 164; James Groms, (P) 165; William Groshong, (P) 152; Jacob Groshong, (P) 152; Peter Grossclose, (P) 169; William Guinn, (P) 157; Benjamin Guinn, (P) 165; Jeptha Haden, (P) 148; Miles Hail, (P) 148; Marcus Hall, (P) 158; James Hall, (P) 158; James Hall, (P) 145; Richard Hancock, (P) 163; Isacc H. Hanes, (P) 164; James Hansen, (P) 167; Henserson Hardesty, (P) 140; John L. Hardy, (P) 173; John Hargrove, (P) 161; Abel Harington, (P) 168; William Harington, (P) 173; Barney Harper, (P) 148; William Harrington, (P) 155; John Harris, (P) 160; John Harris, (P) 147; Isacc Harris, (P) 168; John H. Harris, (P) 144; John Harris, (P) 163; Henry W Harrison, (P) 138; John Hartman, (P) 140; Daniel Hartmen, (P) 140; Jeremiah Haviline, (P) 167; James W. Hayes, (P) 138; John Hays, (P) 160; Hugh Hays, (P) 160; Henry Hays,

(P) 160; Joseph Hederick, (P) 164; Joel Hedgpeth, (P) 162; James Hedgpeth, (P) 162; Samuel Hellards, (P) 154; Elias Hellards, (P) 154; Widdows Henderson, (P) 154; Gelford C. Henderson, (P) 154; Noah Henderson, (P) 173; Robert Henderson, (P) 164; John Hendricks, (P) 143; Isacc Henry, (P) 164; John Henry, (P) 143; John Henry, (P) 165; Henry W. Hensley, (P) 154; William Hickman, (P) 162; Noah Hickman, (P) 169; Thomas Hickman, (P) 162; John I. Hicks, (P) 169; Liman Hide, (P) 138; Richard Hill, (P) 158; Joseph Hill, (P) 158; John Hill, (P) 173; Harlo Hinkston, (P) 159; Jacob Hitribidle, (P) 145; William Hix, (P) 149; Eli Hobble, (P) 173; Jesse Hobbs, (P) 158; Albert Holister, (P) 147; Thomas Holland, (P) 147; John Holland, (P) 169; Wilson Holman, (P) 168; James B Holman, (P) 169; Daniel Holman, (P) 151; William Holman, (P) 169; Timothy Holoway, (P) 150; William Holoway, (P) 150; Loreta Horn, (P) 161; Caleb Hosenmyer, (P) 142; Perry Hoshaw, (P) 145; Abraham Howard, (P) 150; John Howard, (P) 150; James M. Howe, (P) 163; John Howell, (P) 151; Haywood B. Howell, (P) 151; James Howell, (P) 144; Charles B. Huddleston, (P) 154; Prince L. Hudgens, (P) 150; George W. Hudspeth, (P) 159; Joseph Hufft, (P) 161; Abner E. Hugart, (P) 159; Joseph Hughart, (P) 173; Young S. Hughes, (P) 152; Silvester Hughlett, (P) 170; Elias Hughs, (P) 157; Claborn Hughs, (P) 153; Litte Hughs, (P) 153; Major Hungett, (P) 140; Wesley Hunter, (P) 168; Andrew J. Hunter, (P) 173; John Huntquicker, (P) 165; Peter Huntsucker, (P) 164; Thomas Huntsucker, (P) 172; William Huntsucker, (P) 172; John Huntsucker, (P) 169; Joseph Hurst, (P) 150; John Ingleton, (P) 167; Robert Irwin, (P) 171; Haden Jackson, (P) 141; Levi R. Jackson, (P) 169; Nelson James, (P) 163; James James, (P) 142; George Jeffries, (P) 172; Wesley Jenkins, (P) 160; Elijah Jenkins, (P) 170; William Jenks, (P) 147; John Jobe, (P) 149; Aaron Johnson, (P) 145; John L. Johnson, (P) 138; David Johnson, (P) 160; A. M. Johnson, (P) 160; Gebron Johnson, (P) 146; Lewis Johnson, (P) 160; Harvey Jones, (P) 172; Holland Jones, (P) 161; Martha H. Jones, (P) 172; Stephen Jones, (P) 157; Ambros Jones, (P) 173; Robert Jones, (P) 158; Cox Jonithan, (P) 156; Mary M. Jons, (P) 170; Andrew Jourdoin, (P) 162; Eli Judah, (P) 157; Abel Keener, (P) 166; Peter Keepher, (P) 164; Peter Kelley, (P) 146; John Kelley, (P) 140; Edward Kelley, (P) 140; Andrew Kelley, (P) 140; Isaac Kelley, (P) 140; William B. Kelley, (P) 147; Elijah Kellogg, (P) 149; Simon Kemper, (P) 138; William Kerkman, (P) 167; John Kerr, (P) 148; Jacob Kesler, (P) 171; Mastin Kestler, (P) 142; David Kindred, (P) 141; Alford King, (P) 141; Thompson Kinion, (P) 148; Samuel Kinion, (P) 148; John Kinney, (P) 149; George W. Kinney, (P) 149; George Lacey, (P) 138; Andrew Lackey, (P) 146; Joseph Lady, (P) 161; Thomas Langley, (P) 171;

Silvester Lanham, (P) 156; John Lanius, (P) 170; Thomas L. Laseter, (P) 164; Sharon Lawhorn, (P) 149; Edward Lawless, (P) 142; Philip Layman, (P) 170; Joseph Layman, (P) 170; Hiram Lee, (P) 145; Hendrix Lee, (P) 145; David Lee, (P) 159; William Levingston, (P) 141; Jae S. Levingston, (P) 141; Nathaniel Levingston, (P) 141; Charles Lewis, (P) 165; Thomas Lexington, (P) 173; Lemuel Lile, (P) 142; David Lilley, (P) 165; Isacc Linch, (P) 160; David Linch, (P) 156; Wilburn Linville, (P) 160; James Linville, (P) 160; Thomas Linville, (P) 159; George Linville, (P) 163; Zachariah Linville, (P) 159; Chasity Linville, (P) 168; Jacob Lower, (P) 163; John Luman, (P) 148; Jesse Majors, (P) 154; Titus Mark, (P) 173; Philip Marker, (P) 142; Elijah Martin, (P) 144; Nehemiah Martin, (P) 141; Abraham Martin, (P) 161; Margaret Martin, (P) 145; John Martin, (P) 154; Samuel Martin, (P) 161; Isacc Martin, (P) 154; Thomas Martin, (P) 173; Bradberry Martin, (P) 168; Christophe Martin, (P) 155; Litleton Mathis, (P) 143; David May, (P) 162; Isacc May, (P) 161; Robert Mcain, (P) 167; John Mcart, (P) 169; Davis Mcarty, (P) 167; Jobe Mcarver, (P) 173; Thomas McBride, (P) 143; Ambros A B Mcdaniel, (P) 172; Silas McDonald, (P) 157; William Mcdowel, (P) 168; William McDowel, (P) 157; John Mcganthey, (P) 168; Theophilus McGauder, (P) 151; Sarah McGill, (P) 165; Edward McGouder, (P) 152; Alexander Mcguinn, (P) 173; James Mcguinn, (P) 170; Mary Mcguinn, (P) 140; James McGuire, (P) 157; William McGuire, (P) 154; Cornelius McGuire, (P) 154; Bryant McLendon, (P) 150; Thomas McNight, (P) 149; John McOnnel, (P) 162; Jabes Mcorcle, (P) 165; Thomas McOwn, (P) 143; Jeremiah McOwn, (P) 143; Anderson Mcoy, (P) 145; Daniel Mcray, (P) 170; Benjamin Mcray, (P) 169; Hoonigton McRiney, (P) 161; McRoney, (P) 141; Elizabeth Mcubin, (P) 163; William McUmber, (P) 153; Robert Mcutchings, (P) 157; Francis I. Meadows, (P) 169; William C. Means, (P) 143; George W Means, (P) 171; John Meers, (P) 162; Nicholas Meril, (P) 151; Henry Mille, (P) 140; Isacc Miller, (P) 171; Margaret Miller, (P) 171; Jacob Miller, (P) 155; Henry Miller, (P) 157; Jessee Miller, (P) 170; Richard Miller, (P) 151; Asa Mills, (P) 143; James Mitchell, (P) 162; Silas Moland, (P) 156; Jacob Mond, (P) 171; Thomas D Montgomery, (P) 154; Isaac Moody, (P) 152; Thomas Moore, (P) 173; John Moore, (P) 140; William Moore, (P) 161; Sterling Morgan, (P) 154; John Morris, (P) 162; Henry Morris, (P) 145; James Morrison, (P) 150; Robert W Morrison, (P) 150; Samuel Morrow, (P) 173; Samuel Moss, (P) 144; James Motry, (P) 156; Gelford Motry, (P) 156; Ann Motry, (P) 156; Timothy Mozine, (P) 145; George Mufley, (P) 170; James L Mulkey, (P) 159; Daniel Mulkey, (P) 160; Elijah Mulkey, (P) 160; Greenbury Mullinix, (P) 150; Absolem Munkies, (P) 164; Bedman Munkies, (P) 165; Walter

Murphy, (P) 169; Allen Muzings, (P) 141; John Muzings, (P) 141; Joseph Nash, (P) 165; Clayburn Neal, (P) 171; Ahijah Nearis, (P) 143; Edward Neely, (P) 139; Willis Neely, (P) 139; George Nelson, (P) 152; John Nichoels, (P) 139; Benjamin Nicholes, (P) 153; Evan Nichols, (P) 153; John Noble, (P) 149; John Noel, (P) 158; Joel Noland, (P) 144; Henry Noland, (P) 149; James Noland, (P) 144; Jesse Noland, (P) 156; James L. Noland, (P) 144; Abner Norris, (P) 160; Lorenzo D. Nuckles, (P) 147; James O'Tool, (P) 157; William Obanion, (P) 142; James Officer, (P) 144; Thomas Oldham, (P) 142; Hester Olliver, (P) 153; John Orvero, (P) 153; Martha Owen, (P) 160; William M. Owen, (P) 159; William Owens, (P) 152; Nicholas Owens, (P) 156; Nicholas C. Owens, (P) 152; Powell Owensbey, (P) 171; Samuel Owsley, (P) 144; Stephen Parker, (P) 138; Clayburn T Parmer, (P) 138; Harvey Patterson, (P) 150; Green Patterson, (P) 164; Cloborn Patton, (P) 161; William Pearson, (P) 170; Mace Pendleton, (P) 144; Joel H. Penick, (P) 157; Obadiah Persinger, (P) 165; Lewis Persinger, (P) 165; James Person, (P) 170; John Person, (P) 147; Elizabeth Person, (P) 170; James Person, (P) 152; Nathaniel Person, (P) 147; Samuel Peteet, (P) 168; Thomas Peteet, (P) 142; John Petree, (P) 141; Samuel Petyjohn, (P) 145; Ann Philbert, (P) 169; Simeon Pickerell, (P) 162; Jacob P Pierce, (P) 173; Morris Pile, (P) 164; Andrew Pitman, (P) 149; Elias Pitman, (P) 149; Willow Poisel, (P) 154; John Poley, (P) 161; Ephriam Porter, (P) 156; William Portis, (P) 163; Alexander Pounds, (P) 149; James Powell, (P) 159; Charles K Powell, (P) 165; Benjamin F. Price, (P) 147; John Price, (P) 159; William A Price, (P) 150; Joseph Pyburn, (P) 143; William Pyburn, (P) 153; Edward Pyburn, (P) 153; Jacob Pyburn, (P) 150; Jefferson Ragsdale, (P) 163; Milton Randolph, (P) 143; Joseph Rawls, (P) 173; John Ray, (P) 169; Jessee Reams, (P) 158; Alford Rector, (P) 138; James Rector, (P) 159; Tapley Relph, (P) 158; William Reynolds, (P) 144; George L Reynolds, (P) 171; Alford Rice, (P) 142; Gilford Richards, (P) 148; John Richey, (P) 169; John Ritchison, (P) 156; James Roberds, (P) 159; Joseph Roberts, (P) 154; Cornelius Roberts, (P) 163; Hiram Roberts, (P) 163; Richard Roberts, (P) 163; James Roberts, (P) 142; Susanah Roberts, (P) 143; Nicholas Roberts, (P) 143; John Robinett, (P) 159; Stephen Robinett, (P) 159; Emanuel Robinson, (P) 160; Nathan Robison, (P) 161; Asa Rockhole, (P) 164; George Rodes, (P) 154; Absolem Rodes, (P) 139; Hiram Rodgers, (P) 162; Bailey H. Roland, (P) 146; James Ross, (P) 155; John Ross, (P) 155; Samuel Roundtree, (P) 154; John Rousey, (P) 154; George Rubey, (P) 152; Elijah Russel, (P) 156; John D Russel, (P) 151; James Russel, (P) 156; Robert Russell, (P) 153; John C. Russell, (P) 155; Andrew Russell, (P) 161; John Rutledg, (P) 160; James Sale, (P) 157; John Sampson, (P) 157; Glen P. Sampson, (P) 162; Benjamin

Sampson, (P) 154; Benjamin Sampson, (P) 162; James Sanders, (P) 159; John Scaggs, (P) 163; Dudley Scholl, (P) 161; Martin Schultz, (P) 164; David Scott, (P) 168; William Scott, (P) 170; Thomas Sellars, (P) 158; Drewry Sellars, (P) 168; James Sharp, (P) 166; David Sharp, (P) 162; Joseph Shauwood, (P) 167; William Shaw, (P) 151; Haymon Shelton, (P) 151; Tilman H. Shelton, (P) 140; Levi Shelton, (P) 140; David Shelton, (P) 152; James D. Shreve, (P) 143; Jacob Shultz, (P) 172; Samuel Shurlds, (P) 143; Edmund Silence, (P) 149; Peter Silence, (P) 149; William Silence, (P) 149; Elizabeth Silence, (P) 149; Jurdin Silvers, (P) 156; William Silvers, (P) 156; Goalden Silvers, (P) 169; John Silvers, (P) 159; Hugh Silvers, (P) 169; Mikel Simmons, (P) 141; Samuel Simmons, (P) 141; Elizabeth Simmons, (P) 141; Robert Simmons, (P) 141; William Simmons, (P) 141; Robert Simmons jr, (P) 141; Thomas Simpson, (P) 147; John Sipe, (P) 160; Eli Sipe, (P) 159; John Sise, (P) 148; Alexander Skeen, (P) 154; John Slaboy, (P) 171; John G Smedley, (P) 153; Hiram Smith, (P) 152; Delila Smith, (P) 150; George Smith, (P) 166; Pleasant Smith, (P) 139; Jonathan Smith, (P) 167; Tera Smith, (P) 140; Hammilton Smith, (P) 148; Medcalf Smith, (P) 161; George W. Smith, (P) 146; George Smith, (P) 172; David Smith, (P) 173; Ahi Smith, (P) 140; Elias Smith, (P) 151; Anderson Smith, (P) 159; FrederickW. Smith, (P) 151; George Smith, (P) 145; Samuel Smith, (P) 139; George Smith, (P) 149; Elijah Smith, (P) 149; Elijah W. Smith, (P) 158; Burden G. Smith, (P) 171; William Smith, (P) 149; Simpson Smith, (P) 158; Elijah Smith, (P) 173; Thomas Smith, (P) 167; Elisha Smith, (P) 167; Elijah W. Smith, (P) 153; Simon Smith, (P) 147; Elijah Smith jr, (P) 158; Thomas Smither, (P) 149; Oglesby Snead, (P) 154; Edward Snyder, (P) 170; Joseph Snyder, (P) 143; John Sollers, (P) 151; Samuel Son, (P) 162; John Son, (P) 162; William Southward, (P) 155; Benjamin Sparland, (P) 155; John Spence, (P) 151; Obediah M. Spencer, (P) 157; Joseph Stanley, (P) 173; Page Stanley, (P) 140; Harrison Stanley, (P) 140; William Stanton, (P) 147; Jeremiah Stanton, (P) 147; Thomas Stanton, (P) 147; Thomas Stapleton, (P) 138; William A Stephens, (P) 162; William Stephens, (P) 165; Allen Stephens, (P) 170; Archibald Stephenson, (P) 144; Archibald Stewart, (P) 162; Benjamin Stewart, (P) 144; Ezekiael Stewart, (P) 156; Thomas Stewart, (P) 140; Brice Stoller, (P) 145; George Stoner, (P) 145; Thomas Stout, (P) 150; Bonham Stout, (P) 139; William Strickling, (P) 172; John S. Strode, (P) 145; Elizabeth Stufflebeen, (P) 155; James Stutts, (P) 160; Vincent Suitling, (P) 167; James Swan, (P) 143; Robert Swinney, (P) 167; Lowell B. Tassence, (P) 138; James Taylor, (P) 167; Elvis Taylor, (P) 157; George W Taylor, (P) 157; James Taylor, (P) 158; Warner Taylor, (P) 139; Alfred Taylor, (P) 157; John Taylor, (P) 163; Elder Teague, (P) 167; James

Templer, (P) 148; John Tharp, (P) 169; Terry Tharp, (P) 165; Levi Thatcher, (P) 143; John Thermaso, (P) 162; Charles Thermon, (P) 164; Turpen Thomas, (P) 157; David Thomas, (P) 165; James T. Thompson, (P) 151; Moses W. Thompson, (P) 155; David H. Thompson, (P) 162; Larkin F. Thompson, (P) 155; Lemmuel Thornburgh, (P) 166; James Thornburgh, (P) 164; John Thornton, (P) 142; Isaac Thornton, (P) 142; George Tinker, (P) 154; John I. Tinsley, (P) 165; Albert Tipton, (P) 164; John Tobin, (P) 172; Henry Todd, (P) 150; Jeptha Todd, (P) 151; William Tolbey, (P) 152; William Tomas, (P) 161; William H. Tombs, (P) 144; Isaac Tompson, (P) 157; Sebert Tracey, (P) 144; Conrad Travis, (P) 172; Peter Trimble, (P) 166; Robert Trosper, (P) 153; Benjamin Tucker, (P) 149; Nathan Turner, (P) 156; Washington Turner, (P) 155; Silas Turner, (P) 145; Elijah Turner, (P) 140; David Tutheroe, (P) 155; John Underwood, (P) 161; William Underwood, (P) 162; Samuel M. Vance, (P) 151; Isacc Vanhoozier, (P) 163; Abraham Vanmeter, (P) 173; Josiah Vanschoik, (P) 153; Daniel Varvle, (P) 169; Alexander Vaughn, (P) 170; Samuel Vesser, (P) 142; Peter Vesses, (P) 171; Daniel Vestal, (P) 167; Isaac W. Voris, (P) 142; William Wade, (P) 168; Jessee Wadkins, (P) 168; Joseph Walker, (P) 144; Phillip Walker, (P) 169; Mikael Wallice, (P) 168; Elijah Walters, (P) 153; Jonathan B. Ward, (P) 150; George Ward, (P) 138; James Waters, (P) 143; Lorenzo Waugh, (P) 169; James C. Webb, (P) 156; John W. Whisman, (P) 151; Samuel Whitaker, (P) 154; James White, (P) 165; John H. Whitehead, (P) 138; John Whiteley, (P) 166; Daniel T. Whitsman, (P) 146; Hiram Wilburn, (P) 171; John Wilfley, (P) 155; Boss Wilkerson, (P) 155; John Willhite, (P) 146; Jenkin Williams, (P) 157; Henry Williams, (P) 156; Elias Williams, (P) 140; William Williams, (P) 156; James Williams, (P) 160; Catherine Williams, (P) 140; Benjamin Williams, (P) 149; Joseph Williams, (P) 140; Alexander Williams, (P) 172; Benjamin Williams, (P) 151; Catharine Willis, (P) 168; James Wilson, (P) 163; Anderson Wilson, (P) 145; Aaron Wilson, (P) 144; Joseph Wilson, (P) 161; David Winkler, (P) 138; Nelson Witt, (P) 164; George Wolf, (P) 145; Andrew Wollhelm, (P) 166; Abraham Wominash, (P) 163; Allen Wommath, (P) 159; Joseph Wondesley, (P) 142; James W. Wood, (P) 153; Samuel W. Woodcock, (P) 153; Allen B. Woodcock, (P) 153; Williston Woodcock, (P) 153; Stephen C. Woodcock, (P) 147; John W Woods, (P) 145; Alexander Woods, (P) 145; David Worcester, (P) 170; William Worster, (P) 145; Robert Woster, (P) 145; Charles Wright, (P) 167; Francis Writsman, (P) 144; Frederick Wyatt, (P) 141; Washington Yates, (P) 149; Plesant Yates, (P) 167; William Yates, (P) 149; John Yengst, (P) 143; William J. Young, (P) 160; John Young, (P) 155; John P. Younger, (P) 169.

Missourians either Killed in Action (KIA) or Missing in Action (MIA), Regular Army, Korean War

Preston E. Acock : (Id) 55006225, (Svc) Army, (SvcCP) Regular, (Branch) Infantry, (Rank) Pfc, (Grade) E3, (Home) Lawrence County, Mo, (D) March 8, 1951

William R. Akers : (Id) 57502828, (Svc) Army, (SvcCP) Regular, (Branch) Infantry, (Rank) Pfc, (Grade) E3, (Home) Webster County, Mo, (D) April 25, 1951

Richard L. Allen : (Id) 57507293, (Svc) Army, (SvcCP) Regular, (Branch) Infantry, (Rank) Cpl, (Grade) E4, (Home) Wayne County, Mo, (D) February 4, 1951

Ellis L. Anderson : (Id) 17255277, (Svc) Army, (SvcCP) Regular, (Branch) Infantry, (Rank) Cpl, (Grade) E4, (Home) Cole County, Mo, (D) January 4, 1951

John E. Ashby : (Id) 37863491, (Svc) Army, (SvcCP) Regular, (Branch) Infantry, (Rank) Cpl, (Grade) E4, (Home) St Louis County, Mo, (D) April 20, 1951

Kellis B. Baker : (Id) 1339242, (Svc) Army, (SvcCP) Regular, (Branch) Infantry, (Rank) 2lt, (Grade) O1, (Home) Barry County, Mo, (D) June 13, 1951

Granvil L. Bennett : (Id) 17262813, (Svc) Army, (SvcCP) Regular, (Branch) Infantry, (Rank) Pfc, (Grade) E3, (Home) Harrison County, Mo, (D) April 6, 1951

Billy R. Bolin : (Id) 57511810, (Svc) Army, (SvcCP) Regular, (Branch) Artillery, (Rank) Pvt, (Grade) E2, (Home) Atchison County, Mo, (D) February 13, 1951

James H. Boughton : (Id) 57508960, (Svc) Army, (SvcCP) Regular, (Branch) Armor, (Rank) Pfc, (Grade) E3, (Home) Jefferson County, Mo, (D) February 14, 1951

Ernest J. Brendel : (Id) 37863246, (Svc) Army, (SvcCP) Regular, (Branch) Infantry, (Rank) Cpl, (Grade) E4, (Home) St Louis, Mo, (D) March 16, 1951

Kenneth L. Brown : (Id) 17248495, (Svc) Army, (SvcCP) Regular, (Branch) Infantry, (Rank) Cpl, (Grade) E4, (Home) Crawford County, Mo, (D) January 7, 1951

Edward J. Bruno : (Id) 17253136, (Svc) Army, (SvcCP) Regular, (Branch) Infantry, (Rank) Pfc, (Grade) E3, (Home) St Louis County, Mo, (D) April 13, 1951

Damon Burgess : (Id) 6986432, (Svc) Army, (SvcCP) Regular, (Branch) Infantry, (Rank) Sgt, (Grade) E5, (Home) Jackson County, Mo, (D) February 12, 1951

Snowden D. Burnett : (Id) 17163697, (Svc) Army, (SvcCP) Regular, (Branch) Infantry, (Rank) Sgt, (Grade) E5, (Home) Pulaski County, Mo, (D) May 18, 1951

Virgil E. Butler : (Id) 17224114, (Svc) Army, (SvcCP) Regular, (Branch) Infantry, (Rank) Sgt, (Grade) E5, (Home) Montgomery County, Mo, (D) May 19, 1951

John M. Cole, Jr. : (Id) 37649127, (Svc) Army, (SvcCP) Regular, (Branch) Infantry, (Rank) Sfc, (Grade) E7, (Home) St Francois County, Mo, (D) February 12, 1951

Lamonte B. Cook : (Id) 57502791, (Svc) Army, (SvcCP) Regular, (Branch) Medical Department, (Rank) Pfc, (Grade) E3, (Home) St Louis County, Mo, (D) February 3, 1951

Elmer E. Crawford : (Id) 57502842, (Svc) Army, (SvcCP) Regular, (Branch) Infantry, (Rank) Pfc, (Grade) E3, (Home) St Louis County, Mo, (D) May 26, 1951

Roy W. Crawford : (Id) 55007450, (Svc) Army, (SvcCP) Regular, (Branch) Infantry, (Rank) Cpl, (Grade) E4, (Home) Ozark County, Mo, (D) February 14, 1951

James R. Crider : (Id) 17263951, (Svc) Army, (SvcCP) Regular, (Branch) Infantry, (Rank) Pfc, (Grade) E3, (Home) Howell County, Mo, (D) March 7, 1951

Joseph W. Deller : (Id) 57502309, (Svc) Army, (SvcCP) Regular, (Branch) Infantry, (Rank) Pfc, (Grade) E3, (Home) St Louis County, Mo, (D) February 14, 1951

Johnnie R. Duck : (Id) 17262409, (Svc) Army, (SvcCP) Regular, (Branch) Infantry, (Rank) Pvt, (Grade) E2, (Home) Dunklin County, Mo, (D) January 7, 1951

Charles L. Eades : (Id) 17195461, (Svc) Army, (SvcCP) Regular, (Branch) Artillery, (Rank) Cpl, (Grade) E4, (Home) Stoddard County, Mo, (D) February 13, 1951

Floyd N. Faulconer : (Id) 19197417, (Svc) Army, (SvcCP) Regular, (Branch) Infantry, (Rank) Cpl, (Grade) E4, (Home) Johnson County, Mo, (D) February 14, 1951

Joe H. Fisher : (Id) 55006016, (Svc) Army, (SvcCP) Regular, (Branch) Infantry, (Rank) Pfc, (Grade) E3, (Home) New Madrid County, Mo, (D) February 14, 1951

John E. Fletcher : (Id) 17262873, (Svc) Army, (SvcCP) Regular, (Branch) Infantry, (Rank) Pfc, (Grade) E3, (Home) Buchanan County, Mo, (D) February 12, 1951

Justus P. Gallus : (Id) 55007503, (Svc) Army, (SvcCP) Regular, (Branch) Artillery, (Rank) Pfc, (Grade) E3, (Home) De Kalb County, Mo, (D) February 13, 1951

Ivan W. Groom : (Id) 57507207, (Svc) Army, (SvcCP) Regular,

(Branch) Infantry, (Rank) Pfc, (Grade) E3, (Home) Gentry County, Mo, (D) November 28, 1950

Ralph E. Hawkins : (Id) 55007416, (Svc) Army, (SvcCP) Regular, (Branch) Infantry, (Rank) Pfc, (Grade) E3, (Home) Henry County, Mo, (D) January 7, 1951

Cerl V. Head : (Id) 55007423, (Svc) Army, (SvcCP) Regular, (Branch) Infantry, (Rank) Pfc, (Grade) E3, (Home) Camden County, Mo, (D) April 18, 1951

James R. Hedgcoth : (Id) 17253036, (Svc) Army, (SvcCP) Regular, (Branch) Infantry, (Rank) Pfc, (Grade) E3, (Home) Iron County, Mo, (D) February 10, 1951

Elmer E. Holcomb : (Id) 37051547, (Svc) Army, (SvcCP) Regular, (Branch) Infantry, (Rank) Sfc, (Grade) E7, (Home) Shelby County, Mo, (D) May 18, 1951

George S. Kellett : (Id) 37624335, (Svc) Army, (SvcCP) Regular, (Branch) Infantry, (Rank) Pfc, (Grade) E3, (Home) Taney County, Mo, (D) February 12, 1951

Charles W. Kellison : (Id) 16234515, (Svc) Army, (SvcCP) Regular, (Branch) Infantry, (Rank) Sgt, (Grade) E5, (Home) St Louis County, Mo, (D) July 27, 1951

John W. Kimberlin : (Id) 37765050, (Svc) Army, (SvcCP) Regular, (Branch) Infantry, (Rank) Pfc, (Grade) E3, (Home) Jasper County, Mo, (D) February 4, 1951

Oliver B. Kupferle : (Id) 57502655, (Svc) Army, (SvcCP) Regular, (Branch) Infantry, (Rank) Pfc, (Grade) E3, (Home) St Louis, Mo, (D) February 22, 1951

James N. Larkin : (Id) 37057894, (Svc) Army, (SvcCP) Regular, (Branch) Infantry, (Rank) Pfc, (Grade) E3, (Home) St Louis County, Mo, (D) February 12, 1951

Donald E. Laughlin : (Id) 55007533, (Svc) Army, (SvcCP) Regular, (Branch) Infantry, (Rank) Pfc, (Grade) E3, (Home) Nodaway County, Mo, (D) June 16, 1951

Melvin G. Matlock : (Id) 57507078, (Svc) Army, (SvcCP) Regular, (Branch) Infantry, (Rank) Pvt, (Grade) E2, (Home) Howell County, Mo, (D) February 13, 1951

Gaylon L. Mc Claine : (Id) 17256834, (Svc) Army, (SvcCP) Regular, (Branch) Infantry, (Rank) Pfc, (Grade) E3, (Home) Scott County, Mo, (D) January 30, 1951

James W. Mc Connell : (Id) 37731999, (Svc) Army, (SvcCP) Regular, (Branch) Infantry, (Rank) Pfc, (Grade) E3, (Home) Chariton County, Mo, (D) August 27, 1951

Fred G. Mc Cormick : (Id) 17255095, (Svc) Army, (SvcCP) Regular,

(Branch) Infantry, (Rank) Pfc, (Grade) E3, (Home) Randolph County, Mo, (D) February 22, 1951

Harold J. Miller : (Id) 37402486, (Svc) Army, (SvcCP) Regular, (Branch) Infantry, (Rank) Pfc, (Grade) E3, (Home) St Louis, Mo, (D) February 12, 1951

Edward J. Nagel : (Id) 36477624, (Svc) Army, (SvcCP) Regular, (Branch) Infantry, (Rank) Cpl, (Grade) E4, (Home) St Louis, Mo, (D) June 6, 1951

Arnold E. Niewald : (Id) 37862959, (Svc) Army, (SvcCP) Regular, (Branch) Infantry, (Rank) Pfc, (Grade) E3, (Home) Osage County, Mo, (D) January 30, 1951

Mike R. Novak : (Id) 17253750, (Svc) Army, (SvcCP) Regular, (Branch) Infantry, (Rank) Pfc, (Grade) E3, (Home) St Louis, Mo, (D) February 12, 1951

John W. Parkey : (Id) 37180814, (Svc) Army, (SvcCP) Regular, (Branch) Artillery, (Rank) Sgt, (Grade) E5, (Home) Montgomery County, Mo, (D) February 13, 1951

Oliver E. Payne : (Id) 37050647, (Svc) Army, (SvcCP) Regular, (Branch) Infantry, (Rank) Sgt, (Grade) E5, (Home) Franklin County, Mo, (D) February 12, 1951

Arthur J. Perez : (Id) 57509036, (Svc) Army, (SvcCP) Regular, (Branch) Infantry, (Rank) Pfc, (Grade) E3, (Home) St Louis, Mo, (D) March 8, 1951

Donald R. Ross : (Id) 57507210, (Svc) Army, (SvcCP) Regular, (Branch) Infantry, (Rank) Pfc, (Grade) E3, (Home) Harrison County, Mo, (D) February 12, 1951

Walter A. Ross, Jr. : (Id) 37517485, (Svc) Army, (SvcCP) Regular, (Branch) Infantry, (Rank) Sgt, (Grade) E5, (Home) St Louis, Mo, (D) February 14, 1951

Richard A. Saunders : (Id) 55006372, (Svc) Army, (SvcCP) Regular, (Branch) Infantry, (Rank) Pfc, (Grade) E3, (Home) De Kalb County, Mo, (D) January 14, 1951

Lowell D. Scofield : (Id) 17251858, (Svc) Army, (SvcCP) Regular, (Branch) Infantry, (Rank) Pfc, (Grade) E3, (Home) Buchanan County, Mo, (D) May 18, 1951

Lowell D. Shipman : (Id) 57507109, (Svc) Army, (SvcCP) Regular, (Branch) Infantry, (Rank) Pfc, (Grade) E3, (Home) Stone County, Mo, (D) February 12, 1951

Homer H. Shultz : (Id) 17195652, (Svc) Army, (SvcCP) Regular, (Branch) Infantry, (Rank) Pfc, (Grade) E3, (Home) Pulaski County, Mo, (D) February 13, 1951

Hugh N. Sommer, Jr.: (Id) 16234052, (Svc) Army, (SvcCP) Regular,

(Branch) Infantry, (Rank) Pvt, (Grade) E2, (Home) St Louis, Mo, (D) April 22, 1951

Jack N. Stafford : (Id) 17188212, (Svc) Army, (SvcCP) Regular, (Branch) Armor, (Rank) Cpl, (Grade) E4, (Home) Cass County, Mo, (D) October 14, 1951

Gaylord W. Stark : (Id) 37756217, (Svc) Army, (SvcCP) Regular, (Branch) Infantry, (Rank) Sfc, (Grade) E7, (Home) Christian County, Mo, (D) March 19, 1951

James A. Stevens : (Id) 57507113, (Svc) Army, (SvcCP) Regular, (Branch) Infantry, (Rank) Pfc, (Grade) E3, (Home) Laclede County, Mo, (D) February 12, 1951

Henry R. Stutte : (Id) 37396061, (Svc) Army, (SvcCP) Regular, (Branch) Infantry, (Rank) Sfc, (Grade) E7, (Home) Franklin County, Mo, (D) August 10, 1951

Chester E. Tharp : (Id) 57507313, (Svc) Army, (SvcCP) Regular, (Branch) Infantry, (Rank) Pfc, (Grade) E3, (Home) Madison County, Mo, (D) February 12, 1951

Donald M. Thornton : (Id) 17187911, (Svc) Army, (SvcCP) Regular, (Branch) Infantry, (Rank) Pfc, (Grade) E3, (Home) St Francois County, Mo, (D) January 29, 1951

Billy F. Wadkins : (Id) 17281121, (Svc) Army, (SvcCP) Regular, (Branch) Armor, (Rank) Pfc, (Grade) E3, (Home) Greene County, Mo, (D) June 18, 1951

Ralph B. Webb : (Id) 17262264, (Svc) Army, (SvcCP) Regular, (Branch) Infantry, (Rank) Cpl, (Grade) E4, (Home) Butler County, Mo, (D) July 26, 1951

Winston G. Wilson : (Id) 53011041, (Svc) Army, (SvcCP) Regular, (Branch) Infantry, (Rank) Pfc, (Grade) E3, (Home) Pemiscot County, Mo, (D) December 15, 1950

Don Wolfe: (Id) 57502795, (Svc) Army, (SvcCP) Regular, (Branch) Infantry, (Rank) Cpl, (Grade) E4, (Home) St Louis County, Mo, (D) February 15, 1951

Everett J. Woody : (Id) 37753849, (Svc) Army, (SvcCP) Regular, (Branch) Infantry, (Rank) Sgt, (Grade) E5, (Home) Vernon County, Mo, (D) January 30, 1951

Edward C. Wright : (Id) 37515143, (Svc) Army, (SvcCP) Regular, (Branch) Infantry, (Rank) Cpl, (Grade) E4, (Home) Linn County, Mo, (D) February 12, 1951

Missourians either Killed in Action (KIA) or Missing in Action (MIA), Korena War, Army National Guard.

William R. Adams : (Id) 2262254 , (Svc) Army , (SvcCP) National

Guard, (Branch) Artillery, (Rank) 1lt, (Grade) O2, (Home) St Charles County, Mo, (D) November 30, 1950

Frank V. Aston : (Id) 1926738, (Svc) Army, (SvcCP) National Guard, (Branch) Infantry, (Rank) 2lt, (Grade) O1, (Home) Laclede County, Mo, (D) July 24, 1953

Thomas J. Barnes : (Id) 1882511, (Svc) Army, (SvcCP) National Guard, (Branch) Infantry, (Rank) 1lt, (Grade) O2, (Home) Gasconade County, Mo, (D) July 9, 1953

Jerry Barry : (Id) 2208471, (Svc) Army, (SvcCP) National Guard, (Branch) Infantry, (Rank) 2lt, (Grade) O1, (Home) St Louis, Mo, (D) July 12, 1950

Herbert L. Bowman : (Id) 1338435, (Svc) Army, (SvcCP) National Guard, (Branch) Infantry, (Rank) 1lt, (Grade) O2, (Home) Newton County, Mo, (D) November 6, 1950

Lawrence Brunnert : (Id) 964037, (Svc) Army, (SvcCP) National Guard, (Branch) Chaplain's Corps, (Rank) Cpt, (Grade) O3, (Home) St Louis, Mo, (D) December 2, 1950

John O.Crockett : (Id) 2262332, (Svc) Army, (SvcCP) National Guard, (Branch) Infantry, (Rank) 2lt, (Grade) O1, (Home) Buchanan County, Mo, (D) November 28, 1950

Onley T. Davis, Jr. : (Id) 1018995, (Svc) Army, (SvcCP) National Guard, (Branch) Armor, (Rank) 1lt, (Grade) O2, (Home) Randolph County, Mo, (D) November 3, 1950

Thomas E. Dowling : (Id) 2006338, (Svc) Army, (SvcCP) National Guard, (Branch) Infantry, (Rank) Cpt, (Grade) O3, (Home) St Louis, Mo, (D) May 29, 1951

Sherman L. Elwood : (Id) 1315469, (Svc) Army, (SvcCP) National Guard, (Branch) Infantry, (Rank) 1lt, (Grade) O2, (Home) Greene County, Mo, (D) February 12, 1951

Jack C. Gainer : (Id) 2021177, (Svc) Army, (SvcCP) National Guard, (Branch) Infantry, (Rank) 2lt, (Grade) O1, (Home) Moniteau County, Mo, (D) June 6, 1951

Charles L. Gill : (Id) 1913317, (Svc) Army, (SvcCP) National Guard, (Branch) Armor, (Rank) 1lt, (Grade) O2, (Home) Jackson County, Mo, (D) November 2, 1950

Van L. Halferty : (Id) 955252, (Svc) Army, (SvcCP) National Guard, (Branch) Artillery, (Rank) 2lt, (Grade) O1, (Home) Butler County, Mo, (D) September 1, 1950

Alonzo R. Hammock : (Id) 1996714, (Svc) Army, (SvcCP) National Guard, (Branch) Infantry, (Rank) 1lt, (Grade) O2, (Home) St Louis, Mo, (D) February 12, 1951

Douglas D. Harrell : (Id) 979840, (Svc) Army, (SvcCP) National Guard, (Branch) Infantry, (Rank) 1lt, (Grade) O2, (Home) Greene

County, Mo, (D) July 30, 1950

John F. Herdlick : (Id) 947455, (Svc) Army, (SvcCP) National Guard, (Branch) Infantry, (Rank) 1lt, (Grade) O2, (Home) St Louis County, Mo, (D) September 5, 1950

John H. Higgins : (Id) 1048407, (Svc) Army, (SvcCP) National Guard, (Branch) Artillery, (Rank) 1lt, (Grade) O2, (Home) Barry County, Mo, (D) August 31, 1950

Carter Hilgard : (Id) 1325007, (Svc) Army, (SvcCP) National Guard, (Branch) Infantry, (Rank) Cpt, (Grade) O3, (Home) St Louis County, Mo, (D) August 26, 1950

Homer F. Lindsay : (Id) 1173353, (Svc) Army, (SvcCP) National Guard, (Branch) Artillery, (Rank) Cpt, (Grade) O3, (Home) Jackson County, Mo, (D) February 13, 1951

Charles R. Long : (Id) 37504082, (Svc) Army, (SvcCP) National Guard, (Branch) Infantry, (Rank) Sgt, (Grade) E5, (Home) Jackson County, Mo, (D) February 12, 1951

Lawrence E. Loos : (Id) 421727, (Svc) Army, (SvcCP) National Guard, (Branch) Artillery, (Rank) Maj, (Grade) O4, (Home) Nodaway County, Mo, (D) February 19, 1952

Charles McDougal : (Id) 1685564, (Svc) Army, (SvcCP) National Guard, (Branch) Artillery, (Rank) 1lt, (Grade) O2, (Home) Lafayette County, Mo, (D) February 13, 1951

Jack M. McKinney : (Id) 2208414, (Svc) Army, (SvcCP) National Guard, (Branch) Infantry, (Rank) 2lt, (Grade) O1, (Home) Jasper County, Mo, (D) July 20, 1950

George A. Mc Nerney : (Id) 1861677, (Svc) Army, (SvcCP) National Guard, (Branch) Infantry, (Rank) 2lt, (Grade) O1, (Home) Jasper County, Mo, (D) June 16, 1952

Henry M. Moore : (Id) 1180627, (Svc) Army, (SvcCP) National Guard, (Branch) Infantry, (Rank) 1lt, (Grade) O2, (Home) St Louis, Mo, (D) December 1, 1950

Lawrence D. Moss : (Id) 2262677, (Svc) Army, (SvcCP) National Guard, (Branch) Artillery, (Rank) 1lt, (Grade) O2, (Home) Jasper County, Mo, (D) February 9, 1951

Wayne A. Murphy : (Id) 2028399, (Svc) Army, (SvcCP) National Guard, (Branch) Infantry, (Rank) 2lt, (Grade) O1, (Home) Jackson County, Mo, (D) June 22, 1952

Paul A. M. Oechsle : (Id) 2208462, (Svc) Army, (SvcCP) National Guard, (Branch) Infantry, (Rank) 2lt, (Grade) O1, (Home) Cole County, Mo, (D) July 28, 1950

Owen R. Oneill : (Id) 1297934, (Svc) Army, (SvcCP) National Guard, (Branch) Infantry, (Rank) Cpt, (Grade) O3, (Home) Lawrence County, Mo, (D) November 30, 1950

Herman W. Roesch : (Id) 296437, (Svc) Army, (SvcCP) National Guard, (Branch) Infantry, (Rank) Cpt, (Grade) O3, (Home) St Louis, Mo, (D) October 31, 1950

Robert J. Sebacher : (Id) 2208446, (Svc) Army, (SvcCP) National Guard, (Branch) Infantry, (Rank) 1lt, (Grade) O2, (Home) St Charles County, Mo, (D) September 5, 1950

Raymond Smallwood : (Id) 2209587, (Svc) Army, (SvcCP) National Guard, (Branch) Artillery, (Rank) 1lt, (Grade) O2, (Home) Gasconade County, Mo, (D) August 26, 1952

John B. Stanton : (Id) 2017774, (Svc) Army, (SvcCP) National Guard, (Branch) Infantry, (Rank) 1lt, (Grade) O2, (Home) Greene County, Mo, (D) October 16, 1950

Carl S. Wright : (Id) 1340843, (Svc) Army, (SvcCP) National Guard, (Branch) Infantry, (Rank) 1lt, (Grade) O2, (Home) Boone County, Mo, (D) October 1, 1951

Morgan County, Missouri, Miscellaneous Birth and Death Records

Melville Adkins: (B) 6 Feb 1899, (D) Sep. 1973, (RES) Gravois Mills.
Bernie Akin: (B) 21 Dec 1899, (D) Oct 1979, (RES) Versailles.
Ella Allen: (B) 8 Sep 1898, (D) 19-Sep 1990, (RES) Stover.
Robert Armstrong: (B) 21 Jul 1898, (D) Aug 1982, (RES) Gravois Mills.
James Aulgar: (B) 5 Jun 1898, (D) Nov 1985, (RES) Stover.
Bertha Aldrich: (B) 8 Mar 1899, (D) Jan 1975, (RES) Syracuse.
John Anderson: (B) 14 Jan 1899, (D) Nov 1977, (RES) Syracuse.
Floyd Applebury: (B) 20 May 1899, (D) 19 Jan 1996, (RES) Versailles.
Frank Badger: (B) 14 Nov 1899, (D) Oct 1984 , (RES) Versailles.
Lucille Baylard: (B) 27 Aug 1899, (D) 23 Jul 1994, (RES) Gravois Mills.
Henry Boatcher: (B) 13 Jul 1899, (D) 27 Apr 1989, (RES) Stover,
Neva Boyer: (B) 3 Oct 1899, (RES) Gravois Mills.
Ophelia Bowers: (B) 6 Mar 1874, (D) Mar 1970, (RES) Stover.
George Berkstresser: (B) 27 Jul 1875, (D) Jun 1973, (RES) Versailles.
Alfred Cox: (B) 15 May 1874, (D) Dec 1968, (RES) Versailles.
Luther Campbell: (B) 23 Dec 1899, (RES) Versailles.
David Carter: (B) 21 Jan 1899, (RES) Versailles.
Lydia Carver: (B) 31 Jan 1899, (RES)Florence,
Louis Case: (B) 4 Jun 1899, (D) 7 Dec 1992.
My Conley: (B) 19 Feb 1899, (D) 22 Oct 1992 , (RES) Gravois Mills.
Hazel Cook: (B) 31 Aug 1899, (RES) Gravois Mills.
Charley Cooper: (B) 5 May 1899
Catherine Corder: (B) 6 Jan 1899, (RES) Versailles.
Goldie Crum: (B) 18 Feb 1899, (D) Apr 1987, (RES) Versailles.

Samuel Cummins: (B) 7 May 1899, (D) Feb 1981 , (RES) Gravois Mills.
Claude Decker: (B) 2 Apr 1899, (D) Oct 1974, (RES) Versailles.
Robert Forster: (B) 2 Aug 1899, (D) Jun 1978, (RES) Versailles.
Eunice Goff: 14 Jan 1899, (D) Jan 1982, (RES) Florence.
Fannie Gunn: (B) 17 Apr 1899, (D) Oct 1971, (RES) Versailles.
David Hancock: (B) 24 Aug 1899, (RES) Versailles.
Georgiaann Hansen: (B) 10 Dec 1899, (RES) Versailles.
Clyde Hayes: (B) 16 Feb 1899, (D) Nov 1977, (RES) Versailles.
Dixie Hees: (B) 13 Aug 1899, (RES) Versailles.
Cecil Herring: (B) 30 Nov 1899, (D) Jul 1965, (RES) Stover.
Harry Hibdon: (B) 29 Dec 1899, (D) Jan 1977, (RES) Stover.
Joe Hilderbrand: (B) 10 Oct 1899, (D) Oct 1976, (RES) Versailles.
Margaret Hines: (B) 11 Jul 1899, (D) 18 Jul 1989, (RES) Versailles.
Edith Holloway: (B) 22 Jul 1899, (D) May 1979, (RES) Syracuse.
Charles Hutchison: (B) 16 Aug 1899, (RES) Versailles.
Blanche Jones: (B) 13 Sep 1899.
Herbert Jones: (B) 24 Oct 1899, (D) Oct 1976 , (RES) Versailles.
August Kipp: (B) 21 Aug 1874, (D) Feb 1967, (RES) Stover.
Andrew Keith: (B)6 Jun 1899, (D) Feb 1983, (RES) Stover.
Myron Mccollister: (B) 24 Sep 1874,(RES) Versailles.
Nola Kelly: (B)1 Aug 1899, (D) Dec 1992 , (RES) Versailles.
James Kelso: (B) 21 Jul 1899, (D) Dec 1977, (RES) Gravois Mills.
Bessie Kent: (B) 9 Mar 1899, (D) Oct 1982, (RES) Versailles.
Minerva Klein: (B) 10 Jun 1899, (D) Feb 198265354 , (RES) Syracuse.
Peter Koetting: (B) 20 Feb 1899, (D) Dec 1979 , (RES) Versailles.
Minnie Kraxberger: (B) 9 Aug 1899, (D) Oct 1980, (RES) Stover.
Alexander Lambie: (B) 4 Sep 1899, (D) 7 Mar 1989, (RES) Gravois Mills.
Caroline Laughead: (B) 25 Jan 1899, (D) 27 Apr 1990, (RES) Versailles.
Marie Lee: (B) 7 Aug 1899, (D) Jul 1972, (RES) Gravois Mills.
Arthur Leigh: (B) 24 Dec 1899, (D) Mar 1971, (RES) Versailles.
Rose Leonard: (B) 16 Jan 1899, (D) Mar 1976, (RES) Gravois Mills.
Mildred Lyle: (B) 1 Mar 1899, (D) Oct 1980, (RES) Versailles.
Clara May: (B) 19 Jul 1899, (D) 25 Aug 1988, (RES) Versailles.
Moss McDonald: (B) 20 Jan 1899, (D) 15 Jul 1992, (RES) Versailles.
Orlyn Merriott: (B) 10 Jan 1899, (RES) Stover.
Rhoda Metcalf: (B) 8 Jan 1899, (D) Mar 1985, (RES) Gravois Mills.
Robert Miller: (B) 31 Aug 1899, (RES) Gravois Mills.
Mary Mitchell: (B) 8 Feb 1899, (RES) Gravois Mills.
Alice Moore: (B) 23 May 1899, (RES) Versailles.
Newton Neal: (B) 22 Jan 1875, (D) Nov 1969, (RES) Syracuse.

Joe Naylor: (B) 16 Mar 1899, (RES) Versailles.
John Needham: (B) 13 Mar 1899, (RES) Gravois Mills.
Nettie Nolting: (B) 20 Apr 1899, (RES) Versailles.
Doris Pegg: (B) 10 Feb 1899, (D) 22 Dec 1988, (RES) Gravois Mills.
Flossie Phillips: (B) 29 Sep 1899, (D) Nov 1983, (RES) Versailles.
Ida Phipps: (B) 18 Feb 1899, (D) 22 Feb 1989, (RES) Stover.
Ella Rasa: (B) 15 Nov 1899, (D) Nov 1986 (RES) Stover.
Jno Ray: (B) 31 Oct 1899, (D) Sep 1968, (RES) Gravois Mills.
Clarence Schroder: (B) 6 Jun 1899, (RES) Stover.
Adalinde Schroeder: (B) 14 Apr 1899, (RES) Stover.
Edward Schuler: (B) 18 Jun 1899, (RES) Versailles.
Erna Schupp: (B) 21 Nov 1899, (D) Jun 1987, (RES) Stover.
Thomas Shepp: (B) 8 Jan 1899, (D) Dec 1986, (RES) Versailles.
Rex Shineman: (B) 16 Mar 1899, (D) Dec 1984, (RES) Versailles.
W. Silvey: (B) 9 Mar 1899, (RES) Versailles.
Oscar Smith: (B) 22 Sep 1899, (D) May 1985, (RES) Stover.
Edna Snelling: (B) 9 Jan 1899, (D) 10 Jul 1995, (RES) Stover.
Minnie Speaker: (B) 22 May 1899, (D) Nov 1976, (RES) Florence.
H. Thoss: (B) 15 Sep 1899, (D) Sep 1969, (RES) Versailles.
Richard Topper: (B) 19 Oct 1899, (D) Nov 1966, (RES)Versailles.
Alta Urmiller: (B) 29 Apr 1899, (D) 28 Dec 1996, (RES) Gravois Mills.
William Via: (B) 8 Jan 1899, (D) May 1979, (RES) Gravois Mills.
Vasco Waisner: (B) 29 Oct 1899, (D) 24 May 1988, (RES) Versailles.
Marie Walther: (B) 19 Feb 1899, (D) 6 Jul 19946, (RES) Stover.
Carrie Wasson: (B) 20 Jan 1899, (D) Feb 1967, (RES)Versailles.
Lawrence Webb: (B) 20 Nov 1899, (RES) Versailles.
Paul Webb: (B) 17 Aug 1899, (D) Apr 1979, (RES) Gravois Mills.
Cora Weis: (B) 3 Jul 1899, (D) Dec 1983, (RES) Gravois Mills.
Lillie Wittrock: (B) 31 Dec 1899, (RES) Stover.
Mary Zumwalt: (B) 6 Nov 1899, (RES) Versailles.

Carter County, Missouri, Marriage Book A, 1881-1890
Alexander Piles and Seriena Carr, of Reynolds Co., (MD) 4 Jul 1881
Conroe Tyner and Mollie Benton, (MD) 14 Jul 1881
Benjamin P. Darr and Miss Lizzie D. Short, (MD) 21 Aug 1881
William H. Hall and Annie Jane Denning, (MD) 21 Aug 1881
O. H. Day and Miss Cordelia Condray, (MD) 28 Aug 1881
John Wesley Ednigton and Rowda Jane Roark, (MD) 28 Aug 1881
E. C. Benton and Martha Matilda Carpenter, (MD) 16 Oct 1881
W. E. Jordan and Miss Nannie Powell, (MD) 3 Nov 1881
Joseph W. Biffle and Narcissie Oliver, (MD) 10 Nov 1881
Lorenzo C. Click and Ellen Trainar, (MD) 20 Oct 1881

Richard Johnson and Miss Mattie Stewart, (MD) 20 Oct 1881
Milton H. Smith and Miss Annette Carlin, (MD) 16 Nov 1881
A. Wayne Swish and Nannie Sweazea, (MD) 18 Dec 1881
Benjamin C. Windes and Nancy E. Payton, (MD) 8 Jan 1882
A. K. Oliver and Mrs. Margaret Turley, (MD) 29 Jan 1882
Elva G. Turley and Martha J. Payton, (MD) 23 Feb 1882
Joseph Carpenter and Mrs. F. C. Stephens, (MD) 16 Feb 1882
William A. Provance and Charlottie E. Green, (MD) 9 Apr 1882
R. J. Green and Martha Ann V. Brame, (MD) 21 May 1882
George W. Jones and Carolin Dawson, (MD) 3 Jun 1882
Wilson Snider and Maleeta Snider, (MD) 2 Jul 1882
John H. Rector and Mary H. Sartin, (MD) 6 Jul 1882
William A. Bowman and Manda Bridges, (MD) 23 Jul 1882
W. S. Warren and Nancy M. Sw, of ford, (MD) 2 Jul 1882
Isaac N. Butler and Lucinda Toliver, (MD) 20 Jul 1882
William N. Gourley and Malinda C. Richmond, (MD) 16 Jul 1882
William H. Yates and Lucinda Wray, (MD) 24 Aug 1882
Daniel Hughes, of Texas Co., Mo and Lucinda Harris, (MD) 22 Sep 1882
James H. Piles and Lizzie Porter, (MD) 10 Sep 1882
John Carnahan and Emily Smith, (MD) 22 Oct 1882
Samuel Hewit and Malinda Boyer, (MD) 22 Oct 1882
George W. Johnston and Sarida Terry, (MD) 21 Jan 1883
Richard A. Jones and Sina Reed, (MD) 24 Jan 1883
James W. Ballard and Mary Waller, (MD) 4 Feb 1883
Morgan D. Odell and Mary Cate, (MD) 8 Feb 1883
John C. Miller and Susan Parkey, of Wayne Co., (MD) 14 Jan 1883
G. W. Williams and Mrs. Mary Baker, (MD) 8 Mar 1883
Samuel Odell and Sarah Woodward, (MD) 15 Mar 1883
Henry Ballard and C. A. Green, (MD) 1 Apr 1883
George C. Hollis and Emily A. Jones, (MD) 15 Apr 1883
Dach Decker, of Wayne Co., Mo and Susan Rainwater, (MD) 20 May 1883
A. E. Arnold and Lucinda A. Kissinger, (MD) 6 Jun 1883
A. M. Depriest and Martha Windes, (MD) 17 Jun 1883
Millard Fillmore Yates and Martha Jane Yates, (MD) 10 Jul 1883
Thomas Burnham and Martha Ferguson, (MD) 11 July 1883
Aaron Kelley, of Neosho Co., Kansas and Mary Bales, (MD) 2 Aug 1883
James Gardner and Julia Hawkins, (MD) 12 Aug 1883
Marion Decker and Rachel A. Porter, of Ripley Co., Mo, (MD) 26 Aug 1883
Price Hewitt and Rosa Slusher, of Wayne Co., (MD) 16 Aug 1883

James Longbottom and Mary E. Harder, (MD) 22 Aug 1883
W. P. Brinkley, of Reynolds Co., and Jemima Walker, (MD) 31 Aug 1883
William Prichet and Sarah Galbraith, (MD) 2 Sep 1883
William Rongey and Melisa Kinnard, (MD) 6 Sep 1883
William Boyer and Peliza H. Farrar, (MD) 17 Sep 1883
James Holland and Harriet Sigg, (MD) 19 Sep 1883
S. C. Williams and Mary Leach, (MD) 20 Sep 1883, both of Reynolds Co., Mo.
Daniel A. Cowen and Viola Bales, (MD) 30 Sep 1883
Thomas Galbraith and Mary B. Franklin, (MD) 30 Sep 1883
James A. Hopper, of Ripley Co., and Mary J. McDowell, (MD) 11 Oct 1883
James L. A. Kinnard and Amy S. Vermillion, (MD) 17 Nov 1883
Caleb W. Gibbs, of Wayne Co., and Ada S. Buris, (MD) 9 Dec 1883
B. H. Parrott, of Oregon Co., and Sukie Snider, (MD) 23 Dec 1883
George W. Rodgers and Ulicie S. Brame, (MD) 12 Jan 1884
John P. Sigg and Evie Taylor, (MD) 17 Jan 1884
Thomas J. Brame and Lydia Ann Hill, (MD) 27 Jan 1884
Marion Vermillion and Octavia Massie, (MD) 1 Feb 1884
John C. Vermillion and Mary J. Clark, (MD) 4 Feb 1884
J. N. Clark, of Shannon Co., and Laura A. Crandell, (MD) 14 Feb 1884
Jacob Grassum and Margaret Carter, (MD) 22 Feb 1884
James P. Brown and Helen Baker, (MD) 21 Feb 1884
J. R. Carnahan and Missouri J. Short, (MD) 27 Apr 1884
Joseph O'Dell and Alice V. Carpenter, (MD) 8 May 1884
H. H. Haggard and Elvina Harbison, (MD) 18 May 1884
Albert S. Brooks and Emeline Hooper, (MD) 28 May 1884
H. G. Moore and M. G. Lee, (MD) 31 May 1884
Jerome J. Kintz and Mary A. Hill, (MD) 4 Jun 1884
Wesley Kinnard and Belle Rongey, (MD) 8 Jun 1884
John Gillett and Caroline Long, (MD) 21 Jun 1884
Martin Mabery and Nancy E. House, (MD) 22 June 1884
Russell Hewett and Flora Price, (MD) 29 June 1884
James B. Ritter and Katie Harper, (MD) 30 June 1884
James Lewis Brantley and Mary E. Herrin, (MD) 7 aug 1884
Joseph Turley and Loza Jones, (MD) 10 Aug 1884
William P. Thomason, of Shannon Co., and Margaret E. Massie, (MD) 17 Aug 1884
J. H. Grandstaff and Eliza Ellen Norris, (MD) 31 Aug 1884
A. K. Oliver and Perlina E. Windes, (MD) 11 Sep 1884

Anderson Kinnard and Annie D. Massie, (MD) 22 Sep 1884
William G. Turley and Mary R. Payton, (MD) 12 Oct 1884
James M. Mills, of Oregon Co., and Elizabeth Stevenson, (MD) 16 Oct 1884
Joseph F. Sitherland, of Oregon Co., and Hannah A. Jones, (MD) 30 Nov 1884
Harman A. Dildine and Margaret Tinsley, (MD) 27 Nov 1884
Johen E. Jackson and Tennessee Sanders, (MD) 21 Dec 1884
Robert M. Bowman and Susan E. Cole, (MD) 2 Jan 1885
George Sheets, of Reynolds Co., and Ida Bales, (MD) 4 Jan 1885
Millard F. Green and Mary Ann Green, (MD) 8 Jan 1885
John Jonas, of Butler Co., and Nancy E. Hope, (MD) 11 Jan 1885
W. P. Smith, of Wayne Co., and Cynthia Ann Easton, (MD) 15 Feb 1885
Thomas Chilton and Jane Baker, (MD) 21 Mar 1885
Thornton H. Lacy and Manerva J. Mabery, (MD) 3 Mar 1885
Frank Bucey and Mary Jane House, (MD) 19 Mar 1885
J. B. Cargile and Ellen England, (MD) 26 Apr 1885
William N. Sartin and Mary E. Maber, (MD) 24 May 1885
Vincent Rainwaters and Lucinda Walker, (MD) 14 Jun 1885
Newton G. Henson and Mary Ellen Eggars, (MD) 21 Jun 1885
E. Maynard and Linessa Roggers, (MD) 11 Aug 1885
John J. Chilton and Christine Smith, (MD) 3 Sep 1885
Thomas Bowman and Eliza Caroline Williams, (MD) 20 Sep 1885
Cleveland Hawkins and Catherine McGraw, of Reynolds Co., (MD) 27 Sep 1885
William H. Friday and Mary E. Sweazea, (MD) 4 Oct 1885
James M. Brawley, of Oregon Co., and Margaret L. Snider, (MD) 6 Dec 1885
William S. Pickens and Pelona Jane Stratton, (MD) 12 Dec 1885
William A. Hurst and Julia E. McSpadden, (MD) 13 Dec 1885
M. J. Markham, of Wayne Co., and Lizzie E. White, (MD) 24 Dec 1885
John Jordon and Ednas S. Powell, (MD) 27 Dec 1885, both of Reynolds Co., Mo
James C. Pritchet and Nancy Jane Lambert, (MD) 1 Jan 1886
William O. Snider and Melissa Ann Legg, (MD) 3 Jan 1886
G. D. Rector, of Shannon and Cansada Wheeler, (MD) 16 Jan 1886
Francis M. Dildine and Rosella Scott, (MD) 3 Mar 1886
W. J. Markham, of Wayne Co., and Nancy E. Scott, (MD) 3 Mar 1886
John W. Thomas and Sarah E. Massie, (MD) 14 March 1886
Richard Turley and Evy Angle, (MD) 7 Mar 1886

James M. Co., peland and Linah Ellington, (MD) 11 Mar 1886, both of Reynolds Co., Mo

James Daniel and Hildergon Rodgers, (MD) 11 Apr 1886

James Dinwiddie and Margaret House, (MD) 16 May 1886

Sterling P. Rector, of Shannon Co., and Mary E. Lamert, (MD) 30 May 1886

Job Skiles, of Reynolds Co., and Kansas Ann Hanger, (MD) 15 Jul 1886

Jeff D. Hanger and Parthena Campbell, (MD) 26 Aug 1886, both of Reynolds Co., Mo

John B. Pratt and Nancy Jane Hicks, (MD) 2 Sep 1886, both of Reynolds Co., Mo

Charles O. Richardson and Lena M. Smoot, of Ripley Co., (MD) 14 Sep 1886

James N. Leach and Josie B. Freeman, (MD) 3 Oct 1886

Lee Marion Bowman, of Butler Co., and Sarah Margaret Cole, (MD) 14 Oct 1886

R. M. Province and Susie Jane Walker, (MD) 31 Oct 1886

James M. Vermillion and Catherine Lambert, (MD) 1 Nov 1886

John Lester, of Wayne Co., and Louisa E. Boyer, (MD) 14 Nov 1886

William Kinnard and Texas Neel, (MD) 21 Nov 1886

William J. Cowen and Mary E. Crandell, (MD) 25 Dec 1886

John L. Wood and Mary J. Pall, (MD) 23 Jan 1887

Geroge S. Buchanan and Annie E. Sheets, (MD) 20 Jan 1887

Marmaduke Mabery and Josephine Chitwood, of Shannon Co., (MD) 27 Feb 1887

William R. Low and Sarah Anderson, (MD) 20 Mar 1887

Cicero Johnston and Mary A. O'Dell, (MD) 19 May 1887

John F. M. Johnston, of Reynolds Co., and Sarah Porter, (MD) 15 May 1887

Frank J. Jenkins and Theodocia Swafford, (MD) 29 May 1887

John C. Brown and Sarah E. Pool, (MD) 22 Jun 1887

John F. Jones, of Wayne Co., and Martha A. E. Little, (MD) 26 Jun 1887

Lee W. Cotton and Sallie Haskins, (MD) 30 Jun 1887

Caronel W. Neel and Margaret Snider, (MD) 10 Jul 1887

Eli E. Grahma, of Wayne Co., and Elizabeth Carter, of Reynolds Co., Mo, (MD) 22 Jul 1887

George S. Maynard and Paralee Huitt, (MD) 25 Jul 1887, both of Reynolds Co., Mo

Charles W. Clark and Lee Burris, (MD) 24 Jul 1887

William Trammell and Mary Vickery, (MD) 9 Sep 1887

William Giles and Ida Kerby, (MD) 10 Sep 1887
Isaac Boyer and Easter Farrar, (MD) 15 Sep 1887
Hugh McGuire and Sarah J. Lord, (MD) 23 Sep 1887
Alanson Smith and Mary Wills, (MD) 25 Sep 1887
Joseph S. Gresham and Lillie Ann Wallor, (MD) 23 Oct 1887
M. C. Roan and Sarah Malinda Webb, (MD) 30 Oct 1887
William M. Lavay and Emma Josephine Ferguson, (MD) 30 Oct 1887
Andrew J. Cowin and Geneva J. Voile, of Reynolds Co., (MD) 3 Nov 1887
J. W. Tyson, of Wayne Co., and Ella Canton, (MD) 14 Nov 1887
John E. Allen and Phoeby J. Cole, (MD) 19 Nov 1887
Arthur E. Wilson and Candacy Angeline Green, (MD) 30 Nov 1887
Allen Anderson and Amanda Payne, (MD) 21 Dec 1887
Joshua Humphreys, of Ripley Co., and Mary Samantha Emry, (MD) 25 Dec 1887
John B. Barnes and Sarah E. Massie, (MD) 25 Dec 1887
Samuel Van Soyas? and Malinda Banon, (MD) 17 Jan 1888
H. M. Sneed and Elizabeth Davis, (MD) 21 Jan 1888
James Hunter, of Butler Co., and Safronia Stephens, (MD) 29 Jan 1888
James D. Barefield and Rebecca Massongail, of Reynolds Co., (MD) 22 Jan 1888
B. L. Cox and Melvinie H. Clubb, (MD) 5 Feb 1888
Thomas Barrett and Katie McGuerney, (MD) 2 Feb 1888
C. A. Berwich and Sarah Lively, (MD) 5 Feb 1888
Roll Carter, of Reynolds Co., and Bettie Reed, of Shannon Co., (MD) 4 Mar 1888
William Smith and Nancy Parish, (MD) 23 Feb 1888
John D. Williams, of Franklin Co., and Margaret O. Jones, (MD) 4 Mar 1888
Joseph Monz and Gertie Taylor, (MD) 8 Mar 1888
Benjamin Baker and Malinda Kelley, (MD) 25 Mar 1888
William A. Shoemaker and Rebecca Short, (MD) 28 Mar 1888
Ephraim Weese and Nancy E. Webb, (MD) 1 May 1888, both of Shannon Co., Mo
T. M. Hall and Annie M. Little, (MD) 15 Apr 1888
Allen Brown and Francis J. Moore, (MD) 22 Apr 1888
James H. Legg and Lizzie Dent, (MD) 26 Apr 1888
V. V. Barnett and May Belle Howard, (MD) 2 May 1888
John F. Fowler and Judy C. Rouse, (MD) 5 May 1888
John Harmon Rainbolt and Sarah E. Lovings, (MD) 16 May 1888
William R. Gladin, of Howell Co., and Laura O. Evans, (MD) 27 May 1888

John W. Ellis and Tennie Berlseon, (Issue Date) 4 Jun 1888
Anderson Farr and Rocksanna Smith, (MD) 10 Jun 1888, both of Reynolds Co., Mo
Richard Brooks, of Reynolds Co., and Molley Taylor, (MD) 9 Jun 1888
James Dixson and Mary R. Hughes, (MD) 15 Jun 1888, both of Reynolds Co., Mo
Jacob Angle and Hariett Kelley, (MD) 24 Jun 1888
Stephen Hefner and Willie Alice Box, (MD) 1 Jul 1888
Richard Hangar and Emeline Smith, (MD) 28 Jun 1888, both of Reynolds Co., Mo
James Laftey and Susan Paulding, (MD) 2 Jul 1888
Charles Heldt and Minerva J. Leadbetter, (MD) 16 Jul 1888
William J. Mainard and Ettie J. Stratton, (MD) 19 Jul 1888
Nathaniel A. Wagoner, of Ripley Co., and Laura A. Herrington, (MD) 19 Jul 1888
H. C. Shinn and Almira Neel, (MD) 25 July 1888
John G. Marrs and Georgia Belle Harris, (MD) 26 Jul 1888
Harrison Deering and Alice Brewington, (MD) 16 Aug 1888
Charles H. Crowley and Hannah J. Lane, (MD) 24 Jul 1888, both of Butler Co., MO
V. L. Pcket and Mary E. Carpenter, (Issue Date) 6 Aug 1888
James E. Springer and Susan E. Smith, (MD) 12 Aug 1888
Rueben M. Calet and Martha Joplin, (MD) 19 Sep 1888
Robert M. Williams and Mary Windes, (MD) 7 Oct 1888
Joseph R. Snider and Mary J. Oliver, (MD) 21 Oct 1888
A. D. McSpadden and Fannie Dirickson, (MD) 1 Nov 1888
Richard P. Brown, of Reynolds and Cancacy Angaline Green, (MD) 3 Nov 1888
Jasper N. Richmond, of Ripley Co., and Louisa E. Convey, (MD) 11 Nov 1888
Francis M. Whalen and Emma Frazier, (MD) 18 Nov 1888
William J. Leach and Dora L Emery, (MD) 25 Nov 1888
George W. Grindstaff, of Ripley Co., and Martha D. McBay, (MD) 25 Nov 1888
Ephraim M. Berry and Ursula Green, (MD) 20 Nov 1888
Alfred M. Link and Sarah Smith, (MD) 25 Nov 1888
Warner J. Oliver and Minerva A. Holland, (MD) 6 Dec 1888
William C. DeSpain and Sarah A. Beauchamp, of Howell Co., (MD) 10 Dec 1888
William W. Walker and Laura J. Burnley, of Ripley Co., (MD) 23 Dec 1888
John C. Chilton and Emma R. Bales, (MD) 25 Dec 1888

William Lutrell and Martha M. Ballard, (MD) 30 Dec 1888
Arthur B. Cantrill and Zella Graham, of Wayne Co., (MD) 30 Dec 1888
Marques L. Ward, of Ripley Co., and Sarah E. McCarty, (MD) 17 Jan 1889
Thomas J. Parce and Mary E. Campbell, (MD) 29 Jan 1889
John W. Hill and Francis Buchanan, (MD) 22 Jan 1889
Francis M. Tyler, of Shannon Co., and Catherine Snider, (MD) 22 Jan 1889
Richard M. Knight and Susie Killion, (MD) 27 Jan 1889
Jesse B. S. Lawson and Sarah Alley, (MD) 31 Jan 1889
William J. Dyer and Ella Inness, of Shannon Co., (MD) 11 Feb 1889
James Charles Stratto and Mary Condra, (MD) 17 Feb 1889
William N. Burk and Lucy B. Blackwell, (MD) 21 Feb 1889
Jesse A. McKee and Rosa A. Noble, (MD) 28 Feb 1889
William S. Taylor and Martha Ann Myrick, (MD) 3 Mar 1889
Levi Clark and Sarah Box, (MD) 3 Mar 1889
William Bales and Francis Sheets, (MD) 3 Mar 1889
Howard Graham and Louise M. Shepherd, (MD) 10 Mar 1889
Albert L. Raymond and Elizabeth Whitehouse, (MD) 13 Mar 1889
William Buckner and Annie Wiggins, (MD) 17 Mar 1889
Emanual M. Murry and Melvina Lambert, (MD) 21 Mar 1889
Montgomery F. Tucker and Monia Rodgers, (MD) 24 Mar 1889
James W. Copeland and Mary Ann Galbraith, (MD) 31 Mar 1889
Harvey Smith and Mollie Griffen, (MD) 2 Apr 1889
Johnson Huitt and Lillie Hope, (MD) 30 Mar 1889
Phillip Harsch and Mahalia F. Richmond, (MD) 14 Apr 1889
John Toliver and Alice Lampkins, (MD) 14 Apr 1889
John W. Hackworth and Adda C. Toliver, (MD) 14 Apr 1889
Lee W. Cotton and Martha Duncan, of Reynolds Co., (MD) 18 Apr 1889
Edward Lapar? and Willi C. Raymer, (MD) 14 Apr 1889
Andrew J. Woodward and Mintie Blanchard, (MD) 14 Apr 1889
John H. Klumpf and Mandy L. Wilkinson, (MD) 21 Apr 1889
Joseph C. McCarther and Mary Rosa Maine, (MD) 28 May 1889
Thomas J. Heathley, of Shannon Co., and Rosa Bell Hartley, of Iron Co., (MD) 1 May 1889
Thomas J. Beal and Laura E. Lee, (MD) 5 May 1889
Albert O. Evans and Mary E. Shoemaker, (MD) 26 May 1889
J. T. Vandyke and Matilda Skiles, (MD) 27 May 1889, both of Reynolds Co., Mo
N. F. Smith and Caldona Phillips, (MD) 2 Jun 1889
John L. Green and Nancy J. Kinnard, (MD) 4 Jun 1889

H. W. Price and Helen Brown, (MD) 27 Jun 1889
John D. King, of Butler Co., and Stella Hunter, (MD) 30 Jun 1889
James Hargate, of Wayne Co., and Lucinda Allen, (MD) 2 Jul 1889
John B. Pratt and Sarah Elizabeth Price, (MD) 2 Jul 1889, both of Reynolds Co., Mo
William Mabrey and Lillie Rives, (MD) 3 Jul 1889
Alex Mann and Laura Hubble, (MD) 14 Jul 1889 both of Reynolds Co., Mo
Jacob Ratliff and Laura A. Pritchett, (MD) 18 Jul 1889
Albert A. Vance and Artie Wilson, (MD) 2 Aug 1889, both of Bartlett, Shannon Co., Mo
John Hutchins and Martha Ann Boyer, (MD) 5 Aug 1889
Joseph C. Rongley and Jane Williams, of Oregon Co., (MD) 4 Aug 1889
George G. Crawford and Mary Margaret Ann Gatehouse, (MD) 8 Aug 1889
Albert Adams and Melissa Lawrence, (MD) 5 Aug 1889
George W. Meadow and Lydia F. McCain, (MD) 8 Aug 1889
George Smith and Elizabeth Emmons, (MD) 8 Aug 1889
Edward A. Hunter and Mary Ann Collins, (MD) 25 Aug 1889
Clinton Hunter and Harriet Colins, (MD) 25 Aug 1889
Andrew J. Hill and Siffie Mummert?, (MD) 22 Aug 1889
George K. Dawson and Mattie Smith, (MD) 26 Aug 1889
Allen Hixson and Lue Williams, (MD) 25 Aug 1889
Ephraim Farris and Caroline Box, (MD) 1 Sep 1889
Joseph K. Hanna and Nancy Windes, (MD) 2 Sep 1889
William O. Coleman and Lessie Snider, (MD) 4 Sep 1889
James W. Cheers and Mary Belle Neely, (MD) 12 Sep 1889
William E. Matkin and Winnie Taylor, (MD) 19 Sep 1889, both of Cynthia, Reynolds Co., Mo
Mathias Buckingham and Ida M. Ferguson, (MD) 29 Sep 1889
James P. Brame and Sarah J. Robertson, (MD) 13 Oct 1889
T. J. Piles and Mahala M. Bowers, of Reynolds Co., (MD) 27 Oct 1889
James Snider and Nora Neel, (MD) 10 Nov 1889
Zachus Stephens and Barbara Stacy, (MD) 17 Nov 1889
Julian R. Rongey and Lillie Jones, (MD) 17 Nov 1889
Luther J. Hartridge and Amanda Condray, (MD) 8 Dec 1889
George W. Graham, of Wayne Co., and Mary J. Carter, of Reynolds Co., (MD) 22 Dec 1889
James M. Clayton and Liza A. Jones, (MD) 15 Dec 1889
William W. Hall and Stella Myers, (MD) 15 Dec 1889
James W. Taylor and Mrs. Elizabeth Baker, (MD) 19 Dec 1889,

both of Shannon Co., Mo.
George W. Boneman and Mrs. Mary Johnson, (MD) 31 Dec 1889
George W. Jennings and Pearl Kirkpatrick, (MD) 19 Jan 1890
Lewis D. Hill and Ellen O'Dell, (MD) 31 Dec 1889
James A. Frazier and Marinda Maberry, (MD) 19 Jan 1890
Julius Z. Dugdale and Mamie J. Wakefield, (MD) 16 Jan 1890
Charles L. Cain and Nannie Helton, (MD) 19 Jan 1890
John W. Rook and Malisa Hooper, (MD) 19 Jan 1890
Frances M. Dildine and Ellen Hunter, (MD) 26 Jan 1890
William F. Short, Jr. and Mary L. Robertson, (MD) 16 Feb 1890
George Sharp and Hester Tinsley, (MD) 23 Feb 1890
Morgan B. Smith and Emma Baker, (MD) 6 March 1890, both of Reynolds Co.,
Charles Hawkins and Mary Hall, (MD) 23 Feb 1890
Joseph L. Graham, of Wayne Co., and Mollie Brame, (MD) 2 Mar 1890
Lewis S. McCarty and Martha E. Maine, (MD) 2 Mar 1890
Clarence Brown and Alice Jones, (MD) 6 Mar 1890
Harry C. Mooney, of Road House, Ill. and Mattie Hill, (MD) 10 Mar 1890
Joshua H. Lancaster and Liza L. O'Dell, (MD) 13 Mar 1890
Pleasant Holland, of Reynolds Co., and Angeline Brame, (MD) 20 Mar 1890
John Kelley, of Wayne Co., and Ellen Hadley, (MD) 20 Mar 1890
Nathan A. Jetmore and Nancy J. Drake, (MD) 30 Mar 1890
George Preston and Lizzie Coleman, (MD) 28 Mar 1890
Peter Clifton and Ida McFadden, (MD) 30 Mar 1890
J. P. Moore, of Reynolds Co., and Dora Pennington, of Howell Co., (MD) 11 Apr 1890
A. B. Fuller and Alice Mauk, (MD) 20 Apr 1890
Frank W. Jones and Mollie Pipkin, (MD) 11 May 1890

St. Louis County, Missouri, Souvenir of the Golden Jubliee, of Lorretto, Florissant, June. 21-23, 1897, Eddlemon Collection.

Litarary Programme, First Day, Jun. 21, 1897

Name	Event
Miss Olivia Marie Ghio	Piano
Marie Louise Fox	Piano
Elizabeth Hammond	Piano
Mamie Denvir	Piano
Marie Walsh	Piano
Corine Shevnin	Piano
Genevieve Reilly	Piano

Name	Event
Mary Kelly	Piano
Laura Barry	Piano
Anna Redmond	Piano
Stella O'Reilly	Piano
Myra Sicher	Piano
Cecilia Kaune	Piano
Mayme Florida	Piano
Mary Clyde	Piano
Mattie Rankin	Piano
Marie Pujol	Piano
Miss Marie Louise Fox	Address and the Archbishop J. J. Kain
Judith Co., ncone	Vocal Solo
Mrs. Mamie Heine-Ziebold	Vocal Solo
Mrs. Grace Donavan-Gruber	Vocal Solo
* Mrs. Sarah Walsh-Chambers	Recitation
Alecia Chambers *(Grand-daughter)	Recitation
Edna McGinnis	Piano
Edith Daisy McGinnis	Piano
Anna R. Donavan	Piano
Mrs. Margaret Burle-Downing	Loretto's Labors
Mrs. Tabbie Allen-Mara	Vocal Solo
Miss Mary Moran	Piano
Lizzie Hammond	First Mandolin
Mamie Denvir	First Mandolin
Gertie Keating	First Mandolin
Rev. J. J. Glennon	Alumni Addres

<u>Second Day, June 22, 1897.</u>

Name	Event
Miss Olivia Marie Ghio	Piano
Marie Louise Fox	Piano
Elizabeth Hammond	Piano
Mamie Denvir	Piano
Marie Walsh	Piano
Jennie Reilly	Piano
Margaret Bockrath	Piano
Cora Shevin	Piano
Myra Sicher	Piano
Stella O'Reilly	Piano
Cecilia Kaune	Piano
Sara Cunningham	Piano
Name	Event

Laura Barry	Piano
Kathryn Kurth	Piano
Adele Noonan	Piano
Josephine Bockrath	Piano
Anna Redmond	Piano
Gertrude Keating	Piano
Mrs. Mary Murray-Schaefer	Recitation
Miss Bettie Ghio	Vocal Solo
Miss McGinnis	Piano
Miss Daisy McGinnis	Piano Solo
Miss Adele Noonan	Recitation
Mrs. Mamie Heine Ziebold	Piano Solo
Katherine Coery Burke	Essay
Katherine Noel	Eassy Reader
Mrs. Grace Donavan-Gruber	Piano
Mrs. Maggie Larkin-Cooke	Essay
Miss Edna McGinnis	Piano Solo

Missourians at the Reunion, of Civil War Veterans, Centerville, Appanoose Co., Iowa

Name	Co.	Regiment
Ellis, Geo.	L	1st Missouri Cav. M. S M
Gray, A. H.	G	42nd Missouri
Shaffer, W. N.	G	2nd Missouri Cav.
Vespers, Geo. W.	C	7th Missouri Cav.

Missouri Confederate Dead at Rock Island Prison Camp

Adamson, Thomas: (RK) Pvt., (Co) C, (Reg) 10th Mo, (D) Feb. 13, 1864, (GRAVE) 475.

Allega, John: (Co.) Mo Conscript, (D) Dec. 22, 1864, (GRAVE) 1695.

Allen, William: (RK) Pvt., (Co.) E, (Reg) 10th Mo, (D) Jan. 17, 1865, (GRAVE) 1783.

Armstrong, Leonard: (Co.) Missouri Citizen, (D) Mar. 17, 1865, (GRAVE) 1904.

Arnold, Wm. S.: (Rk) Pvt, (Co.) I, (Reg) 15th Mo, (D) Mar. 17, 1865, (GRAVE) 1861.

Austin, James: (Co.) Mo Conscript, (D) Jan. 22, 1865, (GRAVE) 1804.

Baker, Lewis D.: (Co.) Mo Conscript, (D) Dec. 24, 1864, (GRAVE) 1705

Ballance, John: (Rk) Pvt, (Reg) Wood's Mo Battalion, (D) Mar. 12, 1865, (GRAVE) 1912

Basket, Jas. M.: (Co.) Mo Conscript, (D) Jan.23, 1865, (GRAVE) 1805

Best, Eben H.: (Co.) Mo Conscript, (D) Dec. 2, 1864, (Grave) 1635
Bridges, John: (Rk) Pvt, : (Co.) Mo Conscript, (D) Dec.14, 1864, (Grave) 1671
Briggs, James: (Rk) Pvt, (Co.) A2, (Reg) Mo Cav., (D) Aug.27, 1864, (GRAVE) 1458
Brown, Jas.: (Rk) Pvt, (Co.) D, (Reg) 1st Mo Cav., (D) Mar. 12, 1864, (GRAVE) 793
Brown, W. D. T.: (Rk) Pvt, A, (Co.) Wood's Battn Mo Cav., (D) Mar. 17, 1865, (GRAVE)
Bruin, Wm. R.: (Rk) Pvt, (Co.) K, (Reg) Jackson's Mo, (D) Jan.12, 1865, (GRAVE) 1772
Brummett, W.T.: (Co.) Mo Conscript, (D) Feb. 12, 1865, (GRAVE) 1876
Butner, Wallace: (Co.) Mo Conscript, (D) Dec. 29, 1864, (GRAVE) 1721
Cain, A. F.: (Rk) Pvt, (Co.) D, (Reg) Wood's Battn Mo Cav, (D) Jan.15, 1865, (GRAVE) 1779
Calvert, Alfred: (Co.) Mo Conscript, (D) Feb. 4, 1865, (Grave) 1857
Campbell, Thos. C.: (Co.) Mo Conscript, (D) Jan. 24, 1865, (Grave) 1811
Cavanaugh, David: (Co.) Mo Conscript, (D) Nov. 28, 1864, (Grave) 1627
Cheatham, R.A.: (Rk) Pvt, (Co.) I, (Reg) 12th Shank's Mo Cav, (D) Aug. 25, 1864, (Grave) 1450
Chrisam, Nat. B.: (Co.) Mo Conscript, (D) Jan. 24, 1865, (Grave) 1813
Clay, Eli E.: (Co.) Mo Conscript, (D) Feb. 11, 1865, (Grave) 1872
Clay, Wm.S.: (Co.) Mo Conscript, (D) Feb. 6, 1865, (Grave) 1864
Clubb, Jeremiah: (Co.) Mo Conscript, (D) Dec.16, 1864, (Grave) 1682
Cobb, Geo.: (Co.) Mo Conscript, (D) Apr. 10, 1865, (Grave) 1939
Cook, Thos.: (Co.) Mo Conscript, (D) Dec.1, 1864, (Grave) 1658
Dameron, John: (Co.) Mo Conscript, (D) Nov. 27, 1864, (Grave) 1624
Davis, Chas. C.: (Rk) Pvt, (Co.) D, (Reg) Perkins' Mo Cav., (D) Dec. 21, 1864, (Grave) 1692
Davis, Wm. J.: (Co.) Mo Conscript, (D) Dec.5, 1864, (Grave) 1643
Dixon, Thos.: (Co.) Mo Conscript, (D) Jan. 29, 1865, (Grave) 1834
Dodge, Jas. C.: (Rk) Pvt, (Reg) Harris' Mo Battery, (D) Dec.26, 1864, (Grave) 1714
Dodson, Wm.: (Rk) Pvt, (Reg) Cobb's Mo Cav, (D) Jan. 20, 1865, (Grave) 1794
Donaldson, G. R.: (Co.) Mo Conscript, (D) Jun. 14, 1865, (Grave) 1960
Dyson, John: (Rk) Pvt, , (Co.) I, (Reg) 4th Mo Cav., (D) Dec.19, 1864,

(Grave) 1687

Eagan, John: (Co.) Mo Conscript, (D) Jan. 26, 1865, (Grave) 1826

Eaton, Jesse: (Co.) Mo Conscript, (D) Dec.31, 1864, (Grave) 1732

Eaton, John R.: (Co.) Mo Conscript, (D) Jan. 22, 1865, (Grave) 1803

Ellis, William: (Co.) Mo Conscript, (D) Dec.13, 1864, (Grave) 1668

Ervin, Wm. M.: (Co.) Mo Conscript, (D) Dec.6, 1864, (Grave) 1647

Ethridge, J. J.: (Rk) Pvt, (Co.) C, (Reg) Hunter's Mo Cav, (D) Apr. 21, 1865, (Grave) 1947

Ferguson, Bellfield, W.: (Co.) Mo Conscript, (D) Dec.21, 1864, (Grave) 1690

Ferguson, Carroll: (Co.) Mo Conscript, (D) Feb. 13, 1865, (Grave) 1878

Ferrell, W.J.: (Co.) Mo Conscript, (D) Dec.9, 1864, (Grave) 1654

Fletcher, Benj. F.: (Rk) Pvt, , (Co.) C, (Reg) 3th Mo, (D) Feb. 12, 1865, (Grave) 1877

Ford, Samuel: (Rk) Pvt, (Co.) B, (Reg) 7th Mo Cav., (D) Dec.30, 1864, (Grave) 1725

Ford, Wm. C.: (Rk) Pvt, (Co.) D, (Reg) Wood's Mo Cav, (D) Sep. 26, 1864, (Grave) 1533

Forrest, H. L.: (Co.) Mo Conscript, (D) Jan. 4, 1865, (Grave) 1746

Forrest, John H.: (Rk) Pvt, (Co.) B, (Reg) 7th Mo, (D) Jan. 25, 1865, (Grave) 1820

Fowler, Wm. W.: (Rk) Pvt, (Co.) B, (Reg) Greene's 3rd Mo Cav, (D) Jan. 2, 1865, (Grave) 1737

Goforth, Davis: (Co.) Mo Conscript, (D) Dec.7, 1864, (Grave) 1648

Grant, Jas. H.: (Rk) Pvt, (Co.) I, (D) 10 Mo Jan. 10, 1865, (Grave) 1763

Gray, David A.: (Rk) Pvt, (Reg) Baker's Mo, (D) Jan. 23, 1865, (Grave) 1808

Green, David: (Rk) Pvt, (Co.) B, (Reg) Wood's Mo Battalion, (D) Aug. 26, 1864, (Grave) 1455

Griffin, James: (Co.) Mo Conscript, (D) Dec.3, 1864, (Grave) 1638

Griffin, David C.: (Co.) Mo Conscript, (D) Jan. 21, 1865, (Grave) 1797

Hampton, Jas.: (Co.) Mo Conscript, (D) Dec.21, 1864, (Grave) 1694

Harmon, Jas. B.: (Co.) Mo Conscript, (D) Dec.12, 1864, (Grave) 1666

Hartshorn, Thomas A.: (Rk) Pvt, (Reg) 3rd Mo Battery, (D) Apr. 24, 1864, (Grave) Removed

Hendrix, Philip S.: (Rk) Pvt, (Co.) C, (Reg) Wood's Mo Cav, (D) Oct. 4, 1864, (Grave) 1545

Henry, Franklin: (Rk) Pvt, (Co.) B, (Reg) Wood's Mo Cav, (D) Feb. 20, 1865, (Grave) 1888

Herrod, George L.: (Rk) Pvt, (Co.) F, (Reg) 3rd Mo, (D) Mar. 18,

1864, (Grave) 847
Hill, George: (Rk) Pvt, (Co.) Schull's, (Reg) Hodge's Mo, (D) Mar. 6, 865, (Grave) 1905
Hocolm, Wm. F.: (Rk) Pvt, (Reg) Hodge's Mo, (D) Jan. 20, 1865, (Grave) 1793
Holmes, Thomas: (Rk) Pvt, (Co.) Schull's, (Reg) Hodge's Mo, (D) Dec.31, 1864, (Grave) 1731
Horton, Jas. R.: (Rk) Pvt, (Co.) B, (Reg) 10th Mo, (D) Feb. 16, 1864, (Grave) 530
Huffman, Jno A.: (Rk) Pvt, (Reg) Mccullough's Mo, (D) May 7, 1864, (Grave) 1128
Hughs, Elkana: (Rk) Pvt, (Co.) B, (Reg) Wood's Mo Cav, May 30, 1864, (Grave) 1178
Hull, Wm. A.: (Co.) Mo Conscript, (D) Jan. 13, 1865, (Grave) 1785
Hunter, James H.: (Rk) Pvt, , (Co.) E, (Reg) Mo, (D) Dec.1, 1864, (Grave) 1633
Hunter, James P.: (Rk) Pvt, (Co.) Schull's, (Reg) Hodge's Mo, (D) Feb. 1, 1865, (Grave) 1844
Huntsman, W.A.: (Co.) Mo Conscript, (D) Dec.17, 1864, (Grave) 1683
Hutchins, James: (Rk) Pvt, (Co.) H, (Reg) Coffee's Mo, (D) Feb. 1, 1865, (Grave) 1843
Irwin, John: (Co.) Mo Conscript, (D) Feb. 5, 1865, (Grave) 1863
Jackson, Isaiah H.: (Co.) Mo Conscript, (D) Dec.12, 1864, (Grave) 1663
Jackson, W.H.: (Co.) Mo Conscript, (D) Jan. 25, 1865, (Grave) 1817
Jackson, Wm. G.: (Rk) Sgt, (Co.) E, (Reg) 3rd Mo, (D) Mar. 5, 1864, (Grave) 781
Johnson, Andrew: (Co.) Citizen, Mo, (D) Oct. 27, 1864, (Grave) 162
Johnson, John: (Co.) Mo Conscript, (D) Apr. 18, 1865, (Grave) 1945
Johnson, Martin G.: (Co.) Mo Conscript, (D) Dec.16, 1864, (Grave) 1684
Johnson, Thos.: (Co.) Mo Conscript, (D) Apr. 21, 1865, (Grave) 1948
Johnson, William: (Co.) Mo Conscript, (D) Dec.8, 1864, (Grave) 1650
Jones, Reese: (Co.) Mo Conscript, (D) May 12, 1865, (Grave) 1958
Jordan, Chas. F.: (Co.) Mo Conscript, (D) Nov. 6, 1864, (Grave) 1645
Keizer, Wm.: (Co.) Mo Conscript, (D) Jan. 28, 1865, (Grave) 1830
King, Joel: (Co.) Mo Conscript, (D) May 8, 1865, (Grave) 1954
King, Wm. A.: (Rk) Pvt, (Co.) I, (Reg) Wood's Mo Battalion, (D) Dec.9, 1864, (Grave) 1655
Kinzer, Jas. W.: (Co.) Mo Conscript, (D) Jan. 7, 1865, (Grave) 1753
Kizer, John: (Co.) Mo Conscript, (D) Jan. 13, 1865, (Grave) 1775
Knot, Wilson T.: (Rk) Pvt, (Reg) Mo, (D) Jan. 12, 1865, (Grave) 1782

Laplant, Joseph: (Rk) Pvt, (Co.) H, (Reg) Thompson's Mo Battery, (D) Feb. 1, 1865, (Grave) 1845

Lashley, Lemuel: (Rk) Pvt, (Reg) Love's Mo, (D) Oct. 9, 1864, (Grave) 1653

Lawson, W.D.: (Co.) Mo Conscript, (D) Mar. 12, 1865, (Grave) 1911

Leach, Lew: (Co.) Mo Conscript, (D) Oct. 12, 1864, (Grave) 1667

Leach, Wm. H.: (Co.) Mo Conscript, (D) Feb. 4, 1865, (Grave) 1856

Leathers, Wm.: (Rk) Pvt, (Reg) Reve's Mo Cav, (D) Feb. 15, 1864, (Grave) 467

Leech, M.: (Co.) Mo Conscript, (D) Feb. 2, 1865, (Grave) 1849

Leeper, Lester: (Co.) Mo Conscript, (D) Dec.22, 1864, (Grave) 1718

Lewallen, Henry: (Rk) Pvt, (Co.) A, (Reg) Wood's Mo, (D) Aug. 4, 1864, (Grave) 1372

Lile, James P.: (Rk) Pvt, (Reg) Harrison Mo Battery, (D) Feb 12, 1865, (Grave) 1874

Lockard, Moses: (Co.) Mo Conscript, (D) Oct. 12, 1864, (Grave) 1664

Mabrey, Jno. J.: (Rk) Corp, (Co.) E, (Reg) Wood's Mo Cav, (D) Feb. 2, 1865, (Grave) 1848

McDaniel, Abram T.: (Co.) Mo Conscript, (D) Dec. 25, 1864, (Grave) 1707

McDaniel, Jno. W.: (Co.) Mo Conscript, (D) May 8, 1865, (Grave) 1955

McDaniell, Jas. H.: (Co.) Mo Conscript, (D) Mar. 22, 1865, (Grave) 1930

McFall, Aaron F.: (Rk) Pvt, B7 Mo Cav Jan. 16, 1865, (Grave) 1784

McFerren, Jos. N.: (Co.) Mo Conscript, (D) Jan. 25, 1865, (Grave) 1819

McLanahan, Jas.: (Co.) Mo Conscript, (D) Dec.7, 1864, (Grave) 1649

Mclanahan, Tilman: (Rk) Pvt, (Reg) Hodge's Mo, (D) Mar. 17, 1865, (Grave) 1926

Maddox, Benj. F.: (Co.) Mo Conscript, (D) Dec.21, 1864, (Grave) 1693

Manghan, John: (Rk) Corp, (Co.) H, (Reg) 4th Mo Cav, (D) Mar. 2, 1865, (Grave) 1898

Mann, Jasper: (Rk) Pvt, (Reg) Kreves Mo Cav, (D) Mar. 15, 1864, (Grave) 820

Melton, Jno. B.: (Co.) Mo Conscript, (D) Dec.8, 1864, (Grave) 1652

Mills, Thos. R.: (Rk) Pvt, (Co.) H, (Reg) 14th Mo, (D) Jan. 18, 1865, (Grave) 1789

Millsaps, Wiseman: (Rk) Pvt, (Co.) I, (Reg) 7th Mo, (D) Mar. 21, 1865, (Grave) 1928

Moore, Amaziah: (Co.) Mo Conscript, (D) Jan. 2, 1865, (Grave) 1739

Morehan, Thos.: (Co.) Mo Conscript, (D) Feb. 18, 1865, (Grave) 1885

Morgan, Barney: (Rk) Pvt, (Co.) F, (Reg) Love's Mo, (D) Jan. 2, 1865, (Grave) 1736
Morton, John: (Rk) Pvt, (Reg) Hodge's Mo, (D) Mar. 17, 1865, (Grave) 1925
Moxley, Randolph: (Co.) Mo Conscript, (D) Dec. 27, 1864, (Grave) 1719
Muse, Jesse: (Rk) Pvt, (Co.) K, (Reg) 4th Mo Cav, (D) Mar. 25, 1864, (Grave) 920
Neal, Carrol J.: (Co.) Mo Conscript, (D) Jan. 21, 1865, (Grave) 1802
Nicholas, Robt. C.: (Co.) Mo Conscript, (D) Nov. 28, 1864, (Grave) 1626
Noel, Archibald: (Co.) Mo Conscript, (D) Jan. 23, 1865, (Grave) 1810
Norman, Wm.: (Rk) Pvt, (Reg) Harrison's Mo Battery, (D) Feb. 8, 1865, (Grave) 1867
Norton, Wm. C.: (Rk) Pvt, (Co.) A, (Reg) Wood's Battn, Mo Cav, (D) Jan. 21, 1865, (Grave) 1799
Osborne, Joseph: (Rk) Pvt, (Reg) Harrison's Mo Battery, (D) Jan. 21, 1865, (Grave) 1800
Owens, Daniel: (Co.) Mo Conscript, (D) Jan. 18, 1865, (Grave) 1788
Philips, Peter: (Rk) Pvt, (Reg) 10 Mo Battn, (D) Dec.28, 1863, (Grave) 83
Piles, Alfred: (Co.) Mo Conscript, (D) Dec. 3, 1864, (Grave) 1636
Poer, Will.: (Co.) Mo Conscript, (D) Dec. 3, 1864, (Grave) 1644
Porter, Nathaniel B.: (Co.) Mo Conscript, (D) Dec.13, 1864, (Grave) 1669
Prewett, Jno. L.: (Rk) Pvt, (Co.) E, (Reg) 30th Mo Cav, (D) Jun. 3, 1864, (Grave) 1188
Purl, Hezekiah: (Co.) Mo Conscript, (D) 2/4, 1865, (Grave) 1860
Rambo, John W.: (Rk) Pvt, (Co.) C, (Reg) Wood's Battn Mo Cav, (D) Jun.13, 1864, (Grave) 1232
Reed, Jno. S.: (Rk) Pvt, (Co.) B, (Reg) Love's Mo, (D) Jan. 11, 1865, (Grave) 176
Reese, Jno. F.: (Rk) Pvt, A10 Mo Cav Jan. 14, 1865, (Grave) 1776
Reese, Wm.: (Co.) Mo Conscript, (D) Mar. 14, 1865, (Grave) 1916
Rice, Franklin: (Co.) Mo Conscript, (D) Feb. 3, 1865, (Grave) 1853
Roan, Richard S.: (Rk) Pvt, (Co.) A, (Reg) Wood's Battn Mo Cav, (D) Aug. 5, 1864, (Grave) 1377
Robb, William: (Co.) Mo Conscript, (D) Dec.5, 1864, (Grave) 1642
Robertson, Wash.: (Co.) Mo Conscript, (D) Jan. 12, 1865, (Grave) 1773
Rogers, Jno. M.: (Co.) Mo Conscript, (D) Apr. 10, 1865, (Grave) 1941
Rose, Henry: (Rk) Pvt, (Co.) C, (Reg) Wood's Battn Mo Cav, (D) Jun. 5, 1864, (Grave) 1192

Ross, Geo. T.: (Co.) Mo Conscript, (D) Feb. 4, 1865, (Grave) 1858
Ross, Samuel: (Rk) Pvt, (Co.) E, (Reg) Wood's Mo Cav, (D) Jul. 30, 1864, (Grave) 1354
Rowland, Luther: (Rk) Pvt, (Co.) G, (Reg) 12th Mo Cav, (D) Jan. 10, 1865, (Grave) 1764
Rumanus, Daniel: (Co.) Mo Conscript, (D) Apr. 15, 1865, (Grave) 1944
Russell, Thos.: (Rk) Pvt, (Co.) E, (Reg) 12th Mo Cav, (D) Jul. 20, 1864, (Grave) 1332
Sanders, Alfred: (Co.) Mo Conscript, (D) Dec.15, 1864, (Grave) 1676
Sanders, Elias: (Rk) Pvt, (Co.) C, (Reg) Wood's Mo Cav, (D) Jun. 16, 1864, (Grave) 1243
Schroun, David: (Rk) Pvt, C4 Mo Jan. 3, 1865, (Grave) 1734
Scott, Nelins: (Co.) Mo Conscript, (D) Jan. 10, 1865, (Grave) 1759
Scott, William: (Co.) Mo Conscript, (D) Dec.12, 1864, (Grave) 1660
Seay, Joshua: (Rk) Pvt, (Co.) H, (Reg) Mo, (D) Jan. 20, 1865, (Grave) 1796
Shadricks, Jas.: (Co.) Mo Conscript, (D) Jan. 15, 1865, (Grave) 1770
Shaw, Jas. L.: (Rk) Pvt, (Co.)C, (Reg) Wood's Mo Cav, (D) Aug. 5, 1864, (Grave) 1373
Shikel, Samuel: (Rk) Pvt, (Co.) B, (Reg) 10th Mo Cav, (D) Feb. 12, 1864, (Grave) 451
Small, Josiah R.: (Rk) Pvt, (Co.) C, (Reg) Laback's Mo, (D) Feb. 20, 1865, (Grave) 1889
Snelson, Henry: (Rk) Pvt, (Co.) E, (Reg) 8th Mo, (D) Sep. 20, 1864, (Grave) 1519
Speaks, Abisha D.: (Co.) Mo Conscript, (D) Apr. 8, 1865, (Grave) 1936
Speaks, Robt.: (Co.) Mo Conscript, (D) Feb. 7, 1865, (Grave) 1865
Stallions, James: (Co.) Mo Conscript, (D) Apr. 22, 1865, (Grave) 1949
Stephens, L.R.: (Rk) Pvt, (Reg) Stoe's Mo Battery, (D) Nov. 29, 1864, (Grave) 1629
Suggs, James: (Rk) Citizen, Mo, (D) Jan. 29, 1865, (Grave) 1836
Swetman, Benj.: (Co.) Mo Conscript, (D) Feb. 22, 1865, (Grave) 1931
Tudor, John: (Co.) Mo Conscript, (D) Feb. 1, 1865, (Grave) 1846
Tyre, Jerome B.: (Co.) Mo Conscript, (D) Feb. 28, 1865, (Grave) 1897
Vaught, Jacob: (Co.) Mo Conscript, (D) Dec.26, 1864, (Grave) 1712
Waldon, Joseph: (Co.) Mo Conscript, (D) Jan. 2, 1865, (Grave) 1738
Washam, Robert: (Co.) Mo Conscript, (D) Jan. 23, 1865, (Grave) 1806
Wassan, Silas: (Co.) Mo Conscript, (D) Feb. 15, 1865, (Grave) 1882
Webb, Lott: (Co.) Mo Conscript, (D) Mar. 3, 1865, (Grave) 1899
Wells, Jeptha: (Co.) Mo Conscript, (D) Dec.6, 1864, (Grave) 1646

Williamson, Wm.: (Co.) Mo Conscript, (D) Apr. 10, 1865, (Grave) 1940

Williamson, Wm. A.: (Rk) Pvt, (Reg) 2nd Mo Battery, (D) Oct.18, 1864, (Grave) 1573

Winfield, Ephiram: (Co.) Mo Conscript, (D) Nov. 30, 1864, (Grave) 1632

Winkles, Andrew: (Rk) Pvt, (Co.) D, (Reg) Wood's Mo Cav, (D) Jan. 14, 1865, (Grave) 1777

Wright, Hiram: (Co.) Mo Conscript, (D) Jan. 27, 1865, (Grave) 1828

Yates, Jno. W.: (Co.) Mo Conscript, (D) Jan. 9, 1865, (Grave) 1760

Yeager, Alfred: (Co.) Mo Conscript, (D) Feb. 4, 1865, (Grave) 1859.

York, Relay W.: (Rk) Pvt, (Co.) H, (Reg) 9th Mo, (D) Oct. 10, 1864, (Grave) 1560

Young, Jas. W.: (Co.) Mo Conscript, (D) Feb. 7, 1865, (Grave) 1866

Atchinson County, Missouri, Index, 1850 Census

Charles Aikins: (Pg) 280; James R. Aikins: (Pg) 280; Lafayette Aikins: (Pg) 280; Margaret Aikins: (Pg) 280; Martin J. Aikins: (Pg) 280; Thomas Aikins: (Pg) 280; Bethel Allen: (Pg) 274; Bethel Allen: (Pg) 274; Elizabeth Allen: (Pg) 274; Elizabeth Allen: (Pg) 274; Isaac Allen: (Pg) 274; Jesse R. Allen: (Pg) 274; Mathew D. Allen: (Pg) 274; Nancy Allen: (Pg) 274; Nancy A. Allen: (Pg) 281; Precilla Allen: (Pg) 274; Richard J. Allen: (Pg) 274; Susan J. Allen: (Pg) 274; Thomas Allen: (Pg) 281; William R. Allen: (Pg) 274; Alexander Amen: (Pg) 286; Anna Amen: (Pg) 285; Corella Amen: (Pg) 285; Mary E. Amen: (Pg) 285; Mathias Amen: (Pg) 285; Mathias Amen: (Pg) 286; Midleton Amen: (Pg) 285; Ralph Amen: (Pg) 285; Resin Amen: (Pg) 285; Sarah Amen: (Pg) 286; Sylvester Amen: (Pg) 285; Clarinda Aull: (Pg) 302; Clementine Aull: (Pg) 302; Edward Aull: (Pg) 302; Fremont Aull: (Pg) 302; James Aull: (Pg) 302; Thomas M. Aull: (Pg) 302; Charles Baeseley: (Pg) 283; Isom Baeseley: (Pg) 283; Missouri Baeseley: (Pg) 283; Sarah Baeseley: (Pg) 283; Susan Baeseley: (Pg) 283; Susan Baeseley: (Pg) 283; Washington Baeseley: (Pg) 283; Woodson Baeseley: (Pg) 283; Annie Bailey: (Pg) 294; Ely Bailey: (Pg) 294; Grandeson Bailey: (Pg) 294; James Bailey: (Pg) 294; James Bailey: (Pg) 294; Levy Bailey: (Pg) 294; Nancy Bailey: (Pg) 294; Sarah Bailey: (Pg) 294; Sekiel Bailey: (Pg) 294; Benjamin Baldwin: (Pg) 286; Catharine Baldwin: (Pg) 287; Elizabeth Baldwin: (Pg) 287; Frances Baldwin: (Pg) 289; Irina Baldwin: (Pg) 287; James H. Baldwin: (Pg) 289; Martha Baldwin: (Pg) 286; Mary A. Baldwin: (Pg) 287; Elisa Ballard: (Pg) 272; Polina Ballard: (Pg) 272; Richard Ballard: (Pg) 272; Catharine Banzer: (Pg) 288; Charles Banzer: (Pg) 288; Christine Banzer: (Pg) 288; Elise Banzer: (Pg) 288; John Banzer: (Pg)

288; Joseph Banzer: (Pg) 288; Magdalena Banzer: (Pg) 288; Elizabeth Barlow: (Pg) 287; George Barlow: (Pg) 300; Jeremiah Barlow: (Pg) 300; Jeremiah Barlow: (Pg) 287; Judy Barlow: (Pg) 287; Louis Barlow: (Pg) 287; Mary Barlow: (Pg) 300; Mary Barlow: (Pg) 287; Susan M. Barlow: (Pg) 300; Washington Barlow: (Pg) 287; William Barlow: (Pg) 300; Datus Beal: (Pg) 300; Fibia M. Beal: (Pg) 300; George Beal: (Pg) 300; Lucina Beal: (Pg) 300; Lucretia Beal: (Pg) 300; Moses Beal: (Pg) 300; Emma J. Beard: (Pg) 278; George S. Beard: (Pg) 278; Julia A. Beard: (Pg) 278; Martha Beard: (Pg) 278; Sarah F. Beard: (Pg) 278; Elizabeth Beck: (Pg) 299; Mary Beck: (Pg) 299; Percy (f) Beck: (Pg) 299; William Beck: (Pg) 299; Wilson Beck: (Pg) 299; Davis Beers: (Pg) 289; Elisa Beers: (Pg) 289; Jonathin Bell: (Pg) 293; George Bennett: (Pg) 290; Gideon Bennett: (Pg) 290; Jane E. Bennett: (Pg) 290; John Bennett: (Pg) 290; Sarah Blair: (Pg) 287; Almida Blevins: (Pg) 299; Daniel Blevins: (Pg) 299; Daniel M. Blevins: (Pg) 299; Elise A. Blevins: (Pg) 298; Joseph W. Blevins: (Pg) 299; Lucy Blevins: (Pg) 298; Lucy Blevins: (Pg) 299; Nathaniel Blevins: (Pg) 298; Wardeman Blevins: (Pg) 299; Henry Bluhm: (Pg) 267; Dalcina Bony: (Pg) 277; Elizabeth Bony: (Pg) 277; Hiram Bony: (Pg) 277; Joseph Bony: (Pg) 277; Nancy Bony: (Pg) 277; William Bony: (Pg) 277; Augustus Borchers: (Pg) 300; Frances M. Borchers: (Pg) 293; George Borchers: (Pg) 293; Louise Borchers: (Pg) 293; Mary Jane Borchers: (Pg) 293; S. G. Bowen: (Pg) 300; A. A Bradford: (Pg) 303; Emeline Bradford: (Pg) 303; Alfins Bradley: (Pg) 298; Martha Bradley: (Pg) 298; Martha Bradley: (Pg) 298; Susan Bradley: (Pg) 298; Texas Bradley: (Pg) 298; William H. Bradley: (Pg) 298; John Brandenstein: (Pg) 301; Louisa Brandenstein: (Pg) 301; Margaret A. Brandenstein: (Pg) 301; Mary E. Brandenstein: (Pg) 301; Daniel Braziel: (Pg) 280; George Braziel: (Pg) 280; Melinda Braziel: (Pg) 280; Susan Braziel: (Pg) 280; Jane Brissen: (Pg) 269; Willim J. Brissen: (Pg) 269; Carolina Brody: (Pg) 302; Colisty Brody: (Pg) 302; Elizabeth Brody: (Pg) 303; Isabella Brody: (Pg) 302; Jesse Brody: (Pg) 302; Louis K. Brody: (Pg) 302; Mary Brody: (Pg) 303; Mary E. Brody: (Pg) 302; Stephen Brody: (Pg) 302; Stephen Brody: (Pg) 303; William Brody: (Pg) 302; Charlotte Buckham: (Pg) 280; Martha W. Buckham: (Pg) 280; Nancy Buckham: (Pg) 280; Richard Buckham: (Pg) 280; Robert Buckham: (Pg) 300; Robert N. Buckham: (Pg) 280; Susan A. Buckham: (Pg) 280; Carolina Bull: (Pg) 268; John E. Bull: (Pg) 274; William A. Bull: (Pg) 274; Angelina Bulley: (Pg) 290; Antony Bulley: (Pg) 290; Charlotte Bulley: (Pg) 290; Charlotte Bulley: (Pg) 290; Melinda Bulley: (Pg) 290; Henry Bush: (Pg) 296; Martin Bush: (Pg) 296; Susan Bush: (Pg) 296; Thomas Bush: (Pg) 296; Eliza Cameron: (Pg) 266; James Cameron: (Pg) 266; John Cameron: (Pg) 266; Mary

Cameron: (Pg) 266; Rachael Cameron: (Pg) 266; Salite Cameron: (Pg) 266; Sarine Cameron: (Pg) 266; William Cameron: (Pg) 266; Benjamin Campbell: (Pg) 268; Elizabeth Campbell: (Pg) 268; James A. Campbell: (Pg) 268; John Campbell: (Pg) 268; Martha A. Campbell: (Pg) 268; Thomas B. Campbell: (Pg) 268; William B. Campbell: (Pg) 268; Elisa J. Candle: (Pg) 295; James Candle: (Pg) 295; Martha A. Candle: (Pg) 295; Nancy A. Candle: (Pg) 295; Polina A. Candle: (Pg) 295; Sekiel Candle: (Pg) 295; Susan Candle: (Pg) 295; William Candle: (Pg) 295; Albert Casey: (Pg) 275; Benjamin Casey: (Pg) 275; Edward Casey: (Pg) 275; Harriet Casey: (Pg) 275; Janette Casey: (Pg) 275; Janette Casey: (Pg) 275; Levy Casey: (Pg) 275; Margaret Casey: (Pg) 275; Robert Casey: (Pg) 275; Hugh Caudle: (Pg) 295; Mary Caudle: (Pg) 295; Sarah Caudle: (Pg) 295; Charlotte Cer: (Pg) 292; Elizabeth Cer: (Pg) 292; Harry J. Cer: (Pg) 292; John Cer: (Pg) 292; Martha Cer: (Pg) 292; Nancy E. Cer: (Pg) 292; Nicholas W. Cer: (Pg) 292; Sarah A. Cer: (Pg) 292; Louisa Chipman: (Pg) 301; Margaret A. Chipman: (Pg) 301; Martin E. Chipman: (Pg) 301; Mary E. Chipman: (Pg) 301; Glade Choder: (Pg) 290; Mary Choder: (Pg) 290; Patric Choder: (Pg) 290; Elizabeth Christian: (Pg) 301; Mary A. Christian: (Pg) 301; Preston R. Christian: (Pg) 301; M. B. Clark: (Pg) 268; Marion B. Clark: (Pg) 268; Ann E. Claus: (Pg) 286; Elizabeth Claus: (Pg) 286; Simon H. Clayton: (Pg) 302; Thomas Cleveland: (Pg) 278; Cicha Clevinger: (Pg) 265; Elizabeth Clevinger: (Pg) 265; George W. Clevinger: (Pg) 265; Samuel Clevinger: (Pg) 265; Conrad Cloepfield: (Pg) 300; Conrad Cloepfield: (Pg) 286; Elizabeth Cloepfield: (Pg) 286; Magaret Cloepfield: (Pg) 286; Martha Cloepfield: (Pg) 286; Elizabeth Cocine: (Pg) 281; John M. Cocine: (Pg) 281; Martin W. Cocine: (Pg) 281; Mary L. Cocine: (Pg) 281; Abraham Cogdill: (Pg) 271; Daniel Cogdill: (Pg) 271; Jacob Cogdill: (Pg) 271; Kitty A. Cogdill: (Pg) 271; Mahala Cogdill: (Pg) 271; Mary Cogdill: (Pg) 271; Merida Cogdill: (Pg) 271; Totter Cogdill: (Pg) 271; William Cogdill: (Pg) 271; Angelina Cole: (Pg) 297; Angelina Cole: (Pg) 297; Benjamin Cole: (Pg) 297; Burcilla Cole: (Pg) 297; Elise Cole: (Pg) 283; Jane A. Cole: (Pg) 297; Jesse Cole: (Pg) 297; Jesse Cole: (Pg) 297; John Cole: (Pg) 283; Mathilda Collet: (Pg) 284; William Collet: (Pg) 284; Daniel Combs: (Pg) 298; Jackson Combs: (Pg) 298; Jesse Combs: (Pg) 298; Margaret Combs: (Pg) 298; William Combs: (Pg) 298; William T. Combs: (Pg) 298; Amanda M. Cook: (Pg) 265; Annie Cook: (Pg) 265; Elias H. Cook: (Pg) 265; Frances Cook: (Pg) 265; James F. Cook: (Pg) 265; James K. Cook: (Pg) 265; John Cook: (Pg) 265; John C. Cook: (Pg) 265; Joshua Cook: (Pg) 265; Lucas Cook: (Pg) 265; Sarah Cook: (Pg) 265; Daniel Cooley: (Pg) 275; Janice Cornogg: (Pg) 289; Sarah A. Cornogg: (Pg) 289; Daniel Cosley: (Pg) 294; Frances Cosley:

(Pg) 294; Frances Cosley: (Pg) 294; James Cosley: (Pg) 294; Jane Cosley: (Pg) 294; Arelonia Cowles: (Pg) 281; Catharine Cowles: (Pg) 281; Charles Cowles: (Pg) 303; Clayton Cowles: (Pg) 303; George Cowles: (Pg) 303; Henry Cowles: (Pg) 281; Henry C. Cowles: (Pg) 281; Lauris Cowles: (Pg) 303; Martin Cowles: (Pg) 281; Mary Cowles: (Pg) 303; Sarah Cowles: (Pg) 281; Allen Cox: (Pg) 292; Lurena Cox: (Pg) 292; Sarah E. Cox: (Pg) 292; Ester Cummings: (Pg) 303; Israel R. Cummings: (Pg) 303; John Cummings: (Pg) 303; Edward Curry: (Pg) 295; George Curry: (Pg) 295; James Curry: (Pg) 295; Mary Curry: (Pg) 295; Nancy E. Curry: (Pg) 295; Sarah F. Curry: (Pg) 295; Alexander Cuvert: (Pg) 279; Daniel Cuvert: (Pg) 279; Emeline Cuvert: (Pg) 279; Henry Cuvert: (Pg) 279; James Cuvert: (Pg) 279; John W. Cuvert: (Pg) 279; Maria Cuvert: (Pg) 279; Mary A. Cuvert: (Pg) 279; Silas Cuvert: (Pg) 279; William Cuvert: (Pg) 279; : (Pg) ; Elise Daily: (Pg) 303; Favorita Daily: (Pg) 304; John Daily: (Pg) 303; John B. Dallaham: (Pg) 290; Hannah J. Daniel: (Pg) 294; James Daniel: (Pg) 294; Margaret Daniel: (Pg) 294; Mary E. Daniel: (Pg) 294; William Daniel: (Pg) 294; William A. Daniel: (Pg) 294; Andrew J. Davis: (Pg) 290; Isaack Davis: (Pg) 290; John R. Davis: (Pg) 290; Margaret Davis: (Pg) 290; William H. Davis: (Pg) 290; Gilpin Defriece: (Pg) 271; James Defriece: (Pg) 271; James Defriece: (Pg) 271; Philipp Defriece: (Pg) 271; Sarah Defriece: (Pg) 271; Frederick Denicker: (Pg) 303; Maria Denicker: (Pg) 303; James Deputty: (Pg) 280; James Deputty: (Pg) 280; Joseph Deputty: (Pg) 280; Mary A. Deputty: (Pg) 280; Margaret Dickman: (Pg) 270; Mary Dickman: (Pg) 270; Sarah E. Dickman: (Pg) 270; Thomas Dickman: (Pg) 270; Thomas J. Dickman: (Pg) 270; Samuel Doty: (Pg) 266; Milton Dougherty: (Pg) 302; Ada Doughty: (Pg) 302; George Doughty: (Pg) 302; Priphina Doughty: (Pg) 302; Hulda Draper: (Pg) 287; Ira Draper: (Pg) 288; Patience Draper: (Pg) 288; Sophrona Draper: (Pg) 288; Grimes Dryden: (Pg) 296; Hannah Dryden: (Pg) 296; Harrison Dryden: (Pg) 296; Mahala Dryden: (Pg) 296; Sarah E. Dryden: (Pg) 295; Thomas M. Dryden: (Pg) 296; Vincent Dryden: (Pg) 295; William Dryden: (Pg) 296; : (Pg) ; Irina Eckert: (Pg) 289; Charles English: (Pg) 292; Frances E. English: (Pg) 292; Merinda A. English: (Pg) 292; Rebecca J. English: (Pg) 292; Sarah A. English: (Pg) 292; Stephen English: (Pg) 292; : (Pg) ; Elizabeth Farmer: (Pg) 273; Jeremiah Farmer: (Pg) 273; Lucy A. Farmer: (Pg) 273; Nancy Farmer: (Pg) 273; Robert Farmer: (Pg) 273; Scynta Farmer: (Pg) 273; William Farmer: (Pg) 273; Adeline Floyd: (Pg) 281; Elizabeth Floyd: (Pg) 281; Thomas Floyd: (Pg) 281; Louisa Follet: (Pg) 303; Charity D. Forsyth: (Pg) 297; Mary E. Forsyth: (Pg) 297; Albert Fowler: (Pg) 280; Belinda Fowler: (Pg) 278; Belinda Fowler: (Pg) 278; Benjamin Fowler: (Pg) 278; Benjamin Fowler: (Pg)

278; Caleb Fowler: (Pg) 279; Carolina Fowler: (Pg) 280; Elizabeth Fowler: (Pg) 279; Elizabeth Fowler: (Pg) 278; Harvey Fowler: (Pg) 280; Hester Fowler: (Pg) 279; Hugh Fowler: (Pg) 279; Isaack Fowler: (Pg) 278; James Fowler: (Pg) 278; James Fowler: (Pg) 278; James W. Fowler: (Pg) 278; John Fowler: (Pg) 278; John Fowler: (Pg) 280; John J. Fowler: (Pg) 278; John J. Fowler: (Pg) 278; Johnas Fowler: (Pg) 279; Kisina Fowler: (Pg) 278; Luci Fowler: (Pg) 279; Lucinda Fowler: (Pg) 278; Lucinda Fowler: (Pg) 280; Mary Fowler: (Pg) 278; Mary A. Fowler: (Pg) 278; Mary A. Fowler: (Pg) 278; Mary M. Fowler: (Pg) 280; Mathilda Fowler: (Pg) 278; Melissa Fowler: (Pg) 279; Nelson Fowler: (Pg) 279; Samuel C. Fowler: (Pg) 278; Sarah A. Fowler: (Pg) 279; Thomas Fowler: (Pg) 279; Welcome Fowler: (Pg) 278; William Fowler: (Pg) 279; William Fowler: (Pg) 279; William H. Fowler: (Pg) 278; Elenore Francis: (Pg) 268; Elizabeth Francis: (Pg) 268; William Francis: (Pg) 268; Davidson Frazier: (Pg) 265; Nathan Frazier: (Pg) 265; Rebecca Frazier: (Pg) 265; William Frazier: (Pg) 265; William W. Frazier: (Pg) 265; Francis S. Fugitt: (Pg) 299; Sarah A. Fugitt: (Pg) 299; William Fugitt: (Pg) 299; Andreas Gameinaker: (Pg) 268; Barbara Gameinaker: (Pg) 268; Isaack Gibson: (Pg) 287; Isaack Gibson: (Pg) 287; J. Madison Gibson: (Pg) 287; Margaret Gibson: (Pg) 287; Martha Gibson: (Pg) 287; Mary Gibson: (Pg) 287; John Gillpys: (Pg) 270; Louisa A. Gillpys: (Pg) 270; Lucy Gillpys: (Pg) 270; Lucyda E. Gillpys: (Pg) 270; Thomas Gillpys: (Pg) 270; Litia A. Gilmore: (Pg) 300; Nancy Gilmore: (Pg) 300; Robert Gilmore: (Pg) 300; Sarah Gilmore: (Pg) 300; Ann Golden: (Pg) 276; John Golden: (Pg) 277; Maorghe Golden: (Pg) 277; Martha A. Golden: (Pg) 277; Millage Golden: (Pg) 276; Dicy Gray: (Pg) 283; Elise Gray: (Pg) 283; Isaack Gray: (Pg) 283; Jacob Gray: (Pg) 283; Sarah Gray: (Pg) 293; Augusta Grebe: (Pg) 282; Edward Grebe: (Pg) 282; Elise Grebe: (Pg) 282; Martin Grebe: (Pg) 282; Martin Grebe: (Pg) 281; Amelia A. Green: (Pg) 299; James Green: (Pg) 299; Manly Green: (Pg) 300; Martin Green: (Pg) 299; Nancy A. Green: (Pg) 299; Salomon Green: (Pg) 299; Sarah J. Green: (Pg) 299; William Green: (Pg) 299; Maronie Groves: (Pg) 304; Sarah Groves: (Pg) 304; Catharine Hackler: (Pg) 277; David Hackler: (Pg) 277; Elise Hackler: (Pg) 278; Hiram Hackler: (Pg) 278; James M. Hackler: (Pg) 277; James W. Hackler: (Pg) 277; John B. Hackler: (Pg) 277; Julia Hackler: (Pg) 278; Mathilda Hackler: (Pg) 277; Sarah Hackler: (Pg) 277; Talihta Hackler: (Pg) 278; William Hackler: (Pg) 277; James M. Hackley: (Pg) 273; John Hackley: (Pg) 273; Elenore Hale: (Pg) 268; Freeland Hale: (Pg) 300; Samuel Hale: (Pg) 268; Thomas Hale: (Pg) 268; Ann E. Hall: (Pg) 299; Henry B. Hall: (Pg) 281; Henry L. Hall: (Pg) 299; John R. Hall: (Pg) 299; Maria J. Hall: (Pg) 299; Mary A. Hall: (Pg) 299; Nancy C. Hall: (Pg)

299; Sarah J. Hall: (Pg) 281; William Hall: (Pg) 299; Annie Handley: (Pg) 267; Archibald Handley: (Pg) 267; Archibald Handley: (Pg) 267; Archibald Handley: (Pg) 267; Elizabeth Handley: (Pg) 266; Harvey Handley: (Pg) 267; James Handley: (Pg) 267; James Handley: (Pg) 267; John Handley: (Pg) 267; John Handley: (Pg) 267; John Handley: (Pg) 266; Joseph Handley: (Pg) 267; Mary E. Handley: (Pg) 267; Nathan Handley: (Pg) 267; William Handley: (Pg) 267; William Handley: (Pg) 267; Catharine Harmon: (Pg) 266; Elizabeth Harmon: (Pg) 267; Elizabeth Harmon: (Pg) 266; George Harmon: (Pg) 265; George Harmon: (Pg) 266; Henry Harmon: (Pg) 266; James Harmon: (Pg) 266; John Harmon: (Pg) 266; Lian (female) Harmon: (Pg) 265; Louisa Harmon: (Pg) 267; Margaret Harmon: (Pg) 266; Martha Harmon: (Pg) 266; Mary Harmon: (Pg) 266; Mary Harmon: (Pg) 266; Mathew Harmon: (Pg) 267; Nathan Harmon: (Pg) 267; Rebecca Harmon: (Pg) 266; Reuben Harmon: (Pg) 266; Stephen Harmon: (Pg) 265; Thomas Harmon: (Pg) 267; Bardemon Harrington: (Pg) 273; Daniel S. Harrington: (Pg) 273; Elisha Harrington: (Pg) 273; John Harrington: (Pg) 273; Mahala Harrington: (Pg) 273; Merida Harrington: (Pg) 273; William Harrington: (Pg) 273; Johanna Hartman: (Pg) 282; Mina Hartman: (Pg) 282; William Hartman: (Pg) 282; William Hartman: (Pg) 282; Benjamin Hawkins: (Pg) 272; Laticia Hawkins: (Pg) 272; Martha Hawkins: (Pg) 272; Pandesher Hawkins: (Pg) 272; Reuben Hawkins: (Pg) 272; William Hawkins: (Pg) 272; Angelina Hays: (Pg) 302; Carolina Hays: (Pg) 266; Elenore Hays: (Pg) 302; Elizabeth Hays: (Pg) 302; Fibia J. Hays: (Pg) 293; Hiram M. Hays: (Pg) 283; Isaack W. Hays: (Pg) 293; James Hays: (Pg) 302; James Hays: (Pg) 302; James C. Hays: (Pg) 283; Jane Hays: (Pg) 293; Jane Hays: (Pg) 293; John Hays: (Pg) 302; John Hays: (Pg) 266; John Hays: (Pg) 293; Judith Hays: (Pg) 302; Julia A. Hays: (Pg) 266; Louis Hays: (Pg) 266; Martin Hays: (Pg) 302; Mary E. Hays: (Pg) 302; Melinda Hays: (Pg) 293; Sarah A. Hays: (Pg) 293; William Hays: (Pg) 266; Elise Heck: (Pg) 280; Francis M. Heck: (Pg) 280; Martha Heck: (Pg) 280; Martin W. Heck: (Pg) 280; Nathan Heck: (Pg) 280; Samuel Heck: (Pg) 280; John Hildebrandt: (Pg) 272; Mary Hildebrandt: (Pg) 272; Charlotte Hill: (Pg) 266; Emeline Hill: (Pg) 266; George W. Hill: (Pg) 266; Henry Hill: (Pg) 266; Mary Hill: (Pg) 266; Nancy J. Hill: (Pg) 266; William M. Hill: (Pg) 266; Elizabeth Hilvey: (Pg) 265; Ellen Hilvey: (Pg) 265; Helvise Hilvey: (Pg) 265; Heridy Hilvey: (Pg) 265; Jane Hilvey: (Pg) 265; Lakahet Hilvey: (Pg) 265; Elizabeth Hoffman: (Pg) 298; Misouri J. Hoffman: (Pg) 298; Peter Hoffman: (Pg) 298; Richard Hoffman: (Pg) 298; Daniel Hogan: (Pg) 272; Louisa Hogan: (Pg) 272; Sarah A. Hogan: (Pg) 272; Frances Hollen: (Pg) 272; Isom Hollen: (Pg) 272; Mary W. Hollen: (Pg) 272; Nancy J. Hollen: (Pg)

272; Pacha A. Hollen: (Pg) 272; William Hollen: (Pg) 272; John Honk: (Pg) 270; Nancy J. Honk: (Pg) 270; William E. Honk: (Pg) 270; Catharine Hopkins: (Pg) 288; Elise A. Hopkins: (Pg) 288; Joseph A. Hopkins: (Pg) 288; Mary Hopkins: (Pg) 288; Minerva Hopkins: (Pg) 288; Nelson Hopkins: (Pg) 288; Nelson O. Hopkins: (Pg) 288; William Hopkins: (Pg) 288; Josephine Hoppel: (Pg) 288; Elizabeth Houck: (Pg) 270; Francis M. Houck: (Pg) 270; Jasper Houck: (Pg) 270; John Houck: (Pg) 270; Lucinda E. Houck: (Pg) 270; Martha C. Houck: (Pg) 270; Samuel H. Houck: (Pg) 270; William Houck: (Pg) 270; John A. Hoyt: (Pg) 265; Mary E. Hoyt: (Pg) 265; Mary L. Hoyt: (Pg) 265; Stephen F. Hoyt: (Pg) 265; William H. Hoyt: (Pg) 265; Abraham Hughs: (Pg) 302; Benjamin Hughs: (Pg) 288; Charlotte Hughs: (Pg) 288; Clarissa Hughs: (Pg) 288; David Hughs: (Pg) 288; Elizabeth Hughs: (Pg) 288; George C. Hughs: (Pg) 278; Harriet Hughs: (Pg) 302; Henry Hughs: (Pg) 302; Jackson Hughs: (Pg) 266; Jacob Hughs: (Pg) 278; John Hughs: (Pg) 278; John Hughs: (Pg) 302; Joseph Hughs: (Pg) 278; Julia A. Hughs: (Pg) 278; Melinda Hughs: (Pg) 278; Melinda Hughs: (Pg) 302; Sarah Hughs: (Pg) 278; Simon Hughs: (Pg) 288; Thomas Hughs: (Pg) 288; Thomas Hughs: (Pg) 288; William Hughs: (Pg) 278; Ann E. Hull: (Pg) 301; Edwald Hull: (Pg) 301; Elizabeth Hull: (Pg) 303; John Hull: (Pg) 301; John Hull: (Pg) 301; Justus Hull: (Pg) 301; Margaret Hull: (Pg) 302; William Hulliky: (Pg) 297; Elizabeth Hunter: (Pg) 276; Elizabeth Hunter: (Pg) 275; Isabella Hunter: (Pg) 276; James A. Hunter: (Pg) 276; John H. Hunter: (Pg) 275; Robert Hunter: (Pg) 276; Robert T. Hunter: (Pg) 275; William Hunter: (Pg) 276; William Hunter: (Pg) 275; Robert Hutchings: (Pg) 297; Alexander Jackson: (Pg) 276; Asa Jackson: (Pg) 276; Franklin Jackson: (Pg) 276; John Jackson: (Pg) 276; Mary A. Jackson: (Pg) 276; Daniel James: (Pg) 295; Martha James: (Pg) 295; Nancy J. James: (Pg) 295; William James: (Pg) 295; Elenore Jameson: (Pg) 276; James H. Jameson: (Pg) 276; Joeph Jameson: (Pg) 276; Maria Jameson: (Pg) 276; Maria A. Jameson: (Pg) 276; Melinda J. Jameson: (Pg) 276; Thomas Jameson: (Pg) 276; Alonzo F. Johnson: (Pg) 274; Christophe Johnson: (Pg) 279; James Johnson: (Pg) 279; James F. Johnson: (Pg) 278; James M. Johnson: (Pg) 274; John Johnson: (Pg) 279; John N. Johnson: (Pg) 274; John W. Johnson: (Pg) 274; Joseph Johnson: (Pg) 278; Joseph J. Johnson: (Pg) 274; Martha J. Johnson: (Pg) 279; Mary Johnson: (Pg) 279; Melvina Johnson: (Pg) 278; Nancy J. Johnson: (Pg) 274; Richard M. Johnson: (Pg) 274; Sarah Johnson: (Pg) 279; William Johnson: (Pg) 279; Alexander Jones: (Pg) 284; Candis E. Jones: (Pg) 284; Gracy W(f) Jones: (Pg) 284; Martha Jones: (Pg) 268; Marvel Jones: (Pg) 297; Ruly A. Jones: (Pg) 293; Sampson L. Jones: (Pg) 284; Sarah Jane Jones: (Pg) 293; Thomas

J. Jones: (Pg) 293; Wilson Jones: (Pg) 297; A. J. Keeny: (Pg) 293; Anna J. Keeny: (Pg) 293; Hannah Keeny: (Pg) 293; Alfred Keim: (Pg) 294; Carolina Keim: (Pg) 294; Margaret Keim: (Pg) 294; Elisa J. Kellison: (Pg) 266; Joshua Kellison: (Pg) 266; Mary S. Kellison: (Pg) 266; Sarah C. Kellison: (Pg) 266; Louis Kennedy: (Pg) 291; Louis M. Kennedy: (Pg) 291; Roda Kennedy: (Pg) 291; Clarissa Kenney: (Pg) 268; Eliza C. Kenney: (Pg) 268; Emmerine Kenney: (Pg) 268; George W. Kenney: (Pg) 268; James Kenney: (Pg) 268; James Kenney: (Pg) 268; Jane Kenney: (Pg) 268; Joseph C. Kenney: (Pg) 268; Margaret J. Kenney: (Pg) 268; Milbourn B. Kenney: (Pg) 268; Washington Kenney: (Pg) 268; William W. Kenney: (Pg) 268; Fanny R. Kindel: (Pg) 301; Mary A. Kindel: (Pg) 301; Rodgers D. Kindel: (Pg) 301; Kate A. Kinder: (Pg) 300; Sarah Kinder: (Pg) 303; Abraham King: (Pg) 277; Bennett King: (Pg) 276; Berryman King: (Pg) 277; Elijah King: (Pg) 276; Eliza J. King: (Pg) 267; Elizabeth King: (Pg) 267; Elizabeth King: (Pg) 277; Henderson King: (Pg) 277; Hester King: (Pg) 277; Isabella King: (Pg) 277; John King: (Pg) 276; Lurelda J. King: (Pg) 267; Mathilda King: (Pg) 276; Nancy A. King: (Pg) 276; Samuel King: (Pg) 277; Susan King: (Pg) 267; Thomas King: (Pg) 267; Thomas King: (Pg) 277; William King: (Pg) 267; William A. King: (Pg) 277; Christian Kish: (Pg) 303; Ellsaby Kish: (Pg) 303; Jacob H. Kish: (Pg) 303; John M. Kish: (Pg) 303; Louise Kish: (Pg) 303; Michael Kish: (Pg) 303; Peter H. Kish: (Pg) 303; Anton Labbring: (Pg) 286; Elise Labbring: (Pg) 286; D. Lamb: (Pg) 294; Elizabeth Lamb: (Pg) 294; James M. Lamb: (Pg) 294; John K. Lamb: (Pg) 294; Nancy M. Lamb: (Pg) 294; Penscia Lamb: (Pg) 294; Thomas J. Lamb: (Pg) 294; William Lamb: (Pg) 294; John B. Lamorie: (Pg) 291; Julia A. Lamorie: (Pg) 291; Julia A. Lamorie: (Pg) 291; Moses Lamorie: (Pg) 291; Elizabeth Lanhart: (Pg) 268; Edman Lathrop: (Pg) 275; Jacob Lathrop: (Pg) 275; James D. Lathrop: (Pg) 275; Jassom Lathrop: (Pg) 275; John Lathrop: (Pg) 275; Lucynda Lathrop: (Pg) 275; Mary M. Lathrop: (Pg) 275; Raul Lathrop: (Pg) 275; Welcome(m) Lathrop: (Pg) 275; Catharine Law: (Pg) 294; Hester Law: (Pg) 293; Isaack Law: (Pg) 293; Isaack J. Law: (Pg) 294; James H. Law: (Pg) 294; Jesse Law: (Pg) 294; Jesse Dan Law: (Pg) 294; John W. Law: (Pg) 294; Mary J. Law: (Pg) 293; William Law: (Pg) 294; Willis Law: (Pg) 293; Archilles Liebo: (Pg) 291; James Liebo: (Pg) 291; John Liebo: (Pg) 291; Josiah J. Liebo: (Pg) 291; Mary C. Liebo: (Pg) 291; Nancy Liebo: (Pg) 291; Nancy E. Liebo: (Pg) 291; Noah Liebo: (Pg) 291; Noah W. Liebo: (Pg) 291; Unicy Liebo: (Pg) 291; Unicy E. Liebo: (Pg) 291; Alfred Livingston: (Pg) 297; Elizabeth Livingston: (Pg) 297; George W. Livingston: (Pg) 297; Louisa J. Livingston: (Pg) 297; Mary L. Livingston: (Pg) 297; Valentine Livingston: (Pg) 297; Daniel

Lowber: (Pg) 303; Ellen Lowber: (Pg) 303; Ann Lowe: (Pg) 297; Fidelia Lowe: (Pg) 289; Frances Lowe: (Pg) 289; John N. Lowe: (Pg) 297; Mary A. Lowe: (Pg) 297; Mitchel Lowe: (Pg) 289; Nancy Lowe: (Pg) 296; Napoleon Lowe: (Pg) 296; Peter Lowe: (Pg) 289; William H. Lowe: (Pg) 297; WSarah Lowe: (Pg) 297; Charles Mann: (Pg) 269; Elizabeth Mann: (Pg) 271; Eppy Mann: (Pg) 271; Jackson Mann: (Pg) 271; James Mann: (Pg) 271; John W. Mann: (Pg) 269; Lucetta Mann: (Pg) 270; Martha Mann: (Pg) 269; Nancy Mann: (Pg) 271; Nancy J. Mann: (Pg) 270; Nancy J. Mann: (Pg) 269; Polina Mann: (Pg) 271; Ruthy Mann: (Pg) 270; Sarah L. Mann: (Pg) 269; Susan Mann: (Pg) 271; William Mann: (Pg) 270; William D. Mann: (Pg) 269; William P. Mann: (Pg) 270; Daniel Manville: (Pg) 304; Hannah Manville: (Pg) 304; James Manville: (Pg) 293; James Manville: (Pg) 304; John Manville: (Pg) 304; John Manville: (Pg) 304; John Manville: (Pg) 304; Mary Manville: (Pg) 304; Orion M. Manville: (Pg) 304; Abraham Martin: (Pg) 270; Ann M. Martin: (Pg) 285; David Martin: (Pg) 285; Hannah Martin: (Pg) 285; Isaack Martin: (Pg) 285; Margaret Martin: (Pg) 285; Martha Martin: (Pg) 270; McSamiel Martin: (Pg) 285; Thomas Martin: (Pg) 285; Thomas Martin: (Pg) 285; William Martin: (Pg) 270; Elise A. Mathew: (Pg) 291; Job Mathew: (Pg) 291; John H. Mathew: (Pg) 291; Charles Mc Donald: (Pg) 285; Charles Mc Donald: (Pg) 285; E. Jane Mc Donald: (Pg) 285; Elenore Mc Donald: (Pg) 285; James Mc Donald: (Pg) 285; Litia Mc Donald: (Pg) 285; William Mc Donald: (Pg) 285; Zadoc (f) Mc Donald: (Pg) 285; Thomas N. McBride: (Pg) 290; Abel McDaniel: (Pg) 273; Adolphus McDaniel: (Pg) 273; Dillen McDaniel: (Pg) 272; Ephriam McDaniel: (Pg) 273; Frances McDaniel: (Pg) 272; Harriet McDaniel: (Pg) 287; James McDaniel: (Pg) 272; Lucinda McDaniel: (Pg) 272; Martha McDaniel: (Pg) 272; Sarah A. McDaniel: (Pg) 273; Susan McDaniel: (Pg) 273; William McDaniel: (Pg) 287; William McDaniel: (Pg) 272; Catharine McElroy: (Pg) 301; James A. McElroy: (Pg) 301; Mary E. McElroy: (Pg) 301; Mathew McElroy: (Pg) 301; Rachael McElroy: (Pg) 301; Sarah J. McElroy: (Pg) 301; Thomas McFate: (Pg) 293; Ardina S. McKay: (Pg) 268; James A. McKay: (Pg) 268; James M. McKay: (Pg) 268; John D. McKay: (Pg) 268; Joseph C. McKay: (Pg) 268; Eben McKee: (Pg) 296; George W. McKee: (Pg) 296; James McKee: (Pg) 296; Rachael McKee: (Pg) 296; Sarah McKee: (Pg) 296; Warner McKee: (Pg) 296; Joseph Mennois: (Pg) 293; Aydlotte Millsapp: (Pg) 276; Catharine Millsapp: (Pg) 276; Elizabeth Millsapp: (Pg) 276; Pharis Millsapp: (Pg) 276; Pharis Millsapp: (Pg) 276; Russell Millsapp: (Pg) 276; William Millsapp: (Pg) 276; Caldwell Millsaps: (Pg) 277; Emilie J. Millsaps: (Pg) 277; John Mllsaps: (Pg) 277; Joseph Millsaps: (Pg) 277; Robeert 3 Millsaps: (Pg) 277; Samuel Millsaps:

(Pg) 277; Sarah Millsaps: (Pg) 277; Sarah A. Millsaps: (Pg) 277; William Millsaps: (Pg) 277; Ann Mullis: (Pg) 296; Elizabeth Mullis: (Pg) 295; Ennis Mullis: (Pg) 295; Frances Mullis: (Pg) 295; Grimes D. Mullis: (Pg) 295; Henry Mullis: (Pg) 296; James R. Mullis: (Pg) 295; Joel M. Mullis: (Pg) 295; John Mullis: (Pg) 295; John Mullis: (Pg) 295; Lankford Mullis: (Pg) 296; Levinia Mullis: (Pg) 295; Logan Mullis: (Pg) 295; Mahala Mullis: (Pg) 296; Margaret M. Mullis: (Pg) 295; Martha A. Mullis: (Pg) 295; Mary J. Mullis: (Pg) 295; Melvina Mullis: (Pg) 295; Polina Mullis: (Pg) 295; America Needles: (Pg) 275; Elisha S. Needles: (Pg) 275; Frank T. Needles: (Pg) 275; Henry W. Needles: (Pg) 275; John Needles: (Pg) 275; Permilia Needles: (Pg) 275; Sarah Needles: (Pg) 275; Sarah Needles: (Pg) 275; Thomas Neely: (Pg) 270; Afie (female) Neff: (Pg) 269; Catharine Neff: (Pg) 269; Daniel Neff: (Pg) 274; Daniel Neff: (Pg) 269; George Neff: (Pg) 269; Sarah A. Neff: (Pg) 269; Adisson Nobblet: (Pg) 287; Charles Nobblet: (Pg) 287; George Nobblet: (Pg) 287; Isaack Nobblet: (Pg) 287; James S. Nobblet: (Pg) 287; Lucinda Nobblet: (Pg) 287; Nancy Nobblet: (Pg) 287; Ann Nuckolls: (Pg) 303; Lucinda Nuckolls: (Pg) 303; S. F. Nuckolls: (Pg) 303; William E. Nuckolls: (Pg) 303; Samuel O'Neil: (Pg) 274; Mary Orrihood: (Pg) 302; Sarah J. Orrihood: (Pg) 302; Louis Ottman: (Pg) 282; Rosina Ottman: (Pg) 282; Elizabeth Parker: (Pg) 273; Calvin Parry: (Pg) 277; Sarah J. Parry: (Pg) 277; Sylvester Parry: (Pg) 277; William Pennel: (Pg) 300; Abigil Perman: (Pg) 292; Amanda J. Perman: (Pg) 292; Giles Perman: (Pg) 291; Giles Perman: (Pg) 292; Giles Perman: (Pg) 291; Harriet Perman: (Pg) 292; Hely Perman: (Pg) 292; James Perman: (Pg) 291; James Perman: (Pg) 292; Jane Perman: (Pg) 291; Mary A. Perman: (Pg) 291; Mary C. Perman: (Pg) 292; Mary M. Perman: (Pg) 291; Mathilda Perman: (Pg) 292; Misouri Perman: (Pg) 292; Nancy E. Perman: (Pg) 292; Phibia J. Perman: (Pg) 291; Wesley G. Perman: (Pg) 291; William Perman: (Pg) 291; William Perman: (Pg) 292; Davidson Plashers: (Pg) 266; Elizabeth Plashers: (Pg) 266; A. Alford Platte: (Pg) 286; Jane L. Porter: (Pg) 299; Rachael Porter: (Pg) 299; Silas M. Porter: (Pg) 299; William J. Porter: (Pg) 299; John Price: (Pg) 281; Mary L. Price: (Pg) 281; Rebecca Price: (Pg) 281; Robinson Price: (Pg) 281; Susan Price: (Pg) 281; William S. Price: (Pg) 281; Elijah Purdam: (Pg) 282; George F. Purdam: (Pg) 282; Jane Purdam: (Pg) 282; Jeremiah Purdam: (Pg) 282; John W. Purdam: (Pg) 282; Sarah C. Purdam: (Pg) 282; William T. Purdam: (Pg) 282; Charles H. Rafferty: (Pg) 300; Emelia B. Rafferty: (Pg) 300; Mary Rafferty: (Pg) 300; N. Jasper Rafferty: (Pg) 300; Riley A. Rafferty: (Pg) 300; Samuel B. Rafferty: (Pg) 300; Sarah E. Rafferty: (Pg) 300; Adam Rapp: (Pg) 279; Catharine Rapp: (Pg) 279; Charles Rapp: (Pg) 279; Gottlieb Rapp: (Pg) 279; John Rapp: (Pg)

279; Ann Rash: (Pg) 280; Julia Rash: (Pg) 280; Richard Rash: (Pg) 280; Thomas Rash: (Pg) 280; Elizabeth Reed: (Pg) 267; James Reed: (Pg) 267; John Reed: (Pg) 267; Henry C. Rhodes: (Pg) 274; James M. Rhodes: (Pg) 274; Mary R. Rhodes: (Pg) 274; Sarah Rhodes: (Pg) 274; Amen Robbinet: (Pg) 297; Eisa Robbinet: (Pg) 297; Esekiel Robbinet: (Pg) 297; George Robbinet: (Pg) 297; James Robbinet: (Pg) 297; Jeremiah Robbinet: (Pg) 297; Ludinda Robbinet: (Pg) 297; Nathaniel Robbinet: (Pg) 297; David Roberts: (Pg) 296; Elizabeth Roberts: (Pg) 296; Elizabeth Roberts: (Pg) 296; Elizabeth Roberts: (Pg) 277; Elizabeth Roberts: (Pg) 296; Henry B. Roberts: (Pg) 277; James Roberts: (Pg) 296; James Roberts: (Pg) 296; James Roberts: (Pg) 296; James K. P. Roberts: (Pg) 267; Jane Roberts: (Pg) 296; Jimany Roberts: (Pg) 296; John Roberts: (Pg) 295; Louisa Roberts: (Pg) 268; Mary Roberts: (Pg) 277; Nancy Roberts: (Pg) 267; Nancy A. Roberts: (Pg) 296; Nancy J. Roberts: (Pg) 268; Nancy R. Roberts: (Pg) 277; Newton Roberts: (Pg) 296; Rebecca Roberts: (Pg) 296; S. F. Roberts: (Pg) 296; Spencer Roberts: (Pg) 295; Strother Roberts: (Pg) 267; Susan Roberts: (Pg) 295; William Roberts: (Pg) 296; William Roberts: (Pg) 295; William Roberts: (Pg) 268; William S. Roberts: (Pg) 268; Alvis E. Robertson: (Pg) 267; Elizabeth Robertson: (Pg) 267; Janett Robertson: (Pg) 267; Leila A. Robertson: (Pg) 267; Samuel Robertson: (Pg) 267; Samuel W. Robertson: (Pg) 267; Sarah H. Robertson: (Pg) 267; William Robertson: (Pg) 267; Martha Rode: (Pg) 281; Martin Rode: (Pg) 281; Edna Roundtree: (Pg) 274; Elizabeth Roundtree: (Pg) 274; Frances W. Roundtree: (Pg) 274; Irene Roundtree: (Pg) 274; Lucinda Roundtree: (Pg) 274; Mary E. Roundtree: (Pg) 274; Robert Roundtree: (Pg) 274; Samuel Roundtree: (Pg) 274; Susan A. Roundtree: (Pg) 274; Albert G. Rupe: (Pg) 272; Bradford Rupe: (Pg) 298; James D. Rupe: (Pg) 272; John S. Rupe: (Pg) 272; Kisira Rupe: (Pg) 298; Mary J. Rupe: (Pg) 298; Mary M. Rupe: (Pg) 272; Richard Rupe: (Pg) 298; Richard W. Rupe: (Pg) 272; William W. Rupe: (Pg) 271; Caroline Russell: (Pg) 290; Elisa J. Russell: (Pg) 290; Francis M. Russell: (Pg) 290; Jane A. Russell: (Pg) 273; John Russell: (Pg) 290; Joseph H. Russell: (Pg) 273; Lilbourn H. Russell: (Pg) 273; Martha Russell: (Pg) 273; Patten Russell: (Pg) 273; R. D. Russell: (Pg) 290; Rachael Russell: (Pg) 290; Vincent Russell: (Pg) 273; : (Pg) ; Ann M. Sand: (Pg) 288; Joseph Sand: (Pg) 288; Henry Sanford: (Pg) 303; James Sanford: (Pg) 303; Mary Sanford: (Pg) 303; Nancy Sanford: (Pg) 303; Newill W. Sanford: (Pg) 303; William Sanford: (Pg) 303; E. D. Scammon: (Pg) 272; Elizabeth Scammon: (Pg) 273; Nancy Scammon: (Pg) 276; Samuel M. Scammon: (Pg) 276; William Scammon: (Pg) 273; Angelina Schield: (Pg) 289; David Schield: (Pg) 289; Nancy Schield: (Pg) 289; Charles Schmidt: (Pg) 269; Clarissa A.

Schmidt: (Pg) 281; Franciska Schmidt: (Pg) 269; Frederick Schmidt: (Pg) 281; G. A. M. Schmidt: (Pg) 282; George Schmidt: (Pg) 281; Herman Schmidt: (Pg) 269; John G. Schmidt: (Pg) 281; Theresia Schmidt: (Pg) 281; Frank Schnittger: (Pg) 269; Gehrt Schnittger: (Pg) 269; Lena Schnittger: (Pg) 269; Margaret Schnittger: (Pg) 269; Bertha Schubert: (Pg) 281; Cornelius Schubert: (Pg) 281; Emilie Schubert: (Pg) 281; Louise Schubert: (Pg) 281; Oswald Schubert: (Pg) 281; Frances J. Scott: (Pg) 296; Harrison R. Scott: (Pg) 296; Jane Scott: (Pg) 296; Jesse Scott: (Pg) 284; John H. Scott: (Pg) 284; John W. Scott: (Pg) 296; Josiah D. Scott: (Pg) 296; Louisa A. Scott: (Pg) 296; Mary A. Scott: (Pg) 284; Robert R. Scott: (Pg) 284; George W. Scymour: (Pg) 271; John U. Scymour: (Pg) 271; Leander Scymour: (Pg) 271; Louisa Scymour: (Pg) 271; Abigal Shaffer: (Pg) 301; Elizabeth Shaffer: (Pg) 303; Eve Shaffer: (Pg) 301; George H. Shaffer: (Pg) 301; George H. Shaffer: (Pg) 301; Gilliet Shaffer: (Pg) 301; Henry Shaffer: (Pg) 301; John J. Shaffer: (Pg) 301; Joseph R. Shaffer: (Pg) 301; Mary E. Shaffer: (Pg) 301; Nancy Shaffer: (Pg) 301; Nancy Shaffer: (Pg) 301; William H. Shaffer: (Pg) 301; William J. Shaffer: (Pg) 301; Isaack Shaw: (Pg) 265; Andrew Short: (Pg) 289; Frederick Short: (Pg) 290; James Short: (Pg) 290; Joshua Short: (Pg) 290; Orinda Short: (Pg) 290; Filinia Shrum: (Pg) 269; Henry R. Shrum: (Pg) 269; Lydia Shrum: (Pg) 269; Nancy E. Shrum: (Pg) 269; Sarah Shrum: (Pg) 269; Arnen Sickler: (Pg) 282; Elisa J. Sickler: (Pg) 282; Mathilda Sickler: (Pg) 282; William Sickler: (Pg) 282; Carolina Simpson: (Pg) 265; George W. Simpson: (Pg) 265; Jesse F. Simpson: (Pg) 265; John K. Simpson: (Pg) 265; Joshua Simpson: (Pg) 265; Nathan Simpson: (Pg) 265; Nathan T. Simpson: (Pg) 265; Francis Sipes: (Pg) 269; John Sipes: (Pg) 269; John Sipes: (Pg) 272; Nancy E. Sipes: (Pg) 269; Percy Sipes: (Pg) 269; Sarah Sipes: (Pg) 269; William Sipes: (Pg) 269; Alexander Skeen: (Pg) 298; Elizabeth Skeen: (Pg) 298; Kinion Skeen: (Pg) 298; Lucy J. Skeen: (Pg) 298; Margaret Skeen: (Pg) 298; Mary Skeen: (Pg) 298; Mary Skeen: (Pg) 298; Richard Skeen: (Pg) 298; Thom Skeen: (Pg) 298; Jacob Slausher: (Pg) 290; Charles V. Slinow: (Pg) 271; Oliver K. Slinow: (Pg) 271; Sarah E. Slinow: (Pg) 271; James A. Smelser: (Pg) 273; John Smelser: (Pg) 273; Margaret Smelser: (Pg) 273; Martha J. Smelser: (Pg) 273; Mary Smelser: (Pg) 273; Melinda H. Smelser: (Pg) 273; Nancy M. Smelser: (Pg) 273; Sarah E. Smelser: (Pg) 273; Martha Sparks: (Pg) 276; Mary Sparks: (Pg) 276; Oliver G. Sparks: (Pg) 276; Susan H. Sparks: (Pg) 276; William Sparks: (Pg) 276; Ann J. Spellerberg: (Pg) 303; John Spellerberg: (Pg) 303; Nancy J. Spellerberg: (Pg) 303; Altmond Squires: (Pg) 289; Albert M. Stafford: (Pg) 286; Ellen Stafford: (Pg) 286; John Stafford: (Pg) 286; John Stafford: (Pg) 286; Madison

Stafford: (Pg) 286; Mathilda Stafford: (Pg) 286; Newill Stafford: (Pg) 286; Precilla Stafford: (Pg) 286; William Stafford: (Pg) 286; Wilson Stafford: (Pg) 286; David G. Stanford: (Pg) 282; Hiram A. Stanford: (Pg) 282; Jeremiah Stanford: (Pg) 282; Sophia Stanford: (Pg) 282; William J. Stanford: (Pg) 282; Amos Starke: (Pg) 297; John Starke: (Pg) 297; Mary Starke: (Pg) 297; Ansel Steck: (Pg) 281; Antony Steck: (Pg) 281; George Steck: (Pg) 281; Margaret Steck: (Pg) 281; Maria Steck: (Pg) 281; Michael Steck: (Pg) 281; Arlina R. Stevens: (Pg) 289; Casell Stevens: (Pg) 289; Charles R. Stevens: (Pg) 289; Franklin Stevens: (Pg) 289; Hulda AQ Stevens: (Pg) 289; Jane Stevens: (Pg) 289; William G. Stevens: (Pg) 289; Charles Stintzen: (Pg) 285; Elizabeth Stintzen: (Pg) 285; John Stintzen: (Pg) 285; Mary J. Stintzen: (Pg) 285; Narcissa Stintzen: (Pg) 285; Samuel Stintzen: (Pg) 285; Sarah A. Stintzen: (Pg) 285; Sarah Jane Stintzen: (Pg) 285; Augustin Stone: (Pg) 274; Catharine Stone: (Pg) 282; Hesekia Stone: (Pg) 282; Isabella Stone: (Pg) 282; Jeremiah Stone: (Pg) 282; Louisa Stone: (Pg) 282; Catharine Stoner: (Pg) 285; Crosby Stoner: (Pg) 285; Elenore Stoner: (Pg) 285; John Stoner: (Pg) 285; Mary Stuart: (Pg) 270; Mary Stuart: (Pg) 270; Melinda Stuart: (Pg) 270; Nancy Stuart: (Pg) 270; Sarah Jane Stuart: (Pg) 270; William Stuart: (Pg) 270; Drucilla Taylor: (Pg) 272; Elizabeth Taylor: (Pg) 267; Elves Taylor: (Pg) 272; Misouri E. Taylor: (Pg) 272; Terry Taylor: (Pg) 267; James L. Teague: (Pg) 294; Nancy Teague: (Pg) 294; William Teague: (Pg) 294; William H. Teague: (Pg) 294; Acinth Temple: (Pg) 290; George B. Temple: (Pg) 290; George S. Temple: (Pg) 290; Margaret Temple: (Pg) 290; Paris C. Temple: (Pg) 290; Thomas H. Temple: (Pg) 290; James M. Templeton: (Pg) 276; Martha A. Templeton: (Pg) 276; Mary S. Templeton: (Pg) 276; Sarah E. Templeton: (Pg) 276; Andrew Thompson: (Pg) 275; Berryman Thompson: (Pg) 300; David L. Thompson: (Pg) 274; Elenore Thompson: (Pg) 274; George Thompson: (Pg) 300; George C. Thompson: (Pg) 274; J. D. N. Thompson: (Pg) 300; Johanna V. Thompson: (Pg) 275; John A. Thompson: (Pg) 279; L. James Thompson: (Pg) 274; Martha Thompson: (Pg) 300; Martha J. Thompson: (Pg) 279; Mary Thompson: (Pg) 300; Mary E. Thompson: (Pg) 274; Miranda G. Thompson: (Pg) 279; Rachael Thompson: (Pg) 300; Robert Thompson: (Pg) 300; Roda Thompson: (Pg) 279; Sarah E. Thompson: (Pg) 279; Thomas B. Thompson: (Pg) 279; Waughlupy Thompson: (Pg) 300; Winford E. Thompson: (Pg) 279; Ansel Tillman: (Pg) 273; Helvina Tillman: (Pg) 273; James A. Tillman: (Pg) 273; Thomas Tillman: (Pg) 273; Elizabeth Townsend: (Pg) 283; Emeline Townsend: (Pg) 283; John Townsend: (Pg) 284; John M. Townsend: (Pg) 283; Josephus Townsend: (Pg) 284; Louisa Townsend: (Pg) 284; Polina Townsend:

(Pg) 284; Robert Townsend: (Pg) 283; Sarah Townsend: (Pg) 283; William Townsend: (Pg) 283; William Townsend: (Pg) 284; Frederica Traub: (Pg) 280; Frederick Taub: (Pg) 80; Gottlieb Traub: (Pg) 280; Wilhelm Traub: (Pg) 280; Elizabeth Turner: (Pg) 297; John Turner: (Pg) 297; Martha A. Turner: (Pg) 297; Mary J. Turner: (Pg) 297; Thomas Turner: (Pg) 297; Anson Vanluven: (Pg) 299; Benjamin Vanluven: (Pg) 287; Benjamin Vanluven: (Pg) 299; Catharine Vanluven: (Pg) 299; David Vanluven: (Pg) 287; David P. Vanluven: (Pg) 287; Delina Vanluven: (Pg) 287; Ellen Vanluven: (Pg) 286; Fanny Vanluven: (Pg) 287; Frederick Vanluven: (Pg) 288; Frederick Vanluven: (Pg) 287; George Vanluven: (Pg) 287; Hannah Vanluven: (Pg) 288; John Vanluven: (Pg) 299; Levcrett Vanluven: (Pg) 286; Louis Vanluven: (Pg) 299; Lucinda Vanluven: (Pg) 286; Lydia Vanluven: (Pg) 288; Lydia Vanluven: (Pg) 287; Mary Vanluven: (Pg) 286; Mathilda N. Vanluven: (Pg) 286; Melinda Vanluven: (Pg) 287; Orsen Vanluven: (Pg) 287; Precinda Vanluven: (Pg) 287; Ransom Vanluven: (Pg) 286; Rida Vanluven: (Pg) 299; Sabra Vanluven: (Pg) 299; Samitha Vanluven: (Pg) 299; Sarah E. Vanluven: (Pg) 286; Seth Vanluven: (Pg) 286; Sophia P. Vanluven: (Pg) 287; Sydney Vanluven: (Pg) 288; William Vanluven: (Pg) 287; Abraham Vanmeter: (Pg) 288; Olive A. Vanmeter: (Pg) 288; Burril Vaughn: (Pg) 283; Edward Vaughn: (Pg) 283; Merilda Vaughn: (Pg) 283; Wesley Vaughn: (Pg) 283; Andrew J. Waits: (Pg) 298; Catharine Waits: (Pg) 269; Daniel D. Waits: (Pg) 298; Doucilla E. Waits: (Pg) 269; Elisa A. Waits: (Pg) 271; Elizabeth Waits: (Pg) 298; Elizabeth Waits: (Pg) 298; Emeline Waits: (Pg) 298; Hilda Waits: (Pg) 297; James Waits: (Pg) 297; Joseph Waits: (Pg) 298; Margaret Waits: (Pg) 298; Mary Waits: (Pg) 269; Mary A. Waits: (Pg) 269; Melinda E. Waits: (Pg) 269; Misouri Waits: (Pg) 298; Reson Waits: (Pg) 272; Richard Waits: (Pg) 270; Richard Waits: (Pg) 269; Sarah Waits: (Pg) 272; Sarah C. Waits: (Pg) 298; Susan Waits: (Pg) 298; Susan Waits: (Pg) 272; William F. Waits: (Pg) 272; Elenore Walden: (Pg) 293; Hannah Walden: (Pg) 293; Robert Walden: (Pg) 293; Ann M. Walker: (Pg) 269; Frank Walker: (Pg) 269; Helena C. Walker: (Pg) 269; Jacob Walker: (Pg) 269; Augusta Wallhamm: (Pg) 289; Bianca Wallhamm: (Pg) 289; Charles Wallhamm: (Pg) 289; Charles C. Wallhamm: (Pg) 289; Frederick Wallhamm: (Pg) 289; Gustav Wallhamm: (Pg) 289; Mary Wallhamm: (Pg) 289; Mathilda Wallhamm: (Pg) 289; Mathilda Wallhamm: (Pg) 289; Elise J. Wallis: (Pg) 288; Elizabeth Wallis: (Pg) 288; Isaack F. Wallis: (Pg) 288; John Wallis: (Pg) 288; Julia Wallis: (Pg) 288; Mary J. Wallis: (Pg) 288; Warren Wallis: (Pg) 288; D. Ward: (Pg) 268; Archilles Ware: (Pg) 283; Christian Ware: (Pg) 283; Elias Ware: (Pg) 282; Elizabeth Ware: (Pg) 282; James Ware: (Pg) 283; James C.

Ware: (Pg) 282; John Ware: (Pg) 282; Lucy J. Ware: (Pg) 282; Lucy M. Ware: (Pg) 283; Maria F. Ware: (Pg) 283; Mary Ware: (Pg) 283; Mary Ware: (Pg) 282; Mary A. Ware: (Pg) 283; Mary C. Ware: (Pg) 282; Mary F. Ware: (Pg) 282; Montgomery Ware: (Pg) 283; Nancy Ware: (Pg) 283; Robert Ware: (Pg) 282; Thomas H. B. Ware: (Pg) 283; William Ware: (Pg) 283; Frederick Waymeir: (Pg) 290; Charles Wells: (Pg) 289; Elizabeth Wells: (Pg) 289; Mary F. Wells: (Pg) 289; William Wells: (Pg) 289; William H. Wells: (Pg) 289; Anges Welsh: (Pg) 271; James Welsh: (Pg) 284; John W. Welsh: (Pg) 284; Louisa Welsh: (Pg) 284; Mary A. Welsh: (Pg) 284; Nicolaus Welsh: (Pg) 271; Philipp Welsh: (Pg) 271; Maria West: (Pg) 302; Charles White: (Pg) 284; Ellen White: (Pg) 285; Finsey White: (Pg) 272; Hannah White: (Pg) 284; Hesekiah White: (Pg) 283; Jacob White: (Pg) 284; James White: (Pg) 284; Josiah B. White: (Pg) 285; Lorence White: (Pg) 284; Lorence White: (Pg) 284; Nancy White: (Pg) 284; Newton White: (Pg) 280; Rosewell White: (Pg) 272; Sarah White: (Pg) 285; Sarah White: (Pg) 284; Sarah White: (Pg) 283; Eugenius Wilhelm: (Pg) 301; John G. Wilhelm: (Pg) 302; Martha Wilhelm: (Pg) 301; Mary A. Wilhelm: (Pg) 302; Carolina Williams: (Pg) 270; Harvey Williams: (Pg) 270; James H. Williams: (Pg) 270; Louis Williams: (Pg) 290; Louisa N. Williams: (Pg) 270; Lucinda Williams: (Pg) 290; Margaret M. Williams: (Pg) 270; Rebecca J. Williams: (Pg) 290; William H. Williams: (Pg) 290; Benjamin Willis: (Pg) 289; Hannah Willis: (Pg) 289; Hiram Willis: (Pg) 289; John Willis: (Pg) 289; Mary M. Willis: (Pg) 289; Alfred Wilson: (Pg) 300; Ann Wilson: (Pg) 293; Caroline Wilson: (Pg) 293; Elilie J. Wilson: (Pg) 284; Elizabeth Wilson: (Pg) 284; Francis M. Wilson: (Pg) 299; Harriet Wilson: (Pg) 293; Harrison Wilson: (Pg) 293; Isaack Wilson: (Pg) 300; Isaack Wilson: (Pg) 293; Isaack L. Wilson: (Pg) 284; James C. Wilson: (Pg) 284; Jane Wilson: (Pg) 300; John J. Wilson: (Pg) 293; Mary A. Wilson: (Pg) 284; Nancy Wilson: (Pg) 293; Nancy Wilson: (Pg) 284; Nicholas C. Wilson: (Pg) 292; Samuel Wilson: (Pg) 299; Susan Wilson: (Pg) 293; Barbara Wilyard: (Pg) 302; Marion Wilyard: (Pg) 302; Samuel Wilyard: (Pg) 302; John Woerlend: (Pg) 291; Mathilda Woerlend: (Pg) 291; Abner Wolff: (Pg) 286; Amanda Wolff: (Pg) 300; Ann C. Wolff: (Pg) 286; Elizabeth Wolff: (Pg) 286; Emilie Wolff: (Pg) 286; George Wolff: (Pg) 286; George Wolff: (Pg) 286; George Wolff: (Pg) 286; George J. Wolff: (Pg) 286; Johann Wolff: (Pg) 286; Mary J. Wolff: (Pg) 287; Rebecca Wolff: (Pg) 286; Abigil Wolsey: (Pg) 293; Abigil Wolsey: (Pg) 291; Elizabeth Wolsey: (Pg) 293; Gibbert Wolsey: (Pg) 291; Grenville Wolsey: (Pg) 291; Lafayette Wolsey: (Pg) 291; Loveann Wolsey: (Pg) 293; Mary C. Wolsey: (Pg) 291; Rachael Wolsey: (Pg) 293; Susan Wolsey: (Pg) 291; William Wolsey: (Pg) 293; David

Worcester: (Pg) 269; Alexander Works: (Pg) 291; Alexander Works: (Pg) 292; Amanda Works: (Pg) 292; Andrew J. Works: (Pg) 292; Beatruly Works: (Pg) 292; Elizabeth Works: (Pg) 292; Elizabeth Works: (Pg) 291; Flemming Works: (Pg) 292; Frances Works: (Pg) 292; Henderson Works: (Pg) 292; James Works: (Pg) 291; Lucy Works: (Pg) 291; Mary Works: (Pg) 292; Melinda Works: (Pg) 292; Nancy A. Works: (Pg) 291; Rachael Works: (Pg) 292; Robert Works: (Pg) 292; Sarah A. Works: (Pg) 292; Amos Worl: (Pg) 284; Edward Worl: (Pg) 283; Ellen J. Worl: (Pg) 284; Fibia Worl: (Pg) 284; James Worl: (Pg) 284; Joseph Worl: (Pg) 283; Mary Worl: (Pg) 283; Napoleon B. Worl: (Pg) 284; Robert Worl: (Pg) 284; Amos Wright: (Pg) 275; Caleb Wright: (Pg) 275; Fesras Wright: (Pg) 275; Isom Wright: (Pg) 275; J. Wright: (Pg) 280; John Wright: (Pg) 275; Martha Wright: (Pg) 275; Mary J. Wright: (Pg) 275; Scynta Wright: (Pg) 275; Silas Wright: (Pg) 275; Christophe Young: (Pg) 271; Elisa K. Young: (Pg) 271; James W. Young: (Pg) 271; John Henry Young: (Pg) 271; Joseph Young: (Pg) 271; Marinda Young: (Pg) 271; Martha A. Young: (Pg) 271; Rufus Young: (Pg) 271; Sarah Jane Young: (Pg) 271;

Texas County, Missouri, Rocky Branch Normal Music School, 1914.
Ruby Yate, Virdie Farris, Grace Pipkin, Hazel Deck, Bernice Farris, Antha Farris, Florence Parker, Prof. J. W. Dennis, Herbert Flowers, Emery Elliott, Viona Elliott, Mrs. I. W. Durr, Joph. O. Shilling, Edith Miller, Lee Jones, John L. Parker, Marshal Hays, Jime Farris, Amelia Elliott, Frank Stewart, Argie Dean, Cecil Farris, Rosce Goode, Gus Pikin, Tobe Farris, Joel Caylor, Ada Powers, Thelma Parker, Bishop Vines, Maye Flowers, Cook Vevils, Daisy Hogan, Jime Wade, Paul Pipkin, Eugie Dean, Frank Hogan, Nora Powers, Hiram Bishop, Lucy Shilling, Otto Flowers, Zulla Leaverton, Alfred Bishop, Dulcie Flowers, Jack Simmons, Martha Parker, Dorothy Dean, John Craford, Mamie Hogan.

Grundy County, Missouri, Members of the Trenton Lodge of Free Masonry, 1865.
James Austin, Wm. Blew, Jesse Benson, T. B. Clanton, James Cooper, R. A. Collier, Samuel Colley, Elihu Colley, Joseph Davis, James S. Estes, John Fields, John C. Griffin, James C. Gibbs, A. M. Haney, John J. Hobbs, Wm. C. Harvey, G. W. Hendrix, W. W. Hubbell, James Lucas, Wm. H. McGrath, Daniel Markert, Byron Markert, William Pond, Wm. Renfro, John Syres, James St. Clair, Benj. H. Smith, Thos. O. Stepp, James Terril, Thomas Torpey, Rev. David T.

Wright, W. W. Watson, W. T. Wisdom, William Walker, George H. Hubbell, Daniel Rice, B. F. Harding, E. P. Harding, W. P. Sherman, W. W. Brooks, S. K. Witten, J. E. Harris.

Atchison County, Missouri, Democratic Committee Members, 1933.

Name	Townshp/Office	Address
Henry Stapel	Chairman	Rock Port
Mrs. James Thomson	Vice Chairman	Fairfax
Mrs. Minnie Templeton	Secretary	Rock Port
John T. Wells	Treasurer	Rock Port
John Rosenbohm	Benton	Langdon
Mrs. Anna Cooper	Benton	Langdon
Harmon Harmes	Buchanan	Hamburg
Mrs. Cable Brown	Buchanan	Hamburg
Ben Portis	Clark	Fairfax
Mrs. Anna Sheiman	Clark	Fairfax
Mrs. Minnie Templeton	Clay	Rock Port
Harry Clement	Colfax	Tarkio
Mrs. Harry Clement	Colfax	Tarkio
A. R. Carter	Dale	Fairfax
Mrs. James Thomson	Dale	Fairfax
Fred Denkman	Lincoln	Westboro
Blanche E. Tucker	Lincoln	Westboro
J. M. Crockett	Nishnabotna	Watson
Mrs. Gerturde Maupin	Nishnabotna	Watson
Dr. Ray Matkins	Polk	Rock Port
Mrs. Frances Boettner	Polk	Rock Port
W. R. Littell	Tarkio	Tarkio
Mrs. Mollie Curfman	Tarkio	Tarkio
James E. Stevens	Templeton	Phelps City
Mrs. Thelma Harmes	Templeton	Phelps City

Texas County, Missouri, Postmasters of Dykes.

Name	Date
Henry Loorsham	Oct. 26, 1882
David Sebuen	Mar. 30, 1886
John Bauch	Jan. 5, 1889
King Lighfoot	Jan. 15, 1891
Wiley Burch	Apr. 17, 1891
King Lighfoot	Oct. 18, 1892
Melvin Daugherty	May 29, 1900
James Stottlemyre	Jan. 10, 1903
John R. Brooks	Apr. 3, 1905

Name	Date
Joye E. Casebeer	Jul. 16, 1909
Charles L. Hutcheson	Jun. 9, 1914
Vergil Rust	Feb. 21, 1916
Willis E. Smith	Aug. 8, 1918

Missourians on the Pueblo County, Colorado, 1870 Mortality Schedule
Anderson, J. W. : (A) 48Y, (SEX) Male, (D) Aug., (BP) Mo, (CMTS) Typhoid Fever.

Caldwell County, Missouri, Person Listed on the 1897 Atlas. (The names are listed according to the number of times they appear on the Atlas. One individual may have owned several plots of land).

Mary Abbott, Chas. Achenbach, Chas. Ackenbach, G. W. Adair, Agnes Adams, Andrew Adams, Andrew Adams, Andrew Adams, Andrew Adams, C. Adams, G. B. Adams, J. Adams, Mrs. P. Adams, C. C. Alden, C. C. Alden M. G. Alden, Mrs. H. Alden, G. W. Est. Aleson, A. Alexander, A. Alexander, A. Alexander, E. E. Alexander, Jacob Allee, H. W. Allen, H. W. Allen, M. Allen, Marietta Allen, T. P. Allen, J. F. Anderson, John Anderson, John Anderson, Dr. Aplin, W. H. Aplin, J. H. Appleman, G. W. Arey, G. W. Arey, Geo. Arey, Geo. Armstrong, C. Arnold, Clinton Arnold, D. Arnold, Daniel Arnold, Mary Arnold, Mary B. Arnold, O. S. Arnold, O. S. Arnold, P. C. Arnold, P. S. Arnold, A. M. Arnote, J. M. Arnote, J. M. Arnote, W. H. Arnote, W. H. Arnote, W. M. Arnote, W. M. Arnote, Wm. Arnote, Wm. Arnote, Wm. Aster, Chas. Atkinson, E. T. Atkinson, Geo. Atkinson, J. Aubuster, G. L. Austill, Chas. Austin, Mrs. O. Austin, Mrs. I. Austin, Oliver Austin, Oliver Austin, Wm. Austin, Eli Axon, Eli Axon, Henry Axon, Eli Axton, Henry Axton, Mrs. H. D. Ayres, S. C. Bailey, Annie Baker, Annie Baker, C. Baker, E. J. Baker, J. C. Baker, J. C. Baker, J. J. Baker, J. M. Baker, J. M. Baker, J. W. Baker, John Baker, John Baker, O. P. Baker, R. M. Baker, J. C. Baldwin, J. C. Baldwin, W. M. Baldwin, W. W. Baldwin, Daniel Bales, J. C. Bales, G. W. Balkey, G. W. Balkey, J. T. Ball, J. F. Ballinger, J. D. Bancroft, L. D. Bancroft, L. D. Bancroft,W. A. Barcus, Cyrus Barlow, E. L. Barrett, Thos. Barron, Bros. Bartlett John Basseman, S. M. Bassett, G. W. Bateman, G. W. Bateman, G. W. Bateman, G. W. Bateman, Sarah Batemen, H. T. Bathgate, H. T. Bathgate, Thos Bathgate, Thos. Bathgate, J. E. Batson, T. J. Battle, T. J. Battle, Battlefield, Miles Bays, C. T. Beabout, T. C. Beabout, Thos. Beal, A. Bebee, H. C. Bebemyer, H. Bebermeir, B. F. Beckett, B. J. Beckett, Wm. Beckett, H. Belden, Henry Belden, J. D. Bell, N. B. Bell, N. B. Bell, Nelson, Sr. Bell, Saml. Bell, L. Belvins, G. W. Bender, J. P. Benjamin,

David Bennett, H. Bennett, J. Bennett, Thomas Bennett, W. N. Bennett, W. N. Bennett, John Benney, John Bethel, John Bethel, A. A. Bird, L. P. Bisell, A. W. Bishop, C. E. Bishop, J. S. Bishop, J. V. Bishop, T. Blackable, W. B. Blackston, J. C. Blades, W. F. Blair, W. F. Blair, W. J. Blair, A. Blandry, M. A. Blankenship, H. C. Blevins, H. C. Blevins, J. E. Blosseman, R. H. Bogan, T. S. Bona, E. S. Bonar, Chas. Booker, H. Borof, C. H. Boroff, C. H. Boroff, Henry Boroff, John Boseman, John Boseman, G. B. Bothwell, G. B. Bothwell, G. B. Bothwell, G. B. Bothwell, G. B. Bothwell, G. B. Bothwell, J. B. Bothwell, M. Bottom, M. Bottom, M. Bottom, M. Bottom, J. J. Bouce, A. E. Boulton, A. E. Boulton, Ann E. Boulton, H. R. Boulton, E. Boutwell, E. E. Boutwell, R. W. Boutwell, John Bowen, S. L. Bowen, Saml. Bowen, G. D. Bowers, J. F. Bowers, John Bowers, John Bowers, Sarah Bowers, W. E. Bowers, W. E. Bowers, C. L. Bowin, V. Bowman, G. J. Boyd, G. J. Boyd, James Boyd, John Boyd, John Boyd, L. B. Boyd, L. P. Boyle, L. P. Boyle, Mary E. Boyle, C. C. Boyles, F. E. Bradley, F. I. Bradley, T. J. Bradley, W. Bradley, M. V. Bray, Frizeil Braymer D. Braymer, Daniel Braymer, Daniel Braymer, Daniel Braymer, Daniel Braymer, Geo. Braymer, Eliza Brelsford, H. J. Brelsford, H. M. Brelsford, J. G. Brelsford, J. W. Brelsford, M. Brelsford, W. Brennaman, A. A. Brenneman, Susan Brenneman, Susan Brenneman, Henry Brewer, Mary E. Brewer, S. B. Brewer, Wm. Brice, H. Bridgewater, Hal Bridgwater, Est. of Brooing, Edward's Est., ??? Brooing, Edward Martin Brooks, Sam Brooks, J. M. Brookshire, J. R. Brookshire, Jerry Brosnihan, Brown, A. J. Brown, B. F. Brown, B. F. Brown, B. F. Brown, B. F. Brown, Bros. Brown, C. P. Brown, Dan Brown, Dan Brown, E. Brown, Geo. Brown, Geo. Brown, H. Brown, H. H. Brown, H. S. Brown, J. Brown, J. W. Brown, L. W. Brown, Margaret C. Brown, Margaret C. Brown, Margaret C. Brown, Mar-garet C. Brown, Mary Brown, Mary Brown, Mary Brown, P. Brown, R. G. Brown, Tinsley Brown, W. M. Brown, Wm. Brown, Wm. Brown, Brubaker, J. Brubaker, Jane Brumback, A. Brunk, A. Brunk, A. P. Brunk, Geo. Bryant, Geo. Bryant, Henry Bryant, Henry Bryant, James Bryant, T. Bryant, J. Buck, J. H. Buck, Jacob Buck, Jacob Buck, Jacob Burbaker, I. Burbauk, E. Burdett, F. M. Burdick, F. M. Burdick, F. M. Burdick F. M. Burdick, M. Burdick, P. E. Burdick, Frank Burdish, P. J. Burger, P. J. Burger, Julia Burke, & Kendell Burkett, J. E. Burkett, J. P. Burkett, J. P. Burkett, S. Burkett, Timothy Burkett, Wm. Burkett, Chas. Burnett, W. T. Burnett, J. C. Burns, Lewis Burns, T. Burns, J. T. Burris, H. E. Burrows, Lettie Bush, Let-tie Bush, M. Butler, W. Butterfield, T. J. Butts, W. M. Butts, Wm. Butts, A. S. C. , J. Cain, J. Cain, James Cain, Washington Cain, Oscar Calvin, John Campbell, Geo. Campt, F.

Carlile, William Carlisle, W. Carlton, Mary A. Carman, N. J.
Carman, Mary A. Caroll, A. Carr, A. Carr, G. G. Carr, Henry
Carroll, Henry Carroll, J. N. Carter, Jasper Carter, Jasper Carter, W. H.
B. Carter, Wm. B. Carter, W. M. Sr. Cartton, D. W. Caselman,
John Casey, John Casey and George Cash, George Cash, P. S. Cash,
R. S. Cash, R. S. Cash, D. D. Casto, D. D. Casto, D. D. Casto, D. D.
Casto, Eula Cates, P. H. Cates Estate, P. H. Cates Estate, S. H. Cates,
William Cates, W. F. Catron, Wm. Catron, F. Cawthorn Estate,
Cawthron, F. C. Cawthron, R. A. Cenoweith, R. A. Cenoweith, Jeff
Chadwick, John Chaldecut, J. W. Chambers, J. N. Chapman, J. N.
Chapman, J. N. Chapman, J. R. Cheshier, J. R. Cheshier, J. D.
Chivens, J. D. Chivens, B. P. Christianson, M. Christianson, C.
Chubbuck, Estate of Clampit, Estate of Clampitt, Mrs. N. C.
Clampitt, William Clampitt, C. N. Clark, Colby Clark, D. C. Clark,
E. M. Clark, Frank Clark, H. P. Clark, J. Clark, J. C. F. Clark, J. E.
Clark, J. P. Clark, J. P. Clark, J. W. Clark, John M. Clark, John H.
Clark, M. L. Clark, M. L. Clark, J. G. Clayton, J. G. Clayton, J. G.
Clayton, Harris Clelland, Jacob Clem, H. L. Clevenger, H. L.
Clevenger, H. L. Clevenger, H. L. Clevenger, J. M. Clevenger, M. A.
Clevenger, Mary E. Clevenger, W. W. Clevenger, G. W. Clifton, A.
Cline, Andy Cline, C. W. Cline, S. B. Cline, S. B. Cline, Mrs. J. E.
Clough, Mrs. J. E. Clough, Mrs. J. E. Clough, D. W. Coffman, O.
W. Coffman, Z. M. Coffman, A. Coil, A. Coit, Horace Coit, W. C.
Cole, W. M. Cole, G. W. Coleman, Geo. Coleman, J. P. Coleman,
Colman, H. Colvin, H. Colvin, Jas. Colvin Estate, Jno. Colvin Estate,
W. G. Colvin, Seth Combs, C. A. Conner, C. D. Conner, D. N.
Conner, John Conner, S. Conner, W. L. Conner, M. Conners, H. D.
Conrod, J. W. Constant, J. C. Cook, John Cook, Susan H. Cook, D. L.
Cooper, J. S. Cooper, T. W. Cooper, W. F. Cooper, O. C. Cope, O. C.
Cope, Eliz. Corbet, Eliz. Corbet, James Corbet, James Corbett, Eliza
Corbitt, Addie B. Cornish, Addie Cornish, J. Correll, W. Coulson,
W. Cowen, James Cowgill, James Cowgill, James Cowgill, Jesse
Cowgill, Jessie Cowgill, A. A. Cowley, Cox, B. F. Cox, Eliza Cox,
Enoch Cox, Enoch Cox, H. L. Cox, J. D. Cox's Estate, J. D. Cox's
Estate, J. D. Cox's Estate, J. D. Cox, Jr., J. D. Cox, Jr. , J. F. Cox, J.
F. Cox, J. P. Cox, J. S. Cox, J. S. Cox, J. S. Cox, Jerry Cox, Jerry
Cox, John Cox, John, Jr., John Cox, L. P. Cox, L. P. Cox,
Nathan Cox, Nathan Cox, Prof. Cox, S. D. Cox, S. D. Cox, S. E.
Cox, T. Cox, E. E. Cozad, W. Craig, William Craig, W. H. Cramblit,
David Cramer, A. B. Crandal, C. S. & Crane, H. M. Crane, H. M.
Crane, S. & Crane, A. S. Cravens, C. J. Cravens, Chas. Cravens, T.
Cravens, O. L. Crawford, W. H. Crawford, W. H. Crawford, W. H.

Crawford, W. H. Crawford, W. H. Crawford, W. H. Crawford, D. Creswell, D. Creswell, A. D. Crockett, W. W. Crockett, J. F. Cromany, J. A. Cross, J. H. Cross, M. Crouse, M. Crouse, A. Crowley, A. Crowley, G. W. Crowley, S. J. Crowley, W. S. Crowley, M. M. Crumbaugh, S. D. Cudworth, L. R. Cunningham, J. M. Curkbride, Peter Curnow, S. Curnow, Sam Curnow, William Curp, T. G. Curtin Estate, W. C. D., Heirs of Dagley, Geo. Dale, Cooper Daly, F. M. Daniels, E. A. Davidson, Davis, A. G. Davis, A. G. Davis, D. Davis, G. H. Davis, G. W. Davis, G. W. Davis, G. W. Davis, G. W. Davis, Grant Davis, Harmon Davis, Isom G. Davis, J. F. Davis, J. J. Davis, J. J. Davis, J. M. Davis, J. T. Davis, J. T. Davis, J. T. Davis, J. W. Davis, James Davis, Jeff Davis, M. F. Davis, Mary Davis, O. H. P. Davis, P. Davis, P. L. Davis, P. L. Davis, Polly F. Davis, Polly Davis, William Davis, William Davis, Jas. Dawson Estate, O. W. Dawson, W. M. Dawson, W. S. Deam, T. Dean, R. DeHaven, R. DeHaven, A. F. DeLong, Asa DeLong, Heirs Dennis G. W. Dennison, G. W. Dennison, R. DeStiger, G. W. DeVaul, G. W. DeVaul, J. W. DeVaul, J. W. DeVaul, J. M. DeWalt, Wm. DeWalt, W. Deweese, Henry Dickinson, A. W. Diddle, A. W. Diddle, B. F. Diddle, B. F. Diddle, J. T. Diddle, J. T. Diddle, J. T. Diddle, J. W. Diddle, J. W. Diddle, James Diddle, John Diddle, Sarah Diddle, Sarah Diddle, Sarah Diddle, J. Dillard, J. Dillard, David Dillman, J. A. Ditmas, Fred Diven, Ben Divinia, Ben Divinia, J. S. Divinia, W. C. Divinia, Geo. H. Dixon, Job Dixon, Thomas Dixon, Thomas Dixon, Thos. Dixon, E. Doak, T. Dock Estate, Geo. Dockstader, Geo. Dockstader, J. E. Dodd, John Dodd, John Dodd, B. P. Doddridge, J. E. Dodds, D. D. Dodge, J. F. Dodge, J. F. Dodge,. Dodge, L. M. Dodge, F. H. Dolan, Dolan, P. Dolan, F. Dole, Freeman Dole, L. J. Doll, L. T. Doll, J. H. Donaldson, Estate of W. A. Donaldson, J. Doniphant, J. Doniphne, John Dorkens, John Dorkins, C. L. Dorsett, M. A. Douglas, E. S. Douglass, G. W. Downing, P. Doyle, Peter Doyle, Peter Doyle, E. J. Dudley, M. Duffey, L. M. Duke, L. M. Duke, Mary Duncan, G. Dunham, O. Dunham, Robt. Dunkle, Mrs. S. Dunlap, S. Dunlap, Emma Dunn, David Dunnavan, Lewis Dunnavan, E. P. Dunton, J. H. Durnell, H. P. Dustin, H. P. Dustin, J. H. Dustin, J. H. Dustin, J. H. Dustin, Kepley Duston, M. B. E. James' Est. Earl, Jas. Earl, W. T. Earley, J. N. Early, Mildred Early, Mary Eckelberry, Samuel Eckelberry, A. C. Ecton, Amos Edwards, Amos Edwards, Amos Edwards, E. Edwards, E. Edwards, Elisha Edwards, Haywood Edwards, J. E. Edwards, Jabez Edwards, John Edwards, Maggy B. Edwards, Nancy Edwards, Nancy Edwards, S. Edwards, S. E. Edwards, Solomon Edwards, Solomon Edwards, Thos. Edwards, Thos. Edwards, U. F. Edwards, Walter Edwards, C. Eichler, Edw.

Eichler, Harry Eichler, Henry Eichler, Henry Eichler, J. Eichler, John Eichler, John Eichler, Lewis Eichler, Ola Eichler, G. W. Elberton, J. E. Elberton, M. V. Elliot, Bowman Elliott, Eliz. Elliott, G. N. Elliott, G. N. Elliott, G. N. Elliott, J. W. Elliott, R. T. Elliott, J. Ellis, R. B. Ellis, T. Ellsaesser, A. J. Emery, A. J. Emery, A. R. Emery, S. Emery, Sam Emery, Wm. Emery, D. M. Encell, G. J. Ensberger, J. Ensberger, B. Entrican, E. Entrican, Edwin Entriken, C. B. Entrikin, C. B. Entrikin, C. B. Entrikin, E. G. Entrikin, S. L. Entrikin, W. H. Entrikin, Geo. Ernsberger, Hannah Ernsberger, Hannah Ernsberger, J. F. Erwin, E. W. Estabrook, Est. of Estabrook, E. W. Estabrook, E. W. and E. C. Esteb, John T. Esteb, H. Estes Est., James Estes, James Estes, James Estes, Louis Estes, W. M. Estes, W. M. Estes, W. M. Estes, W. M. Estes, G. W. Etherton, J. E. Etherton, J. E. Etherton, H. Etter, Wm. Evans, J. Everett, J. D. Everett, A. M. Evert, John Evert, M. Fairchild, H. B. Fales, H. Farabee, John Farmer, John Farmer, Union Bank Farmers, A. R. Farr, A. R. Farr, A. R. Farr, L. Farr, Lenard Farr, Edward Fauthinger, P. Fauthinger, P. Fauthinger, Perry Fauthinger, Perry Fauthinger, D. C. Feese, D. C. Feese, D. C. Feese, L. B. Feese, L. B. Feese, Frank Felse, Frank Feltis, Frank Feltis, Mrs. W. A. Ferry, Sarah Fesher, Eliza Few, Isaac Fields, John Fields, Susan Est. Fields, Susan Fields Est., W. T. Fields, G. W. Filley, H. C. Filley, Hyram Filley, J. F. Filley, G. W. Filson, W. F. Filson, W. T. Filson, W. T. Filson, W. T. Filson, J. J. Finch, J. J. Finch, J. F. Findley, Gideon Fink, Gideon Fink, Wm. Fink, Wm. Fink, J. Finley, J. F. Finley, J. F. Finley, J. F. Finley, Luke Firth, Fred Fisher, G. E. Fisher, S. C. Fisher, S. C. Fisher, Sarah Fisher, L. Fitzgerald, M. Fitzgerald, Mark Fitzgerald, Wm. Fitzgerald, Jas. Fleming, M. J. Fletcher, Mary E. Flint, Mary E. Flint, W. R. Flint, W. R. Flint, W. R. Flint, Timothy Follett, Timothy Follett, A. B. Ford, Geo. Fort, Geo. Fort, T. C. Fort, T. C. Fort, M. A. Fost, A. Foster, Amy Foster, Amy Foster, J. Foster, E. G. Fowler, M. R. Fowler, Pleasant Fowler, Pleasant Fowler, Susan Fowler, Wm. Fowler, Lewis D. Frank, S. Frank, A. Frazier, G. B. Frazier, G. W. Frazier, G. W. Frazier, Matilda Frazier, Matilda Frazier, Matilda Frazier, F. Frederick, C. Freel, T. H. French, L. L. Frost, L. L. Frost, L. L. Frost, C. Fruett, J. A. Fryer, W. A. Fryer, W. A. Fryer, J. L. Fugitt, W. C. Fugitt, W. C. Fugitt, F. Fulton, G. W. Funk, G. W. Funk, D. G. , W. S. G. , Marcus Gall, Newton Gallaher, S. F. Gallaher, J. D. Gant, J. D. Gant, J. Garett, T. Garret, John Garrett, John Garrett, Jas. Gaunt, Jas. Gaunt, D. H. Gay, W. H. Gearhart, Henry Gee, Henry Gee, C. W. Geilker, T. D. George, T. D. George, Thos. D. George, Thos. D. George, W. W. Gibbs, F. C. Gibson, Geo. Gibson, Geo. Gibson, J. C. Gibson, N. C. Gibson, J. Gier, F. M. Gilbert, James

Gilchrist, B. L. Gildersleeve, James Gilgour, James Gilgour, C. W. Gilker, Chas H. Gill, J. F. Gill, J. F. Gill, John Gill, A. Gillett, W. D. Gillett, W. D. Gillett, W. D. Gillett, W. D. Gilliland, A. Moors-head Glick, E. Glick, E. Glick, J. L. Glick, J. L. Glick, M. Glick, N. Glick, Noah Glick, M. Goddard, Job Goe, Job Goe, C. Gooding, E. Goodman, J. Goodman, Wm. Goodman, Wm. Goodman, Wm. Goodman, F. E. Goodnoe, L. E. Goodnow, L. E. Goodnow, Ed Goodrich, N. Goodrich, T. A. Goodrich, Ed. Goodrick, Mat Gormley, John Gorshe, D. F. Gover, F. A. Graer, N. G. Graff, Eliz. Graham, G. W. Grant, Robert Grant, Robert Grant, E. Gray, E. Gray, E. Gray, E. Gray, E. Gray, J. D. Gray, James Gray, M. B. Gray, T. A. Gray, T. A. T. Gray, Thos. Gray, Perry Green, Joseph Greenwood, Joseph Greenwood, W. Greenwood, W. and Thos. Greenwood, M. K. Gregg, S. R. Griffin, R. A. Griffing, R. A. Griffing, S. P. Griffy, F. A. Grigsby, J. L. Grisby, A. Grove, J. B. Grover, A. Groves, Van Groves, Van H. Groves, A. J. Guffey, J. C. Guffey, W. A. Guffey, W. F. Guffey, W. F. Guffey, S. F. Guffy, Henry Guild, W. E. Gunby, Gurley, Mrs. S. E. Gurley, Mrs. S. E. Gurley, G. W. Hadden, V. Hadden, Anna Haigh, G. B. Hale, J. M. Hale, Frank Haley, J. K. Hall, Melvin Hall, Mr. Hall, U. G. Hall, U. G. Hall, W. S. Hall, J. C. Halstead, J. C. Halstead, J. S. Halstead, J. S. Halstead, J. S. Halstead, Jas. Halstead, J. A. Hamlet, M. Hamlet, T. L. Hamlet, J. B. Handy, C. L. Hanks, Harriet Hanks, J. A. Hanks, J. C. Hanson, J. C. Hanson, A. J. Hansworth, D. C. Hardman, D. C. Hardman, D. C. Hardman, D. C. Hardman, J. R. Hardman, S. B. Hardman, S. B. Hardman, B. F. Hardy, Hardy, R. H. Hargrove, R. N. Hargrove, S. Harlow, J. W. Harper, J. W. Harper, Adam Harpold, John Harpool, John Harpool, Madilean Harpool, Wm. Harpool, Wm. Harpool, A. Harpster, Alvin Harriman, O. P. Harriman, T. S. Harris, J. L. Hart, G. Harter, G. Harter, J. C. Harter, J. C. Harter, J. T. Harter, J. W. Harter, James Hartigan, James Hartigan, M. E. Hartigan, M. E. Hartigan, J. C. Hartley, Wm. Hartley, Fred Hartwig, Fred Hartwig, Fred Hartwig, J. M. Haskinson, J. T. Hatfield, W. H. Hauger, W. H. Hauger, A. W. Havens, John Havens, John Hawk, J. A. Hawks, M. J. Hawks, M. J. Hawks, Mrs. M. J. Hawks, Wm. Hawks, J. W. Hays, J. W. Hays, Nat Hays, Warren Hays, J. G. Hayter, E. Heath, J. F. Heiser, J. F. Heiser, J. M. Helms, A. D. Hemry, E. Hemry, Elizabeth Hemry, Haman Hemry, Haman Hemry, Haman Hemry, Haman Hemry, Isaac Hemry, Isreal Hemry, R. A. Hemry, J. C. Henderson, J. C. Henderson, Louis Henderson, J. H. Hendrickson, Malinda Hendrix, Malinda Hendrix, A. T. Henkins, J. P. Henkins, J. P. Henkins, Raleigh Henkins, Raleigh Henkins, Geo. Henninger, Chas. Henricks, Isaiah Henricks, S. Henry, W. L. Henry, Senora Herald, Senora Herald, E. H. Herbert, Joseph

Herndon, Aaron Herrington, Philip Hewitt, W. S. Hewitt, John Hiatt, John Hiatt, S. P. Hick, A. Hickman, A. Hickman, Fred Hickman, John Hickman, Saml. Hickman, B. C. Hicks, John Hicks, John Hicks, R. H. Hicks, Thos. Hicks, W. J. Hicks, Joseph Higgins, M. A. Higgins, Matilda A. Higgins, Matilda H. Higgins, D. W. Hill, G. B. Hill, G. B. Hill, G. B. Hill, G. B. Hill, J. R. Hill, W. B. Hill, M. O. Hines, M. O. Hines, Attilla Hinson, C. A. Hinson, Geo. Hinz, E. C. Hockstedlar, M. Hockstedler, Frank John Hockstedler, M. Hogan, G. A. Hogsett, W. A. Hogsett, F. M. Holder, F. M. Holder, J. Holder, James Holder, S. Holder, S. E. Holder, W. Holder, W. A. Holder, W. A. Holder, J. A. Holliday, Bros. Holloway Bros. Holloway Bros. Holloway G. B. Holm, Moses Honeycut, Samuel Hooker, Fay Hooper, H. P. Hooper, S. Hootman, Thos. Hootman, Geo. Hopkins, A. Hopper, G. W. Hopper, James Horseman, James Horseman, Chas. Horsman, Jane Hoshinson, Jas. Hoskinson, M. A. Hoskinson, A. M. Hosman, G. W. Houghton, Geo. Houghton, Ira Houghton, Ira Houghton, James Houghton, Jas. Houghton, Jas. Ho-ughton, John Houghton, Wm. Houghton, Wm. Houghton, Nancy A. Houston, Nancy A. Houston, Albert Howard, R. G. Howard, J. F. Howell, A. Hudgens, A. Hudgins, H. J. Hudson, J. F. Hudson, J. H. Hudson, R. L. Hudson, Griff Hughes, J. G. Hughes, M. T. Hughes, P. E. Hughes, R. J. Hughes, R. J. Hughes, A. W. Hughson, A. W. Hugh-son, F. G. Hughson, G. L. Hughson, Adaline F. Hulett, Mrs. A. T. Hulett, Geo. Hulser, Samuel Hulser, Samuel Hulser, Samuel Hulser, J. B. Humphrey, J. B. Humphrey, T. Humphrey, T. Humphrey, William Humphrey, Wm. Humphrey, Agt., Wm. Humphrey, Agt., William Humphrey, Agt., J. M. Hunley, E. A. Hunt, W. H. Hunt, W. W. Hunt, J. D. Hunter Est., Sallie Hunter, Sallie Hunter, Sallie Hunter, R. B. Huston, Huston, J. B. Hutchings, J. B. Hutchings, R. H. Hutchings, W. G. Hutchinson, W. H. Idings, N. A. Impson, J. Irons, J. F. Irwin, E. C. James, Emmit James, Benj. Jennings, C. R. Jewell, G. W. Jewell, J. S. Jewell, Ben John, Alice Johnson, Arthur Johnson, C. Johnson, Clara Johnson, Clara Johnson, Clara Johnson, E. D. Johnson, E. D. Johnson, Ella E. Johnson, Isaac Johnson, J. M. Johnson, J. M. Johnson, T. A. Johnson, W. Johnson, W. F. Johnson, J. W. Johnston, T. W. Johnston, T. W. Johnston, T. W. Johnston, T. W. Johnston, Thos. Est. Johnston, W. J. Johnston, A. G. Jones, A. G. Jones, B. C. Jones, B. C. Jones, B. C. Jones, C. K. Jones, C. K. Jones, Catherine Jones, D. H. Jones, D. H. Jones, E. Jones, Eben Jones, Eben Jones, G. G. Jones, G. W. Jones, Gomer Jones, Hannah Jones, J. Jones, J. E. Jones, J. M. Jones, J. R. Jones, J. R. Jones, J. R. Jones, J. R. Jones, J. R. Jones, J. W. Jones, John Jones, John Jones, Q. T. Jones, S. B. Jones, Soloman Jones, Soloman Jones,

Solomon Jones, Solomon Jones, Strother Jones, T. F. Jones, W. Jones, Warren Jones, Wm. Est. Jones, D. Judd, D. Judd, J. Judy, G. K. , P. Kanan, J. A. Karr, J. A. Karr, James Karr, James Karr, Jas. Karr, Jas. Karr, Mary Kasper, W. Kasper, J. Kaufman, Henry Kaufmann, G. Kautz, Geo. Kautz, George Kautz, H. R. Kautz, H. R. Kautz, S. G. Kearney, Daniel Keef, E. Keefe, E. Keefe, Eugene Keefe, F. B. Kelepper, An-drew Kelley, Andrew Kelley, Chas. Est. Kelley, J. E. Kelley, J. E. Kelley, John Kelley, M. S. Kellogg, John Kelly, John Kelly, John Kelly, Thos. M. Kelsde, Thos. M. Kelsde, Oliver Kelsey, Oliver Kelsey, D. R. Kemble, Benj. Kemper, H. M. Kemper, J. C. Kemper, J. C. Kemper, L. M. Kemper, Q. M. Kemper, Q. M. Kemper, C. H. Kendell, C. M. Kendell, C. M. Kendell, M. C. Kendell, I. Kendrick, J. Kendrick, N. O. Kendrick, V. Kendrick, Mathew Kennedy, Michael Kennedy, Thos. Sr. Kennedy, E. Kenney, M. Kenney, Mrs. E. Kenney, P. E. Kenney, E. Kenny, E. Kenny, J. P. Kenny, Geo. Kepley, Jacob Kerna, G. B. Kerns, C. F. Kerr, C. F. Kerr, J. H. Killion, J. H. Killion, Bros. Kincaid,J. F. & W. Kincaid, W. Kincaid, A. King, Andrew King, D. W. King, Emily King, J. King, J. D. King, Lon King, W. H. King, Wm. King, J. A. Kinne, J. R. Kinne, Jason Kinne, M. B. Kinne, M. J. Kinne, M. J. Kinne, J. Kinney, J. Kinsola, J. Kinsola, M. Kinsola, P. Kinsola, T. Kinsola, T. Kinsola, J. V. & Kiple, J. V. Kiple, F. B. Klepper, W. J. Kline, Wm. Kline, J. W. Knapp, J. Knoch, J. Knoch, J. Knoch, R. L. Knott, Mrs. May. Koyle, J. A. Kresse, Adolphus Kromeick, Albert Kromeick, B. L. , Thos. Laidlaw, W. H. Lake, J. J. Lakey, Harriett Lamson, Lane, J. F. Lane, J. J. Lane, J. R. Lane, W. H. Lane, B. S. Laughlin, Byran Lawrence, J. W. Lawrence, M. Laws, M. Laws, J. L. Leamer, J. S. Leamer, J. S. Leamer, J. S. Leamer, R. R. Leamer, R. R. Leamer, C. C. Leeper, J. Leeper, R. Leeper, J. Legg, Howard Lester, J. B. Les-ter, J. B. Lewellen, Ed Lewis, J. M. Lewis, Wm. Lewis, J. Like, W. H. Lile, R. H. Lindley, S. S. Lindsey, J. Linville, James Linville, Jas. A. Linville, Jas. A. Linville, Jas. A. Linville, Minerva Lister, David Lockridge, E. E. Lollis, G. W. Longstreth, G. W. Longstreth, C. W. Lonstreth, Chas. Loomis, Chas. Loomis, J. M. Loomis, J. M. Loo-mis, H. H. Looney, W. W. Looney, M. Lorette, Eugean Low, Mrs. R. E. Lucky, S. C. Ludington, J. B. Luellen, W. J. Lukins, Martin Lutz, R. M. , Lewis Mabe, A. Mack, Aug. Mack, Aug. Mack, Augustus Mack, Ben Mackey, J. D. Mackey, J. D. Mackey, J. G. Mackey, J. G. Mackey, T. F. MacKorindall, Jas. MacMaster, Richard Maggart, E. Z. Malory, Perl Malory, S. Malory, E. T. Mann, E. T. Mann, J. T. Mann, M. D. Mann, M. D. Mann, M. D. Mann, M. D. Mann, L. Marlatt, J. S. & R. M. Marquis, J. S. & R. M. Marquis, G. B. Martin, J. Martin, J. E. Martin, J. E. Martin, L. F.

Martin, M. F. Martin, Martha F. Martin, W. Martin, J. N. Matchett, J. C. Mayes, J. U. Mayes, Spenser Mayes, T. D. Mayes, W. H. Mayes, W. P. Mayes, Wiley Mayes, Wiley Mayes, Henry Mayfield, J. A. McAdams, A. McArnote, A. McArnote, A. W. McBeath, A. W. McBeath, J. B. McBeath, J. B. McBeath, J. K. McBeath, McBee, David McBee, J. W. McBee, J. W. McBee, J. W. McBee, J. W. McBee, John McBee, Levi McBee, J. W. McBole, W. J. McBrayer, W. J. McBrayer, Jas. McBride, T. D. McBride, T. D. Est. McBride, T. D. Est. McBride, John P. McCartney, F. M. McCauley, John McClain, Stephen McClain, W. N. McClain, D. A. McClelland, Thos. McClelland, Edgar McClintock, Frank McCollum, T. F. McCorkendale, A. F. McCray, Friend McCray, Hortecia McCray, Hortecia McCray, Hortencia McCray, W. H. McCray, Wm. McCray, Wm. McCray, Wm. McCray, Wm. McCray, Wm. McCray, Wm. McCray, Wm. McCray, J. W. McCrea, Mrs. McCree, B. M. McCubbin, J. C. McCubbin, E. A. McDaniel, J. R. McDaniel, W. G. McDaniel, A. A. McDonald, Mrs. M. J. McDonald, Mrs. M. J. McDonald, J. D. McFall, Jas. McFall, W. T. McFall, Wm. McFall, Wm. McFall, Geo. McFee, Geo. McFee, Geo. McFee, Geo. McFee, Robt. McFee, S. McFee, John McGee, John McGee, Wm. McGinnis, Joel McGlothlin, Wm. McGlothlin, W. McGray, Addison McKee, W. McKinzie, Wm. McLain, C. F. McLallen, G. McLallen, G. M. McLallen, G. M. McLal-len, J. E. McLallen, O. F. McLallen, C. McLaughlin, J. L. McLa-ughlin, S. J. McLaughlin, S. J. McLaughlin, G. H. McMangle, John McNaughton, Addie McNeely, E. M. McNew, H. L. McNew, J. F. McNew, Oscar McNew, McNews, A. J. McNight, R. A. McPheeters, R. A. McPheeters, C. G. McQueen, G. W. McQueen, Noah McQuire, O. McWilliams, O. McWilliams, A. J. Meacham, E. L. Meacham, Henry Meacham, T. Meager, M. Meagher, H. B. Meffert, J. P. Meister, J. H. Merideth, G. W. Merryman, G. W. Merryman, John Messenbaugh, John Messenbaugh, R. F. Messimer, John Mether-ingham, C. A. Michael, D. A. Michael, D. A. Michael, D. D. Mic-hael, D. D. Michael, D. D. Michael, Dan Michael, Daniel Michael, J. N. Michael, J. N. Michael, Mrs. L. E. Michael, Sanford Michael, Wm. Middeaugh, Wm. Middeaugh, H. Millard, A. A. Miller, A. E. Miller, Adam Miller, Barbara Est Miller, Chas. Miller, Chas. Miller, Daniel Miller, Daniel Miller, Dr. E. Miller, Dr. E. Miller, J. A. Mil-ler, J. M. Miller, Winfield Miller, Jas. Millett, J. R. Milne, J. R. Mil-ne, G. Milstead, R. M. Milstead, R. M. Milstead, J. H. Misenhelter, L. D. Misenhelter, W. F. Mitcheal, J. M. Mitchell. A. W. Moffit, A. W. Moffitt, G. W. Moffitt, J. G. Mohn, John Mohn, D. W. Monroe, Sam Montgomery, Sam Montgomery, Mrs. C. Montsinger, John Montz, S. A. Mooney, S. A. Mooney,

Edgar Moore, Robt. Moore, S. Moore, S. Moore, T. H. P. Moore, L. F. Moorman, A. Moorshead, A. and Geo. Moorshead, Arthur Moorshead, James Moran, James Moran, Geo. Morey, G. M. Morgan, John Morgan, John Morgan, J. T. Morman, L. F. Morman, A. Morris, C. I. Morris, C. I. Morris, Ed. Morris, Geo. Morris, H. C. Morris, H. C. Morris, H. C. Morris, J. C. Morris, J. F. Morris, J. F. Morris, J. M. Morris, James Morris, Joseph Morris, Joseph Morris, Mary L. Morris, Mary L. Morris, R. M. Mor-ris, Recard Morris, Richard Morris, Wm. Morris, Lewis Morrison, Bliss Morse, J. N. Morton, J. C. Moss, J. C. Moss, R. B. Moss, D. T. Motley, D. T. Motley, Mary Motley, J. A. Motsinger, J. A. Mot-singer, John Mount, John Mount, R. Mount, D. Mulligan, D. Mum-power, E. M. Mumpower, E. M. Mumpower, S. H. Munsell, H. A. Munson, Geo. Murey, Hannah Murphy, John Murphy, Tim Murphy, J. C. Murray, J. C. Murray, J. I. Murrill, W. A. Murrill, J. C. Murry, Mrs. N. Murry, McCook Musser, McCook Musser, S. G. Myers, J. S. Mylar, Mary A. Mylar, R. W. Napier, A. B. Nash, J. F. Naugle, P. Navin, J. F. Naylor, W. Naylor, J. Neff, J. A. Neff, Margaret Neill, G. W. Nelson, G. W. Nelson, J. Nelson, J. Nelson, Geo. Netcher, A. Netzen, A. L. Nevil, G. A. Nevil, G. A. Nevil, M. F. Nevitt, N. C. Newby, W. F. Newton, W. F. Newton, W. F. Newton, W. T. New-ton, C. T. Nichols, Harvey Nichols, Willard Nichols, Willard Nichols, Willard Nichols, T. S. Nicholson, Thos. S. Nicholson, Harvey Nic-kols, Levi Nickols, Mary Nickols, W. C. Nicodemus, H. E. Norris, H. E. Norris, G. W. P. O'Donnald, G. W. P. O'Donnald, G. W. P. O'Don-nald, David O'Donnell, J. C. Oaks, Mary Ogan, S. F. Ogden, E. E. Oldfield, Mrs. L. Oldfield, P. S. Oldfield, E. A. Oliver, E. W. Oliver J. H. Oliver, J. H. Oliver, J. W. Oliver, John Oliver, L. Oliver, Mary ONeil, Orr, B. Orr, Ben Orr, Ben Orr, Chas. Orr, J. H. Orr, J. M. Orr, John Est. Orr, John Est. Orr, John Est. Orr, Moses Orr, Moses Orr, P. Orr, W. Orr, W. F. Orr, Wm. Orr, Wm. Orr, J. Osborn, J. M. Os-born, Conrad Oster, Est. Oster, Est. Oster, A. D. Otto, A. D. Otto, A. D. Otto, A. D. Otto, A. D. Otto, Henry Otto, Henry Otto, J. Owens, John Owens, John Owens, E. P. C. Packard, A. G. Palmer, A. Park, C. H. Parker, G. M. Parker, M. G. Parker, Thos Parker, J. F. Parman, Bros. Parmenter John Parmenter, L. Parmenter, T. A. Parmenter, W. P. Parmenter, W. P. Parmenter, W. R. Parmenter, Chas. Paryman, J. A. Paryman, J. A. Pate, Jas. A. Pate, John A. Pate, John A. Pate, Henry Patton, Joseph Patton, Samuel Patton, Christian Paustian, Christian Paustian, Pawsey, Fred Pawsey, J. P. Pawsey, John Pawsey, John Pawsey, J. R. Paxton, J. R. Paxton, J. R. Paxton, J. R. Paxton, Chas. Payzant, Chas. Payzant, Chas. Payzant, S. Peabody, S. Peabody, Ed. Pearce, R. J. Pearce, R. J. Pearce, J. M. Pearcy, B. A.

Pearson, C. L. Peddicord, T. L. Peddicord, T. L. Peddicord, Thos. Est Peddicord, Thos. Est Peddicord, John Pemberton, John Pemberton, John Pemberton, John Pemberton, Eli Penney, Gertrude Penney, J. C. Est. Penney, E. Penny, E. L. Perkins, Peter Peterson, A. C. Pettis, D. & Petty, Thos. Petty, W. T. Petty, W. T. Petty, Aaron Pfost, Aaron Pfost, Ellen Phares, Ellen Phares, Ellen Phares, James Phares, James Phares, Jas. Phares, John Phelan, L. M. Est. Phelps, A. Phillips, Adaline Phillips, Albert Phillips, D. Phillips, David Phillips, E. D. Phillips, F. Phillips, F. M. Phillips, H. L. Phillips, J. G. Phillips, Jacob Phillips, Mrs. A. Phillips, W. I. Phillips, B. F. Pierce, John Pierce, Wm. Pierce, R. B. Pile, Francis Pilkington, F. Pilkingtun, E. J. Pinkerton, E. J. Pinkerton, J. A. Pinkerton, Wm. Plumb, Wm. Plumb, E. Plummer, Enoch Plummer, T. Plummer, Thos. Plummer, H. W. Plumpton, S. W. Plumpton, D. R. Pollard, E. Pollard, H. T. Pollard, J. M. Pollard, J. R. Pollard, P. J. Pollard, P. J. Pollard, S. W. Pollard, S. W. Pollard, W. G. Pollard, W. M. Pollard, W. M. Pollard, W. M. Pollard, Isaac Sr. Pond, Isaac, Sr. Ponds, Alvin Poor, Alvin Poor, Anderson Poor, R. A. Poor, M. W. Popejoy, W. B. Porter, W. B. Porter, N. L. Post, N. L. Post, G. C. Postlewate, G. C. Postlewate, James Potts, John Potts, M. Potts, P. Potts, P. Potts, Geo. Powell, Isaac Powell, J. W. Powers, C. H. Pratt, A. D. Preston, A. G. Preston, J. B. Price, J. B. Price, John Price, J. C. Primm, N. C. Primm, E. M. Proctor, E. M. Proctor, J. R. Proctor, J. R. Proctor, John M. Proctor, Mr. D. Proctor, Mrs. D. Proctor, P. S. Proctor, P. S. Proctor, P. S. Proctor, R. & Proctor, Robt. Proctor, W. D. Proctor, W. D. Proctor, W. D. Proctor, A. Proffit, A. Proffit, E. Prouty, Pruitt, C. Puckett, C. Puckett, C. Puckett, I. M. Puckett, I. M. Puckett, I. M. Puckett, J. M. Puckett, J. J. Pullin, G. Purple, G. F. Putman, G. S. Putman, Geo. S. Putman, S. Queel, S. Queel, H. T. R. , G. W. Railey, G. W. Railey, G. W. Railey, G. W. Railey, J. T. Railsback, O. I. Randall, John S. Rathbun, Samuel Rathbun, C. Ream, Della Redhair, J. G. Redhair, Jacob Redhair, Peter Redhead, Alf Reed, G. E. Reed, G. E. Reed, J. J. Reed, M. E. Reed, Wm. Reed, H. M. Reeves, H. M. Reeves, H. M. Reeves, J. D. Est. Reeves, A. E. Rehard, A. L. Rehard, A. L. Rehard, K. Rehard, Kinsey Rehard, Kinsey Rehard, M. H. Rehard, Mary A. Rehard, H. W. Reigel, Mary J. Reynolds, C. A. Rhea, C. A. Rhea, Chas. Rhea, Wm. Rhea, Wm. Rhea, Wm. Rhea, Wm. Rhea, G. M. Ribelin, G. M. Ribelin, G. M. Ribelin, G. M. Ribelin, J. N. Ribelin, J. Rice, J. W. Rice, M. A. Rice, Martin Rice, W. Est. Rice, J. L. Richards, Albert Richardson, R. Richardson, Chas. Richey, D. V. Richmond, D. Y. Richmond, A. D. Riddle, J. W. Riddle, Martha A. Riddle, Wm. Riddle, J. Ridinger, H. R. Rigdon, J. F. Rigdon, J. F. Rigdon, W. J. Rigg, Chas. Riggs, Melvin Riggs, Chas. Riley, P.

Riley, J. F.   Roberts, M.   Roberts, M.   Roberts, W. S.   Robertson, J. Robinet, J. S.   Robinson, J. S.   Robinson, J. S.   Robinson, L. P. Robinson, A. E.   Robison, A. E.   Robison, C. O.   Robison, C. O. Robison, D. M.   Robison, E. A.   Robison, E. A.   Robison, J. G. Robison, J. H.   Robison, J. H.   Robison, J. H.   Robison, L.   Robison, L. Robison, Lydia Robison, Lydia Robison, Lydia I.   Robison, H. L. Rodgers, & Noop Rogers & Knoop Rogers D. C.   Rogers, D. C. Rogers, G. F.   Rogers, H. C.   Rogers, J. S.   Rogers, J. S.   Rogers, J. S. Rogers, M. F.   Rogers, Noah Rogers, S. C.   Rogers, S. C.   Rogers, Henry Roloff, Henry Roloff, R. A.   Ronnell, Rosa A.   Ronnell, J. T. Roper, J. T.   Roper, B. B.   Ross, C.   Ross, Carrie Ross, Charlott Ross, Charlott Ross, G. A.   Ross, G. W.   Ross, H. T.   Ross, J. T.   Ross, J. T. Ross, J. T.   Ross, J. S.   Roth, Marion Rozzell, Marion Rozzell, Mrs. A.   Rozzell, Whit Rozzell, A. P.   Rozzelle, A. P.   Rozzelle, A. P. Rozzelle, A. P.   Rozzelle, Marion Rozzelle, Marion Rozzelle, Marion Rozzelle, C. J.   Ruff, C. J.   Ruff's Est.   Ruff C. M.   Russell, G. W. Russell, G. W.   Russell, R. T.   Russell, R. T.   Russell, Samuel Russell, Samuel Russell, W. B.   Rutherford, W. B.   Rutherford, Jonah Rutledge, Josian Rutledge, James Ryan, P.   Ryan, Edward Ryburn, E. D.   Sacket, E. D. Sackett, Chas.   Sackman, G. F.   Sackman, G. F.   Sackman, Isaac Sackman, J. F.   Sackman, J. F.   Sackman, M. D.   Sackman, R. C.   Sackman, R. D.   Sackman, R. D.   Sackman, R. D.   Sackman, W. B.   Sackman, W. B.   Sackman, W. B.   Sackman, W. D.   Sackman, W. I.   Sackman, B. F.   Sadler, Cyrus Sadler, John Sadler, John Sadler, M. J.   Sadler, W. C.   Sadler, A.   Salsbury, Anson Salsbury, Anson Salsbury, Wm. Salsbury, Wm.   Salsbury, Wm.   Salsbury, G. W.   Samuel, G.   Samuels, G.   Samuels, A. M.   Sanders, H. E.   Sanders, W. F.   Sanders, W. T. Sanders, A. L.   Sanderson, R.   Sargent, John Scanlon, John Scharson, Scheson, C.   Schneiter, Chris Schneiter, Susan Schneiter, Chas.   Schultz, J. A.   Schultz, J. C.   Schultz, John Schuster, Leonard A Schuster, Stephen Schuster, Stephen Schuster, J. H.   Scott, James Scott, Walter Scott, Fred Seafert, T.   Sears, T. R. Est.   Sears, C. A.   Seawright, W. W.   Seely, Chris Seitter, Chris Seitter, G.   Seitter, Noah Sell, John Sellers, Thos.   Sellers, Ira Sessions, Paul Shafel, L.   Shafer, Wm.   Shafer, P. M.   Shaffer, P. M.   Shaffer, P. M.   Shaffer, W. N.   Shaffer, W. N. Est.   Shaffer, A.   Sharp, D. C.   Sharp, E.   Sharp, E. A.   Sharp, Eli Sharp, J. F.   Sharp, C. F.   Shaw, Ben Shear, C. D.   Shellaberger, Geo. Shelly, John Shepard, John Shepard, Springer Sherman, Wm. Shevly, S. F.   Shields, W.   Shin, A. P.   Shiner, Eli Shiner, J. A.   Shiner, Mary Shiner, Stewart Shiner, W. F.   Shiner, G. P.   Shirts, W.   Shirts, W. Shirts, J. T.   Shouse, Z. T.   Shouse, F.   Showerman, I.   Shruble, John Shrum, Levi Shrum, Mary Shrum, Mrs. Caroline Shrum, S. S.   Shrum, S. S.   Shrum, S. S.   Shrum, C.   Shultz, J.   Shultz, E.   Shuman, E.   Shuman, U. E. Sidebottom, U. E. Sidebottom, U. E. Sidebottom, John Sigman, G. G. Simpkinson, G. G. Simpkinson, Geo. Simpson, J. Simpson, J. S. Simpson, T. C. Simpson, T. C. Simpson, Mrs. L. Skelton, R. O. & Slater, J. M. Slegbaugh, J. M. Slegbough, A. E. Sloan, A. J. Sloan, G. W. Sloan, Geo. W. Sloan, J. Sloan, J. J. Sloan, J. R. Sloan, J. T. Sloan, M. D. Sloan, M. D. Sloan, N. J. Est. Sloan, R. E. Sloan, Ridge Sloan, Ridge Sloan, S. W. Sloan, T. Sloan, Thomas Sloan, Thomas Sloan, Thos. Sloan, Thos. Sloan, Thos. Sloan, W. Sloan, W. Sloan, C. Sloroff, Amanda J. Smith, Anna M. Smith, Anna M. Smith, C. H. Smith, Chas. Est. Smith, D. P. Smith, G. A. Smith, I. Smith, I. A. Smith, J. A. Smith, J. C. Smith, J. F. Smith, J. H. Smith, J. M. Smith, J. M. Smith, John Smith, John Smith, Margaret Smith, Mary T. Smith, Mrs. S. E. Smith, Mrs. S. E. Smith, Mrs. A. R. Smith, Noah Smith, Susan Smith, W. L. Smith, Wm. Smith, A. J. Smoot, A. J. Smoot, Smylie, D. Snyder, Henry Snyder, J. H. Snyder, J. W. Snyder, Jacob H. Snyder, W. F. Snyder, Gabe Sovereign, C. Sparks, Thos. Sparks, Sarah Spenser, S. J. Spicer, W. R. Spicer, Sarah Splawn, J. R. Sprague, J. R. Sprague, Amelia Spratt, B. G. Spurlock, G. Spurlock, G. W. Spurlock, J. P. Spurlock, J. M. Squires, S. R. Sritter, A. D. Stafford, A. D. Stafford, W. H. Est. Stafford, W. H. Stafford, Ida Stagner, J. Stagner, J. F. Stagner, J. T. Stagner, J. T. Stagner, J. T. Stagner, J. T. Stagner, Aaron Stalk, John Stalk, John Stalk, L. Stanfield, L. Stanfield, J. W. Starret, E. D. Steenrod, E. D. Steenrod, H. E. Steenrod, John Steenrod, John Steenrod, N. E. Steenrod, N. E. Steenrod, Robert Steenrod, Robert Steenrod, Robert Steenrod, F. Steinberg, F. Steinberg, Edw. Est. Stephens, Evens Stephens, J. C. Stephens, John Stephens, Thos. Stephens, Wm. Stephens, Wm. Stephens, Archie Stephenson, Sam Stephenson, H. J. Stevens, Wm. Stevens, W. H. Stevenson, John Stewart, Mrs. A. Stewart, Robert Stewart, S. Stewart, Manerva Stickle, G. Stiles, T. R. Stillfield, W. H. Stillwell, W. N. Stillwell, H. Stock, O. Stockel, Frank Stockwell, J. A. Stockwell, D. Stoller, Matilda Stoller, B. F. Stonam, B. F. Stonam, J. H. Stone, Mary F. Stone, Mary F. Stone, W. C. Stone, A. D. Stoner, J. H. Stoner, J. H. Stoner, J. W. Stoner, S. Stoner, J. W. Stonum, J. W. Stonum, Wilson Stout, I. N. Stoutimore, J. W. Stoutimore, W. H. Stoutimore, Byron Stowell, E. Straub, B. B. Street, C. E. Streeter, C. E. Streeter, C. E. Streeter, D. F. Streeter, G. W. Streeter, G. W. Streeter, H. B. Streeter, M. J. Streeter, Mrs. M. F. Streeter, W. H. Streeter, C. F. Strop, C. F. Strop, Chas. F. Strop, W. K. Strope, W. K. Strope, Isaac Struble, M. E. Stubbenfield, S. S. Stubbinfield, R. M. Stubblefield, J. E. Stubblefield, Mary Stubblefield, R. M. Stubblefield, John Stubbs, T. Stubbs, S. E. Stuck, S. E. Stuck, C. Stucke,

D. Stucke, D. Stucke, Dan Stucke, David Stucke, John Stucke, John Stucke, W. Stucke, A. Stucker, A. Stucker, Al Stucker, O. Stucker, Oscar Stucker, B. C. Sturgis, B. F. Sturgis, Bros. Sturgis, C. H. Sturgis, C. H. Sturgis, C. H. Sturgis, W. H. Sturgis, W. H. Sturgis, W. H. Sturgis, W. H. Sturgis, Wm. Sturgis, J. N. Swaggart, Isaac Swearingen, C. M. Sweatman, Eli Sweatman, C. D. Sweem, I. Sweringen, Franklin Swigart, Celine Swindler, Celine Swindler, H. C. Swindler, H. C. Swindler, J. Swindler, J. C. Swindler, James Swindler, U. H. Swisher, A. R. Switzer, A. R. Switzer, J. Switzer, J. F. Switzer, J. F. Switzer, Jacob Switzer, Jacob Switzer, Jacob Switzer, Jacob Switzer, M. A. Switzer, M. D. Switzer, P. A. Switzer, P. A. Switzer, G. M. T. , Wm. Taft, Eliza Tanner, Eliza Tanner, I. Tarwater, Geo. Tattershall, Geo. Tattershall, Geo. Tattershall, J. Tattershall, J. B. Tattershall, J. B. Tattershall, E. Tayler, Emma Taylor, W. Taylor, Wm. Taylor, C. Temple, C. Temple, C. Temple, John Temple, Joseph Temple, Mary F. Terrill, Mary F. Terrill, Chas. Terry, T. Terry, G. B. Thacker, Gola Thacker, Thacker,Mrs. Wm. Est. Thiel, J. A. Thiel, J. A. Thiel, John Thielman, John Thielman, W. Thielman, A. J. Thomas, E. W. Thomas, J. Thomas, J. Thomas, N. Thomas, O. H. Thomas, A. Thompson, Thompson, F. M. Thompson, Sr.; F. M. Thompson, Flora Thompson, J. A. Thompson, J. K. Thompson, J. W. Thompson, J. Y. Thompson, J. Y. Thompson, J. D. Thomson, Est. Thorn C. G. Thwing, Geo. Tiffney, J. T. Est. Till, V. Tindell, J. W. Tippet, Ray Tippet, J. W. Tippit, Ilet Est. Tobbeen, Est Tobbein,Cathrin Thos. Toner, G. M. Tool, David Toomay, Edw. Too-may, Edw. Toomay, Harker Toomay, M. Toomay, M. J. Toomay, Mike Toomay, Mike Toomay, TimothyToomay, Timothy Toomay, Timothy Toomay, W. H. Tooms, Eliza Tospon, Wm. Tospon, Wm. Tospon, Lenard Town, Lenard Town, Moses Town, Moses Town, Eli Townsend, A. Tracy, A. Tracy, G. Tracy, J. P. Tracy, Miss S. Tracy, R. D. Tracy, W. C. Tracy, W. C. Tracy, Jacob Treon, Jacob Treon, J. J. Trosper, J. J. Trosper, H. Est. Tross, H. Est. Tross, H. W. Trout, Isaac Trumbo, C. B. Trunk, Ilet Tubbein, H. N. Tucker, J. H. Tucker, O. W. Tucker, J. F. Tunnell, J. Turner, J. Turner, J. C. Turner, S. E. Turner, R. M. Tuttle, S. Tuttle, Twing, Jeff Tye, E. C. Uhland, G. A. Umstott, E. Upp, E. Upp, Wm. Sr. Ure, Wm. Ure, G. M. Vanbebber, G. M. Vanbebber, Vance, C. Vance, J. P. Vance, J. Q. Vance, Moses Vance, Wm. Vance, J. Vanderpool, Jas. and Jeff VanNote, Jeff VanNote, Ellen VanOlinda, J. D. VanOlinda, J. D. VanOlinda, J. D. VanOlinda, Lydia VanWinkle, Lydia VanWinkle, Lydia VanWinkle, A. Varndell, M. Vaugh, S. H. Vaughn, Calvin Veach, Geo. Verning, T. S. Virtue, Thos. Virtue, M. A. W. , W. D. Wade, J. M. Waggoner, Wm. Waggoner, Asel Waldo, Asel Waldo, J. Walker, J. H.

Walker, James Walker, John Walker, Ray Wall, D. O. Wallace, E. G. Wallace, E. G. Wallace, Geo. O. Wallace, J. M. Wallace, James Wallace, James Wallace, James Wallace, Wm. Wallace, J. E. Walters, J. H. Walters, J. H. Ward, J. P. Ward, J. P. Ward, John Ward, Mrs. Ward, N. Ward, W. W. Ward, Wm. Ward, M. D. Warmack, A. Warren, Annie Warren, Annie Warren, J. W. Warren, J. E. Waters, J. F. Waters, Joseph Waters, S. J. Waters, U. G. Waters, U. G. Waters, Thos. Jr. Watson, Thos. Watson, Thos. Sr. Watson, J. Wayland, J. W. Wayland, C. Wayman, H. F. Weaver, H. F. Weaver, J. W. Weaver, J. W. Weaver, J. C. Webb, C. B. Webster, E. C. Webster, M. Webster, Mrs. M. Webster, B. G. Weeks, B. G. Weeks, C. Weilkie, Nelson Welker, Norman Welker, Norman Welker, C. W. Wells, C. W. Wells, C. W. Wells, C. W. Wells, C. W. Wells, E. Wells, G. W. Wells, Geo. Wells, Geo. Wells, Geo. Wells, John Wells, John Wells, Mrs. O. Wells, J. B. Welsh, J. B. Welsh, W. S. Est. Welsh, W. S. Est. Welsh, W. S. Est. Welsh, C. Wesbter, W. F. Whaler, C. Y. Wheeler, C. Y. Wheeler, J. F. Wheeler, J. F. Wheeler, admr., Mrs. Aug. Wheeler, Sadie Wheeler, Sadie Wheeler, W. F. Wheeler, W. F. Wheeler, W. F. Wheeler, J. M. Whitaker, J. M. Whitaker, P. J. Whitaker, E. C. White, I. P. White, I. P. White, J. B. White, J. T. White, L. B. White, Wm. White, Wm. White, Wm. White, Wm. White, John Whitelaw, M. A. Whitesell, M. A. Whitesell, A. O. Whiteside, J. Whitlaw, D. Whitmer, J. D. Whitmer, R. H. Whitsitt, J. T. Whitt, J. T. Whitt, W. J. Whitt, Andrew Widmier, Andrew Widmier, C. Widmier, Chris, Sr. Widmier, Geo. Widmier, Gilley Widmier, John Widmier, W. Wilhoit, G. Wilkinson, G. Wilkinson, Thos. Wilkinson, G. S. Will, G. S. Will, N. B. Will, N. B. Will, N. B. Will, Amanda Williams, Amanda Williams, C. Est. Williams, Edgar Williams, Eliza Williams, J. D. Williams, J. D. Williamson, Joseph Willy, C. Wilson, M. O. Wilson, Thos. Wilson, Z. B. Wilson, A. Wingate, A. Wingate, C. J. Winger, M. H. Winger, J. C. Winscott, J. C. Winscott, Sam Wise, H. F. Witehead, A. R. Wolcot, Elmer Wolf, Geo. Wolf, Geo. Wolf, Geo. Wolf, S. Q. Wonsettler, S. Q. Wonsettler, Sarah L Wonsettler, H. L. Wood, G. J. Woodard, Charles Woodbridge, D. A. Woolard, T. J. Woolard, T. J. Woolard, A. R. Woolcott, A. R. Woolcott, D. Woolsey, F. Woolsey, John Woolsey, J. B. Worthington, S. J. Worthington, F. S. Wright, Gibson Wright, J. F. Wright, J. P. Wright, J. P. Wright, Rhoda Wright, S. H. & Wright, W. R. Wright, O. Writt, O. Writt, S. R. Wyant, R. Wyatt, J. P. Wyckoff, G. T. Wycoff, J. T. Wycoff, M. G. Wycoff, G. H. Yoakes, G. H. Yoakes, Edwin Yoakum, W. H. Yoakum, C. Yockey, Alonzo Young, Alonzo Young, Geo. Young, Geo. Young, J. M. Zaner, Abe Zeikle, John Zeikle, John Zeikle, John

Zeikle, N. D. Zeikle, N. D. Zeikle, Margaret Zimmerman, Margaret Zimmerman, Mary Zimmerman, C. Zockery, D. O. Zonker.

Grundy County, Missouri, Charter Member of the Galt Lodge No. 423 of Free Masonry, Oct. 15, 1890.

George A. Smith, R. S. Hutton, Marshall Humphreys, M. M. Keller, J. S. Barbee, J. S. Todd, G. W. Eastwood, J. P. Hamlin, I. N. Moberly, J. W. Tunnell, J. T. Cowhick, A. L. Elder, James Robinson, A. S. Tunnell, F. M. West, Gabriel Williams, John A. Cooper. J. R. Barbee, G. L. Hamblin, J. A. Hedges, N. A. Winters

Taney County, Missouri, Members of the Democratic Committee, 1932.

Name	Office/Township	Address
Joe W. Kenton	Chairman	Branson
Mrs. Ella Dunn	Vice-Chairman	Walnut Shade
Walter Pharris	Secretary	Branson
Mrs. Cecile Stelph	Treasurer	Hollister
D. D. Casey	Swan	Taneyville
Mrs. Etta Boswell	Swan	Forsyth
C. A. Fine	Oliver	Hollister
Mrs. Cecile Stelph	Oliver	Hollister
Robert Brown	Cedar Creek	Cedar Creek
Mrs. Daisey Cornett	Cedar Creek	Groom
T. A. McFarland	Newton	Cedar Valley
Mrs. Tom McFarland	Newton	Cedar Valley
Bail Naish	Jasper	Walnut Shade
Mrs. Ella Dunn	Jasper	Walnut Shade
Joe. W. Kenton	Branson	Branson
Mrs. Glace Flanagan	Branson	Branson
Wm. Ellison	Big Creek	Protem
Mrs. Lou Hart	Big Creek	Protem
W. E. Savage	Scott	Miney
Mrs. Claudia Savage	Scott	Miney
Bryan Wright	Beaver	Bradleyville
Mrs. Bert Patterson	Beaver	Bradleyville

Missourians buried at Lexington National Cemetery

Simmonds, Jas. R.: (D) Jan., 1863, (Rk) Pvt, (Reg) Mo Cav.

Missourians on 1860 Mortality Schedule, Livingston County, Kentucky.

Sail, Mary A.: (A) 35Y, (Race) white, (Status) Married, (BP) Mo, (D)

Nov, (CMTS) pneumonia, ill 8 days.

Stone County, Missouri, 1870 Mortality Schedule
Cass Twp.
Crumpley, Sarah E.: (A) 7Y, (Sex) F, (Race) W, (Status) Single, (BP) Mo, (D) Apr, (Cmts) Diahorea of the bowels
Flat Creek Twp.
Pollard, Scott : (A) 22Y (Sex) Male, (Race) W, (BP) Mo, (D) Oct, (OC) Farm Labor, (Cmts) Jaundice

Berry, Martha: (A) 5 (Sex) Female, (Race) W, (BP) Mo, (D) Sep, (Cmts) Congestive Chill

Case, Sarah E.: (A) 3M, (Sex) Female, (Race) W, (BP) Mo, (D) Jul, (Cmts) Intermittant Fever
James Twp.
Irohn, Mary: (A) 76Y (Sex) Female, (Race) W, (Sex) Female, (BP) Germany, (D) Jul., (Cmts) Paralasis

Surber, Ann Eliza: (A) 8Y (Sex) Female, (Race) W, (BP) Mo, (D) Aug., (Cmts) Typhoid Fever

McNeely, Drucilla B.: (A) 12Y (Sex) Female, (Race) W, (BP) IN, (D) Sep. (Cmts) Typhoid Fever.

McNeely, Hester Ann: (A) 4Y (Sex) Female, (Race) W, (BP) IN, (D) Sep, (Cmts) Brain Fever.
Pierce Twp.
Ohler, James M.: (A) 19Y (Sex) Male, (Race) W, (BP) OH, (D) Jul., (OC) Farm Labor, (Cmts) Congestion Brain

Wheeler, Amanda: (A) 7Y (Sex) Female, (Race) W, (BP) Mo, (D) Sep, (Cmts) Hooping Cough

Brown, Sarah I.: (A) 26Y (Sex) Female, (Race) W, (BP) NC, (D) Apr, (OC) At Home, (Cmts) Consumption

Daniels, Mary E.: (A) 1Y (Sex) Female, (Race) W,(BP) Mo, (D) Sep, (Cmts) Burned To Death
Washington Twp.
Pegram, Milley E.: (A) 4M, (Sex) Female, (Race) W, (BP) Mo, (D) Jul, (Cmts) Brain Fever

Ashe, Hiram L.: (A) 1 (Sex) Male, (Race) W, (BP) Mo, (D) Sep, (Cmts) Dysentery

Smith, Wm. R: (A) . 29 (Sex) Male, (Race) W, (BP) Ar, (D) Sep, (OC) Hulkster, (Cmts) Consumption
Williams Twp.
Gregg, Wm. M.: (A) 2Y (Sex) Male, (Race) W,(BP) Mo, (D) Sep, (Cmts) Brain Fever

Gregg, John Samuel: (A)1Y (Sex) Male, (Race) W,(BP) Mo, (D) Apr,

(Cmts) Lung Fever.

Missouri Civil War Veterans in Illinois
Robert Ball: (Co.) B, (Reg) 14th, Inf Confederate
James W. Bean: (Co.) B, (Reg) 14th, Inf Confederate
Benjamin Bond: (Co.) B, (Reg) 14th, Inf Confederate
Frank Brynes: (Co.) I, (Reg) 30th, Inf
John Clark: (Co.) B, (Reg) 14th, Inf Confederate
Julius V. Cox: (Co.) B, (Reg) 14th, Inf Confederate
George A. Davenport: (Co.) G, (Reg) 11th, Inf
Albert C. Dexter: (Co.) B, (Reg) 14th, Inf Confederate
William F. Dunbar: (Co.) H, (Reg) 72th, Inf
Gottleib Flemming: (Co.) I, (Reg) 43th, Inf
John Forsyth: (Co.) B, (Reg) 14th, Inf Confederate
Robert Forsyth: (Co.) B, (Reg) 14th, Inf Confederate
Douglass Glassgow: (Co.) B, (Reg) 14th, Inf Confederate
Harman Greathouse: (Co.) E, (Reg) 16th, Inf
John Gutjahr: (Co.) I, (Reg) 43th, Inf
Michael Haley: (Co.) B, (Reg) 14th, Inf Confederate
William Hibbs: (Co.) E, (Reg) 16th, Inf
Stephen Hyde: (Co.) B, (Reg) 2nd Art
John Jones: (Co.) B, (Reg) 14th, Inf Confederate
John Kaiser: (Co.) I, (Reg) 43th, Inf
Barney Kets: (Co.) B, (Reg) 14th, Inf Confederate
George Lophink: (Co.) I, (Reg) 43th, Inf
James Mann: (Co.) E, (Reg) 36th, Inf
Isaac Miller: (Co.) B, (Reg) 14th, Inf Confederate
Jacob Musbash: (Co.) I, (Reg) 43th, Inf
Stephen D. Ratliff: (Co.) E, (Reg) 16th, Inf
Samuel Rogers: (Co.) I, (Reg) 16th, Inf
Robert Stephenson: (Co.) B, (Reg) 14th, Inf Confederate
Gregory Vog: (Co.) I, (Reg) 43th, Inf
David W. Walker: (Co.) B, (Reg) 14th, Inf Confederate
William M. Wiatt: (Co.) B, (Reg) 14th, Inf Confederate
George Williams: (Co.) K, (Reg) 9th, Inf
Adam Woltz: (Co.) I, (Reg) 43th, Inf
James E. Yaples: (Co.) B, (Reg) 14th, Inf Confederate

Missourians buried at the National Cemetery, Danville, KY
Buttler, Joseph: (D) 25 Nov 1862, (Rk) Pvt, (Reg) 15th Mo Inf.
Henricks, B.: (D) 14 Jan 1863, (Rk) Pvt, (Reg) 2nd Mo Inf.
Mark, Samuel G.: (D) 15 Mar 1863, (Rk) Pvt, (Reg) 15th Mo Inf.

Texas County, Missouri, Hazelton Postmasters

Name	Date
Marquis Tucker	May 2, 1892
William Craddock	Apr. 24, 1893
Frank Niles	Jun. 20, 1893
Elizabeth Hardester	Mar. 22, 1894
Stark Quick	Apr. 30, 1896
Janey Enlow	May 24, 1897
James A. Farley	May 27, 1899
Janey Enlow	Mar. 28, 1900
William Harrison	Jun. 17, 1901
Charles R. Copeland	Feb. 17, 1902
Williamm R. Harris	May 1, 1903
Stark Quick	Mar. 11, 1904
John Shaw	Dec. 27, 1904

Laclede County, Missouri, Charter members of Washington Christian Church, 1892.

Thomas Conner, Laura Conner, Joseph G. White, Nancy White, Silas Everett, Rachel Sanders, Alonzo Davis, Sarah Ellen Davis, Jesse Manning, Anna Manning, Mary A. Jackson, Aaron T. Anderson.

Nodaway county, Missouri, Individuals Listed on the 1850. Census

Elizabeth Ackison; Robert Ackison; Hannah Aldridge; John Aldridge; Lucinda Aldridge; Melissa E Aldridge; Samuel S. Aldridge; Susan Aldridge; William D. Aldridge; Amy J. Alexander; Angeline Alexander; Elizabeth Alexander; Harry Alexander; Joseph Alexander; Mary Alexander; Mary F. Alexander; Elizabeth Alumbaugh; Harden Alumbaugh; J. B. Alumbaugh; John Alumbaugh; John Alumbaugh; Martin Alumbaugh; Mary I. Alumbaugh; Nancy Alumbaugh; Peter Alumbaugh; William Alumbaugh; Hester Ammons; William Ammons; Candas A. Anderson; Jackson Anderson; James Anderson; Jesse Anderson; Perry Anderson; Mary Ashley; Dixon Ashworth; Elizabeth Ashworth; James Ashworth; Amelia R. Baily; America F. Baily; Bertha E Baily; Ellen G. Baily; George W. Baily; Hannah E Baily; Henry G. Baily; Joshua Baily; Mary Ann Baily; Mary M. Baily; Nancy Baily; Nancy J. Baily; Patience G. Baily; Permilia Baily; Rebecca M. Baily; Sarah M. Baily; William W. Baily; Abraham Banty; Charity F. Banty; Eliza Banty; Mary A. Banty; Susan E Banty; Charles F. Barber; Sarah Barber; William M. Barber; Isaac Bates; Louisa Bates; Marian Bates; Permilia Bates; William Bates; Edith Bayer; Elizabeth Bayer; Francis

M. Bayer; G. P Bayer; Martha Bayer; Melissa Bayer; Parthura Bayer; Phoenix Bayer; Abraham C. Belien; Alvin S. Belien; Belinda C. Belien; Elizabeth Belien; Frances A. Belien; Hannah Belien; Mary Belien; Mary J. Belien; Micagn Belien; Nancy A. Belien; Nancy A. Belien; William H. Belien; James Benson; William P. Bentley; David Best; Humphrey Best; Isaac Best; Mary Best; Silas Best; Silas Best; Susan Best; Susan K Best; William Best; Ann E. Bicket; Edmund J. Bicket; Martha A. Bicket; Permelia Bicket; Richard R. Bicket; Susan M. Bicket; Ann E. Bickett; Joseph Bickett; Martha Bickett; Rebecca Bidwell; William Bidwell; Bird Billings; Charles P. Billings; Elizabeth Billings; Harriet Billings; James Billings; John Billings; Lydia Billings; Lydia A. Billings; Nancy Billings; Thomas Billings; William L. Billings; Carter L. Black; Eleanor E. Black; Mary R. Black; William Black; Agnes P. Blackburn; Elizabeth Blackburn; James T. Blackburn; Jesse Blackburn; John R. Blackburn; Martha S. Blackburn; Mary Blackburn; Nancy Blackburn; Nancy F. Blackburn; Eleanor Blagg; Francis M. Blagg; George W. Blagg; James H. Blagg; Joseph Blagg; Mariah L. Blagg; Mary Blagg; May Blagg; William Blagg; Ann Blakely; Cynthia Blakely; Elizabeth Blakely; James Blakely; Jane Blakely; Jensy Blakely; Jensy A. Blakely; John C. Blakely; Joseph Blakely; Joseph A. Blakely; Joseph T. Blakely; Julince Blakely; Phelix Blakely; Robert A. Blakely; Thomas Blakely; Avery (female) Blakely; James M. Blakly; Jesse F. Blakly; Martha E. Blakly; Mary Blakly; Mary A. Blakly; Susan E. Blakly; Thomas Blakly; Benjamin Boatwright; John A. Boatwright; Mary A. Boatwright; Mary P. Boatwright; Richard Boatwright; William T. Boatwright; William Boen; Abraham Bowman; Elizabeth Bowman; Elizabeth Bowman; Francis M. Bowman; Henry Bowman; Jacob Bowman; James P Bowman; Jane Bowman; Jonathan J. Bowman; Joseph Bowman; Joseph Bowman; Joseph Bowman; Lydia Bowman; Mary A. Bowman; Mary J. Bowman; Missouri A. Bowman; Richard Bowman; Ruth Bowman; Samuel Bowman; Sarah Bowman; Sarah E. Bowman; Sarah K. Bowman; Thomas Bowman; William Bowman; Cornelius Bracking; Mary S. Bracking; Robert L Bracking; Sabitha Bracking; Andrew Braden; Elias Braden; John Braden; Polly Braden; Regaithia Braden; Richard Braden; Rodah Braden; Rodah M. Braden; Ruhamah Braden; Elizabeth Brittain; Fletcher Brittain; John Brittain; L. C. Brittain; Martha J. Brittain; Nancy Brittain; Thomas Brittain; Wiley J. Brittain; Jmes R. Britzen; John Britzen; John Britzen; Martha Britzen; Mary Britzen; William F. Britzen; Levi Brock; Clay A. Broderick; Elizabeth Broderick; Isaac W. Broderick; James K. Broderick; Nancy Broderick; Samuel Broderick; Amanda I. Brown;

Andrew Brown; Andrew Brown; Ann Brown; Elizabeth Brown; Elizabeth Brown; Elizabeth A. Brown; G. L. Brown; Gideon L. Brown; Isaac F. Brown; Isaiah Brown; Jacob Brown; Jane Brown; John Brown; Joseph A. Brown; Joseph C. Brown; Margaret Brown; Mary Brown; Melinda Brown; N. B. Brown; Nancy E. Brown; Philip C. Brown; Priscilla Brown; Sarah A. Brown; Sarah J. Brown; Thomas J. Brown; Wilson W. Brown; Amanda Broyle; Asah Broyle; Elizabeth Broyle; Frances Broyle; Hannah Broyle; James C. Broyle; Jefferson Broyle; John Broyle; Mary J. Broyle; Nancy Broyle; Nathaniel Broyle; Richard Broyle; Samuel Broyle; Sarah Broyle; Sarah E Broyle; Solomon Broyle; Tabitha Broyle; William Broyle; Wilson Broyle; Susannah P Brumfield; William Brumfield; Hugh Burns; Lucinda Burns; Malinda Burns; Nancy A. Burns; Sarah Burns; Susannah Burns; Thomas F. Burns; Cynderella Burris; Cynthia Burris; David Burris; Elijah Burris; Elijah B. Burris; Elizabeth Burris; Ernie Burris; Francis Burris; Jenneta Burris; John Burris; Lewis Burris; Margaret Burris; Margaret E Burris; Moses Burris; Polly A. Burris; Rebecca I. Burris; Sarah E Burris; William Burris; Willim R. Burris; Elizabeth Butts; George Butts; Mariah Butts; Mary Butts; Mary Butts; Sarah Butts; Benjamin Byers; Eliza Byers; Issabella Byers; Lemuel Byers; Martha Byers; Mary J. Byers; Sophiah Byers; William Byers George Cahovn; Ann E Calvin; Eady Calvin; James Calvin; Nancy J. Calvin; Artimissia Campbell; Elizabeth Campbell; James H. Campbell; James M. Campbell; Margaret J. Campbell; Margaret J. Campbell; Mary D. Campbell; Nancy Campbell; Nancy J. Campbell; William Campbell; Elizabeth Careless; John Carless; Joseph Carless; Phebe Carless; Elizabeth Carnutt; John Carnutt; Phiriba Carnutt; Thomas Carnutt; William Carnutt; Dyen Cash; Emanuel Cash; Hannah Cash; John Cash; John Cash; Nancy Cash; Sarah Cash; Thomas B. Cash; William M. Cash; Patsy Cavanaugh; Philmon F. Cavanaugh; Edmund Chestnut; Edmund Chestnut; Elizabeth Chestnut; John Chestnut; Louisa Chestnut; Rachael Chestnut; Sally Chestnut; Samuel Chestnut; Sarah J. Chestnut; Ambrose Clain; Mary H. Clain; Sarah A. Clain; John Clark; Katherine Clark; Wesley Clark; Mary Cleise; Alexander Clellan; Casander Clellan; Elizabeth Clellan; Hester Clifton; John Clifton; William Clifton; Ariana M. Cock; Caroline Cock; D. H. Cock; H. D. Cock; Roxy S. Cock; Susan Cock; William Cock; Abraham Colet; Abraham Colet; Elizabeth Colet; Jane Colet; John Colet; Enoch M. Comer; Mary Comer; Philip Comer; Robert R. Comer; Dartha J. Conlin; Francis Conlin; Francis M. Conlin; Sarah A. Conlin; William Conlin; America J. Cook; Bartlet Cook; Benjamin F. Cook; James Cook; John L

Cook; Jonathan H. Cook; Julia A. Cook; Margaret Cook; Margaret A. Cook; Mary Cook; Samuel Cook; William M. Cook; Eliza Cox; Elizabeth Cox; Elizabeth Cox; Henry D. Cox; Martha Cox; Mary C. Cox; May Cox; Nola Cox; Ruth Cox; Samantha H. Cox; Thomas Cox; Thomas Cox; James Craft; Margaret J. Craft; Polly A. Craft; Sarah Craft; Thomas J. Craft; Jacob Criger; Nancy E Criger; Sarah Criger; William Criger; Eleanor Cubberly; Eveline Cubberly; Jane Cubberly; John R. Cubberly; Joseph Cubberly; Joseph Cubberly; James Curanett; Eliza Curl; Elizabeth Curl; Mary D. Curl; Perlina Curl; Rufina Curl; Abcissa Curmett; Caperton Curmett; William Curmett; Chauncy Dalrymple; Ezra A. Dalrymple; Rebecca Dalrymple; Rebecca J. Dalrymple; Thomas Dalrymple; Richard F. Danaken; Henry Danby; Marth A. Danby; Sarah Danby; Winfield Danby; Benjamin Davenport; Benjamin Davenport; John Davenport; Joseph Davenport; Lucinda Davenport; Sarah Davenport; Timothy Davenport; Allen Davis; Charity Davis; Elizabeth Davis; George W. Davis; John Davis; Martha Davis; Martha J. Davis; Mary A. Davis; Orrin Davis; Thomas Davis; Waid H. Davis; William Demar; Betsy A. Denning; Elizabeth Denning; Hiram Denning; James T. Denning; Martha A. Denning; William Denning; James M. Dewes; Porterfield Dillen; Daniel Dixon; Disey Dixon; Francis M. Dixon; Harriet Dixon; Henry Dixon; Hosa Dixon; Jesse Dixon; Jorden Dixon; Raphail Dixon; Sealy (female) Dixon; Smith Dixon; Susannah Dixon; Willaim Dixon; William Dixon; Asa Downing; Elizabeth Downing; Erastus Downing; Malinda Downing; Marcella Downing; Margaret Downing; Mary Downing; Rebecca Downing; Washington Downing; Actious Drake; Cimeon Drake; Joseph Drake; Mirium Drake; Nancy Drake; Rebecca Drake; David Drewry; T. C. Eastons; Agnes Edster; William Edster; James M. Ellington; Rebecca J. Ellington; Thomas J. Ellington; William H. Ellington; William R. Ellington; Abby D. Elliott; David Elliott; James W. Elliott; James W. Elliott; Jane Elliott; Jeremiah Elliott; John Elliott; Kinnion ? Elliott; Margaret S. Elliott; Mary Elliott; Mary E Elliott; Nancy Elliott; Polly Elliott; Talitha J. Elliott; Telitha Elliott; William Elliott; Willis Elliott; Elizabeth Ellis; Emily Ellis; Isaac Ellis; John Ellis; John C. Ellis; Joseph Ellis; Mary Ellis; Thomas Ellis; William Ellis; Mary K. Elmoir; Elizabeth Estes; Mary Estes; Susannah Estes; Jane Evard; Elizabeth Eversole; John W. Eversole; Mary Eversole; Sarah A. Eversole; Wooling Eversole; Amanda Fanning; Hezekiah Fanning; John J. Fanning; Luaina A. Fanning; Mary Fanning; Matilda Fanning; Melinda Fanning; Permilia Fanning; William H. Fanning; Cynthia A. Farrens; Henry Farrens; John B. Farrens; John

H. Farrens; Rachael Farrens; Sarah Farrens; Sarah J. Farrens; William Farrens; Ann G. Feaster; Cornelius Feaster; John Feaster; Mary E Feaster; Perlina J. Feaster; Sarah R. Feaster; Solomon Feaster; John Felman; Abraham Fletcher; Abraham Fletcher; David Fletcher; Drucilla Fletcher; Francis M. Fletcher; Hiram Fletcher; James Fletcher; James Fletcher; James K Fletcher; John Fletcher; Margaret Fletcher; Martha J. Fletcher; Melinda Fletcher; Rebecca Fletcher; Samuel Fletcher; Thomas B. Fletcher; Vordarman Fletcher; James Francis; Matilda Francis; Matilda Francis; Sarah A. Francis; George Funderburk; Jane Funderburk; Emily J. Gage; Jesse Gage; Margaret Gage; George P Gailon; Mary A. Gailon; Hughy A. Garrett; William S. Garrett; David Gascal; Martha Gascal; Mary A. Gascal; Abidriago Gentry; Alfred Gentry; Allen Gentry; James Gentry; Jesse J. Gentry; John W. Gentry; Sally Gentry; Thomas Gentry; Adaline Gifford; Angeline Gifford; Harvey Gifford; Levi Gifford; Mary Gifford; Patience Gifford; Sylvester Gifford; Edmund Gipson; Elizabeth Gipson; Hannah Gipson; Jesse Gipson; John Gipson; Polly Gipson; Betsy F. Glasgow; Franklin Glasgow; Sarah Glasgow; Archibald Glenn; James Glenn; Jane Glenn; John Glenn; Margaret Glenn; Robert Glenn; William Glenn; Adam Goforth; Carolin Goforth; James H. Goforth; John C. Goforth; Martha Goforth; Mary Goforth; Sarah Goforth; William Goforth; William K Goforth; Charles Good; Gracy A. Good; Joseph Good; Richmond Good; Samuel Good; William Good; Amos Graham; Charles C. Graham; Mary J. Graham; Matthew Graham; Albert C. Graves; Allen P Graves; Amanda E Graves; Amy Graves; Anthony Graves; Aunletha Graves; Elizabeth Graves; Elizabeth Graves; Elvira Graves; George A. Graves; George R. Graves; Henry Graves; Jacob Graves; James Graves; James F. Graves; James M. Graves; John Graves; John Graves; Julia A. Graves; Katharine Graves; Lovina Graves; Lovina Graves; Martha Graves; Martha Graves; Mary E. Graves; Nancy Graves; Rosannah Graves; Rose A. Graves; Sarah Graves; Sarah Graves; Sarah A. Graves; Silas Graves; William Graves; William B. Graves; William T, Graves; Alfred Gray; Alfred Gray; Elizabeth Gray; Emily J. Gray; Frances Gray; James Gray; James F. Gray; James W. Gray; Jennina Gray; John Gray; Lucinda Gray; Martha Gray; Martha Gray; Martha C. Gray; Martha W. Gray; Martin Gray; Martin Gray; Mary Gray; Mary J. Gray; Mary L. Gray; Mary L. Gray; Michael H. Gray; Nancy Gray; Nancy Gray; Robert J. Gray; Sarah E Gray; Sarah J. Gray; Sarah J. Gray; Thomas J. Gray; William Gray; William Gray; William A. Gray; William F. Gray; William M. Gray; America Griffith; Caroline Griffith; Jane Griffith; John T Griffith; Louisa Griffith;

Nancy Griffith; Nancy Griffith; Rebecca A. Griffith; Squire M. Griffith; Uriah Griffith; Walter Griffith; Washington Griffith; William L Griffith; Ahuysa Grove; Eleanor Grove; Elizabeth Grove; Emeline Grove; Francis M. Grove; Jackson Grove; John Grove; John Grove; Mahala A. Grove; Nancy Grove; Susannah Grove; Hiram D. Groves; Alex Guill; Martha M. Guill; Blakely Hall; Elizabeth Hall; Elizabeth Hall; Hiram Hall; J. H. Hall; Jasper Hall; John Hall; Johnson Hall; Margaret Hall; Martin V. Hall; Miranda Hall; Nancy Hall; Newton Hall; Amos Hallsa; John A. Hallsa; Mary K. Hallsa; Nancy Hallsa; Sarah E. Hallsa; William A. Hallsa; Abijah Hampton; Leonard Hampton; Lucinda Hampton; Nancy Hampton; Rosannah Hampton; Ann Hanna; James Hanna; Mary A. Hanna; Sinnura(female) Hanna; Uroy Hannah; Francis M. Harper; James P Harper; Jesse Harper; John T Harper; Mary A. Harper; Benjamin Harris; Ekizabeth Harris; Henry Harris; Henry T. Harris; Hester A. Harris; Isaac Harris; Isaac Harris; James Harris; Jesse Harris; Jesse Harris; John Harris; Marion Harris; Mary Harris; Mary E. Harris; Melissa Harris; Nancy E. Harris; Nancy J. Harris; Reuben Harris; Sarah Harris; Sarah E Harris; William Harris; Willim M. Harris; Woten Harris; Woten Harris; Elizabeth Haws; Elzeplain Haws; Mary K. Haws; Sampson G. Haws; Solomon Haws; William M. Haws; James R. Hays; John P. Hays; Elisha Heddy; Elisha Heddy; Emily Heddy; Emvy Heddy; Ezra Heddy; Ezra Heddy; Joseph Heddy; Kisiah Heddy; Mary Heddy; Mary A. Heddy; Melissa Heddy; Rebecca Heddy; Sarah Heddy; Sarah Heddy; Thomas Heddy; Thomas Heddy; Eleanor Hedgpeth; Eliza Hedgpeth; Elizabeth Hedgpeth; Henry Hedgpeth; I. Hedgpeth; James Hedgpeth; Jane Hedgpeth; Joel Hedgpeth; Joel Hedgpeth; John W. Hedgpeth; Mary E Hedgpeth; Phebe Hedgpeth; Ruth C. Hedgpeth; Thomas R. Hedgpeth; William Hedgpeth; Albert Heflin; Elijah Heflin; Emeline Heflin; James Heflin; James L Heflin; Lewis Heflin; Louvisa Heflin; Marcellus Heflin; Melville Heflin; Nancy Heflin; Robert Heflin; Sylvester Heflin; William Heflin; Clay K Henderson; H. H. Henderson; John W. Henderson; Martha Henderson; Noah Henderson; Susan J. Henderson; Thomas J. Henderson; William R. Henderson; Andrew J. Herring; Elizabeth Herring; George V Herring; Henry A. Herring; J. K Herring; Jacob M. Herring; M. V. Herring; Mary Herring; Nehemiah Herring; Pemela Herring; Benjamin Holland; Letha J. Holland; Thomas Holland; William B. Holland; Cornelia J. Holt; Mary E Holt; Sarah Holt; William R. Holt; Elizabeth Houston; Leander L Houston; Louisa Houston; Mary M. Houston; Parthman Houston; Robert N. Houston; Sarah Houston; William Houston; William

Houston; John F. Howard; John Hudgens; Nancy Hudgens; America Huff; Josephine Huff; Lydia A. Huff; Ruth Huff; Virginia Huff; James L Hughs; Marion Hughs; Mary Hughs; Isaiah Hurlburt; Isiah Hurlburt; Return Hurlburt; Elizabeth Hutson; Franklin Hutson; George W. Hutson; Hannah Hutson; James Hutson; Jasper Hutson; John Hutson; John Hutson; Joseph Hutson; Lucinda Hutson; Margaret Hutson; Margaret Hutson; Nancy Hutson; Nancy Hutson; Rebecca E. Hutson; Resiah (female) Hutson; Sarah Hutson; William Hutson; William Hutson; Alexander Ingals; Anson Ingals; Clarinda Ingals; Cynthia Ingals; Elizabeth Ingals; Lucinda Ingals; Nancy Ingals; Sarah Ingals; William Ingals; Casandra Ingels; Eliza A. Ingels; James Ingels; Joseph Ingels; Josephine Ingels; Lemual Ingels; Phebe Ingels; Samuel Ingels; Thomas J. Ingels; Zacharia T Ingels; Elizabeth Irwin; Joannaeth Irwin; John Irwin; Lafayette Irwin; Missouri Irwin; Nancy Irwin; Rachael Irwin; Elzisar ? Isom; John Isom; Mariba Isom; Archy Jackson; Gashaus Jackson; Harriet Jackson; John Jackson; John ackson; Joseph Jackson; Louisa Jackson; Mary Jackson; Mayna Jackson; Nathan J. Jackson; Obediance Jackson; Sarah A. Jackson; Andrew T Jenkins; Martha A. Jenkins; Elizabeth Jester; James A. Jester; Laura Jester; Martha F. Jester; Benjamin Johnson; E. W. Johnson; Eli B. Johnson; Elizabeth Johnson; Hester Johnson; John A. Johnson; John R. Johnson; Joseph Johnson; Joseph A. Johnson; Levi R. Johnson; Lewis Johnson; Margaret Johnson; Margaret Johnson; Margaret E. Johnson; Nancy Johnson; Polly E. Johnson; Rebecca A. Johnson; Richard A. Johnson; Sally Johnson; Seth Johnson; Elizabeth Jones; Harriet Jones; Jesse Jones; Smith Jones; Eunice Joslin; Harvy E. Joslin; Jonathan C. Joslin; Leonard M. Joslin; Riley Joslin; Sarah A. Joslin; William H. Joslin; Andrew R. Jourdan; Mary Jourdan; Mary J. Jourdan; Matilda M. Jourdan; Nancy H. Jourdan; Rebecca E. Jourdan; William J. Jourdan; Minerva Kelly; Peter W. Kelly; Sarah Kelly; Charity Kennedy; John Kennedy; Lucretia Kennedy; Samuel Kennedy; Elizabeth Kilgore; Levi Kilgore; Sarah A. Kilgore; Enoch King; Sally King; Charles Lamar; John M. Lamar; John M. Lamar; Rutela Lamar; Sarah Lamar; Susannah Lamar; Hiram Lanham; Jane Lanham; Silvester Lanham; Eliza J. Lanning; Isaac A. Lanning; Mary A. Lanning; Nancy J. Lanning; Sarah J. Lanning; Benjamin Lanum; Ema F. Lanum; Andrew J. Lawson; Araminta Lawson; Clarkston Lawson; John B. Lawson; Julia A. Lawson; Mary Lawson; Mary E Lawson; Mary J. Lawson; Nancy J. Lawson; Priscilla Lawson; Samuel Lawson; Sarah H. Lawson; William M. Lawson; George Leader; Sarah Leader; Columbus Lee; Delphuna Lee; Elizabeth Lee; Elizabeth Lee; Hiram Lee; Hiram Lee; James

Lee; Matilda Lee; Melvina Lee; Penina Lee; Hether Linsford; Aaron Linville; Alice Linville; Bethana Linville; Charity Linville; Eleanor Linville; Ernestine Linville; George H. Linville; Granville Linville; Henry C. Linville; Hester A. Linville; Jacob M. Linville; James Linville; James C. Linville; James H. Linville; Joel S. Linville; Lucinda A. Linville; Margaret E. Linville; Martha E. Linville; Mary E, Linville; Mary J. Linville; Nancy C. Linville; Phebe Linville; Rebecca J. Linville; Sarah Linville; Sarah Linville; Sarah Linville; Sarah J. Linville; William R. Linville; Willim J. Linville; Zachariah Linville; Andrew J. Loar; James H. Loar; Nancy Loar; Stephen Loar; Leonard C. Logan; Andrew J. Lowe; Elizabeth Lowe; Isom Lowe; John W. Lowe; Narcissa Lowe; James Lunsford; James Lunsford; John Lunsford; Martha A. Lunsford; Nancy Lunsford; William Lunsford; John S. Malott; George Manly; Harrison Manly; Julia A. Manly; Lebbens Manly; Mary A. Manly; Polly M. Manly; Riley Manly; Roswell Manly; Ruth A. Manly; Sarah A. Manly; Savannah Manly; John Marion; Clarrissa Markwell; Hiram Markwell; James Markwell; John Markwell; Louvisa Markwell; Rodah A. Markwell; Sarah Markwell; Silvester Markwell; Aueia Martin; Betsy Martin; Katharine Martin; Kerson Martin; Levi Martin; Lucinda Martin; Amanda J. Martin; Margaret Martin; Matilda Martin; Minerva Martin; Nancy A. Martin; Polly Martin; Samuel Martin; Thomas Martin; John Mast; Katharine Mast; Noah Mast; Susan Mast; Susannah Mattux; William B. Mattux; Harriet McCarty; Mary J. McCarty; Nancy McCarty; Sally A. McCarty; George McClanahan; M. McClanahan; Mrs McClanahan; Sam McClanahan; Finley McCrary; Finley McCrary; Jefferson McCrary; Rachel McCrary; Charlotte McCulley; Isaac McCulley; John A. McCulley; Mariba McCulley; Martha I. McCulley; Vance T. McCulley; W. B. McCulley; William D. McDonald; Frances McDowell; Jane McDowell; Jesse McDowell; Mary A. McDowell; Mathias McDowell; Melissa McDowell; Sarah J. McDowell; William McDowell; Andrew R. McKinzie; Elizabeth McKinzie; James K McKinzie; Rebecca J. McKinzie; Eleanor A. McKnight; J. E. McKnight; Thomas M. McKnight; Andrew J. McLain; Elizabeth McLain; Elizabeth McLain; Emily McLain; Emily McLain; Farlene McLain; George McLain; George McLain; James McLain; James T. McLain; John McLain; John McLain; Katharine McLain; Rachael McLain; Sarah L McLain; William R. McLain; Greenberry McMichael; Melvina McMichael; America J. Mileham; David F. Mileham; Jacob Mileham; John W. Mileham; Richard J. Mileham; Roena Mileham; Berry Miller; Arminda Minard; Elendor(female) Minard; Frederick Minard; John R. Minard; Julia A. Minard; Mariah

L. Minard; Mary J. Minard; Albert C. Modie; Effe Modie; Jacob Modie; Martha V. Modie; Minerva S. Modie; Rachael Modie; Aramanda Moler; Benjamin F. Moler; Camilla Moler; Christina Moler; Clovy A. Moler; Effe M. Moler; Mary A. Moler; Moses A. Moler; Stinghy Moler; William H. Moler; John Moore; Martha H. Moore; Mary J. Moore; Olivia M. Moore; Susana Moore; William Moore; Elizabeth More; Hannah R. More; Hiram More; Jefferson More; Jesse More; Jesse More; John More; Logan More; Louana More; Louisa More; Mary More; Preston More; Richard More; Samuel More; Adanijah Morgan; Amaziah Morgan; Elizabeth Morgan; James W. Morgan; John B. Morgan; Katherine Morgan; Lecvis Morgan; Margaret Morgan; Pauline Morgan; Ruth A. Morgan; William W. Morgan; Martha Mull; Noah Mull; Elizabeth Musinge; John Musinge; Mary J. Musinge; Matilda Musinge; Selila Musinge; Silas Musinge; Allen Muzinge; Benjamin F. Muzinge; Cornelius Muzinge; Elizabeth Muzinge; John Muzinge; Samuel Muzinge; Sela Muzinge; William Muzinge; Almia A. Myers; Barnabas Myers; Jane B. Myers; Rebecca Myers; Sarah D. Myers; ; Alvina Nash; Amanda J. Nash; Andrew Nash; Elizabeth Nash; George W. Nash; Harriet Nash; Harriet Nash; Julia A. Nash; Katharine Nash; Louisa Nash; Louisa J. Nash; Lovina Nash; Martha E Nash; Nancy Nash; Nancy Nash; Nancy A. Nash; Nancy E Nash; Oliver Nash; Parazetta Nash; Phebe A. Nash; Samuel Nash; Samuel Nash; Samuel Nash; Thomas C. Nash; Timothy Nash; William Nash; William Nash; Sarah Nicholas; Ann E. Noffsinger; Carsa E. Noffsinger; Frances Noffsinger; Frances Noffsinger; Jacob Noffsinger; James Noffsinger; James Noffsinger; John Noffsinger; Margaret E. Noffsinger; Martha Noffsinger; Martha A. Noffsinger; Martin Noffsinger; Matilda Noffsinger; Matilda Noffsinger; Peter Noffsinger; Peter Noffsinger; Rachail Noffsinger; Weslet Noffsinger; William Noffsinger; James C. Noland; Joseph M. Noland; Katharine Noland; Sally Noland; May O'Howel; Amanda J. Owens; Elizabeth Owens; John W. Owens; Louisa Owens; Nancy A. Owens; Nicholas Owens; Nicholas Owens; Prime Owens; Priscilla Owens; Samuel Owens; Calvin Parish; Jesse Parish; Mary E. Parish; Nancy Parish; Susan Parish; Asberry H. Parker; Betsy Parker; Elizabeth Parker; Franklin Parker; Hannah Parker; John Parker; John Parker; John Parker; Mariah Parker; Rebecca Parker; Thomas Parker; Thomas Parsons; Eliza J. Patton; Elizabeth Patton; G. M. Patton; Joseph A. Patton; Louisa M. Patton; Lucinda Patton; Luthena Patton; Lydia A. Patton; Thomas L. Patton; William C. Patton; ClementinePennington; James Pennington; James E Pennington; John T. Pennington; Julia A. Pennington; Nancy

Pennington; Sarah Pennington; Susan Pennington; Telitha Pennington; William W. Pennington; Eliza Perry; George B. Perry; Lorenzo T. Perry; Sarah H. Perry; William Perry; William O. Perry; James Pickerell; Lucinda Pickerell; Margaret E Pickerell; Polly A. Pickerell; David G. Pickwell; Joel Pickwell; Louisa Pickwell; Margaret J. Pigg; Nancy Pigg; Noah Pigg; Delila A. Pistole; George W. Pistole; James C. Pistole; John Pistole; Leander B. Pistole; Lucinda Pistole; Martha Pistole; Stephen C. Pistole; Thomas J. Pistole; William M. Pistole; Howard B. Porter; James C. Porter; John W. Porter; Nancy Porter; Sarah K Porter; Melissa Powell; Cynthia Prather; Elizabeth Prather; Henrietta Prather; Isaac N. Prather; J. N. Prather; James B. Prather; Margaret E Prather; Mariah C. Prather; Mariah S. Prather; Mary V. Prather; Benjamin Price; Mary Price; Samuel Price; Warren Price; William Price; Edward Pugh; Enoch Pugh; Mary Pugh; D. N. Pulley; James CC Pulley; James M. Pulley; Jane Pulley; John Pulley; P B. Pulley; Temperance Pulley; Thomas J. Pulley; W. D. Pulley; Patrick Racraft; Jefferson Ragsdale; Matilda Ragsdale; Melina Ragsdale; Sarah J. Ragsdale; William A. Ragsdale; David Ramsey; Ernie Ramsey; G. R. Ramsey; Hessa Ramsey; Lewis Ramsey; Margaret Ramsey; Willim Ramsey; Elizabeth Ray; Emeline Ray; Gidenren ? Ray; James Ray; Jonathan S. Ray; Rebecca Ray; Sally Ray; Jacob P Retely; George W. Reynolds; Howard Reynolds; Jane Reynolds; John L. Reynolds; Nehemiah Reynolds; Ruth A. Reynolds; Sarah J. Reynolds; Zachariah Reynolds; David Rhoads; Edith Rhoads; George R. Rhoads; Jacob D. Rhoads; James M. Rhoads; John Rhoads; John L. Rhoads; Mary A. Rhoads; Mary L. Rhoads; Melinda A. Rhoads; Sarah Rhoads; Sarah J. Rhoads; Selah Rhoads; Thomas J. Rhoads; William Rhoads; William D. Rhoads; Jasper Rhodes; John M. Rhodes; Rily Rhodes; Susannah Rhodes; Gabriel Rice; Harrison Rice; James M. Rice; Joseph W. Rice; Elizabeth Richards; Gilford Richards; James H. Richards; Lucy A. Richards; Mary F. Richards; Silas A. Richards; Virginia J. Richards; Lydia Richart; Oregon (female) Richart; Sarah Rinehart; Stephen D. Rinehart; Amelina Roads; Ann E Roads; C. C. Roads; Edmonia Roads; J. K Roads; James Roads; John A. Roads; Katharine Roads; Mary M. Roads; Nathan Roads; Sarah K Roads; Adanijah Roberts; Angenine Roberts; B. L Roberts; Baibry (female) Roberts; Benjamin F. Roberts; Cornelius Roberts; Elendu (female) Roberts; Elizabeth Roberts; Elizabeth Roberts; Emily Roberts; Fletcher Roberts; Gracy Roberts; James Roberts; Josiah Roberts; Louisa Roberts; Mariah Roberts; Nathan Roberts; Ruth Roberts; Samuel Roberts; Sarah Roberts; Thomas Roberts; William Roberts; Annette Ross;

Benjamin F. Ross; Henry Ross; Lafayette Ross; Mary J. Ross; Rebecca Ross; Robert Ross; Samuel Ross; Andrew J. Rroils; Andrew Russell; Araminter Russell; Clarissa Russell; Robert R. Russell; Sarah J. Russell; Polly Rutledge; Arthura Sanders; Edray (f) Sanders; Penny Sanders; William Sanders; Elizabeth Saunders; James Saunders; Mary F. Saunders; Rahab M. Saunders; Sara Saunders; Saripta? Saunders; Strapford Saunders; Edwin Schofield; James Schofield; John H. Schofield; Margaret Schofield; Sisaly Schofield; Daniel Seavers; Dicy R. Seavers; Eliza C. Seavers; Elizabeth Seavers; Hughy Seavers; Jane Seavers; John Seavers; John Seavers; Martha A. Seavers; Mary Seavers; Mary K Seavers; Rebecca Seavers; Rebecca Seavers; William Seavers; William Seavers; Sarah A. See; Mary A. Self; Thomas Self; Alexander Sharp; Althina Sharp; Alvin Sharp; Amanda Sharp; Anderson Sharp; Charlotte Sharp; Daniel Sharp; Elmina Sharp; Harvey S. Sharp; Henderson Sharp; Henry Sharp; Henry Sharp; Hester A. Sharp; Isaac Sharp; Isaiah J. Sharp; Jacob Sharp; Jacob Sharp; James Sharp; James Sharp; James A. Sharp; John Sharp; John Sharp; Lavina Sharp; Leroy Sharp; Martha Sharp; Mary A. Sharp; Mary E Sharp; Mary J. Sharp; Mary W. Sharp; Missouri E Sharp; Nancy Sharp; Nicholas Sharp; Nicholas Sharp; Polly A. Sharp; REbecca Sharp; Rebecca Sharp; Rebecca J. Sharp; Sarah Sharp; Sarah Sharp; Sarah A. Sharp; Sarah E. Sharp; Sarah. E Sharp; Sarah J. Sharp; Sarena Sharp; Susannah Sharp; Tebitha Sharp; William Sharp; William H. Sharp; William H. Sharp; John R. Shaw; Joseph Shaw; Maranda E. Shaw; Martha Shaw; Mary E. Shaw; Rachael Shaw; Savannah Shaw; William Shaw; Christina Shelton; David Shelton; India A. Shelton; John Shelton; Levi Shelton; Polly F. Shelton; Andrew Shepherd; Benjamin F. Shepherd; Bryant Shepherd; Clare Shepherd; Decalb Shepherd; Enoch E. Shepherd; George W. Shepherd; Jacob Shepherd; James Shepherd; James H. Shepherd; James M. Shepherd; John W. Shepherd; Johnathan Shepherd; Joseph W. Shepherd; Levi Shepherd; Louisa Shepherd; Lucinda Shepherd; Lucy Shepherd; Lucy A. Shepherd; Mahala Shepherd; Margaret Shepherd; Marion Shepherd; Martha J. Shepherd; Mary Shepherd; Mary M. Shepherd; Missouri F. Shepherd; Nancy Shepherd; Samuel Shepherd; Sarah J. Shepherd; Silvester Shepherd; Susannah Shepherd; Cornelius Short; Eliza Short; Isiah Short; Mary E. Short; Stanly B. Short; Edny L. Sims; Eleanor Sims; Frederick Sims; Joseph T Sims; Telitha A. Sims; William M. Sims; James M. Sitton; John M. Sitton; Joseph Sitton; Lawrence B. Sitton; Mary A. Sitton; Nana N. Sitton; Rebecca Sitton; Silas R. Sitton; Winnifred Sitton; Anny Sizemore; Eastine A. Sizemore; Ephriam

Sizemore; George Sizemore; George W. Sizemore; Rachael Sizemore; Rebecca Sizemore; Alexander Smith; Andrew J. Smith; Buy F. Smith; Christopher Smith; Eliza A. Smith; Elizabeth Smith; Elizabeth Smith; Elon Smith; Elon Smith; Emily J. Smith; Enoch Smith; Isaac Smith; James D. Smith; James K Smith; Jane L Smith; Jesse B. Smith; John Smith; John Smith; John W. Smith; Lewis B. Smith; Lucinda Smith; Michael H. Smith; Minerva Smith; Susan Smith; William C. Smith; William J. Smith; William V. Smith; James Smock; James E .Smock; Joseph Smock; Martha M. Smock; Mathias Smock; Sarah Smock; William H. Smock; Marchel Sollars; Mary Sollars; Nancy A. Sollars; Betsy Spencer; Lafayette Spencer; Sally Spencer; Telitha Spencer; Thomas Spencer; Anderson Spoonsmore; Armilda Spoonsmore; David Spoonsmore; Goodlaw Spoonsmore; Jane Spoonsmore; Melinda Spoonsmore; Nancy Spoonsmore; Perry Spoonsmore; Richard Spoonsmore; Eldy (female) Sroufe; Patsy Stephens; Andrew Stephenson; Hugh A. Stephenson; Jesse Stephenson; Mary J. Stephenson; James Stevens; John Stevens; Mary Stevens; Nancy Stevens; Nancy A. Stevens; Susan Stevens; William Stevens; Camilla Stingley; Eliza Stingley; Elizabeth Stingley; Flora Stingley; Jesse Stingley; Lewis Stingley; Mary Stingley; Orren Stingley; Rachael Stingley; William Stingley; Barret H. Stingly; Eliza Stingly; George R. Stingly; Hiram M. Stingly; Moses Stingly; Rosannah Stingly; Thursey A. Stingly; William A. Stingly; David Stockton; Elizabeth Stockton; John W. Stockton; Mariah Stockton; Pamela Stockton; Rachael Stockton; Robert W. Stockton; Samuel Stockton; William Stockton; Emily J. Stoner; Adaline Stow; Alfred L Stow; Caroline Stow; Eliza E. Stow; Elizabeth Stow; Frances J. Stow; Joel Stow; John Stow; Marion Stow; Marvel T. Stow; Nancy E. Stow; David Surrency; David Swearingen; Eliza Swearingen; Henry Swearingen; Jackson Swearingen; Mary Swearingen; Nicholas Swearingen; Eliza Taply; Elizabeth Taply; Henry C. Taply; James Taply; John Taply; Martha Taply; William Taply; Emelia Tate; Henry Tate; John C. Tate; Louisa J. Tate; Adam Terhune; Amanda Terhune; Betsy Terhune; Courline ? Terhune; Eliza Terhune; John Terhune; Laura Terhune; Martha Terhune; Elizabeth Thomas; William Thomas; John Thomason; Abby Thompson; Eliza Thompson; George C. Thompson; George J. Thompson; Granville Thompson; James H. Thompson; Jasper H. Thompson; John H. Thompson; John R. Thompson; John W. Thompson; Lomira (f) Thompson; Mary K Thompson; Melinda Thompson; Washington789 Thompson; William Thompson; Ajax Torrance; Harriet Torrance; Henry E .Torrance; Hosea Torrance; L. B. Torrance; Milford Torrance; Sophronia

Torrance; Toni (m) Torrance; Anna Trasper; Anna Trasper; George M. Trasper; Hugh Trasper; John Trasper; John D. Trasper; John S. Trasper; Joseph S. Trasper; Mervin A. Trasper; Peter Trasper; Phebe K Trasper; Robert P Trasper; Sarah Trasper; T G. Trasper; Telitha R. Trasper; William Trasper; William H. Trasper; James Trimble; Julia A. Trimble; James Trusty; John Trusty; Nancy Trusty; Ransom Trusty; Sarah Trusty; William Trusty; Levi W. Vandervort; Martha Vandervort; Thomas D. Vandervort; Joseph Vaughhn; Nancy Vaughhn; D. M. Vinsonhaler; Frances Vinsonhaler; George Vinsonhaler; Hellen Vinsonhaler; Henrietta Vinsonhaler; J. Vinsonhaler; James Vinsonhaler; Margaret Vinsonhaler; Mary Vinsonhaler; Nancy Vinsonhaler; Aaron Wallace; Amanda Wallace; Arnistead Wallace; Betsy Wallace; Fanny Wallace; James Wallace; Joseph Wallace; Miller Wallace; Zachariah Wallace; Adam Ware; Elizabeth Ware; Isaac S. Ware; John Ware; John Ware; Joseph L Ware; Lydia J. Ware; Mary Ware; Doctor E Watson; James Watson; John Watson; Mary Watson; Mary A. Watson; Richard Watson; William M. Watson; Elizabeth Watterman; Justin Watterman; Elizabeth Waugh; James Waugh; Robert Waugh; William L. Waugh; Christopher Weatherman; Harriet Weatherman; James W. Weatherman; Jenetta Weatherman; Jesse J. Weatherman; John P Weatherman; Lewis W Weatherman; Martha Weatherman; Miles F. Weatherman; Nathan D. Weatherman; Soloman F. Weatherman; Thomas M. Weatherman; Hannah E Weiser; Robert J. Weiser; Sarah A. Weiser; Johnson West; Margaret R. West; Polly West; Margaret White; William J. White; Elizabeth Whitsett; James H. Whitsett; Sarah J. Whitsett; William C. Whitsett; William G. Whitsett; Ephriam Williams; George Williams; Lucy Williams; David Willis; Elizabeth Willis; George Willis; Jacob S. Willis; John S. Willis; Lucinda Willis; Rachael M. Willis; Rebecca Willis; Sarah L Willis; Suannah Willis; William M. Willis; Eady A. Wood; Elijah C. Wood; Emily J. Wood; George Wood; Henry J. Wood; James Wood; James Wood; Margaret Wood; Martha E Wood; Martin G. Wood; Mary A. Wood; Nancy Wood; Nathan B. Wood; Peter M. Wood; Thomas Wood; William Wood; Jane S. Wright; Jefferson Wright; John Wright; Mary M. Wright; Melinda Wright; Rebecca E Wright; Sally E Wright; Thomas Wright; William Wright; David W. Wyatt; John J. Wyatt; Sidney Wyatt; Elizabeth Young; Francis M. Young; Jesse Young; Lewis Young; Lindeman Young; Louisa Young; Lucretia Young; Margaret Young; Mariah Young; Mary Young; Nancy Young.

Texas County, Missouri, Postmasters, Cabool

Name	Date
William Bradshaw	Apr. 18, 1871
George F. Pettigree	Aug. 21, 1882
Jacob W. Garman	Sep. 26, 1884
George F. Pettigrew	Sep. 30, 1885
Lemuel Hazzard	Apr. 23, 1889
Thomas L. Moore	Jun. 19, 1903
Frank A. Hardin	Jun. 24, 1899
Henry W. Hazzard	May 20, 1897
A. J. McKinney	Jun. 23, 1916
Luther P. Dove	Feb. 2, 1922

Laclede County, Missouri, White Oak Pond Cumberland Presbyterian Church originally known as the Hickory Valley Congregation, Aug. 16, 1868, Charter Members.

Rev. J. R. Alsup, Abner Coffman, Sarah Coffman, George Layman, William McWherter, Mary Ann McWherter, Samuel McMenus, John Smith, Benjamin McFarland, Nancy Jane McFarland, Miriah F. Smith, J. E. Barr.

Buchanan County, Missouri, 1903, Newspaper Editors.

St. Joseph

Paper Name	Politics	Editor
Gazette	Democratic	Lewis Gaylord
News	Independent	C. P. Edgar
Evening Press	Non-Partisan	Howbart Billman
Paper Name	Politics	Editor
Volksblatt	Independent	M. Heckel
Stockyards Journal	Live Stock	W. E. Warrick
Courier	Legal News	Jno. P. Strong
Post	Independent	Jno. Musser
Catholic Tribune	Catholic	M. Lawlor
Report	Local	C.N. VanPool
Foster's Forecast	Scientific	W. T. Foster
St. Joseph Union	Labor	Clato Riley
Spectator	Negro	Wm. H. Jones
Modern Farmer and Busy Bee	General Farm	Emerson Taylor Abbott
Medical Herald	Medical	Dr. Chas. Wood Fassett
Western Fruit Grower	Horticulture	Jas. M. Irving
Dancing Master	Magazine	E. A. Prinz

| Tribune | DeKalb Democratic | E. S. Hays |

Caldwell County, Missouri, 1903, Newspaper Editors

Paper	Poplar Bluff Politics	Name
Citizen	Democratic	Jno. Berner
Republican	Republican	Tromly & Burnsides

Cape Gireardeau County, Missouri, 1903, Newspaper Editors

Paper	Jackson Politics	Name
Cash-Book	Democratic	F. A. McGuire
Volksfreund	Republican	Fred Kles & Bro.
Herald	Republican	B. F. Lusk
Progress	Cape Girardeau Democratic	C. D. Tresemriter
Democrat	Republican	B. H. Adams

Polk County, Missouri, "Bolivar Herald," Jul. 28, 1937
    Historical And Descriptive Sketch Of Polk County Prepared For The Centennial Celebration On The Fourth Of July, 1876
By A. C. Lemmon

    In celebrating the Centennial year of our National existence, the President of the United States has deemed it eminently wise and proper to recommend to each county within the vast domain of the Republic, to gather up the scattered and fast decaying fragments of her early history and settlement, down to the present hour of our national rejoicings. And he has further suggested that the same be read, on this anniversary occasion, to the assembled millions who have this day suspended their usual employments to participate in celebrating the One Hundredth birthday of American Independence.
  Polk County was organized in the early part of 1835. It included all the territory lying between the range lines which divide ranges 17 and 18, on the east, and 26 and 27 on the west, and the township lines dividing 31 and 32, on the south and 36 and 37 on the north. Length from east to west, 54 miles; width from north to south, 31 1/2 mile; total area 1,701 square miles, or nearly three times the present limits. When organized it embraced portions of territory subsequently added to surrounding sister counties, as follows: All of Dallas, except 12 square miles in the southwest corner of said county, 147 square miles on the south side of Hickory, 54 square miles to the southeast corner of St. Clair, 105

square miles on the east side of Cedar, 48 square miles of the north corner of Dade and 36 square miles in the northwest corner of Webster, taken from Dallas, though originally belonging to Polk. The present limits of Polk were established in 1845. The eastern boundary is the range line between ranges 20 and 21; western the range line dividing 24 and 25; the southern boundary begins at the southeast corner of section 12, township 31, range 21; thence running due west to the western boundary, already described. The northern boundary begins at the northeast corner of section 12, township 35, range 24; thence north to the northeast corner of said section; thence west to the range line dividing range 24 and 25. Length, from north to south, 26 1/2 miles; width, from east to west, 24 miles; area 640 square miles, or but a little more than one-third of her original limits. When first organized the county was in a wild, unimproved state. Several settlements had, however, been made previous to its formation. Some as early as 1828. Bears and panthers were occasionally met with. Deer and wild turkeys were very plentiful. Sporting and hunting constituted a large share of the employments and pleasures of the first settlers. Bee-hunting was both a pleasant and profitable source of amusement, and as much as a hundred, to a hundred and fifty pounds were frequently taken from a single tree. It supplied the place of sugar, and syrup, and was an article of diet in almost every family; and like the people of Palestine they rarely sat down to the table without it. The county was mostly a wild prairie, covered with a luxuriant growth of grass, frequently taller than a man on horseback.

It is estimated that at the time of its organization the population of the entire county scarcely exceeded 175 or 200 persons; or about one to every ten square miles. The inhabitants were chiefly Tennesseans and Kentuckians. The county did not, however, long remain in this condition. Our enterprising settlers soon began the work of improvement. Log cabins were erected, small farms opened, counties organized, and temporary seats of justice established. Flattering reports of the grandeur and fertility of the country soon reached the older States -- vivid descriptions of our broad undulating prairies, alluvial bottoms and fertile valleys, with their clear sparkling springs and brooks, soon induced hundreds to seek their future homes in the new country where their friends before them had so correctly described. Immigration poured in constantly, and every year brought fresh arrivals who entered at once upon the work of settling and improving the country. Churches, school houses, mills and other necessary public improvements, were constructed as circumstances demanded. The country being but thinly settled, and in neighborhoods distant from each other, the settlers frequently had many miles to travel to reach a mill, post office or trading point. Springfield was for a long time the nearest office to our county, and was then, as now, the most important town in the Southwest. Most of the trade centered at that point, and all of the mail matters was there received and delivered.

The first meeting of the county court was held on the 9th day of February, 1835, at the house of Daniel M. Stockton, at present the residence of James M. Henslee, Esq., five miles southwest of Bolivar, on the West Bend road, Jeremiah N. Sloan and Richard Saye, constituted the court; Joseph Inglish was the sheriff, and Wm. Henry was appointed Clerk, pro tem, J. N. Sloan was President of the court, and E. M. Campbell was made county surveyor. The court adjourned on the first day, to meet on the next at the house of Wm. C. Campbell. At this court the county was divided into three Municipal Townships; the central portion was called Marion, the eastern part, Washington; and the western, Jackson. The first election in Marion township was ordered to be held at the house of Ephriam Jamison. The Judges of election were Wm. Lunceford, Josiah Dent and Wm. Owens. In Jackson township at the house of William Davidson; Judges of election, William Crisp, Joseph Allen and James Stockton. In Washington township at the house of Richard Riddles; Judges of election, Daniel R. Brown, Richard Riddles and William Marlin. The same court made the following appointments; Rodham R. Payne, Assessor; Thos. Marlin, Wm. Montgomery, Richard Saye, Wm. Lunceford, Abner Spence, Thomas W. Johnson, John Riddles, Henry Akard, Isaac Ruth, James Stockton and Wm. Penn, Justices of the Peace. Richard Riddless was appointed Constable of Washington township; William M. Payne of Marion township; John S. Campbell, of Jackson township, and Jeremiah Sloan, Collector. The first county court warrant issued was in favor of J. N. Sloan for the sum of $3.50 for two days services as county court Justice; the second was in favor of Richard Saye for the same amount and services; the third in favor of Joseph Inglish for $3.00, for services as Sheriff in waiting on court. Total amount of warrants issued at first term of county court $10.

The following is a list of the members of the county Court from first organization to the present time including the date of election or appointment and length of term: Names Elected of Terms when Length J. H. Sloan 1835 3 mos.; Richard Saye 1835 1 yr.; Winfrey Owens 1835 2 yrs.; Thomas Martin 1836 1 yr.; James G. Human 1836 2 yrs.; Wm. Fourshee 1836 8 yrs.; Isaac Ruth 1837 2 yrs.; Henry Ackard 1837 2 yrs William Lunceford 1837 2 yrs A. W. Temple 1838 4 mos.; Wm. Henry 1839 1 yr.; Winfrey Owens 1840 4 mos.; Thomas Rountree 1841 3 yrs.; Benjamin C. Mitchell 1844 8 yrs Francis Dunnegan 1844 2 yrs Caleb Lutrell 1844 5 yrs John Burns 1846 2yrs

Wm. R. Devin 1848 2 yrs Wm. H. Newland 1849 3yrs Leander Wilson 1851 1 yr.; T. W. Cunningham 1852 4 yrs.; Wm. Lunceford 1852 4 yrs.; David M. McClure 1853 8 yrs.; Wm. H. Lemmon 1856 4 yrs.; Moses P. Hart 1856 6 yrs.; Thos. D. Hall 1860 2 yrs.; James Jump 1862 2 yrs.; Moses L. Carter 1862 6 yrs.; James Potts 1862 4 yrs.; Thos. Higginbotham 1864 2 yrs.; Thos. Fox 1866 4 yrs.; Thos. Burros 1866 4 yrs.; Hiram Hopkins 1868 1 yr.; John W. Ratcliff 1868 1 yr.; 6 mos.; W. H. Branham 1870 6 mos.; Jesse H. Murray 1870 3 yrs.; J. B. Barnett 1870 3 yrs.; L. J. Mitchell 1872 8 mos.; Wm. McVanZandt 1873 2 yrs.; J. W. Farmer, 1873; Enoch Plumer, 1873; re-elected Benj. Rodgers, 1873; Hiram Hopkins, 1873, re-elected in 1876; B. W. Appleby; 1875

The five last named constitute the members of the present court. Wm. Henry Clerk Pro Tem 1835, 3 mos.; Wm. C. Campbell, 1835, 3 yrs.; Isreal W. Davis, 1838, 9 yrs.; Abram Fenley, Jr., 1847; 5 yrs.; Isreal D. Davis, 1853, 6 yrs.; James M. Jones, 1859., 3 yrs.; T. W. Cunningham, 1862, 3 yrs.; T. H. B. Dunnegan, 1866, 1 yr.; Jas. B. Burros 1866, 7 yrs.; A. C. Lemmon, 1874.Present Sheriffs: Joseph Inglish, 1835, 2 yrs.; James Ables, 1837, 2 yrs.; N. McMinn 1839, 3 yrs.; Samuel H. Bunch, 1842, 2 yrs.; David D. Stockton, 1844, 2 yrs.; Richard Saye, 1846. 4 yrs.; James W. Johnson, 1850., 2 yrs.; Morris Mitchell, 1852, 2 yrs.; James M. Jones, 1854, 4 yrs.; Joseph McBroom, 1862, 2 yrs.; 9 mos.; John Caldwell, 1864, 4 yrs.; T. H. B. Dunnegan, 1868, 4 yrs.; Robert Greer, 1872, 2 yrs.; Thos. Greer, 1874, present sheriff.

Circuit Court Clerks: Joseph Allen, Clerk pro tem, 1835, 1 yr.; Thos. Jones, 1836, 2 yrs.; Israel W. Davis, 1839, 9 yrs.; Abram Fenley, Jr., 1847, 5 yrs.; Thomas Rountree, 1852, 1 yr.; Israel W. Davis, 1853, 6 yrs.; James M. Jones, 1859., 2 yrs.; Vacancy; M. G. Devin 1862, 2 yrs.; W. L. Snodgrass, 1864, 10 yrs.; A. J. Hunter, 1874, present clerk

Recorders : In 1869, the office of Recorder was, by an act of the Legislature separated from the office of the Circuit Court, and made a distinct office, entitled "Recorder of Deeds". At the general election in 1870, A. J. Hunter was elected Recorder, and in 1874, Andrew J. Lower, the present incumbent was elected to said office.

County Treasurers: Wm. M. Payne, 1835, 1 yr.; Joseph L. Young, 1836, 3 yrs.; Nath. T. Williams, 1839, 8 yrs.; Neil McKenzie, 1847, 1 yr.; Wm. Fourshee, 1848, 5 yrs.; Wm. M. Griggs, 1853, 1 yr.; Wm. R. Devin 1854, 9 yrs.; John E. Rains, 1863, 4 yrs.; G. W. Drake, 1867, 3 yrs.; John Watson ,1870, present treasurer.

Representatives In State Legislature: Thomas Marlin, 1836, 1 term; Nicholas McMinn, 1840, 1 term; Robert E. Acock, 1842, 2 terms Winfrey Owens, 1844, 1 term; John Hurt, 1846, 1 term; B. F.

Robinson, 1848, 1 term; R. E. Acock, 1850, 1 term; James G. Human, 1852, 1 term; R. E. Acock, 1854, 1 term; Geo. M. Williams, 1856, 1 term; T.W. Cunningham, 1858, 1 term; T.W. Freeman, 1860, 1 term; W. R. Devin, 1862, 1 term; David D. Stockton, 1864, 1 term; James J. Akard, 1866, 2 terms; John D. Abbe, 1870, 1 term; Wm. Lemmon, 1872, 1 term; John Carson, 1874, 1 term.

Member From Polk County In State Constitutional Convention: R. E. Acock, S. H. Bunch, 1845; R. C. Cowden, 1861; James W. Johnson, 1861; John W. Ross, 1875.

Prosecuting Attorneys: The office of Circuit Attorney was abolished in, 1872, and that of Prosecuting for each county, substituted therefor: C.A. Milliken, 1872, 2 yrs.; W.F. Freeman, 1874 present attorney.

The first Circuit Court was held in Bolivar, in a log cabin, near the ground upon which the Circuit House now stands, on the 7th day of September, 1835, C. H. Allen (familiarly known as Horse Allen), presided as Judge. Joseph Allen clerk pro tem, and Joseph Inglish, Sheriff, But two cases were on the docket, and only one was tried, namely, that of David Welch vs. Robert Grahm, an action of replevin, resulting in judgment for the defendant. The grand jurors at that term; were Thomas Jones, foreman; Peter Ruyle, Richard Stout, Wm. Penn, Elijah Milliken, Wm. M. Crisp, Henry Akard, Joseph H. Miller, Wm. Lunceford, Amos Richardson, Thos. Gilliham, Absalom Rentfrow, Caswell Beckham, Winfrey Owens, John Burch, Josiah Dent and Thomas Martin. This jury retired and after a short consultation returned one true bill of indictment against David O. George, for peddling without a license. Not a member of this court of jury is now living. Amos Richardson, the last survivor, died during the past year at Humansville, in this county, at the advanced age of 83 years.

The first name on the list of attorneys, is that of John S. Phelps, under date of August 7th, 1837. Then follow, in order, Littleberry Hendricks, Charles S. Yancey, Robert W. Crawford and Jas. Winston, at the same term;.

The office of Probate Judge was established in, 1860. Previous to that time the county court held probate jurisdiction. W. R. Cowden was appointed first Judge, and was succeeded by Wm. Boren, in, 1862, who filled the office until, 1863, when it was abolished, but was re-established in, 1867. J. D. Abbe, 1868 2 yrs.; H. B. Watson, 1870 2 yrs.; Thos. J. Poage, 1872 2 yrs.; J. G. Simpson, 1874.

Of the veterans of, 1812, but few are now living in our midst. They have nearly all passed away. Of the living, we are able to name the following, all of whom have attained to advanced ages, to-wit: John Burns, Evan Stewart, John Jump, Allen Bridges, Rev. Jas. Kennon,

Phillip Watkins, Mattias Chilton and Samuel Sherwood--numbering in all 8 pensioners. One of them, Hartwell Johnson died near Morrisville a few years since, in the 91st year of his age. For several years previous to his death his strength, memory and sight were greatly impaired. Alexander Blair and David Hunter died in, 1874, which Henry Potts lived to witness the dawn of the Centennial year.

Soldiers Of The Mexican War: The County furnished two full Cavalry companies, and a part of a third one, for this war, the number exceeding our required quota. The first was organized in Bolivar, in July, 1846, and numbered 101 men, including commissioned and non-commissioned officers. B. F. Robinson was captain and Samuel Hughes, Nathaniel T. Williams and John Miller, were Lieutenants. This company, with others, was organized into an extra battalion at Fort Leavenworth, under command of Lieutenant-Colonel Whillock; but subsequently attained to the Second Missouri regiment, commanded by Colonel (afterwards General), Sterling Price. The second company was organized in, 1847, under Captain B. F. Smithton, who remained in command but a very short time, being succeeded by Captain D. D. Stockton, who remained its commander until the company was regularly disbanded. This company formed a part of Col. Ralls' third Missouri regiment. A part of another company from this county was attached to Lieutenant Col. Gillespie's battalion. These troops were stationed at Santa Fe, and vicinity, and consequently were not engaged in the great battles of that war. They had, however, several engagements and skirmishes with hostile Indians, and foraging parties of the enemy. At the battle of Wagon Mound the lost one man (killed) Charles Casteel; and Joseph Derrick and Charles Wilson were slightly wounded. In the other engagements out troops sustained no loss. An infantry company, under command of Capt. Thomas Ruffle, was also organized, and went as far as Fort Leavenworth, but the war was about over, and our victorious troops had already conquered the Mexicans, this company was not received into the service, but disbanded and returned home. Of our two hundred and twenty-five soldiers, who saw active service in this war, but very few of them are now living in the county. Indeed, one would be surprised at the very small number that now remains in our midst. In a recent conversation with one of them (John E. Rains), he gave me the following list who are living at present in the county, to-wit: S. A. Morgan, Alexander Moore, John Parrish, H. D. Wilson, W. B. Mitchell, J. H. C. Mitchell, R. W. Menefee, John E. Rains, Chas. L. Lane, Thomas A. Robertson, Wm. M. Wilson, Johnathin Bradford, James Jump, John Hurt, Hiram Thompson, and John Caldwell, in all, sixteen persons. Many of them have removed, but the larger portion of them have passed off the stage of action.

The Late Rebellion: In this war, Polk County furnished many gallant soldiers for contending armies, but as the scenes and events of this conflict are still fresh in the memories of all, it is deemed prudent at this time to make merely a passing allusion to it, hoping that the bitterness and animosities of that period may be buried in oblivion's tomb--that the peace and happiness of the present hour, and the patriotic impulses that have called us together, may not be marred by any unpleasant rehearsal of its sad reminiscences. "Peace to the ashes of the dead, love and respect to the living."

Churches, Schools And Benevolent Societies: We have about seventy-five churches, or congregations, representing various denominations, principally Methodist, Baptist, Presbyterian and Christian; eighty-eight public schools; one college at Morrisville; two high schools, Pleasant Hope and Humansville; one graded public school, at Bolivar; five Masonic lodges; Bolivar, Morrisville, Humansville, Halfway and Pleasant Hope; and three lodges, I. O. O. F., Bolivar, Halfway and Humansville.

Agricultural Productions: Corn, wheat, oats, rye, tobacco, potatoes, and grapes of all kinds are the staples. Apples, peaches, pears, grapes and small fruits are grown abundantly. Wheat, tobacco, wool, bacon, eggs and butter are the principal exports.

Stock Raising: The county is well adapted to the raising of stock and in earlier years the luxuriant growth of grass on the prairies and timbered lands furnished fine pasturage for large herds of cattle, sheep and horses. Stock roamed at will, and lived nearly the entire year upon the range. But little care or attention was given to improve the breeds, but with the steady march of improvement vast portions of these pasture lands have been reduced to cultivation. The wild grass in so many parts has given way to the introduction of tame grasses, such as timothy, clover and blue grass. Consequently, the farming community has become more interested in raising live stock, which must eventually take the place of the common breeds.

Mineral Resources: Many indications of rich leads of lead, zinc, and coal are to be found in various portions of the county; but the absence of transportation facilities have delayed any extensive developments. As soon, however, as these facilities are afforded we may look for rich and paying mines to be opened.

Railroads: Our county has not kept pace with the spirit of internal improvement, although she is, in wealth, population and fertility of soil, one of the foremost counties in this part of the State; yet she has no railroads or navigable streams to bear away the productions of her industry. She has two important railways in process of construction but work for some time has been suspended on each of them in consequence of pecuniary embarrassments and legal complications. These roads certainly will be completed at no distant future. The Laclede and Fort Scott is already graded from Lebanon on the Atlantic and Pacific railroad to this point, a distance of fifty miles. The other, the Kansas City and Memphis, is graded from Kansas City to Osceola, St. Clair county, thirty-five miles northwest of Bolivar.

Towns And Villages: Bolivar, the county seat, located in Marion township, is the largest and most important. It was laid out and established in, 1835, shortly after the organization of the county. A few houses had been built previous to that time. The first building was erected in, 1832 or, 1833 by Gustavus Gunter, near the present residence of A. J. Hunter. He afterwards sold his improvements to Edmund Kneeling who occupied the same for several years. Joseph C. Montgomery was appointed commissioner to select the seat of Justice of Polk County on the 20th day of March, 1835. William Jamison succeeded him as the commissioner and as such purchased from the general government the land on which the town now stands, being the first cash entry made in the county. He laid off the town and sold the lots as such commissioner. Bolivar was first incorporated some time before the civil war, but during the war the offices became vacant, and the corporation ceased to act. It was reincorporation in, 1867 under a statutory provision. This corporation has continued in force ever since. The town at this time contains three hotels with excellent accommodations, three churches, one large brick public school house, one private banking house, six dry goods stores, two family groceries, one bakery, four drug stores, one millinery establishment, two boot and shoe shops, one saddle and harness store, one tin and hardware store, three blacksmith and two wagon shops, one music store, one jewelry store, two weekly newspapers, the Free Press by H. B. Knoght and the Herald by C. D. Lyman, one fine streak flouring mill and carding machine, one steam shingle and saw mill, three ministers, thirteen licensed attorneys, six practicing physicians, and liberal representation of other professions. The first store was opened by Wm. M. Payne in, 1834. The present court house was completed in, 1841, under the management and direction of John Toler. The town has received several additions at different times, the most important of which is the Hendrick's addition laid out by, 1870 by the administrator of the estate of Gibson Hendricks. Bolivar is noted for it's healthy climate, fine water, and the sociability of its citizens. There has never been a dwelling or business house burned in the town; it therefore, has never suffered from the incendiarism, not even during the late war. The town contains several good substantial business houses and quite a number of neatly constructed and desirable private residences. Its population is estimated at one thousand inhabitants, and it's retail trade is about one hundred thousand dollars per year. Humansville, in Johnson township, seventeen miles northwest of Bolivar, is a flourishing little town of about 450 inhabitants, its trade is almost as large as that of Bolivar, has several dry goods, family groceries and drug stores, and picture gallery, tin shop, two hotels and some other business houses, two attorneys and three physicians. The town carries on an active trade with the adjoining counties. A new woolen factory has been recently established in the place and does an excellent business. Humansville has an industrious and enterprising population and with Bolivar in business importance. It is named in honor of its founder, James B. Human, the first settler in the township. Morrisville in Looney township, ten miles southwest of Bolivar, is a neat and growing town, has an active trade and fine surrounding country. It is the seat of Morrisville College, an institution founded in, 1873 under the auspices of the M. E. church, South, and is rapidly growing into popularity and importance, has a good corp of professors, is liberally patronized by the southwestern counties. The town was founded in, 1870 by Morris Mitchell Esq. Fair Play is a small village in Madison township, ten miles west of Bolivar, contains two dry goods stores, one drug store, a blacksmith shop, church, school house and post office. Pleasant Hope, Halfway, Bright, Rondo and West Bend are smaller places, reference to which will be found in the history of the townships to which they respectively belong.

  First Entry Of Lands, Recording Of Deeds, Etc.: From the records of the U. S. Land Office at Springfield, we learn that government lands in Polk County were first opened to entry in the fall of, 1837. The first entry was made by William Jamison, commissioner of Polk County, October 5th, 1837. The land first entered was that on which the town of Bolivar was built. R. K. Payne, John Looney, and Washington Williams entered lands in the same year, which are now embraced within the limits of Looney township. The first warranty deed filed for record in the Recorder's office was made by Washington Williams and wife to Joseph Tuck, acknowledged January 3rd, 1838, before Richard Saye, J. P. The first recorded instrument of any kind is that of a power of attorney made by Wm. Ross to Wesley Robertson and acknowledged before Thomas Jones, clerk of the Circuit Court, May 11th, 1837. The first marriage solemnized after the organization of the county was that of Jeremiah Yancy to Miss Mary Thompson, August 11th, 1835, Isaac Ruth, J. P. officiating.

The Oldest Citizen: Rev. James Mitchell living near Morrisville is supposed to be the oldest person in the county. He was born October 19th, 1786, and is consequently in his nintieth year. He entered the Methodist ministry in, 1810 and has remained in the same chiefly as a local preacher for the last sixty-six years He raised a family of fourteen children by his first marriage, eight boys and six girls, all of whom lived to be grown. The number of his offspring living and dead is two hundred and sixty-six. Notwithstanding his advanced age and active life he has never called a physician to practice in his family. His mind is still clear and active, though his body is frail and his limbs feeble. By special request he delivered a sermon at Mitchell's Camp Ground last August. Mr. Mitchell emigrated to Polk County in, 1834, before the organization of the county, from Blount County, East Tennessee. Old Uncle Dick, a colored inmate at the poor house, is supposed to be the next oldest, though his precise age is not known. Having given a limited history of the county generally we will now give a brief sketch of the townships.

Mooney Township: Mooney Township, named in honor of John Mooney, one of the earliest settlers, lies in the southeast corner of the county, is eight miles square containing 64 square miles. Population in, 1870, 1,260 estimated at present to be 1,400. This township is well timbered, with some small prairies. The surface of the township is somewhat broken. The soil on the stream valley prairies is generally rich. Timbered uplands usually produce fine wheat. The people are alive upon the subject of education and their schools are well patronized. The township contains several churches, eleven school houses, three saw and grist mills and one post office. Pleasant Hope is the only town; population one hundred. One store, one flouring and saw mill, two blacksmith shops, one shoe shop, academy and church. John Mooney, Wm. Patterson, Dr. Hamilton Bradford, John McClure, Samuel Beckley, Anthony Agnes, James Smithton and others whose names we are unable to learn were among the earliest settlers of this township. Mrs. Lucretia H. Bradford, widow of Dr. H. Bradford has in her possession a relic of the revolution. It is a bottle shaped gourd raised on the farm of Eli Coffee, Albemarle County, Virginia, in the year 1776. Mr. Coffee presented it to Dr. Bradford about 40 years ago. This gourd was used as a powder horn during the war of the revolution and is now in a good state of preservation. There are many fine farms in Mooney, but much of the land is unfit for cultivation. Pomme de Terre and Dry Sac are the principal streams.

Looney Township: Looney Township, named in honor of Benj. Looney, who settled there in, 1833 and died in, 1875, is bounded on the south by Marion on the east by Mooney, west, Jackson, and on the south by the Greene county line, is 8 miles square and contains 64 square miles; population in, 1860-1750, estimated at present at 2,000; the soil upon the prairies and uplands has a red clay foundation and produces well; the valleys and bottoms are quite rich. Wheat is extensively grown. The principal streams are Dry and Little Sacs, Slagle and Asher creeks; the growth of timber on these streams is white and shell-bak hickory, black and white walnut, hackberry, linn, pawpaw, elm, red-bud, maple, sycamore, ash and many species of oak. This township was about the first settled part of the county. Among the earliest may be mentioned John Mooney who settled near the present town of Brighton, Richard Saye, Samuel Asher, John and David Ross; Aaron, Gideon and Nelson Ruyle, J. N. Sloan, John and Benj. Looney, Jacob, Thomas and Smith Lemmon, Joseph Tuck, Pittman and Thomas Woolard, W. W. McNight, James Faulkner, Charner DeGraffenreid, Nathaniel Herndon, Daniel and Martin Harpool, Wm. Maxey, William Daly, Hartwell Johnson, Wm. Winton, Hugh Boyd, Robert E. Acock, Abram and John Slagle and Abram Sears. This township is well timbered and has many fine springs located in Pleasant Prairie in a rich and healthful portion of the county. A more extended description is given in another part of this sketch. Brighton, on the Bolivar and Springfield road. twelve miles from the former place, is a small town but has a considerable trade, and contains one dry goods store, one drug store, post office, blacksmith shop, and one stream saw mill. West Bend, on Little Sac, has one dry goods store and one water mill. Slagle Creek has one store and post office. The second entry of land made in the county was located in this township in the year, 1837. There were several settlers here before the Indians retired. They required rent of the whites and soon became quite troublesome, and made threats which alarmed the settlers. The danger became so alarming that the whites assembled together and selected one of the number, J. N. Sloan to visit and petition the Governor for relief. He immediately mounted his horse and rode to St. Louis, consulted with His Excellency, and returned with gratifying assurances of protection. After this the Indians became more quiet, and remained friendly until their removal. These early pioneers were remarkable for generosity and hospitality, and were always ready and willing to lend assistance to a neighbor when he needed it. When a newcomers house was to be built, or, his land to be cleared, or a friends corn to be husked, his neighbors for miles around gathered to assist him and soon made quick work of it. Mrs. Marth Smith, near Brighton, widow of the late J. H. M. Smith, is said to have woven the first piece of cloth in the county in, 1830.

Jackson Township: Jackson Township lies in the southwest corner adjoining Greene and Dade Counties. In the southern and western parts are some very fine farming lands. Crisp and Coat prairies are noted for their rich soil and well improved farms. The northern part is generally broken and hilly. Orleans on Sac eleven miles southwest of Bolivar is the only town. It contains one dry goods and drug store, and one grist and saw mill. In the first settlement of the county this store was quite a trading point. There were many business houses and the name of Orleans was familiar throughout the Southwest, but for many years past there have been but traces of its former existence. The township is 8 miles square, containing 64 square miles. Population in, 1870, 1,483, estimated at present to be about 1,650. It was settled as an early day. Among the first settlers were Isaac Looney, Michael Crow, Adam Zumwalt, Isaac Ruth, James Malicoat, Jeremiah Acuff, Woods Hamilton, Berry Coats, Jonathin Rice, Thomas Burros, Joseph Linn, Middleton Lane, Henry and James King, John McClure, Anguish New, Thomas J. Kelly, Bletcher Holder and several families of the Potters and Mitchells. Little Sac, Walnut and Turkey Creeks are the principal streams.

Madison Township: Madison Township lies north of Jackson, west of Marion, south of Johnson and east of the Cedar County line. It is eleven miles long and six miles wide, containing an area of 66 square miles. Population in, 1870-1,361; estimated at present to be 1,550. It is the second township in taxable wealth, fourth in extent and fifth in population. It is well timbered and has but little prairie. Soil is generally good and produces well. Little Sac, Brush and Bear Creeks are the principle streams. Considerable interest is manifested in public schools and the spirit of popular education is steadily increasing; contains ten school houses, several churches, one steam and two water mills, and one post office. The old town of New Market laid out by Wm. Campbell once had an active trade, but the building of the town of Orleans near by so deprived it of its trade that it soon went down and is not now known on the map of the county. The first settlers were S. H. Bunch, Ransom Cates, Abnor Renfrow, Peter Ruyle, Wm. Campbell, John Hunt, James Stockton, Robert Evans, Henry and James Akard, Jacob Seigler, Joseph Ferguson, Silas Fox, John Crain, James Watson, Ahab Bowen, James Hopkins, Benj. Craighead, Francis, William and Matthew Dunnegan, William Webb, Drury Kersey, Alfred Frieze, and David Rountree. In, 1857 there was, but one school house which was used for both church and school purposes.

Benton Township: Benton Township is situated east of Marion, north of Mooney, south of Greene and west of the Dallas County line.

It is the second in extent and third in population, being eleven miles long and eight miles wide, containing 88 square miles; population in, 1870, 1,650, estimated at present at 1,900. The township is well watered with springs and creeks; along the banks of the latter the surface is broken and hilly. Immense quarries of cotton rock are to be found in the hills adjoining Pomme De Terre. This rock is said to be found nowhere else in the state except along the streams and its tributaries. It is quite valuable for building purposes and has been used extensively as a substitute for marble. Wolfe, Shultze, Coon and Brush creeks are tributaries of Pomme de Terre. Buffalo-head prairie in the eastern part is one of the prettiest and most fertile in the county. Flint and Elkhorn are smaller prairies. Halfway, ten miles east of Bolivar, is the only town; has two retail stores, blacksmith shop, school house post office, one lodge each of the Masons and I. O. O. F. David Bartley first settled the township. After him came John and Maynard Vanderford, Stephen Jones, Noah and Elijah Gorden, James Shaw, David Hendrickson, John and Benj. Gordon. This township is well adapted to stock raising, both grass and water being plentiful. Benton contains two post offices, nine school houses and several churches.

Marion Township: Marion Township occupies the central portion of the county, and is first in wealth, population and extent. It is ten miles from east to west, and eleven miles from north to south, containing 110 square miles. Population in, 1870, including the town of Bolivar, 2,489; estimated at present 2,800. The Three-mound prairie embraces nearly all of the southern and western part. The western portion of this prairie is highly productive; the eastern is less fertile and more adapted to pasturage. It is named from three large mounds which contain immense quantities of what is known as vermicular sandstone, and are covered only with grass and rocks from the base to summit; not a tree to be seen. In the southern part of this prairie as a place known as Hickory Point, was built the first retail store in the county., Wm. Jamison, proprietor. The northern portion of the township is timbered, the surface being undulating and hilly. Bolivar is the only town. Among the first settlers were Gustavus Gunter, Wm. Lunceford, James W. Johnson, Winfrey Owens, Wm. Piper, E. M. Campbell, Caleb Jones, Samuel and John W. Wilson, Joseph L. Young, David D. and Daniel M. Stockton, William and Ephriam Jamison, Edmund Keeling, Abram Fenley, I. W. Davis, Thos. McAllister, R. B. Price, John E. Rains, Wm. Henry, Rev. Elijah Williams, W.R. and Clayton Devin, A. C. Denny, Isham and Jas. Ables, J. R. Calloway, Darling and Scudder Smith, Amos Richardson, and Lewis Morgan. The greatest part of the history and statistics of this township is more or less connected with that of the town of Bolivar, which has already been given.

Greene Township: Greene Township is located in the northeast corner of the county, length from east to west 10 miles, width from north to south 7 1/2 miles, containing 75 square miles; population in, 1870- 1904, estimated in, 1876 at 1,200. There are no towns or villages, but one retail store, two post offices, several churches and schoolhouses, no mills of manufactories. Sentinal prairie is the best and wealthiest portion. The bottom lands on Lindsay creek are rich and well timbered. There are many indications of mineral deposits. Lead is supposed to exist in paying quantities and will doubtless be developed sometime in the near future. The hills and prairies furnish a fine pasture for live stock. This township was not so early settled as some of the others. B. L. Stephens, Joseph Inks, Jacob Ballinger, John and James Jump, John Howe, Samuel Rutherford, Brice Stewart, Leonard Richards, Derrit Barclay, Hugh Estes, Evan Stewart, Rev. Gallison and John Burns were among the first settlers. John Jump is the oldest citizen in the township is now eighty-four years of age. He was a soldier of the war of, 1812 so were Evan Stewart and John Burns.

Johnson Township: Johnson Township is located in the northeast corner of the county and embraces some of its most desirable and best portions. The township is about equally divided in prairie and timber. The prairie portion is generally very productive. The timbered lands are rough and hilly. This portion of the county was not settled so early as the central and western parts. James Human was the first pioneer. He settled at the big spring at Humansville in the fall of , 1834, having emigrated from Illinois the same year. Judge Human frequently filled important positions of trust. Once represented the county in the state legislature, once a member of the county court, besides at different times fulfilling the duties of several other offices. He died in, 1875. Shortly after him came David Moulder, W. B. B. George, James Renfrow, Larkin Williams, John and George Yoast, Thomas W. King, Wesley Savely and many others. David R. Murphy, who died in Humansville last fall, was among the oldest citizens, having lived in different localities in the county for the last forty years or more. He was a minister of the Baptist Church and a zealous and devoted Christian. Humansville is the only town, reference to which has already been made. Brush creek is the principle stream. Twenty-Five Mile and Valley Prairies, comprising a large portion of the township, are fine agricultural districts. The citizens are generally industrious, social and full of thrift and enterprise. This township contains 48 square miles. Population in, 1870, 799, estimated in, 1876, 1,150.

Jefferson Township: Jefferson Township was the last settled part of the county. It was bounded on the East by Greene, on the south by Marion, on the west by Johnson, and on the north by Hickory County. George W. Kelly made the first settlement at Dry Fork, at the Bolivar, and Warsaw road, at the present residence of his son, William Kelly. James Black, Ezekial Flint, Russell K. Kelly, S. A. Morgan, J. C. Davis, and Leander Wilson were also early settlers. Weaver and Twenty-five mile prairies embrace about half the township. The latter is inclined to be wet, but produce immense crops of corn, oats and grass, but the soil is unfavorable to the growth of wheat. The other portions of this township are admirably adapted to the growth of the important cereal. Pomme De Terre and Dry Fork are the only water courses. A new mill propelled by a wire cable has recently been constructed on the former stream by Dr. P. C. Sherwood. It is the only one of the kind in this part of the state and is regarded as quite an improvement on the water mills now in use. The are of this township is 65 1/2 square miles. Population in, 1870, 480; estimated in, 1876 at 750. Rondo on the Twenty-five Mile prairie is the only post office. Having given a short sketch of each township we return to the county in general.

Financial Condition: In August, 1869, the county court of this county made a conditional subscription to the Laclede & Fort Scott Railroad Company to the amount of $250,000 to be paid in county bonds, in denominations not less than $500, said bonds payable in twenty years and bearing seven per cent interest payable semi-annually. In, 1870 and, 1871 bonds to the amount of $33,000, were issued and delivered to said railroad company, but on the 9th day of August, 1872, the county court rescinded the order subscribing the aforesaid stock to said road. The above mentioned amount of bonds, $33,500, constitute the outstanding bonded indebtedness of the county, the interest on which has always been promptly paid when due. In addition to these railroad bonds the county owes a debt of one thousand dollars to capital stock of her county school funds. The floating indebtedness of the county has been reduced for the last three years, but in the last twelve months there has been a greater reduction than during any previous year. The total amount of outstanding warrants at the present time will not exceed in round numbers the sum of six thousand dollars. If the delinquent taxes due the county revenue fund were all paid in it would be sufficient to redeem all outstanding warrants and leave a balance in the treasury.

Conclusion: Having now reached the conclusion of this historical and descriptive sketch we beg leave to state that the brief space of time allotted us for its preparation, together with the difficulty and delay in obtaining facts outside of official records have prevented the introduction of many events and occurrences that ought not to be omitted in a sketch of this character. Many of the incidents and circumstances herein recorded are taken from the recollection of the parties furnishing them, and as they cover a long period of time, they may not in all cases be substantially as the occurred, but in the main we think their correctness will not be disputed. In making personal reference we have not intentionally omitted and person whose name should have occurred in connection with the early settlement of the townships or county. We have in most instances given them as they were furnished by others. To the following gentlemen, we are under many obligations for the information furnished by them in reference to their respective localities, viz: Col. James M. Johnson, John E. Rains, and John Watson of Bolivar. Capt. J. W. Burns of Halfway, Geo. W. Williams of Humansville, Dr. A. C. Sloan of Walnut Grove, Henry Gardner of Pleasant Hope, James M. Zumwalt of Sentinal Prairie, Milton Brown of Jefferson Township, James Stockton and Silas Fox of Madison and W. H. King of Jackson, also to A. J. Hunter, circuit clerk, and A. J. Lower, Recorder, for statistics and historical facts gathered from the records in their offices, and we are especially indebted to James W. Rains, Esq. for his arduous labors in searching through and examining official records, and for other valuable assistance rendered in the preparation of the sketch. A. C. Lemmon County Historian

Chariton County, Missouri, Land Owners Atlas
    C. P. Nordmeyer: (PO) Glascow, Mo, (OC) Farmer, (BP) Chariton Co. Mo, (ARVD), 1850.
    Charles Sanders: (PO) Glascow, Mo, (OC) Farmer and carpenter, (BP) Lippe Detmold, Germany, (ARVD) 1854.
    J.C. Minor: (PO) Forest Green, (OC) Farmer and TWP Clerk, (BP) Chariton Co., Mo, (ARVD)1841.
    Marion Moore: (PO) Forest Green, (OC) Farmer and Stock Raiser (BP) Chariton Co., Mo, (ARVD) 1844.
    M. Guerin: (PO) Forest Green, (OC) Physician and Surgeon, (BP) Clare Co. Ireland, (ARVD) 1854.
    C. Heimann: (PO) Glasgow, Mo, (OC) Farmer and Tobacco Grower, (BP) Switzerland, (ARVD)1855.
    H.D. Kothe: (PO) Glasgow, Mo, (OC) Farmer and Tobacco Grower Hanover, Germany, (ARVD) 1855.
    Gebhardt, Rohwer and Co: (PO) Glasgow, Mo, (OC) Grist and Saw Mill, (BP) Germany, (ARVD) 1855.
    G. Nauerth: (PO) Glasgow, Mo, (OC) Farmer State of Bavaria, Germany, (ARVD) (ARVD) 1865.

Christopher Noll: (PO) Glasgow, Mo, (OC) Farmer and Tobacco Grower, (BP) New Orleans, LA, (ARVD) 1851.

M.D. Bagley: (PO) Glasgow, Mo, (OC) Farmer, (BP) Susquehanna Co. PA, (ARVD) 1847.

Z. Locke Dalton: (OC) Farmer and Stock Raiser, (BP) Madison Co. KY, (ARVD) 1870.

Ferdinand Smith: (PO) (PO) Glasgow, Mo, (OC) Farmer, (BP) Chariton Co., Mo, (ARVD) 1846.

Frank M. Meyer : (PO) Shannondale, Mo, (OC) Farmer, (BP) Chariton Co., Mo, (ARVD) 1844.

H. C. Hurt: (PO) Forest Green, Mo, (OC) Farmer, (BP) Chariton Co., Mo, (ARVD) 1842.

I. K. Stephenson: (PO) Forest Green, Mo, (OC) Farmer and School Master, (BP) Madison Co., KY, (ARVD) 1844.

J. Brodie Hyde: (PO) Dalton, Mo, (OC) Farmer and Stock Raiser (BP) Chariton Co., Mo, (ARVD) 1840.

Ephraim Moore: (PO) Keytesville, Mo, (OC) Farmer and Stock Raiser (BP) Chariton Co., Mo, (ARVD) 1843.

E. Finnell : (PO) Keytesville, MO Farmer & Stock Raiser (BP) Chariton Co., MO (ARVD) 1843.

G. M. Dewey, M.D.: (PO) Dalton, Mo, (OC) Tobacconist, (BP) Erie Co., NY, (ARVD) 1846.

George Young: (PO) Salisbury, Mo, (OC) Farmer and Miller, (BP) Germany, 1849

Jackson Cloyd: (PO) Shannondale, Mo, (OC) Farmer and Stock Raiser Howard Co, Mo, (ARVD) 1850.

S. Johnson: (PO) Salisbury, Mo, (OC) Farmer and Tobacco Raiser, (BP) Howard Co, Mo, (ARVD) 1848.

Eliza J. Hurt Salisbury, Mo, Resident (BP) Chariton Co., Mo, 1848

G. W. Cravens Salisbury, Mo, (OC) Farmer and Tobacco Grower Howard Co, Mo, 1849.

L. R. Perkins : (PO) Keytesville, Mo, (OC) Physician and Surgeon, (BP) Buchanan Co., VA, (ARVD) 1856.

J. F. Draper: (PO) Shannondale, Mo, Mechanic Jackson Co., IN, 1867.

W. H. Metcalf : (PO) Keytesville, Mo, (OC) Farmer and Stock Raiser, (BP) Frederick Co., VA, (ARVD) 1858.

J. J. Moore : (PO) Keytesville, Mo, (OC) Farmer and Stock Raiser, (BP) Chariton Co., Mo, (ARVD) 1843.

A. J. Cuddy: (PO) Keytesville, Mo, (OC) Farmer and Stock Raiser, (BP) Chariton Co., Mo, (ARVD) 1846.

W. T. Spence: (PO) Salisbury, Mo, (OC) Farmer and Stock Raiser, (BP) Howard Co, Mo., (ARVD)1866.

Wm Bitter: (PO) Dalton, Mo, (OC) Farmer and Stock Raiser, (BP) Germany, (ARVD)1848.

F. T. Dysart : (PO) Keytesville, Mo, (OC) County Clerk, (BP) Macon Co, Mo., (ARVD)1867.

O.F. Smith : (PO) Keytesville, Mo, (OC) Prosecuting Attorney, (BP) Columbia, KY, (ARVD) Nov, 1867.

Wm. E. Jones : (PO) Keytesville, Mo, (OC) Owner Keytesville Herald, (BP) Missouri (ARVD) Sep 16, 1872.

Wm. E. Hill: (PO) Keytesville, Mo, (OC) Cashier Bank Massachusetts, (ARVD) 1846.

John P. Jones : (PO) Keytesville, Mo, (OC) Post Master, (BP) Massachusetts, (ARVD) 1865.

J. Miller De Moss : (PO) Keytesville, Mo, (OC) Attorney, (BP) Harrison Co., KY, (ARVD) 1875.

Thos J. Martin: (PO) Keytesville, Mo, (OC) Dealer in Drugs, (BP) Meade Co., KY, (ARVD) 1857.

B. E. Johnson : (PO) Keytesville, Mo, (OC) Merchant, (BP) Spotsylvania Co, VA, (ARVD)1875.

M. J. Rucker : (PO) Keytesville, Mo, (OC) Physician and Surgeon, (BP) Orange Co., VA, (ARVD)1852.

A. Mackay, Jr. : (PO) Keytesville, Mo, (OC) Attorney, (BP) Henderson Co., KY, (ARVD) 1857.

A. Mackay, Sr. : (PO) Keytesville, Mo, (OC) Owner Chariton House, (BP) Henderson Co., KY, (ARVD) 1857.

Hugo Bartz: (PO) Keytesville, Mo, (OC) Owner Grist Mill, (BP) Prussia, (ARVD) 1867.

D.B. Kellogg : (PO) Keytesville, Mo, (OC) Saloon Owner, (BP) Pennsylvania, (ARVD)1852.

John L. Potts: (PO) Keytesville, Mo, (OC) Merchant, (BP) Howard Co. Mo, (ARVD)1873.

Jno A. Fuqua: (PO) Keytesville, Mo, (OC) Owner Oldham Hotel, (BP) Prince Edward Co., VA, (ARVD) 1843.

B. M. Featch : (PO) Keytesville, Mo, (OC) Fruit Grower, (BP) Harrison Co., IN, (ARVD) 1864.

James M. Johnson : (PO) Keytesville, Mo, (OC) Farmer (BP) Chariton Co., Mo, (ARVD) 1847.

Walter E. Hyde : (PO) Keytesville, Mo, (OC) Farmer and Stock Raiser (BP) Chariton Co., Mo, 1845.

A.W. McCampbell : (PO) Keytesville, Mo, (OC) Farmer and Stock Raiser, (BP) Shelby Co., KY, (ARVD) 1858.

H. T. Garnett : (PO) Keytesville, Mo, (OC) Physician and Surgeon Shelby Co., KY, (ARVD) 1865.

Robert J. Brown: (PO) Keytesville, Mo, (OC) Farmer and Stock Raiser, (BP) Ireland, (ARVD) 1851.

Robert Duff: (PO) Keytesville, Mo, (OC) Farmer and Stock Raiser, (BP) Ireland, (ARVD) 1851.

C. Courtney: (PO) Keytesville, Mo, (OC) Farmer and Stock Raiser, (BP) Clark Co., KY, (ARVD)1869

A. S. Cunningham: (PO) Keytesville, Mo, (OC) Farmer and Stock Raiser, (BP) Randolph Co., Mo, (ARVD) 1866

Joel Elam: (PO) Keytesville, Mo, (OC) Farmer and Stock Raiser, (BP) Prince Edward Co., VA, (ARVD) 1843.

L. Reister : (PO) Keytesville, Mo, (OC) Farmer, (BP) Baden, Germany, (ARVD) 1874.

D. W. Carter : (PO) Keytesville, Mo, (OC) Farmer Bedford Co., TN, (ARVD) 1843.

James M. Welch: (PO) Keytesville, Mo, (OC) Farmer (BP) Chariton Co., Mo., (ARVD) 1847.

B.F. Welch Muscle Fork, Mo, (OC) Farmer and Stock Raiser (BP) Chariton Co., Mo., (ARVD) 1840.

John W. Worsham: (PO) Keytesville, Mo, (OC) Farmer and Stock Raiser (BP) Chariton Co., Mo., 1849.

A. S. Pound : (PO) Muscle Fork, Mo, (OC) Farmer, (BP) Platte Co., Mo., (ARVD) 1856.

Geo. B. Oldman : (PO) Muscle Fork, Mo, (OC) Farmer and Teacher, (BP) Chariton Co., Mo., (ARVD) 1848.

T. P. Chrane : (PO) Muscle Fork, Mo, (OC) Farmer (BP) Chariton Co., Mo., (ARVD) 1852.

H. G. McEuen : (PO) Muscle Fork, Mo, (OC) Physician and Surgeon, (BP) Montgomery Co., Mo., (ARVD)1869.

Harden Scott : (PO) Muscle Fork, Mo, (OC) Farmer, (BP) Russell Co., KY, (ARVD) 1841.

John Callahan: (PO) Westville, Mo, (OC) Farmer and Stock Raiser, (BP) Clay Co., IL, (ARVD) 1866.

John H. Walker: (PO) Brunswick, Mo, (OC) Farmer and Tobacco Grower, (BP) Gallia Co, Ohio, (ARVD) 1845.

John Saunders : (PO) Muscle Fork, Mo, (OC) Farmer and Stock Raiser, (BP) Fauquier Co., VA, (ARVD) 1841.

Daniel Eastridge: (PO) Muscle Fork, Mo, (OC) Farmer and Stock Raiser Pulaski Co., KY, (ARVD) 1851.

G. W. Minnick : (PO) Keytesville, Mo, (OC) Farmer and Stock Dealer, (BP) Fulton Co., IL, (ARVD)1874.

John Huenten: (PO) Brunswick, Mo, (OC) Farmer, (BP) Prussia, (ARVD) 1853.

R. P. Clarkson: (PO) Keytesville, Mo, (OC) Farmer and Tax Collector : (PO) Mucle Fork Twp., (BP) Breckenridge Co., Ky., (ARVD)1868.

G.M. Maupin: (PO) Westville, Mo, (OC) Farmer and Stock Raiser, (BP) Madison Co., Ky, (ARVD) 1865.

Wm O. Phillips: (PO) Westville, Mo, (OC) Farmer and Stock Raiser, (BP) Campbell Co., VA, (ARVD) 1867.

George Langley: (PO) Rothville, Mo, (OC) Farmer and Stock Raiser, (BP) Alexander Co., VA, (ARVD) 1868.

Wm F. Morris : (PO) Westville, Mo, (OC) Farmer and Tobacco Grower (BP) Howard Co., Mo., (ARVD) 1873.

James T. Robinson : (PO) Westville, Mo, (OC) Farmer and Stock Raiser, (BP) Clark Co., KY, (ARVD) 1866.

G.A. Newson : (PO) Westville, Mo, (OC) Farmer and Stock Raiser, (BP) Adair Co., KY, (ARVD) 1867.

James Mulholland: (PO) Westville, Mo, (OC) Farmer, (BP) Terre Haute, Ind., (ARVD) 1854.

Francis Clark: (PO) Bucklin, Mo, (OC) Farmer and Stock Raiser, (BP) Cavan Co., Ireland, (ARVD) 1867.

David R. Hall : (PO) Westville, Mo, (OC) Farmer and Carpenter, (BP) Montgomery Co., VA, (ARVD) 1875.

Jermiah Lynch: (PO) Bucklin, Mo, (OC) Farmer and Stock Raiser, (BP) Clare Co., Ireland, (ARVD) 1871.

John Patterson: (PO) Bucklin, Mo, (OC) Farmer and Stock Raiser, (BP) Mayo Co., Ireland, (ARVD) 1872.

Timothy McAndra: (PO) Bucklin, Mo, (OC) Farmer and Stock, (BP) Raiser Sligo Co., Ireland, (ARVD) 1868.

Thomas Sportsman : (PO) Westville, Mo, (OC) Farmer and Stock Raiser, (BP) Linn Co., Mo., (ARVD) 1872.

James Sportsman: (PO) Westville, Mo, (Cmts) Served in War of, 1812, (BP) Mercer Co., KY, (ARVD) 1872.

Wm W. Riddell : (PO) Rothville, Mo, (OC) Farmer and Stock Dealer, (BP) Boone Co., KY, (ARVD) 1857.

C.E. Allen : (PO) Rothville, Mo, Prairie (OC) Farmer, (BP) Cumberland Co., VA, (ARVD) 1852.

Eli Riggle and Son : (PO) Rothville, Mo, (OC) Rothville Mills, (BP) Lycoming Co., PA, (ARVD) 1867.

James M. Riddell : (PO) Rothville, Mo, (OC) Retired Farmer (BP) Boone Co., KY, (ARVD) 1874.

Felix A. Cameron : (PO) Rothville, Mo, (OC) Farmer and Merchant, (BP) Polk Co., Tn, (ARVD) 1872.

N. J. Haskell : (PO) Rothville, Mo, (OC) Farmer, (BP) Hancock Co., ME, 1869.

Chas B. Allen : (PO) Rothville, Mo, (OC) Farmer, (BP) Cumberland Co., VA, (ARVD) 1851.

James F. Allen : (PO) Rothville, Mo, (OC) Farmer and Carpenter, (BP) Kanawha Co., W Va, (ARVD) 1852.

Milton B. Bishop : (PO) Brookfield, Mo, Prairie (OC) Farmer, (BP) Ross Co., Ohio, (ARVD) 1867.

Alex W. Adams : (PO) Rothville, Mo, (OC) Farmer (BP) Chariton Co., Mo., (ARVD) 1843.

James Carpenter: (PO) Brookfield, Mo, (OC) Farmer and House Builder, (BP) Chenango Co., NY, (ARVD) 1870.

T. P. Wilkinson : (PO) Rothville, Mo, (OC) Farmer and Justice of the Peace, (BP) Cumberland Co., VA, (ARVD) 1842.

J. Upp: (PO) Mendon, Mo, (OC) Farmer and Stock Raiser, (BP) Perry Co., Ohio, (ARVD) 1868.

Edward Saylor: (PO) Mendon, Mo, (OC) Farmer and Fruit Grower, (BP) Somerset Co., PA, (ARVD) 1870.

Martin O. Stoner: (PO) Mendon, Mo, (OC) Farmer and Fruit Grower, (BP) Westmoreland Co., PA, 1869.

John McClelland : (PO) Mendon, Mo, (OC) Farmer and Twp. Clerk, (BP) Ireland, (ARVD) 1869.

J.W. Simpson : (PO) Mendon, Mo, (OC) Farmer and Tobacco Grower, (BP) Grant Co., KY, (ARVD) 1867.

George Bower : (PO) Mendon, Mo, (OC) Farmer and Tobacco Grower, (BP) York Co., PA, (ARVD) 1870.

Mrs. Jane B. Dickey: (PO) Mendon, Mo, (OC) Farmer and Tobacco Grower, (BP) Kenton Co., KY, (ARVD) 1869.

J. S. Dickey: (PO) Mendon, Mo, (OC) Paints and Portraits, (BP) Kenton Co., KY, (ARVD) 1869.

Wm J. Enyeart : (PO) Mendon, Mo, Prairie (OC) Farmer, (BP) Miami Co., Ohio, (ARVD) 1865.

John McClure: (PO) Mendon, Mo, (OC) Farmer and Stock Raiser, (BP) Broome Co., NY, (ARVD) 1872.

J. P. Hess : (PO) Mendon, Mo, (OC) Farmer and Manufacturer of Sorgam, (BP) Jefferson Co., Ohio, (ARVD) 1868.

J. D. Cameron : (PO) Rothville, Mo, (OC) Farmer and Blacksmith, (BP) Polk Co., TN, (ARVD) 1871.

Robt. Pickens : (PO) Rothville, Mo, Retired (OC) Farmer, (BP) Pendleton Dist. SC, (ARVD) 1870.

T. J. Berry : (PO) Mendon, Mo, Prairie (OC) Farmer (BP Hopkins Co., KY, (ARVD)1853.

Mrs. Elizabeth Weaver : (PO) Rothville, Mo, (OC) Prairie Farmer (BP) Howard Co., Mo., (ARVD) 1855.

J. Schmidt : (PO) Rothville, Mo, (OC) Prairie Farmer , (BP) Prussia, (ARVD) 1851.

B.J. Pollard : (PO) Mendon, Mo, (OC) Farmer , (BP) Harrison Co., KY, (ARVD) 1867.

J.C. Bennett : (PO) Mendon, Mo, (OC) Farmer and School Master, (BP) Greene Co., PA, (ARVD) 1873.

H.M. Sullivan : (PO) Mendon, Mo, (OC) Farmer and Road Overseer, (BP) Augusta Co., VA, 1853.

P. R. Dunham : (PO) Mendon, Mo, (OC) Farmer, BP) Wayne Co., IN, (ARVD) 1867.

Thos J. Grace : (PO) Mendon, Mo, (OC) Farmer and Carpenter, (BP) Washington Co., VA, (ARVD) 1857.

Wm S. Pickens : (PO) Rothville, Mo, Prairie (OC) Farmer , (BP)McMinn Co., TN, (ARVD) 1869.

Charles Mahan : (PO) Mendon, Mo, Stock Trader, (BP) Cincinnati, Ohio, (ARVD) 1869.

C. Kelly : (PO) Mendon, Mo, (OC) Farmer and Tobacco Grower, (BP) Mercer Co., KY, (ARVD) 1867.

J.T. Swain : (PO) Keytesville, Mo, (OC) Farmer and Stock Dealer, (BP) Logan Co., KY, (ARVD) 1851.

Cpt. J.W. Allen : (PO) Dalton, Mo, (OC) Farmer and Stock Dealer, (BP) Augusta Co., VA, (ARVD) 1870.

R. H. Tisdale : (PO) Keytesville, Mo, (OC) Farmer and Tobacco Grower, (BP) Lunenberg Co., VA, (ARVD) 1843.

John Dailey : (PO) Keytesville, Mo, (OC) Farmer and Tobacco Grower, (BP) Wayne Co., Ohio, 1859.

Wm. Burr : (PO) Keytesville, Mo, (OC) Farmer and Stock Raiser, (BP) Cortland Co., NY, (ARVD) 1867.

C. J. Hampton : (PO) Keytesville, Mo, (OC) Farmer and Stock Raiser, (BP) Clark Co., KY, 1863.

Thos Palmer : (PO) Dalton, Mo, (OC) Retired Farmer, (BP) Ireland, (ARVD) 1857.

H. J. Britt Brunswick, Mo, (OC) Farmer and Tobacco Grower, (BP) Bertie Co., NC, (ARVD) 1857.

H.C. Hudnall : (PO) Keytesville, Mo, (OC) Farmer and Tobacco Grower, (BP) (BP) Chariton Co., Mo., (ARVD) 1844.

R.F. Ringer Brunswick, Mo, (OC) Farmer and Stock Dealer, (BP) Butler Co., Ohio, (ARVD) 1867.

B.H. Cooke: (PO) Brunswick, Mo, (OC) Prairie Farmer Culpepper Co., VA, (ARVD) 1867.

E. M. Williams : (PO) Salisbury, Mo, (OC) Farmer and Stock Raiser, (BP) (BPq) Chariton Co., Mo, (ARVD) 1841.

C. J. Hurt : (PO) Salisbury, Mo, (OC) Farmer and Tobacco Grower, (BP) (BP) Howard Co., Mo, 1849.

H. Dean : (PO) Roanoke, Mo, (OC) Farmer, (BP) Adams Co., IL, (AVRD) 1858.

G. J. Allen : (PO) Roanoke, Mo, (OC) Farmer (BP) Boone Co., KY, (ARVD) 1840.

D.H. Burton : (PO) Clifton Hill, Mo, (OC) Farmer and Stock Dealer, (BP) Caswell C. NC, 1858.

W.J. Tillotson : (PO) Clifton Hill, Mo, (OC) Farmer and Tobacconist, (BP) Tennessee, (ARVD) 18??.

N. J. Windsor : (PO) Clifton Hill, Mo, (OC) Farmer and Stock Dealer, (BP) Caswell Co., NC, (ARVD) 1845.

W.B. Hurt : (PO) Salisbury, Mo, (OC) Farmer and Stock Raiser, (BP) (BP) Chariton Co., Mo, (ARVD) 1841.

Lewis Lusher : (PO) Salisbury, Mo, (OC) Farmer and Stock Raiser, (BP) Cabell Co., VA, (ARVD) 1844.

Asa Gunn : (PO) Salisbury, Mo, (OC) Farmer and Stock Raiser, (BP) Caswell Co. NC, (ARVD) 1847.

G. G. Dameron : (PO) Salisbury, Mo, (OC) Farmer and Stock Dealer, (BP) Caswell Co. NC, (ARVD) 1857

T. J. Jackson : (PO) Salisbury, Mo, (OC) Farmer and Stock Raiser, (BP) Nelson Co., VA, (ARVD) 1874

A. G. Houston : (PO) Salisbury, Mo, (OC) Farmer and Stock Raiser, (BP) Scott Co., KY, (ARVD), 1850.

Thomas Barnes: (PO) Prairie Hill, Mo, (OC) Farmer and Stock Raiser, (BP) Howard Co., Mo, (ARVD) 1870.

W. F. Waterfield : (PO) Salisbury, Mo, (OC) Farmer, (BP) Linn Co., Mo, (ARVD) 1871.

James A. Houston : (PO) Salisbury, Mo, (OC) Farmer and Stock Raiser, (BP) Scott Co., KY, (ARVD) 1852.

Franklin S. Loudon: (PO) Prairie Hill, Mo, (OC) Farmer and Stock Dealer, (BP) Missouri, (ARVD) 1857.

Wm I. Twyman: (PO) Thomas Hill, Mo, (OC) Farmer and Stock Raiser, (BP) Orange Co., VA, (ARVD) 1860.

John C. Sears: (PO) Prairie Hill, Mo, (OC) Farmer and Stock Dealer, (BP) Randolph Co., Mo, (ARVD) 1858.

Michael Grant : (PO) Salisbury, Mo, (OC) Farmer and Stock Dealer, (BP) Washington Co., PA, (ARVD) 1875.

W.F. Carlsted: (PO) Thomas Hill, Mo, (OC) Farmer and Stock Raiser, (BP) Germany, 1853.

Henry Conard: (PO) Prairie Hill, Mo, (OC) Farmer and Stock Raiser, (BP) Butler Co., PA, (ARVD) 1857

G.W. Epperly: (PO) Prairie Hill, Mo, (OC) Farmer and Stock Dealer, (BP) Randolph Co., Mo, (ARVD) 18??.

A. J. Smith: (PO) New Cambria, Mo, (OC) Farmer and Stock Raiser, (BP) Morris Co., NJ, (ARVD) 1865.

J.W. Proctor: (PO) New Cambria, Mo, (OC) Physician and Surgeon Macon Co, Mo, (ARVD) 1865.

S. J. Lowe: (PO) New Cambria, Mo, (OC) Blacksmith, (BP) Sussex Co., Del., (ARVD) 1870.

James Johnson: (PO) New Cambria, Mo, (OC) Farmer and Stock Dealer, (BP) Howard Co., Mo., (ARVD) 1874.

J. P. Ramsey: (PO) New Cambria, Mo, (OC) Farmer and Stock Raiser, (BP) Wayne Co., KY, (ARVD)1853.

E.Q. Blankenship: (PO) New Cambria, Mo, (OC) Farmer and Stock Raiser, (BP) Russell Co., KY, (ARVD) 1874

William Whiteaker: (PO) Bynumville, Mo, (OC) Farmer and Miller, (BP) Pulaski Co., KY, 1862

W.H. Brewer : (PO) Bynumville, MO, (OC) Farmer and Stock Raiser, (BP) Fulton Co., NY (ARVD) 1868.

H. Yocum : (PO) Bynumville, MO, (OC) Farmer and Stock Dealer, (BP) Montgomery Co., KY (ARVD) 1867.

Charles B. James : (PO) Bynumville, MO, (OC) Farmer and Stock Raiser, (BP) Randolph Co., MO (ARVD) 1872.

Mrs. Parmelia R. Dewey : (PO) Bynumville, MO, (OC) Farming, (BP) Jefferson Co., NY (ARVD) 1868.

W. Yocum : (PO) Bynumville, MO, (OC) Farmer and Road Commissioner, (BP) Schuyler Co., IL (ARVD) 1870.

D. H. James : (PO) Bynumville, MO, (OC) Farmer and Stock Raiser, (BP) Montgomery Co., KY (ARVD) 1873.

S.C. Sharp (PO) Wein, MO, (OC) Farmer and Stock Raiser, (BP) Pickaway Co., Ohio (ARVD) 1871.

Sarah J. Chrisman (PO) Wein, MO, (OC) Farming (BP) Chariton Co., MO.

Wm. A. Howell : (PO) Bynumville, MO, (OC) Merchant, (BP) Essex Co., NJ (ARVD) 1874.

John Tyson : (PO) Bynumville, MO, (OC) Farmer and Stock Raiser, (BP) St. Louis Co., MO (ARVD) 1868.

W. P. Davis : (PO) Bynumville, MO (OC) Merchant, (BP) Schuylkill Co., PA (ARVD) 1873.

D. B. Baldwin : (PO) Bynumville, MO, (OC) Merchant, (BP) Indiana (ARVD) 1873.

W. H. Bradley : (PO) Bynumville, MO, (OC) Attorney At Law, (BP) Brown Co., Ohio (ARVD) 1866.

D. Spear : (PO) Bynumville, MO, (OC) Physician and Surgeon, (BP) Orange Co., VT (ARVD) 1870.

J. T. Spear : (PO) Bynumville, MO, (OC) Physician and Surgeon, (BP) Menard Co., IL (ARVD) 1870.

Luther Logan: (PO) Bynumville, MO, (OC) Notary Public and Counselor at Law, (BP) Highland Co., Ohio (ARVD) 1867.

John Garhart : (PO) Salisbury, MO (OC) Farmer and Stock Dealer, (BP) Crawford Co., Ohio (ARVD) 1873.

John Girvin: (PO) Hamden, MO (OC) Farmer and Stock Raiser, (BP) Ireland (ARVD) 1866.

John McSparren: (PO) Bynumville, MO (OC) Farmer and Stock Raiser, (BP) Pennsylvania (ARVD) 1851.

Anthony Pleyer: (PO) Bynumville, MO (OC) Farmer and Stock Dealer, (BP) Germany, (ARVD) 1858.

James McDowell: (PO) Bynumville, MO (OC) Farmer and Stock Raiser, (BP) Pulaski Co., KY 1858.

Peter Krager: (PO) Bynumville, MO (OC) Farmer and Stock Dealer, (BP) Germany, (ARVD) 1853.

J. H. Hise: (PO) Bynumville, MO (OC) Farmer and Stock Raiser, (BP) Mercer Co., KY (ARVD) 1840.

James Hise: (PO) Bynumville, MO (OC) Farmer and Stock Raiser, (BP) Chariton Co., MO (ARVD) 1855.

E. B. Downer : (PO) Bynumville, MO (OC) Farmer and Stock Raiser, (BP) Jefferson Co., NY (ARVD) 1868.

E. Defayette Hamden, MO (OC) Farmer and Stock Raiser, (BP) Morgan Co., IL (ARVD) 1870.

Wm. M. Smith: (PO) Hamden, MO (OC) Farmer and Stock Raiser, (BP) Morgan Co., IL, (ARVD) 1860.

Henry Krager: (PO) Bynumville, MO (OC) Farmer and Stock Raiser, (BP) Howard Co., MO, (ARVD) 1853.

W. L. Pattison : (PO) Bynumville, MO (OC) Farmer and Stock Raiser, (BP) Chatauqua Co., NY (ARVD) 1868.

Joseph Headley: (PO) Hamden, MO (OC) Farmer and Carpenter Colombian Co., MO 1859.

Henry Ehrhardt : (PO) Salisbury, MO (OC) Farmer and Stock Dealer, (BP) Brooke Co., VA (ARVD) 1844.

Peter Merrill : (PO) Salisbury, MO (OC) Farmer and Stock Raiser, (BP) New Hamshire, (ARVD) 1865.

H. S. Bosworth : (PO) Salisbury, MO (OC) Farmer and Stock Dealer, (BP) Preble Co., Ohio (ARVD) 1869.

Valentine Giesler : (PO) Salisbury, MO (OC) Farmer and Stock Raiser, (BP) Offen Hurisk, Baden, Germany (ARVD) 1868.

Henry Hurkelroth : (PO) Salisbury, MO (OC) Farmer and Stock Raiser, (BP) St. Louis Co., MO (ARVD) 1868.

Arthur Price : (PO) Salisbury, MO (OC) Farmer and Stock Raiser, (BP) Howard Co., MO (ARVD) 1868.

Robert Terrill : (PO) Salisbury, MO (OC) Farmer and Stock Raiser, (BP) Boone Co., KY, (ARVD) 1860.

J. W. Terrill: (PO) Salisbury, MO (OC) Farmer and Stock Raiser, (BP) Howard Co., MO 1860.

George Ehrhardt : (PO) Salisbury, MO (OC) Farmer and Stock Dealer, (BP) Germany (ARVD) 1847

G. W. Finnell : (PO) Salisbury, MO (OC) Farmer and Stock Raiser, (BP) Chariton Co., MO (ARVD) 1841.

Frank Kraissig : (PO) Salisbury, MO (OC) Farmer and Stock Raiser, (BP) Germany (ARVD) 1868.

Fred. Reppenhagen : (PO) Salisbury, MO (OC) Farmer and Stock Raiser, (BP) Germany (ARVD) 1869.

J. T. McDonald : (PO) Salisbury, MO (OC) Farmer and Stock Raiser, (BP) Garrard Co., KY, (ARVD) 1856.

J.C. Elliott : (PO) Salisbury, MO (OC) Farmer and Stock Dealer, (BP) McMinn Co., TN (ARVD) 1871.

J. M. Gallemore : (PO) Salisbury, MO, (OC) Owner Salisbury Press Garrard Co., KY, (ARVD) 1862.

P. H. Foster : (PO) Salisbury, MO (OC) Farmer and Stock Raiser, (BP) (BP) Chariton Co., MO (ARVD) 1842.

W.D. Whilhite : (PO) Salisbury, MO Physician and Druggist (BP) Boone Co., KY (ARVD) 1867.

James L. Frazier : (PO) Salisbury, MO Carpenter, (BP) Harrison Co., Ohio (ARVD) 1870.

Frank Kistner : (PO) Salisbury, MO Contractor Baden Germany (ARVD) 1869.

F.C. Wicks : (PO) Salisbury, MO, (OC) Livery Stable, (BP) Pike Co., MO (ARVD) 1867.

W. S. Stockwell: (PO) Salisbury, MO, (OC) Attorney At Law Onieda Co., NY (ARVD) 1866.

Geo. Baier : (PO) Salisbury, MO Wines and Liquors Baden, Germany (ARVD) 1875

F. Blakey : (PO) Salisbury, MO, (OC) Dealer in Livestock, (BP) Orange Co., VA, (ARVD) 1865.

B. F. Dameron : (PO) Salisbury, MO, (OC) Resident (BP) Chariton Co., MO, (ARVD) 1859.

B.F. Moore : (PO) Salisbury, MO, (OC) Manufacturer of plows, (BP) Howard Co., MO (ARVD) 1874.

L. Silvey : (PO) Salisbury, MO (OC) Merchant (BP) Howard Co., MO (ARVD) 1872.

J.S. Robertson : (PO) Salisbury, MO (OC) Merchant (BP) Howard Co., MO (ARVD) 1872.

Edward Waller : (PO) Salisbury, MO, (OC) Painter, (BP) Baden, Germany (ARVD) 1872.

Albert Petrus : (PO) Salisbury, MO, (OC) Manufacturer of wagons, (BP) Prussia (ARVD) 1873.

Isaac Moorhead : (PO) Salisbury, MO, (OC) Dealer in Tinware, (BP) Franklin Co., PA (ARVD) 1866.

T. G. Dulany : (PO) Salisbury, MO, (OC) Dealer in lumber and tobacco, (BP) Monroe Co., MO (ARVD) 1868.

B. F. Wilson : (PO) Salisbury, MO Physician and Surgeon, (BP) Kentucky, (ARVD) 1872.

T. J. Banning : (PO) Salisbury, MO, (OC) Physician and Surgeon, (BP) Macon Co, MO, (ARVD) 1861.

Wm. Wack : (PO) Salisbury, MO (OC) Farmer and Stock Raiser, (BP) Fulton Co., IL (ARVD) 1867.

J. C. Grimes : (PO) Salisbury, MO, (OC) Manufacturer of plows and wagons, (BP) Clark Co., KY, (ARVD) 1862.

A. Fisher : (PO) Salisbury, MO, (PO) Manufacturer of Farm implements and blacksmith, (BP) Germany (ARVD) 1870.

Lucius McAdam : (PO) Salisbury, MO (OC) Farmer and Stock Raiser, (BP) Chariton Co., MO 1845.

W. W. Whilhite : (PO) Salisbury, MO, (OC) Saloon Owner (BP) Boone Co., MO (ARVD) 1868.

J.A. Taylor: (PO) Salisbury, MO, (OC) Saloon Owner, (BP) Buckingham Co., VA (ARVD) 1844.

W. R. Slaughter : (PO) Salisbury, MO (OC) Farmer and Tobacco Dealer, (BP) Jackson Co., MO (ARVD) 1870.

T. H. Allin, Jr. : (PO) Salisbury, MO (OC) Farmer and Stock Dealer, (BP) Chariton Co., MO (ARVD) 1846.

J. W. Goe: (PO) Shannondale, MO, (OC) Carpenter, (BP) Monroe Co., MO (ARVD) 1871.

Wm. Lewis: (PO) Shannondale, MO (OC) Farmer (BP) Chariton Co., MO, (ARVD) 1860.

Y.C. Blakey : (PO) Salisbury, MO (OC) Farmer and Stock Raiser, (BP) Overseer of Roads Orange Co., VA (ARVD) 1866.

Wm Cook : (PO) Salisbury, MO (OC) Farmer and Stock and Tobacco Raiser, (BP) Prussia 1860.

Benjamin F. Horton: (PO) Shannondale, MO (OC) Farmer and Stock and Tobacco Raiser, (BP) Russell Co., VA (ARVD) 1847.

T. Brooks : (PO) Salisbury, MO (OC) Farmer Preble Co., (BP) Ohio, (ARVD) 1860.

Geo W. Johnson : (PO) Salisbury, MO (OC) Farmer Madison Co., KY, (ARVD) 1860.

Wm. H. Johnson : (PO) Salisbury, MO (OC) Farmer Marion Co., MO, (ARVD) 1861.

W. C. Wright : (PO) Salisbury, MO (OC) Farmer and Town Collector (BP) Howard Co., MO (ARVD) 1854.

J.C. Cravens : (PO) Salisbury, MO (OC) Farmer and Stock Dealer, (BP) Howard Co., MO, (ARVD) 1848.

J. M. Hamilton : (PO) Salisbury, MO (OC) Farmer and Public Administrator Russell Co., VA, (ARVD) 1865.

Francis Elmore : (PO) Salisbury, MO (OC) Farmer and Stock Raiser, (BP) Hanover, Germany (ARVD) 1852.

T. Holliday : (PO) Salisbury, MO, (OC) Teacher, (BP) Shelby Co., MO (ARVD) 1867.

B.F. Davis : (PO) Salisbury, MO (OC) Farmer Callaway Co., MO (ARVD) 1870.

C.B. Landrum : (PO) Salisbury, MO, (OC) Tobacco Factory Mercer Co., KY 1860.

Edward Leach : (PO) Salisbury, MO (OC) Farmer, (OC) Yorkshire England (ARVD) 1869.

G. H. Robbins: (PO) Shannondale, MO (OC) Farmer and Stock Raiser, (BP) Russell Co., VA, (ARVD) 1854

P. R. Nickerson : (PO) Salisbury, MO (OC) Farmer, (BP) Madison Co., KY (ARVD) 1846

Henry Horton : (PO) Salisbury, MO (OC) Farmer (BP) Howard Co., MO (ARVD) 1847.

J. H. Ford : (PO) Salisbury, MO (OC) Farmer (BP) Howard Co., MO, (ARVD) 1861.

L. T. Embree : (PO) Salisbury, MO (OC) Farmer (BP) Howard Co., MO (ARVD) 1869.

G. D. Johnson : (PO) Salisbury, MO (OC) Farmer and Town Clerk Platte Co., MO (ARVD) 1869.

John F. Johnson (PO) Glasgow, MO (OC) Farmer and Stock Raiser, (BP) Woodford Co., KY, (ARVD) 1857

W.S. O'Bannon: (PO) Glasgow, MO (OC) Farmer and Stock Raiser, (BP) Fauquier Co., VA (ARVD) 1846.

M. B. Williams: (PO) Forest Green, MO (OC) Merchant (BP) Howard Co., MO (ARVD) 1874.

L. A. Spencer: (PO) Forest Green, MO (OC) Farmer and Justice of the Peace, (BP) Portage Co., Ohio 1859.

K. Kothe: (PO) Glasgow, MO (OC) Farmer and House Builder,

(BP) Hanover, Germany, (ARVD) 1850.

Lewis Coleman: (PO) Glasgow, MO (OC) Farmer and Tobacco Grower, (BP) Chariton Co., MO (ARVD) 1840.

H. Imgarten: (PO) Glasgow, MO (OC) Farmer and Tobacco Grower, (BP) Hanover, Germany (ARVD) 1852

M. Nauerth: (PO) Glasgow, MO Fruit and Wine (OC) Farm Bavaria, Germany (ARVD) 1868.

A. F. Rector: (PO) Dalton, MO, (BP) Campbell Co., VA (ARVD) 1870.

J. W. Jeter : (PO) Dalton, MO Physician and Surgeon, (BP) Fayette Co., KY, (ARVD) 1862.

J. C. Beck : (PO) Dalton, MO (OC) Merchant, (BP) Germany, (ARVD) 1856.

S. H. Franklin : (PO) Dalton, MO, (OC) Constable and Collector, (OC) Farmer, (BP) Campbell Co., VA (ARVD) 1869.

Wm. H. Price : (PO) Dalton, MO (OC) Farmer and Stock Raiser, (BP) Prince Edward Co., VA (ARVD) 1844.

Henry Bucksath : (PO) Dalton, MO (OC) Farmer and Tobacco Grower, (BP) Germany, (ARVD) 1844.

John A. Goll : (PO) Dalton, MO (OC) Farmer, (BP) Montgomery Co, Ohio, (ARVD) 1869.

Garet Sleyster : (PO) Dalton, MO (OC) Farmer and Tobacco Raiser, (BP) Holland (ARVD) 1846.

J. H. Grotjan : (PO) Dalton, MO (OC) Farmer and Stock Raiser, (BP) Chariton Co., MO, (ARVD) 1848.

E. A. Grotjan : (PO) Dalton, MO (OC) Farmer and Stock Raiser, (BP) Chariton Co., MO, (ARVD) 1853.

H. H. F. Brandt: (PO) Brunswick, MO (OC) Farmer and Stock Raiser, (BP) Germany (ARVD) 1857.

C.W. Brandt: (PO) Brunswick, MO (OC) Farmer and Stock Raiser, (BP) Germany, (ARVD) 1851.

G.S. Lutzi: (PO) Brunswick, MO (OC) Farmer and Stock Raiser, (BP) Butler Co., Ohio, (ARVD) 1865.

M. Filser: (PO) Brunswick, MO (OC) Farmer and Stock Raiser, (BP) France or Germany (ARVD) 1851.

Margaret Straub: (PO) Brunswick, MO (OC) Farmer, (BP) Germany (ARVD) 1851.

A. R. Voorhees: (PO) Brunswick, MO (OC) Farmer and Stock Raiser, (BP) Yates Co., NY, (ARVD) 1865.

R. H. Hodge: (PO) Brunswick, MO (OC) Farmer and Stock Dealer, (BP) Livingston Co., KY, (ARVD) 1849.

C. J. Warden: (PO) Brunswick, MO (OC) Farmer and Stock Raiser, (BP) (BP) Howard Co., MO 1845.

August Grotjan : (PO) Dalton, MO (OC) Farmer and Tobacco Dealer, (BP) Germany, (ARVD) 1845.

John Laker : (PO) Dalton, MO (OC) Farmer and Tobacco Raiser, (BP) Germany (ARVD) 1855.

Louis Grotjan : (PO) Dalton, MO (OC) Farmer and Tobacco Dealer, (BP) Germany, (ARVD) 1845.

Wm. Munson; (PO) Brunswick, MO (OC) Farmer and Stock Raiser, (BP) Germany (ARVD) 1842.

Andrew Storm: (PO) Brunswick, MO (OC) Farmer and Stock Dealer, (BP) Germany (ARVD) 1866.

J. B. Naylor: (PO) Brunswick, MO (OC) Owner Brunswicker, (BP) McDonough Co., IL (ARVD) 1866.

W. H. Balthis: (PO) Brunswick, MO (OC) Merchant, (BP) Warren Co., VA (ARVD) 1866.

John N. Coudrey: (PO) Brunswick, MO, (OC) Insurance and Real Estate Dealer, (BP) Pennsylvania, (ARVD) 1865.

Jas. A. Armstrong: (PO) Brunswick, MO, (OC) Owner Andes House, (BP) Steuben Co., NY, (ARVD) 1865.

E. C. Stowe: (PO) Brunswick, MO, (OC) Photographer, (BP) Adams Co., IL (ARVD) 1870.

Louis Benecke: (PO) Brunswick, MO, (OC) Attorney At Law, (BP) Germany (ARVD) 1857.

W. C. Davis: (PO) Brunswick, MO, (OC) Ex Editor of the Randolph Citizen, (BP) Johnson Co., MO, (ARVD) 1865.

J. W. McGuire: (PO) Brunswick, MO, (OC) Dentist, (BP) Hardeman Co., TN (ARVD) 1871.

L. S. Prosser: (PO) Brunswick, MO, (OC) Physician and Surgeon, (BP) Mason Co., W Va, (ARVD) Nov. 6, 1842.

Chas Hammond: (PO) Brunswick, MO, (OC) Attorney At Law, (BP) Brooke Co., W Va, (ARVD) 1858.

R. Wylie Hammond: (PO) Brunswick, MO, (OC) Attorney At Law, Brooke Co., W Va, (ARVD) 1865.

Wm. Bierbower: (PO) Brunswick, MO, (OC) Dealer in Stoves and Tinware, (BP) Dauphin Co., Pa (ARVD) 1866.

John F. Cunningham: (PO) Brunswick, MO (OC) Merchant, (BP) Warren Co., NY (ARVD) 1852.

Henry L. Bosworth: (PO) Brunswick, MO, (OC) Professional Harness Maker (BP) Chariton Co., MO, (ARVD) 1849.

W. T. Graham: (PO) Brunswick, MO, (OC) Lumber and hardware (BP) Chariton Co., MO (ARVD) 1874.

A. Griffen: (PO) Brunswick, MO (OC) Merchant, (BP) Albany Co., NY, (ARVD) 1859.

R. A. Scott: (PO) Brunswick, MO, (OC) City Marshal and Auctioneer, (BP) Augusta Co., Va, (ARVD) 1859.

B. Strub: (PO) Brunswick, MO (OC) Merchant, (BP) Baden, Germany, (ARVD) 1864.

A. Meyer: (PO) Brunswick, MO (OC) Merchant , (BP)Baden Germany, (ARVD) 1853.

John Knappenberger: (PO) Brunswick, MO, (OC) Abstract of Titles Real Estate Agent, (BP) Westmoreland Co., PA (ARVD) 1866.

John Kuechler: (PO) Brunswick, MO, (OC) Owner Brunswick House, (BP) Bavaria, Germany, (AVRD) 1850.

C. W. Bell: (PO) Brunswick, MO, (OC) Attorney At Law, (BP) Lunenberg Co., Va, (ARVD) 1843.

L. P. Beatty: (PO) Brunswick, MO, (OC) Owner Brunswick Republican, (BP) Lunenberg Co., VA (ARVD) 1875.

G. Gritzmacher: (PO) Brunswick, MO, (OC) Saloon Owner , (BP) Prussia, (ARVD) 1864.

P. M. Smith: (PO) Brunswick, MO, (OC) Miller, (BP) Ireland (ARVD) 1869.

Louis Sasse: (PO) Brunswick, MO, (OC) Groceries and Produce , (BP) Prussia (ARVD) 1851.

J. M. Peery: (PO) Brunswick, MO, (OC) Lumber and Hardware (BP) Howard Co., MO (ARVD) 1854.

J. J. Heisel: (PO) Brunswick, MO, (OC) Post Master and Merchant, (BP) Bavaria, Germany (ARVD) 1846.

L.W. Axton: (PO) Brunswick, MO (OC) Farmer and Stock Raiser, (BP) Breckenridge Co., KY, (ARVD) 1858.

Samuel Stabler (PO) Brunswick, MO, (OC) Architect and Builder Baltimore Co., MD (ARVD) 1867.

Michael Sonreil: (PO) Brunswick, Mo, (OC) Contractor and Builder, (BP) Montreal, Canada, (ARVD) 1859.

John E. Foggins: (PO) Brunswick, Mo, (OC) Painter and Grainer, (BP) Yorkshire, England (ARVD) 1852.

R. N. Davis: (PO) Brunswick, Mo, (OC) Minister of Christian Church, (BP) Daviess Co., Mo, (OC) (ARVD) 1875.

Jacob Ament: (PO) Brunswick, Mo, (OC) Manufacturer of Boots and Shoes, (BP) Bavaria, Germany (ARVD) 1852.

J. E. Lewis: (PO) Brunswick, Mo, (OC) (OC) Farmer and Stock Raiser, (BP) Holmes Co., Ohio (ARVD) 1869.

A.G. Kennedy: (PO) Brunswick, Mo, (OC) Merchant and Tobacco Raiser, (BP) Canada (ARVD) (ARVD) 1865.

Wm. Ostermann: (PO) Brunswick, Mo, (OC) Saloon Owner, (BP) Hanover, Germany (ARVD) 1868.

Louis Kinkhorst: (PO) Brunswick, Mo, (OC) Saloon Owner, (BP)

Hanover, Germany (ARVD) 1867.

J. X. Mitchell: (PO) Brunswick, Mo, (OC) Carpenter and Joiner, (BP) Otsego, NY, (AVRD) 1858.

A. L. Wires: (PO) Brunswick, Mo, (OC) Carpenter and Joiner, (BP) Wood Co., W Va 1850.

Albert J. Wires: (PO) Brunswick, Mo, (OC) Carpenter and Joiner (PO) Brunswick, Mo, (ARVD) 1858.

C. A. Winslow: (PO) Brunswick, Mo, (OC) Attorney At Law, (BP) Kennebec Co., ME, (ARVD) 1853.

John Strub: (PO) Brunswick, Mo, (OC) Merchant , (BP)Baden, Germany, (ARVD) 1854.

Henry Strub: (PO) Brunswick, Mo, (OC) Merchant (BP) Chariton Co., Mo, (OC) 1858.

Samuel E. Everly: (PO) Brunswick, Mo, (OC) Blacksmith, (BP) Shenandoah Co., VA (ARVD) 1866.

C. T. Kimmel: (PO) Brunswick, Mo, (OC) Physician and Surgeon, (BP) Cape Girardeau Co., Mo, (OC) 1858.

R. Love: (PO) Brunswick, Mo, (OC) Owner Barber Shop, (BP) Caldwell Co., KY (ARVD) 1855.

E. T Allin: (PO) Brunswick, Mo, (OC) Farmer and Stock Raiser, (BP) Chariton Co., Mo, (OC) 1845.

J. E. Owen: (PO) Brunswick, Mo, (OC) Farmer and Stock Dealer, (BP) Howard Co., Mo, (OC) 1856.

Henry Newcomer : (PO) Mendon, Mo, (OC) Farmer and Stock Raiser, (BP) Fayette Co., KY (ARVD) 1866.

Richard H. Clements (PO) Brunswick, Mo, (OC) Farmer and Stock Raiser, (BP) Fluvanna Co., VA 1862.

JohnJ. Burrus (PO) Brunswick, Mo, (OC) Farmer and Stock Dealer, (BP) Henry Co., Va, (ARVD) 1854.

Wm N. Riddle (PO) Brunswick, Mo, (OC) (OC) Farmer and Stock Dealer, (BP) Pendleton Co., KY (ARVD) 1867.

Robert T. Morehead: (PO) Triplett, Mo, (OC) Farmer and Stock Raiser, (BP) Howard Co., Mo, (ARVD) 1869.

John E. M. Triplett: (PO) Triplett, Mo, (OC) Farmer and Notary Public, Land Agent , (BP) Franklin Co., KY (ARVD) 1846.

Benj. F. Fleetwood: (PO) Triplett, Mo, (OC) Farmer and Stock Dealer, (BP) (BP) Chariton Co., Mo, (ARVD) 1840.

T. J. Marshal: (PO) Brunswick, Mo, (OC) Farmer and Stock Raiser, (BP) Madison Co., NY (ARVD) 1857.

W. O. McLeod: (PO) Triplett, Mo, (OC) Physician and Surgeon, (BP) Hancock Co., Ohio (ARVD) 1873.

S. B. Noel: (PO) Brunswick, Mo, (OC) Farmer and Stock Raiser, (BP) Hopkins Co., KY, (ARVD) 1871.

Thos. S. Anderson: (PO) Triplett, Mo, (OC) Farmer and Stock Raiser, (BP) Salem Co., NY, (ARVD) 1843.

John P. Randolph: (PO) Brunswick, Mo, (OC) Farmer and Stock Raiser, (BP) Adams Co., IL (ARVD) 1866.

Henry O. Overholt: (PO) Brunswick, Mo, (OC) Farmer and Stock Raiser, (BP) Westmoreland Co., PA (ARVD) 1868.

Wm B. Bruce: (PO) Brunswick, Mo, (OC) Farmer and Stock Raiser, (BP) Nottoway Co., VA (ARVD) 1844.

Christain Staubus: (PO) Brunswick, Mo, (OC) Farmer and Stock Raiser, (BP) Augusta Co., VA (ARVD) 1870.

James H. Harper: (PO) Triplett, Mo, (OC) Farmer and Stock Raiser, (BP) Chariton Co., Mo, (ARVD) 1840.

L. W. Axton: (PO) Brunswick, Mo, (OC) Farmer and Stock Raiser, (BP) Breckenridge Co., KY, (ARVD) 1858.

Jacob Sharp: (PO) Mendon, Mo,(OC) Farmer and Stock Raiser, (BP) Southampton Co., VA (ARVD) 1874.

Valentine Kahler: (PO) Brunswick, Mo, (OC) Farmer and Stock Raiser, (BP) Germany, (ARVD) 1845.

John D. Ruddell: (PO) Mendon, Mo, (OC) Farmer and Stock Raiser, (BP) Adams Co., IL (ARVD) 1866.

J. W. Nichols : (PO) Mendon, Mo, (OC) Farmer and Stock Dealer, (BP) Bourbon Co., KY (ARVD) 1866.

J. M. Herndon : (PO) Mendon, Mo, (OC) Farmer and Stock Dealer, (BP) Campbell Co., VA (ARVD) 1857.

E. M. Shupe and Co.: (PO) Mendon, Mo, (OC) Farmer and Merchant, (BP) Adams Co., IL (ARVD) 1868.

T. Dade Palmer: (PO) Mendon, Mo, (OC) Physician and Surgeon, (BP) Hinds Co., MS (ARVD) 1870.

William W. Felt: (PO) Mendon, Mo, (OC) Farmer and Stock Raiser, (BP) Adams Co., IL (ARVD) 1867.

Winslow L. Felt : (PO) Mendon, Mo, (OC) Farmer and Stock Raiser, (BP) Adams Co., IL (ARVD) 1867.

J. N. Hern : (PO) Mendon, Mo, (OC) Farmer and Stock Dealer, (BP) Adams Co., IL (ARVD) 1867.

J. P. Chapman: (PO) Mendon, Mo, (OC) Farmer and Stock Raiser, (BP) Tolland Co., Ct (ARVD) 1869.

A. F. Wood : (PO) Mendon, Mo, (OC) Farmer and Stock Raiser, (BP) Adams Co., IL (ARVD) 1867.

G. H. Ruddell : (PO) Mendon, Mo, (OC) Farmer and Stock Raiser, (BP) Adams Co., IL (ARVD) 1870.

Daniel Newcomer : (PO) Mendon, Mo, (OC) Farmer and Stock Raiser, (BP) Fayette Co, PA (ARVD) 1866.

S. M. Moore : (PO) Mendon, Mo, (OC) Farmer and Stock Dealer, (BP) Shenandoah Co., Va, (ARVD) 1854.

J. L. Riddell : (PO) Rothville, Mo, (OC) (OC) Farmer and Stock Dealer, (BP) (BP) Boone Co., KY 1859.

Wm. E. Taylor Cunningham, Mo, (OC) Farmer, Grain and Stock Dealer, (BP) Northampton Co., NC (ARVD) 1866.

I. N. Long Cunningham, Mo, (OC) Farmer and Grain Dealer, (BP) Mason Co., W Va (ARVD) 1855.

John H. Deem : (PO) Rothville, Mo, (OC) Farmer, (BP) Pennsylvania (ARVD) 1871.

H. Dewey : (PO) Rothville, Mo, (OC) Farmer, (BP) Steuben Co., NY (ARVD) 1868.

Cyrus Williams: (PO) Rothville, Mo, (OC) Farmer and Stock Raiser, (BP) Canada (ARVD) 1869.

Noah Dean: (PO) Rothville, Mo, (OC) Farmer and Stock Raiser, (BP) Lawrence Co., PA (ARVD) 1869.

J. D. Hartzell : (PO) Rothville, Mo, (OC) Farmer and Stock Raiser, (BP) Northampton Co., PA (ARVD) 1869.

Joseph Ebbert: (PO) Rothville, Mo, (OC) Farmer and Stock Raiser, (BP) Westmoreland Co., PA (ARVD) 1869.

James H. Gray : (PO) Rothville, Mo, (OC) Farmer and Stock Raiser, (BP) Bath Co., KY (ARVD) 1868.

M. H. Dewey : (PO) Brookfield, Mo, (OC) Farmer and Stock Raiser, (BP) Jefferson Co., NY (ARVD) 1867.

D. E. Grommons : (PO) Brookfield, Mo, (OC) Farmer and Stock Raiser, (BP) Jefferson Co., NC (ARVD) 1868.

H. N. Armstrong : (PO) Brookfield, Mo, (OC) Farmer and Stock Raiser, (BP) Philadelphia, PA (ARVD) 1874.

Otis A. Carpenter : (PO) Rothville, Mo, (OC) Farmer, (BP) Steuben Co., NY (ARVD) 1868.

James Devore : (PO) Rothville, Mo, (OC) Farmer, Brick and Stone Mason, (BP) Chemung Co., NY, (ARVD) 1873.

W. W. Pease: (PO) Brookfield, Mo, (OC) Farmer, (BP) Jasper Co., NY, (ARVD) 1865.

H. W. Wilson: (PO) Cunningham, Mo, (OC) Farmer and Merchant, (BP) Gabbia Co., Va, (ARVD) 1871.

R. Baker : (PO) Brookfield, Mo, (OC) (OC) Farmer and (OC) Merchant Schoharie Co., NY (ARVD) 1866.

Wm. Fulbright: (PO) Cunningham, Mo, (OC) Farmer and Stock Dealer, (BP) Jackson Co., IN, (ARVD) 1865.

Wm. McKee: (PO) Cunningham, Mo, (OC) Farmer and Stock Dealer, (BP) County Down, Ireland (ARVD) 1873.

Charles Stothard: (PO) Laclede, Mo, (OC) Farmer and Sheep Raiser, (BP) New York City, NY, (ARVD) 1866.

John Gould: (PO) Cunningham, Mo, (OC) (OC) Farmer Mo, (BP) England, (ARVD) 1865.

P. W. Post: (PO) Cunningham, Mo, (OC) Farmer, (BP) Hancock Co., IL, (ARVD) 1865.

Jas McCullough: (PO) Triplett, Mo, (OC) Farmer and Stock Raiser, (BP) Page Co., VA, (AVRD) 1853.

Logan H. Shipp: (PO) Triplett, Mo, (OC) Farmer and Stock Raiser, (BP) Howard Co., Mo, (ARVD) 1870.

J. Pointer: (PO) Triplett, Mo, (OC) Farmer and Stock Dealer, (BP) Barren Co., KY (ARVD) 1874.

Milton Cross: (PO) Triplett, Mo, (OC) Farmer and Stock Dealer, (BP) Chariton Co., Mo, (ARVD) 1841.

Phillip Hooper: (PO) Triplett, Mo, (OC) Farmer and Stock Dealer, (BP) Allegheny Co., PA. (ARVD) 1840.

Wm. Fulbright: (PO) Cunningham, Mo, (OC) Farmer and Stock Dealer, (BP) Jackson Co., IN, (ARVD) 1865.

Texas County, Missouri, Charter Members of the Freedom Baptist Church, July 1, 1916.

Joseph L. and Hattie B. Snow; George W. Booker; Dixie Emily Garrett; Lee and Francis Norris; Mary E. Skelton; Amy Means; Clara, Ida and Alice McCart; Christene Booker; Violet Whited; Jesse Garret; Sis. M. J. Woodyard; Elberta Maine; James Hine; Nannie Booker; Clara Smith; Fred D. Garrell; Ada, James L., Anna and Jessie Ellis; Nicholas and Julia LaLoy; William C. Gooker; Freed Goodman; Nora Thornton; Johanah Kruse; Annie Buzzell; Jessie Kruse; Perry and Mary Buzzell; Cora Booker; Florence Krose; Nathan Garrett.

Surname Index

ABBE, 167
ABBINGTON, 66
ABBOT, 66
ABBOTT, 8 131 162
ABBY, 72
ABERNATHA, 51
ABLES, 166 175
ABNEY, 74
ACHENBACH, 131
ACKARD, 165
ACKENBACH, 131
ACKISON, 149
ACOCK, 87 166-167 173
ACUFF, 174
ADAIR, 131
ADAMS, 4-5 7 72-74 91 104 131 163 183
ADAMSON, 74 107
ADDICKS, 49
ADDISON, 51
ADKINS, 68-69 78 94
AGNES, 172
AGNEW, 68
AIKINS, 114
AKARD, 165 167 174
AKERS, 60 87
AKIN, 66 75 94
AKINS, 70
ALBIN, 66
ALDEN, 131

ALDRICH, 10 94
ALDRIDGE, 149
ALESON, 131
ALEXANDER, 3 5 68-69 71 131 149
ALFORD, 78
ALLCORN, 60
ALLEE, 131
ALLEGA, 107
ALLEN, 52 54 59-60 63 66 70 72-74 78
   87 94 101 104 107 114 131 165-167
   182-185
ALLEN-MARA, 106
ALLEY, 71 78 103
ALLIN, 189 194
ALLISON, 7 78
ALLRED, 52
ALMOND, 78
ALNUT, 78
ALSUP, 162
ALUMBAUGH, 149
ALVARADO, 36
ALVERSON, 66
AMBURGH, 1
AMEN, 114
AMENT, 193
AMES, 68
AMMERMAN, 13
AMMONS, 149
AMSDEN, 3

ANDERSON, 16 52 68 72 75 78 87 94 100-101 131 149 195
ANDREWS, 9 16 18
ANGLE, 99 102
ANIBAL, 2
ANKENEY, 4
ANNIN, 1
ANTHONY, 6 52
ANTLE, 78
APLIN, 131
APPLEBURY, 94
APPLEBY, 1 166
APPLEMAN, 131
ARBUCKEE, 68
ARBUTHNOT, 1
ARCHER, 5
AREY, 131
ARGYETE, 78
ARHUR, 4
ARMSTRONG, 5 14 72 76 94 107 131 192 196
ARNET, 59 63
ARNETT, 52 60 69 78
ARNOLD, 5 51-52 78 97 107 131
ARNOTE, 131
ARROWSMITH, 5
ARTERBERRY, 74
ARTHUR, 71-72
ASHBY, 87
ASHE, 147
ASHER, 78 173
ASHLEY, 72 78 149
ASHLOCK, 52 57
ASHMORE, 3
ASHWORTH, 149
ASMON, 53
ASTER, 131
ASTON, 92
ATKINSON, 71 73 131
AUBUSTER, 131
AUL, 8
AULGAR, 94
AULL, 114
AUSTILL, 131
AUSTIN, 60 68 73 107 129 131
AUZIER, 78
AVERILL, 2
AVIS, 70
AXON, 131
AXTON, 131 193 195

AYRES, 4 61 131
BABBITT, 10
BABCOCK, 66 76
BABER, 72
BACHELLER, 5
BACON, 67
BADGER, 94
BAESELEY, 114
BAGAN, 75
BAGBEY, 78
BAGLEY, 179
BAGNELL, 52
BAIER, 188
BAILEY, 8 73 114 131
BAILY, 73 149
BAIN, 5
BAINTER, 4
BAINTON, 78
BAIRD, 59
BAITY, 5
BAKER, 4 6 8-9 71 78 87 97-99 101 104-105 107 131 196
BALDWIN, 6 52 114 131 186
BALES, 97-99 102-103 131
BALKEY, 131
BALL, 68 131 148
BALLANCE, 107
BALLARD, 78 97 103 114
BALLINGER, 131 176
BALTHIS, 6 192
BALTIMORE, 78
BANCROFT, 131
BANES, 78
BANEY, 78
BANKER, 52
BANKSON, 2
BANKUS, 13 23
BANNING, 189
BANO, 78
BANON, 101
BANTY, 149
BANZER, 114-115
BAPPLE, 76
BARBEE, 146
BARBER, 7 149
BARCLAY, 176
BARCUS, 131
BARDEAUX, 6
BAREFIELD, 101
BARETT, 62

BARKER, 78
BARLEY, 5
BARLOW, 115 131
BARNARD, 4 7
BARNES, 51 68-69 72 78 92 101 185
BARNETT, 2-3 6 76 78 101 166
BARNOLLY, 68
BARNS, 60
BARR, 15 162
BARRET, 67
BARRETT, 8 58 60 101 131
BARRIER, 78
BARRON, 4 8 55 131
BARRY, 92 106-107
BARTLETT, 131
BARTLEY, 175
BARTON, 2 60 63 71
BARTZ, 180
BARUTHOUSE, 2
BASKET, 73 107
BASSEMAN, 131
BASSETT, 131
BAST, 76
BATEMAN, 131
BATEMEN, 131
BATES, 3 14 19 149
BATHGATE, 131
BATIE, 71
BATSON, 131
BATTLE, 131
BATTLEFIELD, 131
BAUCH, 130
BAUDON, 5
BAUGHMAN, 8
BAXTER, 8
BAYER, 149-150
BAYLARD, 94
BAYS, 131
BEABOUT, 131
BEACH, 10
BEAGLE, 73
BEAIRD, 58
BEAL, 41 64 103 115 131
BEALE, 36 39-40
BEALER, 71
BEAN, 148
BEARD, 115
BEARER, 69
BEASLEY, 78
BEATTY, 193
BEAUCHAMP, 71 102
BEAVER, 52
BEAVIN, 78
BEBEE, 131
BEBEMYER, 131
BEBERMEIR, 131
BECK, 78 115 191
BECKETT, 60 68 78 131
BECKHAM, 167
BECKLEY, 172
BECKNER, 74
BEDES, 63
BEDFORD, 78
BEELS, 71
BEEMAN, 8
BEERS, 115
BEESON, 9
BEETS, 68
BEEVE, 60
BEEVES, 53
BEGGS, 10
BEGNOLD, 78
BELCHEO, 78
BELDEN, 131
BELIEN, 150
BELIESO, 78
BELIEU, 78
BELK, 78
BELL, 3 10 72 78 115 131 193
BELLMORE, 71
BELMAR, 52
BELMIRE, 52
BELTZHOOVER, 16
BELVINS, 131
BENCE, 6
BENDER, 131
BENECKE, 192
BENJAMIN, 131
BENNETT, 52 54 60 69 78 87 115 132 184
BENNEY, 132
BENSON, 4-5 129 150
BENT, 78
BENTLEY, 150
BENTON, 34 79 96
BERCY, 79
BERD, 52
BERGER, 70
BERHOFF, 58
BERKSTRESSER, 94

BERLSEON, 102
BERMONT, 79
BERNARD, 68
BERNER, 163
BERNIER, 52
BERRY, 52 57 59 70 75 79 102 147 183
BERRYHILL, 79
BERRYMAN, 52-53 55 62-63
BERWICH, 101
BESS, 54 59-60 62
BEST, 79 108 150
BETHEL, 132
BETT, 58
BETTER, 71
BEVE, 52
BEWER, 60
BIBB, 79
BICHEY, 79
BICKET, 150
BIDDLE, 34
BIDDLEMAN, 10
BIDWELL, 150
BIERBOWER, 192
BIFFLE, 96
BIGGIN, 79
BIGLER, 47
BILDERBACK, 79
BILLINGS, 150
BILLMAN, 162
BINFORD, 4
BINGHAM, 10
BINGLE, 79
BIRD, 6 60 132
BISELL, 132
BISHOP, 10 70 73-74 129 132 183
BITTER, 180
BIVENS, 52
BIVIN, 79
BIXLER, 73
BLACK, 49-50 68 79 150 177
BLACKABLE, 132
BLACKBURN, 150
BLACKMAN, 79
BLACKSTON, 72 132
BLACKWELL, 103
BLADES, 132
BLAGG, 150
BLAINE, 6
BLAIR, 18 40 72 115 132 168
BLAKE, 69

BLAKELY, 74 150
BLAKEMAN, 2
BLAKEY, 188-189
BLAKLEY, 79
BLAKLY, 150
BLANCHARD, 103
BLANDRY, 132
BLANKENSHIP, 79 132 186
BLANTON, 52 73
BLASETON, 79
BLASS, 75
BLEDSOE, 15 67-68 79
BLEVIN, 79
BLEVINS, 79 115 132
BLEW, 129
BLEWETT, 50
BLISS, 2
BLOESS, 76
BLOOM, 60
BLOOMER, 4
BLOSSEMAN, 132
BLOUCHARD, 71
BLUHM, 115
BLYDES, 11
BOAN, 52
BOARDWINE, 52
BOATCHER, 94
BOATWRIGHT, 150
BOBINS, 79
BOCKLEMAN, 76
BOCKRATH, 106-107
BOEN, 150
BOETTNER, 130
BOGAN, 132
BOGGS, 23 26 33 68
BOGSTON, 71
BOHANNON, 79
BOHART, 74 79
BOHMER, 51
BOHRES, 79
BOITSTON, 79
BOLEN, 72
BOLES, 75
BOLIN, 87
BOLLINGER, 1 6 52 60
BOMARD, 79
BONA, 132
BONAR, 132
BOND, 60 66 148
BONDS, 62

BONEMAN, 105
BONFIELD, 71
BONY, 115
BOOKER, 132 197
BOOKOUT, 13
BOON, 74
BOONE, 2
BOOTH, 52 60 71
BORCHERS, 115
BOREN, 167
BORNETTE, 75
BOROF, 132
BOROFF, 132
BOSEMAN, 132
BOSS, 79
BOSSIER, 60
BOSTON, 72
BOSWELL, 52 146
BOSWORTH, 187 192
BOTHWELL, 132
BOTT, 52
BOTTOM, 132
BOTTS, 6 61
BOUCE, 132
BOUGHTON, 87
BOULTON, 4 132
BOUNDS, 55
BOUTON, 75
BOUTWELL, 132
BOWEN, 115 132 174
BOWER, 183
BOWERMAN, 8
BOWERS, 75 94 104 132
BOWGERS, 79
BOWIN, 132
BOWLES, 4
BOWLING, 79
BOWLS, 74
BOWLY, 70
BOWMAN, 73 79 92 97 99-100 132 150
BOWSER, 76
BOWYERS, 79
BOX, 102-104
BOYD, 6 52 69 73 79 132 173
BOYER, 94 97-98 100-101 104
BOYERS, 79
BOYES, 79
BOYLE, 76 132
BOYLES, 132
BOZE, 64

BRACKING, 150
BRADBURY, 68
BRADEN, 71 150
BRADFORD, 11 79 115 168 172
BRADIN, 74
BRADLEY, 9 73-74 115 132 186
BRADSHAW, 162
BRADY, 52 59 68 71-72 74 79
BRAGG, 79
BRAINARD, 11
BRAINERD, 9
BRAME, 97-98 104-105
BRANDENSTEIN, 115
BRANDT, 11 76 191
BRANFIELD, 73
BRANHAM, 166
BRANTLEY, 98
BRASFIELD, 74
BRASHEAR, 5
BRAWLEY, 79 99
BRAY, 132
BRAYMER, 132
BRAZIEL, 115
BREKER, 8
BRELSFORD, 132
BRENDEL, 87
BRENNAMAN, 132
BRENNEMAN, 132
BRENNING, 11
BRETZ, 71
BREWER, 61 63 132 186
BREWIN, 52
BREWINGTON, 102
BREYSON, 72
BRIANS, 67
BRICE, 132
BRIDGEMAN, 78
BRIDGES, 97 108 167
BRIDGEWATER, 132
BRIDGMAN, 79
BRIDGWATER, 132
BRIES, 79
BRIGGS, 10 51 74 108
BRIGHT, 52
BRINES, 79
BRINKLEY, 98
BRISCOE, 7
BRISSEN, 115
BRITT, 184
BRITTAIN, 52 72 150

BRITTLE, 79
BRITZEN, 150
BROCK, 72 79 150
BRODERICK, 41-43 47 150
BRODY, 115
BROOING, 132
BROOK, 70
BROOKE, 53
BROOKS, 68 73 98 102 130 132 190
BROOKSHIRE, 132
BROSNIHAN, 132
BROTHER, 5
BROTHERTON, 58
BROUS, 3
BROWN, 2-5 7 9 11 52 55 61 67-69 71-75 79 87 98 100-102 104-105 108 130 132 146-147 150-151 165 178 181
BROWNE, 67
BROWNING, 71 74
BROYLE, 151
BRUBAKER, 74 132
BRUCE, 79 195
BRUIN, 108
BRUMBACK, 132
BRUMFIELD, 151
BRUMMETT, 78 108
BRUNER, 2
BRUNK, 132
BRUNNERT, 92
BRUNO, 87
BRUTON, 7
BRYAN, 2 7 9-10 76
BRYANT, 9 26 29 31 50 72 132
BRYNES, 148
BUCEY, 99
BUCH, 71
BUCHANAN, 1 8 100 103
BUCHHAUMAN, 75
BUCK, 5 8 67 132
BUCKHAM, 8 115
BUCKINGHAM, 104
BUCKMAN, 75
BUCKMASTER, 1
BUCKNELL, 79
BUCKNER, 52 55-56 61 103
BUCKSATH, 191
BUDILY, 66
BUFFUM, 66
BUILTEMAN, 7
BUKAM, 74

BULL, 115
BULLARD, 53
BULLEY, 115
BUNCH, 68 166-167 174
BUNKER, 16
BUNNER, 68
BUNNING, 62
BUNTON, 79
BURBAKER, 132
BURBAUK, 132
BURCH, 130 167
BURCHAM, 54 64
BURDETT, 132
BURDICK, 132
BURDISH, 132
BUREN, 4
BURGDORF, 51
BURGER, 47 132
BURGESS, 26-27 69 79 87
BURIS, 98
BURK, 76 103
BURKE, 8-9 107 132
BURKETT, 132
BURKS, 22
BURLE-DOWNING, 106
BURLESON, 23
BURNETT, 42-43 67-68 79 88 132
BURNHAM, 97
BURNLEY, 102
BURNS, 1 53-54 57 79 132 151 165 167 176 178
BURNSIDES, 163
BURR, 184
BURRIS, 79 100 132 151
BURROS, 166 174
BURROWS, 8 30 64 132
BURRUS, 194
BURTON, 66 185
BUSCH, 10
BUSH, 6 22 79 115 132
BUSHNELL, 71
BUSICK, 23
BUTCHER, 70
BUTENHOLER, 53
BUTLER, 7 9 69 88 97 132
BUTNER, 108
BUTS, 68
BUTTERFIELD, 132
BUTTLER, 148
BUTTS, 132 151

BUZZELL, 197
BYERS, 151
BYLER, 19
BYRON, 71
CABBAGE, 13
CABLE, 23
CACY, 62
CAHOVN, 151
CAIL, 69
CAILLOTE, 53
CAIN, 55-56 61 105 108 132
CAINS, 79
CALAMAN, 53
CALDWELL, 166 168
CALET, 102
CALHOUN, 34
CALLAGHAN, 67
CALLAHAN, 181
CALLAWAY, 53-54 60
CALLOWAY, 175
CALLUE, 67
CALVERT, 9 79 108
CALVIN, 79 132 151
CAMBELL, 11
CAMERON, 22 115-116 182-183
CAMMACK, 4
CAMMERON, 66
CAMPBELL, 5 9-10 61 72 79 94 100 103 108 116 132 151 165-166 174-175
CAMRON, 79
CANDLE, 116
CANDLER, 7
CANFIELD, 16 18
CANNON, 48
CANTER, 79
CANTON, 101
CANTRILL, 103
CAPLES, 79
CARATHERS, 57
CARBAN, 74
CARELESS, 151
CARGILE, 99
CARLESS, 151
CARLILE, 133
CARLIN, 97
CARLISLE, 76 133
CARLSTED, 185
CARLTON, 133
CARMACK, 53 56 61
CARMAN, 133

CARMON, 68
CARN, 11
CARNAHAN, 97-98
CARNES, 79
CARNUTT, 151
CAROLINE, 50
CAROLL, 133
CARPENTER, 4 6 51 79 96-98 102 183 196
CARR, 9 96 133
CARROL, 53
CARROLL, 2 10 14 67 76 133
CARSON, 32 71 167
CART, 16
CARTER, 3 68-69 71-72 94 98 100-101 104 130 133 166 181
CARTLON, 59
CARTTON, 133
CARUTHERS, 52 57
CARVER, 94
CARY, 79
CASE, 68 94 147
CASEBEER, 79 131
CASELMAN, 133
CASEY, 5 116 133 146
CASH, 79 133 151
CASHADY, 79
CASSELL, 10
CASTEAL, 53 61
CASTEEL, 68 168
CASTIEL, 61
CASTILE, 53 61
CASTO, 133
CASTRO, 37
CASY, 71
CATE, 97
CATES, 69 79 133 174
CATHERINE, 51
CATLET, 79
CATRON, 133
CATTIN, 71
CAUDLE, 116
CAULREED, 62
CAUSBY, 61
CAUTHORN, 2
CAVANAUGH, 108 151
CAWLFIELD, 79
CAWTHORN, 14 133
CAWTHRON, 133
CAYLOR, 129

CELLARS, 69
CENOWEITH, 133
CER, 116
CERNICK, 11
CHADWICK, 133
CHALDECUT, 133
CHALLAS, 73
CHAMBERLAIN, 72
CHAMBERLIN, 67
CHAMBERS, 9 64 106 133
CHAMLER, 6
CHANCE, 79
CHANCEY, 76
CHANDLER, 71 73
CHANEY, 79
CHAPEL, 79
CHAPLIN, 49
CHAPMAN, 13 133 195
CHAPPELL, 13
CHARLES, 75
CHASE, 2 5 9
CHE, 79
CHEACK, 64
CHEATHAM, 108
CHEERS, 104
CHELANDER, 75
CHENYWORTH, 73
CHESHIER, 133
CHESTNUT, 151
CHILDERS, 22 68
CHILTON, 53 61 99 102 168
CHINAWORTH, 53
CHINN, 2 66
CHIPMAN, 116
CHITTENDEN, 23 25
CHITWOOD, 100
CHIVENS, 133
CHOATE, 9
CHODER, 116
CHOUTEAU, 75
CHRANE, 181
CHRISAM, 108
CHRISMAN, 22 186
CHRISTIAN, 7 116
CHRISTIANSON, 133
CHUBBUCK, 133
CHUDYS, 71
CHURCHMAN, 75
CHURK, 68
CINCLEARE, 61

CISLIFEE, 72
CITIHEN, 79
CLACKSTON, 61
CLAIN, 151
CLAMPIT, 133
CLAMPITT, 133
CLANTON, 79 129
CLARK, 2 9 68 75 79 98 100 103 116 133 148 151 182
CLARKE, 70 74
CLARKSON, 15 182
CLASBY, 80
CLAUS, 116
CLAY, 53 80 108
CLAYTON, 104 116 133
CLEATON, 68
CLEEK, 80
CLEISE, 151
CLELLAN, 151
CLELLAND, 133
CLEM, 133
CLEMENT, 130
CLEMENTS, 194
CLEMMONS, 71
CLENDENNIN, 66
CLERK, 166
CLEVELAND, 8 116
CLEVELEN, 53
CLEVENGER, 133
CLEVINGER, 116
CLICK, 96
CLIFFIELD, 80
CLIFTON, 61 105 133 151
CLINE, 133
CLOEPFIELD, 116
CLORY, 71
CLOUD, 18
CLOUGH, 133
CLOUSER, 80
CLOYD, 179
CLUBB, 61 101 108
CLYDE, 10 106
COALE, 73
COATES, 61
COATS, 174
COBB, 55 61 66 80 108
COBURN, 3
COCINE, 116
COCK, 151
COCKERILL, 3

206

COCKFIELD, 66
COCKRELL, 15
COFFEE, 172
COFFEY, 7
COFFMAN, 68 80 133 162
COGDELL, 80
COGDILL, 116
COGGINS, 8
COIL, 7 80 133
COIT, 133
COKER, 68
COKLEY, 74
COLE, 88 99-101 116 133
COLELEASURE, 80
COLEMAN, 6 8 68 104-105 133 191
COLET, 151
COLINS, 104
COLLET, 116
COLLETT, 67
COLLEY, 129
COLLIER, 53-54 58 61 129
COLLINER, 53
COLLINS, 2 50 63 71 104
COLMAN, 66 133
COLVIN, 133
COMBS, 80 116 133
COMER, 151
COMES, 61
COMPTON, 19 53 57
CONARD, 185
CONDRA, 103
CONDRAY, 96 104
CONGREVE, 73
CONLEY, 94
CONLIN, 151
CONNALLY, 7
CONNER, 13 133 149
CONNERS, 133
CONNETT, 80
CONRAD, 17
CONRAN, 7
CONROD, 133
CONSTANT, 133
CONVEY, 102
CONVILLE, 69
COOK, 53 67-69 71 73 80 88 94 108 116 133 151-152 189
COOKE, 184
COOLEY, 116
COOLY, 73
COOMNAN, 74
COOPER, 54 56-57 59 61 94 129-130 133 146
COOTS, 70
COPE, 4 133
COPELAND, 20 73 80 100 103 149
COPLAND, 72 80
COPLIN, 68
CORBET, 133
CORBETT, 133
CORBITT, 133
CORDER, 94
CORDINEER, 71
CORKEN, 1
CORNELIUS, 80
CORNETT, 146
CORNISH, 133
CORNOGG, 116
CORNYN, 17
CORRELL, 133
COSLEY, 116-117
COTNER, 61
COTTEREL, 73
COTTON, 100 103
COUCH, 9
COUDREY, 192
COULSON, 133
COULTER, 6
COURTNEY, 13 181
COUSLEY, 75
COVEY, 68
COWDEN, 167
COWEN, 80 98 100 133
COWGILL, 133
COWHICK, 146
COWIN, 101
COWLES, 117
COWLEY, 133
COX, 53 60-61 64 68 71 80 94 101 117 133 148 152
COZAD, 133
COZZENS, 17
CRABTREE, 80
CRADDICK, 58
CRADDOCK, 53 66 149
CRAFORD, 129
CRAFT, 72 152
CRAFTON, 7
CRAIG, 8 133
CRAIGHEAD, 49 174

207

CRAIN, 174
CRAMBLIT, 133
CRAMER, 133
CRANDAL, 133
CRANDELL, 98 100
CRANE, 66 133
CRAVENS, 54 65 133 190
CRAWFORD, 15 23 57 73 88 104 133-134 167
CREAL, 72
CREEK, 74
CREEL, 2
CRENSHAW, 19 22
CRESWELL, 134
CRIDER, 88
CRIGER, 152
CRIPPEN, 72
CRISP, 165 167
CROCKET, 3
CROCKETT, 67 92 130 134
CROMANY, 134
CROMWELL, 80
CRONEE, 67
CRONENS, 73
CROOKS, 67
CROPP, 80
CROSEN, 6
CROSS, 11 134 197
CROSSLIN, 76
CROSWAIT, 5
CROTHERS, 9
CROUSE, 134
CROW, 174
CROWDER, 5
CROWE, 4
CROWLEY, 70 80 102 134
CROWTHER, 3
CROY, 80
CROZEER, 71
CRUM, 94
CRUMBAUGH, 134
CRUMMER, 67
CRUMP, 5
CRUMPLEY, 147
CRUST, 74
CUBBERLY, 152
CUDDY, 179
CUDWORTH, 134
CULEGHER, 53
CULP, 80

CULTON, 69
CUMMING, 1 11
CUMMINGS, 73 117
CUMMINS, 67 80 95
CUNNINGHAM, 15 71 73 76 80 106 134 166-167 181 192
CURANETT, 152
CURD, 51
CURFMAN, 130
CURKBRIDE, 134
CURL, 80 152
CURLEW, 67
CURMETT, 152
CURNOW, 134
CURP, 134
CURRAN, 1
CURRY, 26 67 117
CURTIN, 134
CURTIS, 9 11 72
CUSIGER, 70
CUTLER, 75
CUVERT, 117
DAGLEY, 134
DAILEY, 184
DAILY, 117
DALE, 68 134
DALLAHAM, 117
DALLAS, 74
DALRYMPLE, 152
DALTON, 179
DALY, 134 173
DAMERON, 108 185 188
DAMRON, 78
DAMSON, 68
DANAKEN, 152
DANBY, 152
DANG, 9
DANIEL, 10 68 100 117
DANIELS, 68 80 134 147
DARNALL, 5
DARNELL, 53
DARR, 96
DAUGHERTY, 130
DAVALT, 55
DAVENPORT, 148 152
DAVIDOSN, 68
DAVIDSON, 67 80 134 165
DAVIS, 1 3 10-11 54 61 67-68 70-74 76 80 92 101 108 117 129 134 149 152 166 175 177 186 190 192-193

DAVISON, 80
DAWLEY, 5
DAWSON, 80 97 104 134
DAY, 67 80 96
DAYTON, 47
DEACON, 71
DEAKINS, 80
DEAM, 134
DEAN, 74 80 129 134 185 196
DEARNIER, 73
DEATHERAGE, 3
DEBERNATES, 11
DEBOLT, 11
DECK, 129
DECKER, 95 97
DEEM, 196
DEEN, 56
DEERING, 102
DEFAYETTE, 187
DEFRIECE, 117
DEGUIRE, 53 61 64-65
DEHAVEN, 134
DEHONEY, 68
DEISTEN, 11
DEITZLER, 16-17
DELANO, 4
DELLER, 88
DELONG, 134
DEMAND, 5
DEMAR, 152
DEMOSS, 180
DENBO, 53
DENBOW, 63
DENICKER, 117
DENKMAN, 130
DENNING, 96 152
DENNIS, 74 129
DENNISON, 134
DENNY, 5 175
DENT, 101 165 167
DENTON, 62
DENVIR, 105-106
DEPEE, 2
DEPPEN, 8
DEPRIEST, 97
DEPUTTY, 117
DERRICK, 168
DERVINT, 68
DESLOUS, 71
DESPAIN, 102

DESTIGER, 134
DEVAUL, 134
DEVAULT, 55
DEVIN, 166-167 175
DEVORE, 196
DEVORT, 70
DEWALT, 134
DEWEESE, 134
DEWES, 152
DEWEY, 179 186 196
DEWITT, 4 13
DEXTER, 148
DEYS, 72
DGRAFFENREID, 173
DIAL, 80
DICKENGD, 11
DICKENS, 73
DICKERSON, 73
DICKEY, 67 183
DICKINSON, 134
DICKMAN, 117
DICKSON, 80
DIDDLE, 134
DIETRICH, 2
DIKE, 80
DILDINE, 99 105
DILL, 52 61 80
DILLA, 73
DILLARD, 134
DILLEN, 61 152
DILLENBACK, 5
DILLENBECK, 4
DILLMAN, 134
DILLON, 68 72
DIMOND, 61
DINGEN, 68
DINGER, 57
DINWIDDIE, 100
DIRICKSON, 102
DISON, 80
DITMAS, 134
DITYMORE, 71
DIVEN, 134
DIVINIA, 134
DIX, 2
DIXON, 80 108 134 152
DIXSON, 102
DOAK, 134
DOBBIN, 4
DOBYNS, 9

DOCK, 134
DOCKSTADER, 134
DODD, 5 8 134
DODDRIDGE, 134
DODDS, 134
DODGE, 74 108 134
DODSON, 7 108
DOGGETT, 6
DOLAN, 134
DOLE, 134
DOLL, 134
DOLLEN, 61
DOLON, 72
DONALDSON, 15 70 75 108 134
DONALLY, 53
DONAVAN, 106
DONAVAN-GRUBER, 106-107
DONEEN, 71
DONELL, 68 80
DONIPHANT, 134
DONIPHNE, 134
DONLEY, 71
DONNEL, 73
DONNELL, 80
DONOVAN, 80
DOOLIN, 68
DORKENS, 134
DORKINS, 134
DORLAND, 69
DORRELL, 67
DORSETT, 134
DOTY, 117
DOUGHERTY, 117
DOUGHTY, 117
DOUGLAS, 62 67 73 134
DOUGLASS, 4 9 42 134
DOVE, 162
DOW, 2
DOWD, 76
DOWLING, 11 92
DOWNER, 187
DOWNES, 11
DOWNEY, 74
DOWNING, 7 23 73 80 134 152
DOWRY, 73
DOYLE, 134
DRACE, 1
DRAGOO, 3
DRAKE, 5 62 105 152 166
DRAPER, 117 179

DREESER, 69
DREIER, 53
DRENNON, 69
DREWRY, 152
DRIER, 62
DRIESSELMIER, 72
DRISKELL, 68
DRYDEN, 80 117
DRYLE, 72
DUBOIS, 17
DUCAN, 6
DUCK, 88
DUCKWORTH, 20
DUDLEY, 62 68 134
DUEST, 9
DUFF, 3 80 181
DUFFEY, 134
DUFRENE, 70
DUGAN, 8
DUGDALE, 105
DUGGINS, 6
DUKE, 80 134
DULANY, 3 189
DULEY, 11
DUMMER, 75
DUNBAR, 148
DUNCAN, 6 54 68 72 75 80 103 134
DUNGAN, 80
DUNHAM, 74 134 184
DUNHOUPT, 9
DUNIGAN, 68
DUNKLE, 134
DUNLAP, 10 13 134
DUNN, 2 5 7 9 54 64 80 134 146
DUNNAVAN, 134
DUNNEGAN, 165-166 174
DUNNING, 71 80
DUNTON, 134
DURELL, 80
DURNELL, 134
DURONY, 73
DURR, 129
DUSSER, 75
DUSTIN, 134
DUSTON, 134
DUTTON, 6
DUVANET, 72
DYER, 9 15 70 80 103
DYSART, 10 180
DYSE, 73

DYSON, 108
DYZE, 71
EADES, 88
EAGAN, 109
EAMES, 11
EARL, 134
EARLE, 74
EARLEY, 134
EARLS, 80
EARLY, 134
EASLEY, 80
EASTIN, 3 74
EASTON, 9 59 61 76 80 99
EASTONS, 152
EASTRIDGE, 181
EASTWOOD, 146
EATON, 54 62 109
EBBERT, 196
EBERTS, 5
ECKELBERRY, 1 134
ECKERT, 117
ECKLES, 13 73
ECTON, 134
EDDLEMAN, 20
EDGAR, 80 162
EDMISTON, 4
EDMONDS, 54
EDNIGTON, 96
EDSTER, 152
EDWARD, 72
EDWARDS, 1 6 54 69 80 134
EGGARS, 72 99
EHRHARDT, 187-188
EICHLER, 134-135
EIDSON, 68
ELAM, 66 181
ELBERT, 75
ELBERTON, 135
ELDER, 146
ELIFF, 4
ELINGTON, 80
ELLINGTON, 100 152
ELLIOT, 135
ELLIOTT, 1 6 68 71 73-74 80 129 135 152 188
ELLIS, 3 7 65 68 73 80 102 107 109 135 152 197
ELLISON, 11 67 80 146
ELLSAESSER, 135
ELMOIR, 152
ELMORE, 190
ELSTON, 5
ELWOOD, 92
EMBERSON, 2
EMBREE, 190
EMERY, 49 102 135
EMMONS, 104
EMRY, 101
ENCELL, 135
ENDICOTT, 69
ENGLAND, 54 99
ENGLISH, 80 117
ENLOW, 149
ENSBERGER, 135
ENSIGN, 2
ENTREKIN, 4
ENTRICAN, 135
ENTRIKEN, 135
ENTRIKIN, 135
ENYART, 46
ENYEART, 183
EOFF, 63
EPLINGER, 80
EPPERLY, 186
EPPSTEIN, 20
ERICKSON, 80
ERNSBERGER, 135
ERNST, 9
ERVIN, 109
ERWIN, 135
ESININGER, 80
ESTABROOK, 135
ESTEB, 135
ESTEPS, 68
ESTES, 80 129 135 152 176
ETEN, 52
ETHERTON, 135
ETHINGTON, 11
ETHRIDGE, 109
ETTER, 135
ETTNER, 9
EUBANKS, 70
EVANS, 7 54 67 69-71 73 80 101 103 135 174
EVARD, 152
EVERETT, 80 135 149
EVERHART, 68
EVERLY, 194
EVERSOLE, 152
EVERT, 135

EVRARD, 3
EWELL, 80
EWIN, 4 71
FABYAM, 2
FAGER, 75
FAIRBANKS, 8
FAIRCHILD, 135
FALES, 135
FALKNER, 54
FANNING, 152
FARABEE, 135
FARGY, 11
FARLEY, 1 80 149
FARMER, 68 117 135 166
FARMERS, 135
FARR, 54 102 135
FARRAND, 16
FARRAR, 98 101
FARRENS, 152-153
FARRIS, 104 129
FARWELL, 73
FASRON, 13
FASSETT, 162
FATH, 55
FAULCONER, 88
FAULKENDER, 4
FAULKNER, 22 173
FAUTHINGER, 135
FAWTS, 68
FEASTER, 153
FEATCH, 180
FECK, 67
FEDERLY, 62
FEESE, 135
FEILDS[SIC], 72
FELMAN, 153
FELSE, 135
FELT, 195
FELTIS, 135
FENLEY, 9 166 175
FENNEA, 80
FENNY, 80
FERGUSON, 97 101 104 109 174
FERNAN, 67
FERREL, 81
FERRELL, 109
FERRIL, 81
FERRY, 135
FESHER, 135
FEURT, 3

FEWELL, 15
FICKLIN, 5
FIDLER, 81
FIELD, 11 68 81
FIELDS, 65 81 129 135
FILLEY, 135
FILLMORE, 44
FILMORE, 44
FILSER, 191
FILSON, 3 135
FINCH, 54 57 81 135
FINDLEY, 74 135
FINE, 146
FINK, 9 135
FINKS, 7
FINLEY, 81 135
FINNELL, 179 188
FIRTH, 135
FISER, 73
FISHER, 3-6 23 69 76 88 135 189
FITZGERALD, 81 135
FITZPATRICK, 54 71
FLANAGAN, 146
FLANIGIN, 72
FLANNERY, 73 81
FLEETWOOD, 69 194
FLEMING, 68 135
FLEMMING, 148
FLETCHER, 4 36 51 54 67 81 88 109 135 153
FLINT, 11 135 177
FLOIS, 70
FLORES, 30
FLORIDA, 106
FLOURNOY, 5
FLOWERS, 129
FLOYD, 117
FLUHARTY, 2
FLY, 69
FOGGINS, 193
FOLLET, 117
FOLLETT, 135
FOLMIRE, 54
FORD, 8 10-11 68 109 135 190
FOREMAN, 71
FORGARSON, 62
FORMAN, 71
FORNDON, 62
FORREST, 109
FORSTER, 95

FORSYTH, 117 148
FORT, 135
FOSHER, 81
FOST, 135
FOSTER, 9 15 41 54 81 135 162 188
FOURSHEE, 165-166
FOUTS, 81
FOWLER, 3 9 69 81 101 109 117-118 135
FOWLES, 81
FOX, 4 54 68 71 105-106 166 174 178
FRAKES, 81
FRANCE, 62 68
FRANCIS, 62 64 69 118 153
FRANK, 6 9 13 135
FRANKLIN, 7 98 191
FRAZEE, 81
FRAZIER, 13 54 102 105 118 135 188
FRAZUER, 75
FRAZURE, 81
FREAKS, 68
FREDAY, 62
FREDERICK, 135
FREEL, 135
FREELAND, 73-74
FREEMAN, 20 81 100 167
FRELAND, 81
FREMONT, 25 29-34 36-40 42 44
FRENCH, 11 66 135
FRETWELL, 2
FRIDAY, 99
FRIER, 6 54 56
FRIEZE, 174
FRIGETT, 81
FRILY, 73
FRISBEE, 43
FRIZEL, 62
FRIZELL, 52 54
FROHN, 58
FRONGAN, 71
FROST, 81 135
FRUCHTE, 9
FRUETT, 135
FRY, 72
FRYER, 135
FUGETT, 81
FUGITT, 118 135
FULBRIGHT, 196-197
FULKS, 74 81
FULLER, 49 51 105

FULTON, 5 11 81 135
FUNDERBURK, 153
FUNK, 135
FUQUA, 180
FURGISON, 81
FURGUSON, 6
GABBERT, 81
GABERTS, 74
GABRIEL, 72
GADLING, 68
GAGE, 153
GAILON, 153
GAINER, 92
GAINES, 2 81
GAINS, 71
GALBARD, 71
GALBRAITH, 98 103
GALE, 73
GALL, 135
GALLAHER, 8 135
GALLATIN, 7
GALLEMORE, 188
GALLENKAMP, 10
GALLIHER, 15
GALLISON, 176
GALLOWAY, 10
GALLUS, 88
GALSGOW, 3
GAMEINAKER, 118
GANARVA, 68
GANETT, 75
GANN, 75 81
GANT, 135
GARASCHE, 9
GARBER, 10
GARDINNER, 72
GARDNER, 6 71 81 97 178
GAREHEART, 64
GARETT, 135
GARHART, 187
GARMAN, 162
GARMEN, 76
GARNER, 62
GARNETT, 180
GARRELL, 197
GARRET, 81 135 197
GARRETT, 8 67 70 135 153 197
GARRIGUES, 9
GARRITT, 74
GARSS, 67

GASAWAY, 68
GASCAL, 153
GASTON, 81
GATEHOUSE, 104
GATES, 73 81
GATEWOOD, 65
GAUNT, 135
GAY, 71 135
GAYLORD, 162
GEARHART, 135
GEARY, 44
GEBHARDT, 178
GEE, 81 135
GEERE, 81
GEIER, 4
GEILKER, 135
GELLOND, 71
GENTRY, 67 81 153
GEORGE, 60 62 75 135 167 176
GEPPERICH, 62
GERARDUS, 50
GERDING, 7
GERLAS, 9
GESST, 81
GEYERT, 4
GHIO, 105-107
GHOLSON, 62
GIBBONS, 71
GIBBS, 15 98 129 135
GIBSON, 9 74 81 118 135
GIDDENS, 81
GIER, 135
GIERNN, 74
GIESLER, 187
GIFFORD, 13 153
GILAM, 81
GILBERT, 16 18 67 73 135
GILCHRIST, 136
GILDAY, 5
GILDERSLEEVE, 136
GILES, 101
GILFILLAN, 9
GILGOUR, 136
GILKER, 136
GILL, 68 81 92 136
GILLAM, 81
GILLESPIE, 68 168
GILLET, 81
GILLETT, 98 136
GILLIHAM, 167

GILLILAND, 136
GILLMORE, 70
GILLPYS, 118
GILMORE, 69 81 118
GINNINGS, 3
GIPSON, 153
GIRVIN, 187
GIVENS, 81
GLADDEN, 75
GLADDIN, 72
GLADDON, 74
GLADIN, 101
GLASGOW, 153
GLASSGOW, 148
GLAZE, 81
GLEASON, 5
GLEN, 56 81
GLENN, 9 153
GLENNON, 106
GLICK, 136
GLOVER, 68 76
GODBEY, 9
GODDARD, 12 73 136
GODFREY, 69
GOE, 136 189
GOEBEL, 75
GOFF, 95
GOFORTH, 109 153
GOLDEN, 68 118
GOLL, 191
GOOD, 68 153
GOODE, 129
GOODING, 136
GOODMAN, 61-62 136 197
GOODNIGHT, 81
GOODNOE, 136
GOODNOW, 136
GOODRICH, 136
GOODRICK, 136
GOODWIN, 2 67-68
GOOKER, 197
GORDEN, 175
GORDON, 2 68 175
GORMLEY, 136
GORSHE, 136
GOSHON, 71
GOSSING, 9
GOULD, 197
GOURLEY, 97
GOVER, 136

GOWDY, 7
GRACE, 71 184
GRAER, 136
GRAFF, 136
GRAHAM, 54-55 58 60 62 73 81 103-105 136 153 192
GRAHM, 167
GRAHMA, 100
GRANDSTAFF, 98
GRANGER, 17-18
GRANT, 5 81 109 136 185
GRANTHAM, 6
GRASSUM, 98
GRAVES, 5 14-15 68-69 153
GRAVIL, 71
GRAY, 1-2 8 81 107 109 118 136 153 196
GRAYHAM, 54
GREATHOUSE, 148
GREBE, 118
GREEN, 2-3 7 41 44 49 54 66 76 81 97 99 101-103 109 118 136
GREENFIELD, 72
GREENWOOD, 4-5 136
GREER, 1 68 166
GREEWOOD, 11
GREGG, 136 147
GREGOIRE, 62
GREGORY, 68 74 81
GRESHAM, 81 101
GREVE, 11
GRIFFEN, 54 103 192
GRIFFEY, 81
GRIFFIN, 18 54 109 129 136
GRIFFING, 136
GRIFFITH, 3 5 7 9 59 72 81 153-154
GRIFFY, 136
GRIGGS, 166
GRIGSBY, 54 136
GRIMES, 189
GRINDSTAFF, 102
GRISBY, 136
GRISHAM, 5
GRIT, 81
GRITZMACHER, 193
GROMES, 72 81
GROMMONS, 196
GROMS, 81
GROOM, 8 88
GROSHONG, 81
GROSSCLOSE, 81
GROTJAN, 191-192
GROTOFF, 62
GROUNDS, 59
GROVE, 136 154
GROVER, 73 136
GROVES, 8 50 118 136 154
GROVNER, 54 59
GUERIN, 178
GUFFEY, 10 136
GUFFY, 136
GUILD, 136
GUILL, 154
GUINN, 81
GUNBY, 136
GUNN, 11 95 185
GUNTER, 170 175
GUNTHEY, 69
GURLEY, 136
GUTJAHR, 148
GWINN, 2 4
HACKLER, 118
HACKLEY, 118
HACKMAN, 62
HACKWORTH, 103
HADDEN, 136
HADEN, 81
HADLEY, 105
HAGGARD, 98
HAGLEWOOD, 73
HAIGH, 136
HAIGHT, 50
HAIL, 81
HAININE, 3
HALCOMB, 5-6
HALCUM, 68
HALDERMAN, 17
HALE, 1 118 136
HALEY, 73 136 148
HALFERTY, 92
HALL, 3 10 15 74 81 96 101 104-105 118-119 136 154 166 182
HALLOWAY, 68
HALLSA, 154
HALSTEAD, 136
HAM, 4
HAMBLIN, 55 146
HAMEBLEN, 65
HAMELTON, 55
HAMILTON, 5 68 71 174 190

HAMLET, 136
HAMLIN, 146
HAMMACK, 64
HAMMERSTEIN, 9
HAMMOCK, 92
HAMMOND, 4 74 105-106 192
HAMMONS, 2
HAMPTON, 13 60 63 68 109 154 184
HAMS, 6
HANAN, 72
HANCOCK, 58 73 81 95
HANDLEY, 119
HANDY, 136
HANES, 81
HANEY, 129
HANFORD, 36
HANGAR, 102
HANGER, 100
HANKS, 4 136
HANLEY, 70
HANLIN, 74
HANNA, 104 154
HANNAH, 154
HANNOND, 36
HANSBRAUGH, 68
HANSEN, 81 95
HANSON, 136
HANSWORTH, 136
HARBER, 65
HARBISON, 98
HARD, 75
HARDER, 98
HARDESTER, 149
HARDESTY, 81
HARDIN, 56 72 76 162
HARDING, 130
HARDMAN, 136
HARDY, 8 81 136
HARGATE, 104
HARGIS, 68
HARGRAVE, 68
HARGROVE, 81 136
HARINGTON, 81
HARIS, 52 62 68
HARKNESS, 12
HARLOW, 136
HARMES, 130
HARMON, 109 119
HARMONY, 68
HARN, 73

HARNSBY, 67
HARPER, 15 55 67 72 81 98 136 154 195
HARPOLD, 78 136
HARPOOL, 136 173
HARPSTER, 136
HARRELL, 92
HARRIMAN, 4 136
HARRINGTON, 67 75 81 119
HARRIS, 10 52 54 56 60-62 66 68 70 74 76 81 97 102 130 136 149 154
HARRISON, 66-67 74 149
HARRISS, 6 51 55 57
HARSCH, 103
HART, 65 74 136 146 166
HARTER, 136
HARTIGAN, 136
HARTLEY, 103 136
HARTMAN, 68 72 81 119
HARTMEN, 81
HARTRIDGE, 104
HARTSELL, 74
HARTSHORN, 109
HARTWELL, 67
HARTWIG, 136
HARTZELL, 196
HARVEY, 12 76 129
HARWOOD, 6
HASKELL, 182
HASKINS, 100
HASKINSON, 136
HASLER, 63
HASTING, 35
HASTINGS, 27
HATFIELD, 136
HATTON, 50 67
HAUGER, 136
HAUN, 62
HAVENS, 136
HAVILINE, 81
HAWK, 136
HAWKINS, 6-7 10 55 89 97 99 105 119
HAWKS, 136
HAWLEY, 73
HAWS, 154
HAXWELL, 74
HAY, 55
HAYDEN, 14 22 55
HAYES, 7 13 55 68 70 72 81 95
HAYNE, 73
HAYNES, 65

HAYS, 81 119 129 136 154 163
HAYTER, 136
HAZE, 73
HAZELHANAN, 72
HAZZARD, 162
HEAD, 72 89
HEADLEY, 187
HEARNES, 12
HEATH, 68 136
HEATHLEY, 103
HECK, 119
HECKEL, 162
HEDDY, 154
HEDERICK, 82
HEDGCOTH, 89
HEDGES, 146
HEDGPETH, 82 154
HEES, 95
HEFLIN, 154
HEFNER, 102
HEHN, 62
HEIMANN, 178
HEINDRICKS, 67
HEINE-ZIEBOLD, 106
HEISEL, 193
HEISER, 136
HEIX, 67
HELBER, 1
HELDT, 102
HELLARDS, 82
HELMS, 136
HELTON, 62 105
HELTZELL, 9
HEMBE, 62
HEMBY, 64
HEMENWAY, 49
HEMRY, 136
HENDERSON, 6 56 58 71 73-74 82 136 154
HENDRICKS, 67-68 82 167 170
HENDRICKSON, 136 175
HENDRIX, 2 109 129 136
HENINGER, 5
HENKINS, 136
HENNINGER, 136
HENNON, 8
HENRICKS, 136 148
HENRY, 2 50 78 82 109 136 165 175
HENSLEE, 165
HENSLER, 73

HENSLEY, 68 82
HENSLY, 63
HENSON, 73 99
HERALD, 136
HERBERT, 136
HERDLICK, 93
HERMAN, 6
HERN, 195
HERNDON, 76 137 173 195
HERNLEBEN, 2
HERREL, 1
HERRIN, 98
HERRING, 5 8 95 154
HERRINGTON, 102 137
HERRIOTT, 5
HERROD, 109
HERRON, 18
HERTHEL, 12
HERTZINGER, 55
HERZINGER, 55
HESS, 7 9 183
HEUX, 63
HEWETT, 98
HEWIT, 97
HEWITT, 97 137
HEYDENFELT, 44
HEYDON, 22
HIATT, 137
HIBBS, 148
HIBDON, 95
HICHMAN, 9
HICK, 137
HICKEY, 9
HICKLAN, 68
HICKMAN, 1 74 82 137
HICKS, 76 82 100 137
HIDE, 82
HIGBEE, 5
HIGBY, 73
HIGDON, 8
HIGGINBOTHAM, 166
HIGGINS, 4 67 93 137
HIGHGATE, 66
HILDEBRANDT, 119
HILDENBRANDT, 9
HILDERBRAND, 95
HILGARD, 93
HILL, 8 50 52 59 64 67-68 72 82 98 103-105 110 119 137 180
HILVEY, 119

HINCHMAN, 12
HINDE, 6
HINE, 197
HINES, 95 137
HINKSTON, 82
HINSON, 137
HINTON, 70
HINZ, 137
HIOB, 12
HISE, 187
HITRIBIDLE, 82
HIX, 59 68-69 74 82
HIXSON, 104
HOBBLE, 82
HOBBS, 82 129
HOBIE, 12
HOCKLER, 67
HOCKSTEDLAR, 137
HOCKSTEDLER, 137
HOCOLM, 110
HODGE, 191
HODGES, 10 74
HODSHEIR, 4
HOEFFER, 49
HOFFMAN, 2 119
HOFMAN, 61
HOGAN, 70 119 129 137
HOGANS, 68
HOGSETT, 137
HOLCOMB, 89
HOLDER, 55 71 137 174
HOLISTER, 82
HOLLAND, 71 82 98 102 105 154
HOLLEN, 119-120
HOLLENBOCH, 71
HOLLIDAY, 4 137 190
HOLLINGSWORTH, 73
HOLLIS, 97
HOLLOWAY, 95 137
HOLM, 137
HOLMAN, 3 82
HOLMES, 4 70 110
HOLMESLEY, 76
HOLOWAY, 82
HOLT, 8 55 154
HOLTER, 55
HOMBERGER, 8
HONEYCUT, 137
HONK, 120
HOOD, 1 78

HOOG, 50
HOOK, 63
HOOKER, 137
HOOPER, 71 74 98 105 137 197
HOOTMAN, 137
HOOVER, 1 7
HOPE, 99 103
HOPEWELL, 71
HOPKINS, 8 120 137 166 174
HOPPEL, 120
HOPPER, 67 98 137
HORN, 22 82
HORNWOOD, 16
HORSEMAN, 137
HORSMAN, 137
HORTON, 62 110 189-190
HOSENMYER, 82
HOSHAW, 82
HOSHINSON, 137
HOSKINSON, 137
HOSLER, 64
HOSMAN, 137
HOUCK, 120
HOUGH, 4-5
HOUGHTON, 47 137
HOUSE, 73 98-100
HOUSTON, 6 137 154 185
HOVER, 72
HOVIES, 55
HOWALD, 74
HOWARD, 11 63 67-68 72 82 101 137 155
HOWE, 67 82 176
HOWELL, 72 74 82 137 186
HOWISON, 51
HOWLAND, 2 51 67 74
HOYT, 120
HUBBARD, 2 70
HUBBELL, 129-130
HUBBLE, 104
HUDDLE, 71
HUDDLESTON, 63 82
HUDGENS, 82 137 155
HUDGINS, 137
HUDNALL, 184
HUDSON, 76 137
HUDSPETH, 82
HUENTEN, 181
HUFAKER, 67
HUFF, 52 55 59 63 68 155

HUFFAKER, 70
HUFFMAN, 6 110
HUFFT, 82
HUGART, 82
HUGHART, 82
HUGHES, 1 12 68 82 97 102 137 168
HUGHLETT, 82
HUGHS, 82 110 120 155
HUGHSON, 137
HUITT, 100 103
HULETT, 9 137
HULING, 72
HULL, 30 110 120
HULLEN, 71
HULLIKY, 120
HULSER, 137
HULSON, 55
HUMAN, 165 167 171 176
HUME, 10
HUMPHREY, 3 137
HUMPHREYS, 69 101 146
HUNGETT, 82
HUNLEY, 137
HUNT, 2 4 68 73-74 137 174
HUNTER, 12 68 71 82 101 104-105 110 120 137 166 168 170 178
HUNTQUICKER, 82
HUNTSMAN, 110
HUNTSUCKER, 82
HURKELROTH, 188
HURLBURT, 155
HURST, 15 82 99
HURT, 72 166 168 179 185
HUSLEY, 67
HUSTON, 16 18 137
HUTCHESON, 131
HUTCHINGS, 74 120 137
HUTCHINS, 104 110
HUTCHINSON, 137
HUTCHISON, 95
HUTSON, 155
HUTTON, 146
HUVER, 55
HYDE, 65 148 179-180
HYDEN, 70
HYE, 72
IDDINGS, 74
IDINGS, 137
ILSE, 72
IMGARTEN, 191

IMMENSCHUH, 75
IMPSON, 137
INGALS, 155
INGELS, 155
INGERSON, 11
INGHAM, 69
INGLEHART, 72
INGLETON, 82
INGLISH, 165-166
INGOLD, 9-10
INKS, 176
INNESS, 103
IROHN, 147
IRONS, 137
IRVIN, 71
IRVING, 162
IRWIN, 77 82 110 137 155
ISAACS, 73
ISBELL, 12
ISHMEL, 55
ISOM, 155
ISRAIL, 55
IVES, 1
IVIE, 5
IVY, 60
JACKSON, 5 12 52 63 68 72 82 99 110 120 149 155 185
JACOB, 31 68
JACOBS, 26 29 77
JACQUEMOT, 4
JAMES, 6 54 68-69 82 120 137 186
JAMESON, 68 120
JAMISON, 2 6 72 165 170-171 175
JANIS, 62
JANNY, 69
JAQUITH, 7
JAVENS, 68
JEFFERSON, 26 74
JEFFRIES, 82
JENKINS, 5 66 82 100 155
JENKS, 82
JENNINGS, 105 137
JESSE, 70
JESSUP, 75
JESTER, 155
JETER, 191
JETMORE, 105
JEWELL, 137
JIBBS, 71
JOACHIM, 2

JOBE, 82
JOHN, 8 71 137
JOHNSON, 3 5 12 19 42 55 58-59 64 67-68 70 72-73 75 78 82 97 105 110 120 137 155 165-168 173 175 178-180 186 190
JOHNSTON, 8 49 97 100 137
JOINER, 50
JOLER, 73
JONAS, 99
JONES, 4-5 9 12 50 55 66-68 70 72-74 82 95 97-101 104-105 110 120-121 129 137-138 148 155 162 166-167 171 175 180
JONITHAN, 82
JONS, 82
JONSON, 55 63
JONT, 71
JOPLIN, 102
JORDAN, 2 9 63 96 110
JORDON, 72 99
JOSLIN, 155
JOURDAN, 155
JOURDOIN, 82
JOYCE, 3
JUDAH, 82
JUDD, 138
JUDSON, 9
JUDY, 138
JUMP, 166-168 176
JUSTICE, 67
KAEPPEL, 50
KAGS, 68
KAHLER, 195
KAHN, 4
KAISER, 148
KANAN, 138
KARLESKIND, 71
KARR, 138
KASPER, 138
KAUFMAN, 9 138
KAUFMANN, 138
KAUFMON, 75
KAUNE, 106
KAUTZ, 138
KAUZLARICH, 13
KAY, 73
KEARNEY, 138
KEARNY, 30-31 34
KEATING, 106-107

KEEF, 138
KEEFE, 138
KEELE, 55
KEELING, 175
KEENER, 82
KEENY, 121
KEEPHER, 82
KEETON, 68
KEIM, 121
KEITH, 4 95
KEIZER, 110
KELEPPER, 138
KELLER, 74 146
KELLETT, 89
KELLEY, 70 72 74 82 97 101-102 105 138
KELLISON, 89 121
KELLOGG, 82 138 180
KELLY, 8 14 54-55 59 63 73-74 95 106 138 155 174 177 184
KELSDE, 138
KELSEY, 4 138
KELSO, 95
KELTON, 14
KEMBLE, 138
KEMPER, 58 63 82 138
KEMPERS, 55
KENCE, 73
KENDALL, 9 35
KENDELL, 138
KENDRICK, 138
KENNEDY, 2-3 121 138 155 193
KENNETT, 55
KENNEY, 121 138
KENNON, 167
KENNY, 138
KENT, 5 95
KENTON, 146
KENY, 63
KEPLEY, 138
KERBY, 101
KEREN, 68
KERKMAN, 82
KERNA, 138
KERNS, 12 138
KERR, 82 138
KERSEY, 174
KESER, 68
KESLER, 82
KESTLER, 82

KETS, 148
KEUPER, 77
KEY, 61
KIDWELL, 56
KIEFFER, 2
KILGORE, 155
KILLE, 1
KILLION, 103 138
KIMBERLIN, 89
KIMMEL, 194
KINCADE, 67
KINCAID, 138
KINCAIDE, 68
KINDEL, 121
KINDER, 121
KINDERMANN, 12
KINDRED, 82
KINFROW, 74
KING, 6 15 19 42 44 56 70 82 104 110 121 138 155 174 176 178
KINION, 82
KINKEAD, 5
KINKHORST, 193
KINNARD, 98-100 103
KINNE, 138
KINNEY, 82 138
KINNION, 63
KINSEY, 12
KINSOLA, 138
KINTZ, 98
KINZER, 110
KIPLE, 138
KIPP, 95
KIRK, 68
KIRKENDALL, 71
KIRKMAN, 73
KIRKPATRICK, 72 105
KISH, 121
KISINGER, 73
KISSINGER, 74 97
KISTLER, 10
KISTNER, 188
KITTS, 75
KIZER, 110
KLEIN, 95
KLEINSCHMIDT, 4
KLEPPER, 138
KLES, 163
KLINE, 138
KLUMPF, 103

KLYCE, 12
KNAPP, 6 138
KNAPPENBERGER, 1 193
KNEELING, 170
KNIE, 8
KNIGHT, 5-6 103
KNOCH, 138
KNOCHE, 62
KNOGHT, 170
KNOT, 110
KNOTT, 138
KNOW, 9
KNOWLES, 9
KNOX, 73
KOCH, 20
KOENTZ, 75
KOERN, 12
KOETTING, 95
KOLBOHN, 77
KOTHE, 178 190
KOYLE, 138
KRAGER, 187
KRAISSIG, 188
KRAXBERGER, 95
KREAM, 72
KRESSE, 138
KROMEICK, 138
KROSCHEN, 77
KROSE, 197
KRUSE, 197
KUECHLER, 193
KUPFERLE, 89
KURTH, 107
KUTES, 67
KUYKENDALL, 26
KYLE, 74
LABBRING, 121
LACEY, 56 67 82
LACHANCE, 56 60 63 65
LACKEY, 82
LACY, 73 99
LADD, 67
LADY, 82
LAFTEY, 102
LAHAY, 67
LAIDLAW, 138
LAIGE, 74
LAINE, 54
LAKE, 138
LAKER, 192

LAKEY, 138
LALOY, 197
LAMAR, 155
LAMB, 121
LAMBERT, 99-100 103
LAMBIE, 95
LAMERT, 100
LAMM, 4
LAMORIE, 121
LAMPKINS, 103
LAMSON, 138
LANCASTER, 105
LANCE, 56-57
LANDEN, 68
LANDIES, 71
LANDON, 72
LANDRUM, 190
LANE, 6 102 138 168 174
LANGLEY, 57 82 182
LANGSCHMIDT, 12
LANGSHER, 55
LANHAM, 83 155
LANHART, 121
LANIERS, 56
LANIUS, 51 53 56 83
LANKFORD, 68
LANNING, 155
LANTZ, 57
LANUM, 67 155
LAPAR, 103
LAPLANT, 111
LARBERGE, 11
LARGE, 73-74
LARKIN, 30-32 89
LARKIN-COOKE, 107
LASETER, 83
LASHANT, 52 60
LASHIENA, 72
LASHLEY, 111
LATGEN, 53
LATHROP, 121
LAUGHEAD, 95
LAUGHLIN, 5 89 138
LAVAY, 101
LAVERY, 5
LAVINE, 5
LAW, 13 68 121
LAWHORN, 72 83
LAWITSKY, 9
LAWLESS, 83

LAWLOR, 162
LAWRENCE, 104 138
LAWS, 138
LAWSON, 74 103 111 155
LAYMAN, 83 162
LAYTON, 74
LEACH, 98 100 102 111 190
LEADBETTER, 102
LEADER, 155
LEAMER, 138
LEARY, 74
LEATHERS, 111
LEAVERTON, 129
LEBAUN, 69
LECLARE, 56
LECOMPTE, 71
LEDLIE, 12
LEE, 2 56 78 83 95 98 103 155-156
LEECH, 111
LEEPER, 111 138
LEGG, 99 101 138
LEIGGAN, 74
LEIGH, 95
LEMMON, 166-167 173 178
LEONARD, 42 95
LESTER, 100 138
LETTS, 8
LEVINE, 68
LEVINGSTON, 83
LEVINN, 74
LEVSEE, 72
LEWALLEN, 111
LEWELLEN, 138
LEWIS, 3 14 51 53 56 67 69 72 74-75 83 138 189 193
LEXINGTON, 83
LICE, 12
LICHLITER, 4
LIEBO, 121
LIGHFOOT, 130
LIGHT, 73
LIKE, 138
LILE, 83 111 138
LILLEY, 83
LILLY, 6
LINCH, 83
LINCOLN, 52 56-57 63
LIND, 5
LINDLEY, 138
LINDSAY, 56 93

LINDSEY, 138
LINDSLY, 12
LINK, 5 67 102
LINKHORN, 56
LINN, 69 174
LINSFORD, 156
LINVILLE, 74 83 138 156
LIPPINCOTT, 25 32 36 40-41 43 45-47
LISBY, 73
LISLE, 55
LISTER, 138
LITTELL, 130
LITTLE, 100-101
LITTLEJOHN, 68
LIVELY, 101
LIVINGSTON, 121
LOAR, 156
LOCHRIDGE, 68
LOCKARD, 111
LOCKHART, 49
LOCKRIDGE, 138
LOGAN, 1 156 187
LOHRIE, 63
LOLLIS, 138
LOMSECK, 59
LONG, 23 56 68-69 93 98 196
LONGAN, 8
LONGBOTTOM, 98
LONGSTRETH, 138
LONSTRETH, 138
LOOMIS, 6 138
LOONEY, 138 171-174
LOORSHAM, 130
LOOS, 93
LOPHINK, 148
LORANCE, 56
LORANS, 53
LORD, 101
LORETTE, 138
LORT, 74
LOSTEN, 73
LOT, 56
LOTHROP, 16 18-19
LOUDON, 185
LOUIS, 56 71
LOVE, 69 194
LOVELACE, 70
LOVELADY, 73
LOVELANDY, 73
LOVELL, 72

LOVINGS, 101
LOW, 100 138
LOWBER, 122
LOWE, 7 70 122 156 186
LOWELL, 6
LOWEN, 76
LOWER, 83 166 178
LOWRY, 70
LUBY, 5
LUCAS, 70 129
LUCENSON, 69
LUCK, 69 74
LUCKY, 138
LUDINGTON, 138
LUELLEN, 138
LUKINS, 138
LUMAN, 83
LUNCEFORD, 165-167 175
LUNCH, 7
LUNSFORD, 60 63 156
LUSHER, 185
LUSK, 4 163
LUTRELL, 103 165
LUTZ, 138
LUTZI, 191
LYELL, 8
LYKING, 70
LYKINS, 69
LYLE, 95
LYMAN, 170
LYNCH, 3 7 182
LYNN, 9 67 78
LYON, 9 12 15-17 69
M'CLIMANS, 77
M'CURDY, 77
M'NEIL, 77
MABE, 138
MABER, 99
MABERRY, 105
MABERY, 98-100
MABREY, 104 111
MACDONALD, 12
MACK, 138
MACKAY, 180
MACKEY, 5 77 138
MACKORINDALL, 138
MACLEAN, 15
MACMASTER, 138
MACRAKEN, 49
MADDOX, 111

MADISON, 71
MAGGART, 138
MAHAN, 184
MAHBEY, 10
MAINARD, 102
MAINE, 103 105 197
MAIZE, 54
MAJOR, 2
MAJORS, 83
MALICOAT, 174
MALLORY, 10
MALLOX, 69
MALORY, 138
MALOTT, 156
MAM, 74
MANDEVILLE, 46
MANGHAN, 111
MANKER, 77
MANLY, 156
MANN, 104 111 122 138 148
MANNING, 149
MANVILLE, 122
MARDIS, 13
MARE, 12
MARGROVE, 69
MARING, 8
MARION, 69 156
MARK, 83 148
MARKER, 83
MARKERT, 129
MARKHAM, 99
MARKLEY, 1
MARKWELL, 156
MARLATT, 138
MARLER, 63
MARLIN, 165-166
MARLOW, 63
MARON, 72
MARQUIS, 10 138
MARR, 7
MARROW, 72
MARRS, 102
MARSHAL, 194
MARSHALL, 56 70
MARSTON, 8
MARTIN, 12-15 50-51 59 70-71 73 83 122 138-139 156 167 180
MASON, 19 34 67
MASSIE, 98-99 101
MASSONGAIL, 101
MAST, 156
MASTER, 63
MASTERS, 63
MATCHETT, 139
MATHEW, 122
MATHEWS, 51 56 63 65 71 75
MATHIS, 60 83
MATKIN, 56 104
MATKINS, 130
MATLOCK, 12 89
MATTERSON, 72
MATTHEWS, 9 52 56 58
MATTUX, 156
MAUK, 105
MAUPIN, 2 14 130 182
MAXEY, 173
MAXWELL, 6 10
MAY, 83 95
MAYBURN, 53
MAYES, 139
MAYFIELD, 13 139
MAYHEW, 4
MAYNARD, 99-100
MCABOYS, 69
MCADAM, 189
MCADAMS, 66 139
MCAFEE, 49
MCAIN, 83
MCALLISTER, 175
MCANDRA, 182
MCARNOTE, 139
MCART, 83
MCARTY, 83
MCARVER, 83
MCBAY, 102
MCBEATH, 139
MCBEE, 67 139
MCBOLE, 139
MCBRAYER, 139
MCBRIDE, 63 73 83 122 139
MCBROOM, 166
MCCAFFERTY, 72
MCCAIN, 104
MCCALL, 67
MCCALLISTER, 2
MCCALLUM, 65
MCCAMPBELL, 180
MCCARGO, 12
MCCART, 197
MCCARTHER, 103

MCCARTNEY, 139
MCCARTY, 103 105 156
MCCAULEY, 139
MCCHESNEY, 51
MCCLAIN, 71 139
MCCLAINE, 89
MCCLANAHAN, 67 156
MCCLANE, 34
MCCLEAN, 15
MCCLELAND, 72
MCCLELLAND, 70 139 183
MCCLEMENT, 1
MCCLINTOCK, 139
MCCLUNEY, 76
MCCLURE, 2 166 172 174 183
MCCLURG, 2
MCCOLLISTER, 95
MCCOLLUM, 139
MCCONNELL, 68 89
MCCORKENDALE, 139
MCCORMAC, 71
MCCORMICK, 89
MCCOWAN, 19
MCCOWN, 19
MCCRARY, 156
MCCRAY, 139
MCCREA, 139
MCCREE, 139
MCCUBBIN, 139
MCCULLA, 14
MCCULLAH, 12
MCCULLEY, 156
MCCULLOCH, 15
MCCULLOUGH, 1 197
MCCURDY, 5
MCCUSE, 70
MCDADE, 56
MCDANIEL, 4 57 69 83 111 122 139
MCDANIELL, 111
MCDERMITH, 52
MCDONALD, 74 83 95 122 139 156 188
MCDONELL, 74
MCDONNEL, 67
MCDOUGAL, 42-43 93
MCDOWAL, 61
MCDOWEL, 56 83
MCDOWELL, 98 156 187
MCELRATH, 15
MCELREE, 8
MCELROY, 122

MCELVAIN, 5
MCEUEN, 181
MCFADDEN, 105
MCFADDIN, 52
MCFALL, 111 139
MCFARLAND, 67 146 162
MCFATE, 122
MCFEE, 139
MCFERREN, 111
MCGANTHEY, 83
MCGAUDER, 83
MCGEE, 70 74 139
MCGILL, 83
MCGINNIS, 106-107 139
MCGLENN, 67
MCGLOTHLIN, 139
MCGOUDER, 83
MCGOWAN, 8
MCGRATH, 129
MCGRAW, 99
MCGRAY, 139
MCGREER, 72
MCGREW, 72
MCGUERNEY, 101
MCGUINN, 83
MCGUIRE, 60 83 101 163 192
MCINTIRE, 3 10
MCKALUP, 9
MCKANNA, 13
MCKAULER, 71
MCKAY, 122
MCKEE, 103 122 139 196
MCKENNY, 15
MCKENSIE, 8
MCKENZIE, 166
MCKINEY, 69
MCKINLEY, 8
MCKINNEY, 69 93 162
MCKINZIE, 139 156
MCKISSICK, 14
MCKNIGHT, 5-6 156
MCLAIN, 139 156
MCLALLEN, 139
MCLANAHAN, 111
MCLAUGHLIN, 5 18 139
MCLEAN, 12
MCLENDON, 83
MCLEOD, 194
MCMAHAN, 12 15
MCMANGLE, 139

225

MCMENUS, 162
MCMICHAEL, 156
MCMILLAN, 6
MCMINN, 166
MCMURRY, 7
MCMURTNY, 74
MCNAUGHTON, 139
MCNEELY, 139 147
MCNEILL, 8
MCNERNEY, 93
MCNEW, 69 139
MCNEWS, 139
MCNIGHT, 83 139 173
MCONNEL, 83
MCORCLE, 83
MCOWN, 83
MCOY, 83
MCPHEETERS, 139
MCQUEEN, 139
MCQUIRE, 139
MCRAY, 83
MCRINEY, 83
MCRONEY, 83
MCSPADDEN, 99 102
MCSPARREN, 187
MCSPIRING, 72
MCSWEEN, 63
MCUBIN, 83
MCUMBER, 83
MCUTCHINGS, 83
MCVANZANDT, 166
MCVAY, 73
MCVEY, 63
MCWHERTER, 162
MCWILLIAMS, 7 139
MCWINDERS, 74
MEACHAM, 139
MEADOW, 104
MEADOWS, 83
MEAGER, 139
MEAGHER, 7 139
MEANS, 83 197
MEAR, 71
MECHLMAN, 70
MEDLIN, 69
MEEKS, 75
MEERS, 83
MEFFERT, 139
MEGGULER, 49
MEIGE, 71

MEISTER, 139
MELCHER, 3
MELOY, 74
MELTON, 111
MENCHAM, 67
MENDAZY, 18
MENEES, 54
MENEFEE, 168
MENNOIS, 122
MERIDETH, 139
MERIL, 83
MERRIL, 72
MERRILL, 5 187
MERRIOTT, 95
MERRITT, 18-19
MERRYMAN, 139
MERVIN, 30
MESSENBAUGH, 139
MESSIMER, 139
METCALF, 95 179
METHER-INGHAM, 139
MEYER, 63 179 193
MEYERS, 77
MIBNXKWITZ, 4
MICHAEL, 139
MICHAELS, 71
MICHER, 74
MIDDEAUGH, 139
MIDDLETON, 10
MILEHAM, 156
MILES, 50
MILLAMAN, 71
MILLARD, 139
MILLE, 83
MILLER, 1 5-6 9 12 14 53 56 58 63-64
    69 71-72 77 83 90 95 97 129 139 148
    167-168
MILLETT, 139
MILLIGAN, 10
MILLIKEN, 167
MILLION, 50 72
MILLS, 7 9-10 69 83 99 111
MILLSAP, 122
MILLSAPS, 111 122-123
MILNE, 139
MILSTEAD, 139
MINARD, 156-157
MINGS, 15
MINICK, 181
MINOR, 69 178

MINTCER, 71
MIRE, 74
MISENHELTER, 139
MISSINGER, 12
MITCHEAL, 139
MITCHELL, 9 16 18 69 74 83 95 139
 165-166 168 171-172 174 194
MITTELBACK, 1
MIZE, 74
MLLSAPS, 122
MOBERLY, 146
MODIE, 157
MOFFIT, 139
MOFFITT, 139
MOHN, 139
MOLAND, 83
MOLER, 157
MOLLOY, 62
MOND, 83
MONKASS, 70
MONROE, 139
MONSEES, 77
MONTAGUE, 1
MONTGOMERY, 30 56 67 72 76 83 139
 165 170
MONTSINGER, 139
MONTZ, 139
MONZ, 101
MOODY, 69 83
MOON, 56 61
MOONEY, 57 71 105 139 172-173
MOONY, 73
MOOR, 57
MOORE, 2 5 14 49 52 57 64-65 69 71 74
 83 93 95 98 101 105 111 140 157 162
 168 178-179 188 196
MOORHEAD, 189
MOORMAN, 140
MOORSHEAD, 140
MOOYARD, 69
MORAN, 106 140
MORE, 57 157
MOREHAN, 111
MOREHEAD, 194
MOREY, 4 140
MORGAN, 61 64 69 83 112 140 157 168
 175 177
MORINE, 16 18-19
MORMAN, 140
MORRIS, 7 15 20-21 72 77 83 140 182

MORRISON, 3 5 12 71 83 140
MORRISSEY, 13
MORROW, 47-48 71 83
MORSE, 69 140
MORTON, 73 112 140
MOSEN, 70
MOSS, 55 72 76 83 93 140
MOTLEY, 140
MOTRY, 83
MOTSINGER, 140
MOULDER, 176
MOUNT, 140
MOUSER, 64
MOXLEY, 74 112
MOYERS, 62 64
MOZINE, 83
MUDD, 51
MUEHLSIEPEN, 51
MUELLER, 9
MUFLEY, 83
MUIR, 2 14
MULFORD, 9 73
MULHOLLAND, 182
MULKEY, 83
MULL, 157
MULLEN, 3 57 71
MULLER, 12
MULLIGAN, 140
MULLINIX, 83
MULLIS, 123
MUMMERT, 104
MUMPOWER, 140
MUNDERHOFF, 62
MUNGLE, 57
MUNKIES, 83
MUNROE, 12
MUNSELL, 140
MUNSON, 140 192
MUNTHELY, 70
MURCHISON, 67
MUREY, 140
MURPHY, 5 84 93 140 176
MURRAY, 15-16 53 60 69 140 166
MURRAY-SCHAEFER, 107
MURRILL, 140
MURRY, 57 64 103 140
MURY, 56
MUSBASH, 148
MUSE, 15 112
MUSINGE, 157

MUSSER, 140 162
MUSTARD, 5
MUZINGE, 157
MUZINGS, 84
MYERS, 8 49 57 69 73 104 140 157
MYLAR, 140
MYRES, 72
MYRICK, 103
NAGEL, 90
NAISH, 146
NALL, 64
NALLE, 64
NAPEYEAR, 55
NAPIER, 140
NAPPER, 7
NARVEY, 73
NASH, 84 140 157
NATHAN, 74
NATIONS, 71
NAUERTH, 178 191
NAUGLE, 140
NAVIN, 140
NAYLOR, 96 140 192
NEAL, 84 95 112
NEALE, 4
NEARIS, 84
NEEDHAM, 96
NEEDHARDT, 57
NEEDLES, 123
NEEL, 100 102 104
NEELEY, 9
NEELY, 84 104 123
NEET, 8
NEFF, 123 140
NEILL, 140
NEITZERT, 77
NELLES, 44
NELSON, 6 66 69 84 140
NERMIER, 72
NETCHER, 140
NETT, 71
NETZEN, 140
NEVIL, 140
NEVITT, 140
NEW, 174
NEWBY, 140
NEWCOM, 57
NEWCOMER, 194-195
NEWELL, 8
NEWKIRK, 7 58

NEWLAND, 166
NEWLEE, 6
NEWMAN, 8 71-72
NEWSON, 182
NEWTON, 2 15 71 74 140
NICHOELS, 84
NICHOLAS, 112 157
NICHOLES, 84
NICHOLS, 6 69 84 140 195
NICHOLSON, 140
NICKERSON, 190
NICKOLS, 140
NICODEMUS, 140
NIEWALD, 90
NIFONG, 57
NIGHTFONG, 57
NILES, 149
NISE, 6
NISINGER, 69
NOBBLET, 123
NOBLE, 72 74 84 103
NOEL, 8 69 84 107 112 194
NOELL, 57
NOFFSINGER, 157
NOLAND, 84 157
NOLL, 179
NOLTING, 96
NOONAN, 107
NORDMEYER, 178
NORMAN, 112
NORRIS, 3 73 76 84 98 140 197
NORTH, 56
NORTHUP, 74
NORTON, 8 73-74 112
NORVILLE, 2
NOVAK, 90
NOVEL, 73
NOWELS, 23
NOWLIN, 4
NOYES, 13 73
NUCKLES, 84
NUCKOLLS, 123
O'BANNON, 1 52 55-56 63 190
O'CONNELL, 71
O'DELL, 98 100 105
O'DONEGHEA, 9
O'DONNALD, 140
O'DONNELL, 140
O'HAVER, 19
O'HOWEL, 157

O'NEIL, 123 140
O'NEILL, 22
O'REAR, 9
O'REILLY, 106
O'TOOL, 84
O'TOOLE, 72
OAKS, 140
OBANION, 84
ODELL, 97
ODOM, 58
ODOR, 1
OECHSLE, 93
OEN, 58
OFFICER, 84
OGAN, 140
OGDEN, 140
OGIER, 8
OGLESBY, 2 22
OHLER, 147
OKES, 52
OLDAKER, 22
OLDFIELD, 140
OLDHAM, 53 57 60 62 84
OLDMAN, 181
OLDSON, 71
OLIVER, 7 96-98 102 140
OLLIVER, 84
OLSON, 75
ONEILL, 93
ORAHOOD, 10
ORCHARD, 20
ORR, 1 140
ORRIHOOD, 123
ORVERO, 84
ORVINS, 67
OSBORN, 140
OSBORNE, 5 69 112
OSBORN[SIC], 72
OSBOURN, 72
OSBOURNE, 73
OSBURN, 9 69
OSGOOD, 5
OSTER, 140
OSTERHAUS, 16
OSTERMANN, 193
OTT, 8
OTTMAN, 123
OTTO, 140
OUSBOIN, 69
OUTEN, 51

OVERFIELD, 59
OVERHOLT, 195
OVIATT, 9
OWEN, 2 84 194
OWENS, 69 75 84 112 140 157 165-167 175
OWENSBEY, 84
OWSLEY, 84
PACE, 77
PACKARD, 140
PAGE, 1 5 14 57 67
PAGET, 74
PAINTER, 69
PALFREY, 13
PALL, 100
PALMER, 4 13 67 72 140 184 195
PANISH, 75
PANKAKE, 74
PAPEN, 71
PAPIN, 71
PAR, 69
PARCE, 103
PARISH, 101 157
PARK, 14 50-51 69 140
PARKE, 58
PARKER, 13 53 57 69 73 84 123 129 140 157
PARKEY, 57 90 97
PARKIN, 3 57
PARKS, 57 64-65 69 74
PARMAN, 140
PARMENTER, 140
PARMER, 84
PARRISH, 168
PARROTT, 98
PARRY, 2 123
PARSELL, 9
PARSON, 69
PARSONS, 157
PARYMAN, 140
PASSLY, 74
PATE, 71 140
PATTEE, 74
PATTEN, 57
PATTERSON, 2 4 9 84 146 172 182
PATTISON, 187
PATTON, 1 84 140 157
PATY, 31
PAUL, 8
PAULDING, 102

PAUSTIAN, 140
PAWSEY, 140
PAXTON, 7 140
PAYNE, 66 74 90 101 165-166 170-171
PAYTON, 97 99
PAYZANT, 140
PCKET, 102
PEABODY, 9 140
PEACE, 63-64
PEARCE, 1 14 140
PEARCY, 140
PEARSON, 13 84 140
PEAS, 62
PEASE, 55 196
PECKOVER, 5
PECKTOL, 53
PEDDICORD, 140
PEERY, 193
PEGG, 96
PEGRAM, 147
PELHAM, 3 66
PELTIER, 9
PEMBERTON, 71 140
PENDERGRAFT, 4
PENDEY, 64
PENDLETON, 72 84
PENICK, 84
PENN, 51 165 167
PENNEL, 123
PENNEY, 140
PENNICK, 73
PENNINGTON, 105 157-158
PENNY, 140
PENYMAN, 1
PEPPERS, 71
PEREZ, 90
PERKINS, 14 57 140 179
PERMAN, 123
PERRINGER, 54 56-57
PERRY, 8 73 158
PERSINGER, 84
PERSON, 84
PETEET, 84
PETER, 72
PETERMAN, 59 65
PETERS, 3-5
PETERSON, 140
PETREE, 84
PETRUS, 189
PETTIGREE, 162

PETTIGREW, 162
PETTIS, 140
PETTY, 140
PETYJOHN, 84
PFOST, 140
PHARES, 140
PHARR, 74
PHARRIS, 146
PHELAN, 140
PHELPS, 140 167
PHILBERT, 84
PHILIPS, 74 112
PHILLIPS, 2 5-6 67 96 103 140 182
PHIPPS, 3 96
PICKENS, 99 183-184
PICKERAL, 70
PICKERELL, 84 158
PICKTON, 73
PICKWELL, 158
PIEPER, 51
PIERCE, 6 74 84 140
PIERSON, 74
PIGG, 14 158
PIKE, 7
PIKIN, 129
PILE, 6 84 140
PILES, 70-71 96-97 104 112
PILKINGTON, 140
PILKINGTUN, 140
PINKERTON, 140
PINKLEY, 60
PIPER, 175
PIPKIN, 105 129
PISTOLE, 158
PITCHER, 74
PITKIN, 23
PITMAN, 84
PLASHERS, 123
PLATT, 3
PLATTE, 123
PLEYER, 187
PLOGER, 5
PLUMB, 140
PLUMER, 166
PLUMMER, 16 18 140
PLUMPTON, 140
POAGE, 167
POENA, 73
POER, 112
POINTER, 197

POISEL, 84
POISSE, 10
POLEY, 84
POLK, 56-57 69 71
POLLARD, 1 50 140 147 184
POLLER, 54
POMEROY, 67
POND, 129 140
POOL, 100
POOLE, 69
POOR, 140
POPEJOY, 140
PORTER, 9 13 18-19 23 84 97 100 112 123 140 158
PORTIS, 84 130
POST, 20 71 140 197
POSTLEWATE, 140
POTJOFF, 9
POTTER, 2 6 55 57 73 174
POTTS, 69 140 166 168 180
POUND, 181
POUNDS, 84
POWEL, 62
POWELL, 13-14 67 84 96 99 140
POWER, 73
POWERS, 26-27 129 140
PRATHER, 67 158
PRATT, 2 100 104 140
PRATTE, 57
PRESTON, 105 140
PREWETT, 112
PREWITT, 13
PRICE, 70 73 84 98 104 123 140 158 168 175 188 191
PRICHET, 98
PRIMM, 140
PRINZ, 162
PRITCHARD, 13
PRITCHET, 99
PRITCHETT, 49-50 104
PROCTOR, 140 186
PROFFIT, 140
PROSSER, 192
PROUTY, 140
PROVANCE, 97
PROVENCE, 56
PROVINCE, 100
PRUETT, 57
PRUIT, 56
PRUITT, 140
PRYER, 72
PUCKETT, 140
PUGH, 158
PUJOL, 106
PULLEN, 73
PULLEY, 158
PULLIN, 140
PULTZ, 68
PURDAM, 123
PURDY, 46
PURIFICATION, 50
PURKITT, 71
PURL, 112
PURMTON, 67
PURPLE, 140
PUTMAN, 140
PYBURN, 84
PYLE, 74
PYLES, 7
QUEEL, 140
QUICK, 149
QUINN, 9
QUISENBERRY, 2
RACRAFT, 158
RAFFERTY, 123
RAGAN, 69
RAGIN, 54 57
RAGSDALE, 3 84 158
RAILEY, 140
RAILSBACK, 140
RAINBOLT, 101
RAINS, 9 14 19 166 168 175 178
RAINWATER, 97
RAINWATERS, 99
RALLS, 168
RALPH, 72
RAMBO, 112
RAMSEY, 158 186
RANDALL, 6 69 75 140
RANDOLPH, 67 84 195
RANFRO, 52
RANKIN, 74 106
RAPP, 72 123
RASA, 96
RASH, 124
RATCLIFF, 70 166
RATCLIFFE, 70
RATHBUN, 140
RATHBURN, 1
RATLIFF, 104 148

RAUTENSTRAUCH, 8
RAWLS, 84
RAY, 69-70 84 96 158
RAYMER, 103
RAYMOND, 103
RAZOR, 57 64
REAM, 140
REAMS, 84
REAVES, 52 65
RECTOR, 84 97 99-100 191
REDDISH, 6
REDER, 64
REDHAIR, 140
REDHEAD, 140
REDMOND, 106-107
REDMUND, 74
REED, 2 33 57 64 67 70 74 97 101 112 124 140
REEDE, 64
REEDER, 56
REESE, 112
REESLEY, 69
REEVES, 76 140
REGAN, 77
REGISTER, 74
REHARD, 140
REID, 3 5 67
REIGEL, 140
REILLY, 105-106
REISTER, 181
RELPH, 84
RENALDS, 65
RENFRO, 56 129
RENFROW, 174 176
RENIER, 62
RENNY, 8
RENTFROW, 167
REPP, 75
REPPENHAGEN, 188
REPPTA, 75
RESE, 69
RESER, 50
RESLLY, 69
REST, 71
RETELY, 158
REVEL, 57 64
REVELL, 56
REVES, 58
REYNOLDS, 58 84 140 158
RHEA, 7 140
RHOADES, 9
RHOADS, 158
RHODES, 58 67 72-73 124 158
RIALL, 49
RIBELIN, 140
RICE, 49 71 84 112 130 140 158 174
RICH, 73-74
RICHARDS, 84 140 158 176
RICHARDSON, 1 4-5 8 69 71-72 77 100 140 167 175
RICHART, 158
RICHEY, 84 140
RICHMOND, 97 102-103 140
RICKLE, 74
RICKMAN, 58
RIDDELL, 182 196
RIDDLE, 71 140 194
RIDDLES, 165
RIDINGER, 140
RIGDON, 140
RIGG, 140
RIGGLE, 182
RIGGS, 2 6 140
RILEY, 4 72 140 142 162
RINEHART, 158
RING, 69
RINGER, 184
RITCHER, 72
RITCHISON, 84
RITTER, 98
RIVES, 104
ROACH, 69
ROADS, 158
ROAN, 101 112
ROARK, 72 96
ROBB, 112
ROBBENS, 70
ROBBINET, 124
ROBBINS, 51 190
ROBERDS, 84
ROBERSON, 9-10
ROBERTS, 6 69 74 84 124 142 158
ROBERTSON, 6 104-105 112 124 142 168 171 189
ROBINET, 142
ROBINETT, 84
ROBINS, 73
ROBINSON, 49 51 67 69 75 84 142 146 167-168 182
ROBISON, 84 142

ROCKHOLE, 84
RODE, 124
RODES, 7 84
RODGERS, 71-72 84 98 100 103 142 166
RODY, 72
ROE, 69
ROESCH, 94
ROGERS, 9 64 67 74 112 142 148
ROGGERS, 55 99
ROLAND, 84
ROLOFF, 142
RONALDS, 54
RONGEY, 98 104
RONGLEY, 104
RONNELL, 142
ROOD, 2
ROOK, 105
ROPER, 142
ROSCIE, 70
ROSE, 1 112
ROSENBERGER, 5
ROSENBOHM, 130
ROSS, 71 84 90 113 142 158-159 167 171 173
ROSSER, 15
ROSSLEN, 13
ROSTER, 9
ROTH, 13 142
ROUNDTREE, 84 124
ROUNTREE, 165-166 174
ROUSE, 23 101
ROUSEY, 84
ROW, 58
ROWLAND, 1 113
ROWLEY, 1 6
ROY, 4 71
ROZIER, 13
ROZZELL, 142
ROZZELLE, 142
RROILS, 159
RUBEY, 84
RUBLE, 65
RUCKER, 6 180
RUDDELL, 195
RUDHOMME, 71
RUFF, 142
RUFFLE, 168
RULE, 58 67
RUMANUS, 113
RUMMELL, 70

RUPE, 124
RUSCAL, 73
RUSH, 4
RUSSEL, 84
RUSSELL, 26-27 29 31-32 34 67 70 74 84 113 124 142 159
RUST, 131
RUTH, 165 171 174
RUTHERFORD, 142 176
RUTLEDG, 84
RUTLEDGE, 77 142 159
RUTLIDGE, 75
RUYLE, 167 173-174
RYAN, 142
RYBURN, 142
SABERT, 8
SACKET, 142
SACKETT, 142
SACKMAN, 142
SADLER, 142
SAIL, 146
SAINTCLAIR, 129
SAINTDAVIS, 67
SAINTGEMME, 53 56 65
SALE, 84
SALLE, 2
SALLEE, 6 29
SALOMON, 14
SALSBURY, 142
SAMPSON, 67 84-85
SAMUEL, 142
SAMUELS, 64 142
SAND, 124
SANDER, 60
SANDERS, 58 69-71 85 99 113 142 149 159 178
SANDERSON, 142
SANFORD, 2 124
SANSBERRY, 7
SAPP, 73
SARGENT, 5 142
SARTIN, 97 99
SARVIN, 67
SASSE, 193
SAUNDERS, 4 53 74 90 159 181
SAUNTMAN, 58
SAVAGE, 41 146
SAVELY, 176
SAYE, 165-166 171 173
SAYLOR, 183

SCAGGS, 74 85
SCAMMON, 124
SCANLON, 142
SCHARSON, 142
SCHESON, 142
SCHIELD, 124
SCHILMER, 72
SCHMIDER, 72
SCHMIDT, 124-125 184
SCHNEIDER, 9
SCHNEITER, 142
SCHNITTGER, 125
SCHOFIELD, 17 19 159
SCHOLL, 66 85
SCHOUTE, 65
SCHRODER, 96
SCHROEDER, 96
SCHROUN, 113
SCHUBERT, 125
SCHULER, 96
SCHULT, 2
SCHULTZ, 85 142
SCHUPP, 96
SCHUSTER, 142
SCHUYLER, 9
SCOFIELD, 90
SCOTT, 6 9 13 74 85 99 113 125 142 181 193
SCOTTEN, 2
SCRUGGS, 74
SCYMOUR, 125
SEAFERT, 142
SEAL, 64
SEALS, 58 71
SEARCY, 23-24
SEARLES, 71
SEARS, 3 51 69 142 173 185
SEATON, 7
SEAVERS, 159
SEAWRIGHT, 142
SEAY, 113
SEBACHER, 94
SEBASTIN, 58
SEBASTION, 58 67
SEBRING, 4
SEBUEN, 130
SEDUCKE, 67
SEE, 159
SEELY, 142
SEIGLER, 174
SEITTER, 142
SEITZ, 5
SELF, 159
SELL, 64 142
SELLARS, 85
SELLERS, 50 67 142
SEMANS, 5
SESSIONS, 142
SETTLE, 6 58
SEYMOUR, 14
SHACKELFORD, 7
SHACKLEFORD, 9 51
SHADRICKS, 113
SHAFEL, 142
SHAFER, 9 142
SHAFFER, 107 125 142
SHALLWOOD, 72
SHANKES, 72
SHANNON, 69 72
SHARP, 6 51 57-58 63-64 72-73 85 105 142 159 186 195
SHARPER, 72
SHAUWOOD, 85
SHAW, 5 50 64 71 85 113 125 142 149 159 175
SHEA, 6
SHEAR, 142
SHEAREIR, 70
SHEARIN, 74
SHEETS, 99-100 103
SHEIMAN, 130
SHELBY, 2
SHELLABERGER, 142
SHELLY, 142
SHELTON, 53 58 64 85 159
SHEPARD, 17 73 142
SHEPHERD, 103 159
SHEPP, 96
SHERIFF, 70
SHERMAN, 9 130 142
SHERNER, 53 58
SHERRY, 8
SHERWOOD, 168 177
SHETLEY, 58
SHETTER, 68
SHEVIN, 106
SHEVLY, 142
SHEVNIN, 105
SHIELDS, 5 142
SHIKEL, 113

SHILLING, 129
SHIN, 142
SHINEMAN, 96
SHINER, 142
SHINN, 102
SHIPMAN, 90
SHIPP, 197
SHIRLEY, 13 67
SHIRTS, 142
SHOEMAKER, 101 103
SHOEMATE, 65
SHOOP, 23
SHORT, 53 96 98 101 105 125 159
SHOUGHNESSY, 9
SHOULTS, 52
SHOUSE, 142
SHOUTH, 63
SHOWERMAN, 142
SHREVE, 85
SHRUBLE, 142
SHRUM, 125 142
SHRYNBERRY, 7
SHUBRICK, 34
SHUGARS, 69
SHULTZ, 63 85 90 142
SHUMAN, 142-143
SHUPE, 195
SHURLDS, 85
SHUTTS, 76
SIBERT, 9
SIBLEY, 46
SICHER, 106
SICKLER, 125
SIDEBOTTOM, 143
SIEGEL, 15
SIGEL, 14-16
SIGG, 98
SIGMAN, 143
SILENCE, 85
SILVERS, 85
SILVEY, 96 189
SIMMANS, 64
SIMMONDS, 146
SIMMONS, 9-10 67 85·129
SIMONS, 70
SIMONSON, 3
SIMPKINSON, 143
SIMPSON, 70 85 125 143 167 183
SIMS, 159
SINCLAIR, 58 64
SINGLEY, 23
SINKLER, 58
SIPE, 85
SIPES, 125
SISE, 85
SITHERLAND, 99
SITTLER, 6
SITTON, 159
SITZE, 58-59 64
SITZES, 60 63
SIZEMORE, 159-160
SKAGGS, 58 65 74
SKEEN, 85 125
SKELTON, 72 143 197
SKIDMORE, 68
SKIDWELL, 69
SKILES, 100 103
SKINNER, 77
SLABOY, 85
SLAGLE, 77 173
SLATER, 65 143
SLAUGHTER, 189
SLAUSHER, 125
SLEGBAUGH, 143
SLESIN, 71
SLEYSTER, 191
SLINOW, 125
SLOAN, 5 71 143 165 173 178
SLOAT, 32
SLOROFF, 143
SLOUGH, 13
SLUSHER, 97
SMALL, 113
SMALLWOOD, 94
SMART, 47-48
SMEDLEY, 85
SMELSER, 125
SMIDT, 70
SMITH, 1-2 4-6 8-9 13 44 49-50 52 58
    61-62 65 67 69-74 77 85 96-97 99
    101-105 129 131 143 146-147 160
    162 173 175 179-180 186-187 193
    197
SMITHER, 85
SMITHTON, 168 172
SMOCK, 160
SMOOT, 100 143
SMYLIE, 143
SNEAD, 14 85
SNEED, 101

SNELL, 76
SNELLING, 96
SNELSON, 113
SNIDER, 70 73 75 97-100 102-104
SNODDY, 73
SNODGRASS, 166
SNOW, 197
SNYDER, 5 70 77 85 143
SOKALSKI, 17
SOLDAN, 9
SOLLARS, 160
SOLLERS, 72 85
SOMERS, 67
SOMERVILLE, 8
SOMMER, 90
SON, 85
SONNAMAKER, 70
SONREIL, 193
SOOTER, 70
SOUTHWARD, 85
SOVEREIGN, 143
SPAIN, 55 58 65
SPANE, 58
SPARGO, 9
SPARKMAN, 69
SPARKS, 74 125 143
SPARLAND, 85
SPAULDING, 22
SPEAKER, 96
SPEAKS, 113
SPEAR, 187
SPEARS, 70
SPEER, 2
SPELLERBERG, 125
SPENCE, 5 85 165 179
SPENCER, 6 85 160 190
SPENSER, 143
SPICER, 143
SPIVA, 58 65
SPLAWN, 143
SPOONSMORE, 160
SPORTSMAN, 182
SPOTSWOOD, 13
SPOTWOOD, 69
SPRAGUE, 17 143
SPRATT, 70 143
SPRAY, 49
SPRINGER, 102
SPURLOCK, 67 143
SQUIRES, 125 143
SRITTER, 143
SROUFE, 160
STABLER, 193
STACY, 104
STAFFORD, 74 91 125-126 143
STAGNER, 49 143
STAHL, 70
STALK, 143
STALLIONS, 113
STAMPER, 3
STANCILL, 1
STANFIELD, 143
STANFORD, 69 126
STANLEY, 85
STANLY, 74
STANTON, 69 71 85 94
STAPEL, 130
STAPLETON, 85
STARK, 52 91
STARKE, 126
STARN, 52
STARR, 9
STARRET, 143
STATEN, 66
STAUBUS, 195
STEALEY, 58
STEARNS, 74
STECK, 126
STEEL, 69
STEELE, 5 16 18 77
STEELY, 53
STEENROD, 143
STEGNER, 1
STEIN, 69
STEINBERG, 4 143
STELPH, 146
STEPHEN, 70
STEPHENS, 7 25 33 36 41 43 45 58 69 74 85 97 101 104 113 143 160 176
STEPHENSON, 85 143 148 160 179
STEPP, 129
STEPS, 74
STERGEON, 69
STERITT, 64
STEVENS, 2 24 65 72 91 126 130 143 160
STEVENSON, 4 59 77 99 143
STEWARD, 61
STEWART, 67 69-70 85 97 129 143 167 176

STICKLE, 143
STIGALL, 2
STILES, 143
STILL, 50 67
STILLFIELD, 143
STILLWELL, 143
STINGLEY, 160
STINGLY, 160
STINSON, 72
STINTZEN, 126
STIPES, 4
STOCK, 143
STOCKARD, 50
STOCKEL, 143
STOCKTON, 30-31 33-34 160 165-168 174-175 178
STOCKWEL, 70
STOCKWELL, 143 188
STOKES, 9
STOLEN, 69
STOLLER, 85 143
STONAM, 143
STONE, 7 59 67 72 126 143
STONER, 85 126 143 160 183
STONUM, 143
STORM, 192
STORMS, 10
STORY, 59 64
STOTHARD, 197
STOTTLEMYRE, 130
STOUT, 8 85 143 167
STOUTIMORE, 143
STOW, 160
STOWE, 192
STOWELL, 143
STRAIN, 13
STRATTO, 103
STRATTON, 99 102
STRAUB, 143 191
STREET, 58 143
STREETER, 143
STRICKLAND, 75
STRICKLEN, 65
STRICKLIN, 61
STRICKLING, 85
STRINGFELLOW, 73
STRODE, 85
STROETER, 2
STRONG, 162
STROP, 143
STROPE, 143
STRUB, 193-194
STRUBLE, 143
STUARD, 59
STUART, 126
STUBBENFIELD, 143
STUBBINFIELD, 143
STUBBLEFIELD, 143
STUBBS, 143
STUCK, 143
STUCKE, 143-144
STUCKER, 144
STUFFLEBAM, 4
STUFFLEBEEN, 85
STURGES, 77
STURGIS, 16 18 144
STUTTE, 91
STUTTS, 85
STUTZ, 73
SUELL, 73
SUGG, 71
SUGGS, 113
SUITLING, 85
SULLIVAN, 59 67 184
SUMERS, 70
SUMMERS, 9
SUMPTER, 74
SURBER, 147
SURMAN, 69
SURRENCY, 160
SUTERMEISTER, 4
SUTHERLAND, 7 75
SUTTEN, 52 64-65
SUTTON, 57 59 61 65
SWAFFORD, 100
SWAGGART, 144
SWAIN, 184
SWAIRANGAIN, 63
SWAN, 85
SWEARINGEN, 7 144 160
SWEARINGIN, 57
SWEAT, 70
SWEATMAN, 144
SWEAZEA, 97 99
SWEEM, 144
SWEENY, 17 72
SWEETEN, 71
SWERINGEN, 144
SWETMAN, 113
SWEZER, 67

SWIGART, 144
SWINDLER, 144
SWINNEY, 85
SWISH, 97
SWISHER, 144
SWITZER, 144
SYLVESTER, 9
SYRES, 129
TAFT, 144
TALBOT, 32 36 67
TANKERSLY, 10
TANNER, 144
TAPLY, 160
TARWATER, 144
TASSEER, 70
TASSENCE, 85
TATE, 69 160
TATTERSHALL, 144
TAUB, 127
TAYLER, 144
TAYLIN, 68
TAYLOR, 1 3 9 13 59 64 73 77 85 98 101-104 126 144 189 196
TEAGUE, 85 126
TEEL, 65
TEMPLE, 126 144 165
TEMPLER, 86
TEMPLETON, 126 130
TERE, 72
TERHUNE, 160
TERRIL, 129
TERRILL, 144 188
TERRY, 23 97 144
TESSEREAU, 59 63 65
TESSEROU, 52
THACKER, 144
THARP, 14 86 91
THATCHER, 4 86
THAYER, 9
THEILMAN, 49
THERMASO, 86
THERMON, 86
THIEL, 144
THIELMAN, 144
THOMAS, 1 22 69 73-74 77 86 99 144 160
THOMASON, 62 73 98 160
THOMPSON, 3 5 23 49-50 53 61 66 70 72-74 86 126 144 160 168 171
THOMSON, 48 130 144

THORN, 144
THORNBURGH, 86
THORNBURY, 73
THORNTON, 86 91 197
THOSS, 96
THROWER, 3
THUDIUM, 4
THWING, 144
TIBLELS, 8
TIFFNEY, 144
TILL, 144
TILLMAN, 126
TILLOTSON, 185
TINDALL, 69
TINDELL, 144
TINDLE, 72
TINKER, 70 86
TINSLEY, 86 99 105
TIPPET, 144
TIPPIT, 144
TIPTON, 23 86
TISDALE, 184
TITTLE, 59
TOBBEEN, 144
TOBBEIN, 144
TOBIN, 86
TOBURS, 71
TODD, 72 74 86 146
TODHUNTER, 67
TOLBEY, 86
TOLER, 170
TOLIVER, 97 103
TOMAS, 86
TOMBS, 86
TOMLIN, 9
TOMPSON, 86
TONER, 144
TONG, 56 59 63
TONGATE, 77
TOOL, 144
TOOMAY, 144
TOOMS, 144
TOPPER, 96
TORPEY, 129
TORRANCE, 160-161
TOSPON, 144
TOTTEN, 14 16-17
TOWN, 144
TOWNSEND, 126-127 144
TRACEY, 86

TRACY, 15 72 144
TRAILS, 10
TRAINAR, 96
TRAMMEL, 8
TRAMMELL, 100
TRANSAWAY, 72
TRAP, 71
TRASPER, 161
TRAUB, 127
TRAVERS, 9
TRAVIS, 86
TRENT, 72
TREON, 144
TRESEMRITER, 163
TRIBBLE, 72
TRIGMAN, 15
TRIMBLE, 5 86 161
TRIP, 59 63
TRIPLETT, 194
TRIPP, 65
TRITE, 74
TRITT, 74
TROMLY, 163
TROSPER, 86 144
TROSS, 144
TROTMAN, 72
TROUT, 144
TROWBRIDGE, 5
TRUMBO, 1 144
TRUNK, 144
TRUSTY, 161
TRYGLE, 69
TUBB, 49
TUBBEIN, 144
TUCK, 71 171 173
TUCKER, 69 86 103 130 144 149
TUDOR, 113
TULL, 1
TULLEY, 1
TUNER, 6
TUNNEL, 73
TUNNELL, 144 146
TURLEY, 97-99
TURNER, 67 69-70 77 86 127 144
TURRENTINE, 6
TUTHEROE, 86
TUTTLE, 144
TWEED, 4
TWENDLE, 4
TWING, 144

TWITTY, 57
TWOMBLEY, 74
TWOMBLY, 70
TWYMAN, 185
TYE, 144
TYLER, 69 74 103
TYNER, 74 96
TYRE, 113
TYSON, 101 186
UHLAND, 144
UMSTOTT, 144
UNDERHILL, 70
UNDERWOOD, 4 53 58-59 86
UNWERTH, 4
UPMAN, 59
UPP, 144 183
UPTON, 70
URE, 144
URMILLER, 96
USHER, 9
VALLE, 57 59
VALLEJO, 43
VANBEBBER, 144
VANCE, 60 67 86 104 144
VANDERFORD, 175
VANDERPOOL, 144
VANDERVORT, 161
VANDYKE, 9 103
VANHOFF, 77
VANHOOZIER, 86
VANHORN, 69
VANLUVEN, 127
VANMETER, 86 127
VANMETRE, 5
VANNEMAN, 2
VANNOTE, 144
VANOLINDA, 144
VANPOOL, 162
VANSCHOIK, 86
VANSOYAS, 101
VANWINKLE, 144
VARNDELL, 144
VARVLE, 86
VAUGH, 144
VAUGHAN, 15
VAUGHHN, 161
VAUGHN, 1 9 86 127 144
VAUGHT, 113
VEACH, 144
VEERKAMP, 7

VELLARS, 61
VENABLE, 7
VERMILLION, 98 100
VERMULE, 38 40 47
VERNICE, 51
VERNING, 144
VERTEFEILLE, 71
VESPERS, 107
VESSER, 86
VESSES, 86
VESTAL, 86
VESTALL, 70
VEVILS, 129
VIA, 96
VICKERY, 100
VINCEN, 60
VINCENT, 52-53 61
VINES, 129
VINSONHALER, 161
VIRTUE, 144
VIVIS, 71
VOG, 148
VOILE, 101
VOLENTINE, 65
VONSTRUVE, 4
VOORHEES, 5 191
VORIS, 86
WACK, 189
WADDELL, 16
WADDILL, 74
WADDLE, 73
WADE, 69 73 86 129 144
WADKINS, 86 91
WAFAL, 67
WAGENER, 65
WAGGONER, 59 62 144
WAGONER, 69 102
WAISNER, 96
WAITS, 127
WAKEFIELD, 70 105
WALCH, 77
WALDEN, 127
WALDO, 144
WALDON, 113
WALDRON, 19
WALKER, 4-5 7 13-14 57 59 63 69 71 73-74 77 86 98-100 102 127 130 144-145 148 181
WALL, 145
WALLACE, 4 59 67 72-73 145 161

WALLER, 97 189
WALLHAMM, 127
WALLICE, 86
WALLIS, 127
WALLOR, 101
WALSH, 105-106
WALSH-CHAMBERS, 106
WALTERS, 86 145
WALTHER, 96
WALTON, 1 50
WAMMACK, 73-74
WAMPLER, 10
WANEY, 9
WANGELIN, 10
WARD, 36 50 67 70 72 86 103 127 145
WARDEN, 191
WARDER, 67
WARDIN, 10
WARE, 2 127-128 161
WARING, 9
WARMACK, 145
WARNECKE, 59
WARREMAN, 59
WARREN, 7 97 145
WARRICK, 162
WASHAM, 113
WASSAN, 113
WASSON, 96
WATERFIELD, 185
WATERMAN, 13
WATERS, 86 145
WATKINS, 69 168
WATKINSON, 1
WATNY, 70
WATSON, 4 13 56 59 130 145 161 166-167 174 178
WATTERMAN, 161
WATTERS, 8
WATTS, 3 58-59
WAUGH, 86 161
WAYLAND, 145
WAYMAN, 145
WAYMEIR, 128
WEATHERMAN, 161
WEAVER, 6 70 145 183
WEBB, 70 86 91 96 101 113 145 174
WEBER, 5 59 64-65
WEBSTER, 145
WEEKS, 145
WEESE, 101

WEIGHTMAN, 14-15
WEILKIE, 145
WEIS, 96
WEISE, 63
WEISER, 161
WEIST, 75
WELBURN, 63
WELCH, 4 50 70 167 181
WELDING, 72
WELKER, 145
WELLS, 13 72-74 113 128 130 145
WELLSCD, 13
WELSH, 128 145
WENDELL, 67
WERNER, 55 65
WESBTER, 145
WEST, 68 128 146 161
WESTON, 13
WEVER, 65
WHALEN, 102
WHALER, 145
WHALEY, 3
WHEALDON, 4
WHEELER, 1 5 13 99 145 147
WHEN, 3
WHERRY, 17
WHILHITE, 188
WHILLOCK, 168
WHIPPLE, 5
WHISMAN, 86
WHISTLER, 69
WHITACRE, 3
WHITAKER, 6 51 86 145
WHITBY, 2
WHITE, 1 4 9 14 59-60 67 69 71-72 74-75 77 86 99 128 145 149 161
WHITEAKER, 186
WHITED, 197
WHITEFORD, 6
WHITEHEAD, 72 86
WHITEHOUSE, 103
WHITELAW, 145
WHITELEY, 86
WHITENER, 54 59 64
WHITESELL, 145
WHITESIDE, 145
WHITFIELD, 15
WHITLAW, 145
WHITLOCK, 67
WHITMER, 145

WHITNER, 52 55 58-59 62
WHITSETT, 161
WHITSITT, 145
WHITSMAN, 86
WHITSON, 67
WHITT, 145
WHITTEN, 4
WHITWORTH, 56 65
WHYBARK, 2 20
WIATT, 148
WICKARD, 11
WICKS, 188
WIDMIER, 145
WIGGINS, 74 103
WIKLE, 69
WILBURN, 69 86
WILCOX, 9 65
WILDE, 5 13
WILDER, 4
WILES, 14
WILEY, 8 65
WILFLEY, 86
WILHELM, 128
WILHITE, 73
WILHOIT, 145
WILKERSON, 8 86
WILKIN, 73
WILKINS, 54
WILKINSON, 1 4 59 74 103 145 183
WILL, 145
WILLA, 73
WILLBAHAN, 72
WILLET, 52
WILLHITE, 86
WILLIAMS, 3 5-6 10 26 32 50 53 59-60 64-70 73-74 77 86 97-99 101-102 104 128 145-146 148 161 166-168 171 175-176 178 184 190 196
WILLIAMSON, 7 13 114 145
WILLIS, 3 60 65 72 86 128 161
WILLOCK, 7
WILLS, 101
WILLY, 145
WILSON, 5 8 13 46 60 65 70-72 86 91 101 104 128 145 166 168 175 177 189 196
WILYARD, 128
WINBARGER, 60
WINCHESTER, 3
WIND, 13

WINDES, 97-98 102 104
WINDSOR, 185
WINEBARGER, 65
WINFIELD, 114
WINGATE, 145
WINGER, 145
WINKLE, 71
WINKLER, 86
WINKLES, 114
WINN, 74
WINNINGHAM, 10
WINSCOTT, 145
WINSLOW, 194
WINSTON, 167
WINTERS, 146
WINTON, 173
WIRES, 69 194
WIRT, 1 4
WISDOM, 67 130
WISE, 10 145
WISEMAN, 66
WISER, 73
WITEHEAD, 145
WITHERS, 7 14
WITMER, 3
WITSETT, 72
WITT, 86
WITTEN, 130
WITTROCK, 96
WITZONG, 69
WOERLEND, 128
WOLCOT, 145
WOLF, 86 145
WOLFE, 91
WOLFF, 128
WOLLHELM, 86
WOLSEY, 128
WOLTZ, 148
WOMINASH, 86
WOMMATH, 86
WONDESLEY, 86
WONSETTLER, 145
WOOD, 16 18-19 60 67 86 100 145 161 195
WOODARD, 145
WOODBRIDGE, 145
WOODCOCK, 86
WOODFORD, 6 8
WOODRUFF, 1 14
WOODS, 61 86
WOODSON, 69
WOODWARD, 2 51 70 97 103
WOODY, 91
WOODYARD, 197
WOOLARD, 145 173
WOOLCOTT, 145
WOOLFORD, 65
WOOLSEY, 145
WOONS, 74
WORCESTER, 86 129
WORKS, 129
WORL, 129
WORSHAM, 181
WORSTER, 86
WORTHINGTON, 145
WOSTER, 86
WOY, 14 23
WRAY, 13 23 97
WRIGHT, 1 13 72 74 86 91 94 114 129-130 145-146 161 190
WRITSMAN, 86
WRITT, 145
WYANT, 145
WYATT, 86 145 161
WYCKOFF, 145
WYCOFF, 145
WYNN, 7 15
YANCEY, 167
YANCY, 171
YAPLES, 148
YATE, 129
YATES, 67 86 97 114
YEAGER, 5 114
YENGST, 86
YOAKES, 145
YOAKUM, 145
YOAST, 176
YOCKEY, 145
YOCUM, 186
YOGAN, 72
YOKEM, 73
YONDER, 72
YONGER, 54
YORK, 114
YOUNG, 10 60 64 70-71 86 114 129 145 161 166 175 179
YOUNGER, 86
ZANER, 145
ZEIGLER, 14
ZEIKLE, 145-146

ZIEBOLD, 107
ZIEGLER, 60
ZIMMERMAN, 8 146
ZOCKERY, 146
ZONKER, 146
ZUMWALT, 96 174 178

Other Heritage Books by Sherida K. Eddlemon:

Missouri Genealogical Records and Abstracts:
Volume 1: 1766-1839
Volume 2: 1752-1839
Volume 3: 1787-1839
Volume 4: 1741-1839
Volume 5: 1755-1839
Volume 6: 1621-1839
Volume 7: 1535-1839

Missouri Genealogical Gleanings 1840 and Beyond, Volumes 1-9

1890 Genealogical Census Reconstruction: Mississippi, Volumes 1 and 2

1890 Genealogical Census Reconstruction: Missouri, Volumes 1-3

1890 Genealogical Census Reconstruction: Ohio, Volume 1
(with Patricia P. Nelson)

1890 Genealogical Census Reconstruction: Tennessee, Volume 1

A Genealogical Collection of Kentucky Birth and Death Records

Callaway County, Missouri, Marriage Records: 1821 to 1871

Cumberland Presbyterian Church, Volume One: 1836 and Beyond

Dickson County, Tennessee Marriage Records, 1817-1879

Genealogical Abstracts from Missouri Church Records and Other Religious Sources, Volume 1

Genealogical Abstracts from Tennessee Newspapers, 1791-1808

Genealogical Abstracts from Tennessee Newspapers, 1803-1812

Genealogical Abstracts from Tennessee Newspapers, 1821-1828

Tennessee Genealogical Records and Abstracts, Volume 1: 1787-1839

Genealogical Gleanings from New York Fraternal Organizations Volumes 1 and 2

Index to the Arkansas General Land Office, 1820-1907 Volumes 1-10

Kentucky Genealogical Records and Abstracts, Volume 1: 1781-1839

Kentucky Genealogical Records and Abstracts, Volume 2: 1796-1839

Lewis County, Missouri Index to Circuit Court Records, Volume 1, 1833-1841

Missouri Birth and Death Records, Volumes 1-4

Morgan County, Missouri Marriage Records, 1833-1893

Our Ancestors of Albany County, New York, Volumes 1 and 2

Our Ancestors of Cuyahoga County, Ohio, Volume 1
(with Patricia P. Nelson)

Ralls County, Missouri Settlement Records, 1832-1853

Records of Randolph County, Missouri, 1833-1964

Ten Thousand Missouri Taxpayers

The "Show-Me" Guide to Missouri: Sources for Genealogical and Historical Research

CD: Dickson County, Tennessee Marriage Records, 1817-1879

CD: Index to the Arkansas General Land Office, 1820-1907 Volumes 1-10

CD: Missouri, Volume 3

CD: Tennessee Genealogical Records

CD: Tennessee Genealogical Records, Volumes 1-3

www.ingramcontent.com/pod-product-compliance
Lightning Source LLC
Chambersburg PA
CBHW051043160426
43193CB00010B/1044